D0944686

Social Referencing and the Social Construction of Reality in Infancy

Social Referencing and the Social Construction of Reality in Infancy

Edited by
Saul Feinman

University of Wyoming
Laramie, Wyoming

Withdrawn
University of Waterloo

Plenum Press • New York and London

Library of Congress Cataloging in Publication Data

Social referencing and the social construction of reality in infancy / edited by Saul Feinman.
     p.   cm.
Includes bibliographical references and index.
ISBN 0-306-43850-X
1. Socialization. 2. Reference groups. 3. Infant psychology. I. Feinman, Saul.
[DNLM: 1. Cognition — in infancy and childhood. 2. Interpersonal Relations. 3. Social Environment. 4. Socialization. WS 105.5.S6 S6784]
BF720.S63S67   1992
303.3'2 — dc20
DNLM/DLC   92-11922
for Library of Congress   CIP

ISBN 0-306-43850-X

© 1992 Plenum Press, New York
A Division of Plenum Publishing Corporation
233 Spring Street, New York, N.Y. 10013

All rights reserved

No part of this book may be reproduced, stored in a retrieval system, or transmitted in any form or by any means, electronic, mechanical, photocopying, microfilming, recording, or otherwise, without written permission from the Publisher

Printed in the United States of America

To the Faculty and Students, 1970–1973,
of the Department of Social Relations
at The Johns Hopkins University
for showing me the way
the pieces fit together

Contributors

MARY D. SALTER AINSWORTH, Department of Psychology, University of Virginia, Charlottesville, Virginia 22903.

ALBERT BANDURA, Department of Psychology, Stanford University, Stanford, California 94305.

INGE BRETHERTON, Child Development and Family Studies, School of Family Resources and Consumer Sciences, University of Wisconsin, Madison, Wisconsin 53706.

NORMAN K. DENZIN, Department of Sociology, University of Illinois at Urbana-Champaign, Urbana, Illinois 61801.

ROBERT N. EMDE, Department of Psychiatry, University of Colorado Health Sciences Center, Denver, Colorado 80262.

SAUL FEINMAN, Child and Family Studies, Department of Home Economics, University of Wyoming, Laramie, Wyoming 82071.

CANDICE FEIRING, Institute for the Study of Child Development, Robert Wood Johnson Medical School, University of Medicine and Dentistry of New Jersey, New Brunswick, New Jersey 08903.

MARTHA FOSCHI, Department of Anthropology and Sociology, University of British Columbia, Vancouver, British Columbia, V6T 2B2, Canada.

JAMIE GERMOND, Department of Psychology, University of Maine at Orono, Orono, Maine 04473.

JACOB L. GEWIRTZ, Department of Psychology, Florida International University, University Park Campus, Miami, Florida 33199.

MEGAN R. GUNNAR, Institute of Child Development, University of Minnesota, Minneapolis, Minnesota 55455.

ROBIN HORNIK PARRITZ, Department of Psychology, Hamline University, St. Paul, Minnesota 55104.

KUEI-FANG HSIEH, Child and Family Studies, Department of Home Economics, University of Wyoming, Laramie, Wyoming 82071.

JAN C. KRUPER, Department of Psychology, Clark University, Worcester, Massachusetts 01610.

MICHAEL LEWIS, Institute for the Study of Child Development, Robert Wood Johnson Medical School, University of Medicine and Dentistry of New Jersey, New Brunswick, New Jersey 08903.

SARAH MANGELSDORF, Department of Psychology, University of Illinois, Champaign–Urbana, Illinois 61820.

JAYANTHI MISTRY, Department of Child Study, Tufts University, Medford, Massachusetts 02155.

MARTHA PELÁEZ-NOGUERAS, Department of Psychology, Florida International University, University Park Campus, Miami, Florida 33199.

BARBARA RADZISZEWSKA, Institute for Prevention Research, University of Southern California, Alhambra, California 91803.

DEBRA ROBERTS, Child and Family Studies, Department of Home Economics, University of Wyoming, Laramie, Wyoming 82071.

BARBARA ROGOFF, Department of Psychology, University of Utah, Salt Lake City, Utah 84112.

DARBY SAWYER, Child and Family Studies, Department of Home Economics, University of Wyoming, Laramie, Wyoming 82071.

DEE SWANSON, Child and Family Studies, Department of Home Economics, University of Wyoming, Laramie, Wyoming 82071.

INA Č. UŽGIRIS, Department of Psychology, Clark University, Worcester, Massachusetts 01610.

MURRAY WEBSTER, JR., Department of Sociology, San Jose State University, San Jose, California 95192.

Preface

Virtually every realm of human activity carries with it the vision of a lost paradise, a time when life was simple and satisfying, a place in which things made sense and fit together into a meaningful, integrated whole. This tranquility often is destroyed by a single act, whether a bold stroke or a sniveling swipe, an act which unintentionally brings down the old order. In some mythologies, this deed is followed almost immediately by the fall from grace and the emergence of a new reality, as in the biblical expulsion from Eden and the subsequent emergence of self-consciousness (and the self-conscious emotions). In others, the critical stroke sets into motion, as the clockmaker winds the timepiece, a sequence of events which build toward the inevitable cataclysm; in Richard Wagner's *Der Ring des Nibelungen*, Wotan sets in motion the forces that will lead to the eventual destruction of the old order, the Twilight of the Gods (Götterdämmerung) foretold in the Norse legend of Ragnarok, by the single act of breaking off a branch of the world ash tree to make the spear on which to carve the covenants that govern the world. Typically, in such transformations, there is gain as well as loss, birth as well as death. With the loss of innocence comes the emergence of consciousness. We are compensated for the loss of tranquility by the gain of creativity. The fall of the old deities makes way for the new.

In the world of scholarship (in its broadest sense), this lost paradise is the time and place in which knowledge was whole, in which the various strands and threads of philosophy (in *its* original and broadest sense) were intertwined in one tapestry. Not really all that long ago, any one scholar might still focus on a wide range of phenomena, and there was a strong sense of wholeness and unity. That intellectual utopia was lost once we began to tease apart the threads of the cloth, and to specialize in the study of these individual strands. As the holistic activities of philosophy were deconstructed into evermore minute, specialized bits and pieces, we came to acquire increasingly detailed and technical information within each of these precisely focused domains. This trend—despite its benefits—moved forward at the expense of making it increasingly difficult to see how all these pieces of particulate matter might fit back together into some semblance of unity. Indeed, sometimes it seems as though the fracturing of knowledge over the last century is irreversible, much like Humpty Dumpty after his fall.

Being somewhat more sanguine about the possibilities of academic reunification, in spirit and thought (if not in bureaucratic structure), my intention in editing this volume was to reduce the odds that the study of social referencing in infancy would go the way of many other specialized domains of research, becoming ever more arcane and insular, if nonetheless technically proficient and correct. Referencing is a phenomenon that stretches beyond infancy to meander on through the lifespan. It lies at the razor's edge interface of the individual and society, as one of the critical ways in which the individual's construction of reality is socially influenced. It is of relevance to developmental and social psychology, and to sociology's and anthropology's basic interest in how individuals become encultured into their societies. As such, it is essential that the study of social referencing in infancy be informed and guided by what is known about related processes. In that spirit, the goal of this edited collection is to evaluate what is known about the thread of social referencing by examining it within the broad, integrated perspective of the tapestry that is the social construction of reality in human social relations.

The scholars who participated in this effort, and wrote chapters for the present volume, first came together at a study group funded by the Society for Research on Child Development. We are most grateful in the society for supporting our efforts to integrate social referencing within the broader fabric of the study of human social relations. Joseph Campos was a member of this group but was unable to contribute a chapter to the volume. Nonetheless, his views, as a member of the "Denver Collaborative Group," which contributed so much to the initial formulation and later explication of the concept of social referencing in infancy, is reflected and represented in this volume.

In this great age of specialization, there may be some intrinsic limit upon how adeptly the pieces can be put back together again. It is probably more difficult now, with our minds set for specialized knowledge, than it was in earlier days, to reconstruct the parts into a unified whole. Nonetheless, I believe that we have had some success in our efforts, in this volume, to put the piece that is infant social referencing back into the puzzle of how definitions of the situation arise within the context of social relations.

SAUL FEINMAN

Contents

III. COGNITION AND INFORMATION PROCESSING

IV. RELATIONSHIPS AND INTERACTION

V. CONNECTIONS AND DIRECTIONS

I

Orientations and Beginnings

1

In the Broad Valley
An Integrative Look at Social Referencing

Saul Feinman

Human relations can serve a variety of functions. They can offer comfort, caring, and socioemotional support, especially when a person is stressed or scared. They can help to satisfy physical needs and wants, such as those for nutrition, shelter, and thermoregulation. People can help one another learn about the world around them (the exterior environment) and about their selves (the interior environment). It is this guiding and learning function of social relations which is our focus as we examine, in this book, the topic of social referencing in infancy.

The social guidance of learning can be found throughout the lifespan, from infancy to old age, and, despite developmental differences, operates through basically the same mechanisms at all ages. This process lies at the interface of the individual with society, and is one of the most important methods through which persons are socialized into both the near environment of kith and kin, and the far environment of society. As such, guidance of learning is very much a central strand in the fabric of everyday life. It represents one of the various ways in which social influence can occur when people interact, but in no way can it be considered to be isomorphic with that bigger and broader phenomenon. Indeed, social influence operates in ways other than the social guidance of learning—as can be noted

SAUL FEINMAN • Child and Family Studies, Department of Home Economics, University of Wyoming, Laramie, Wyoming 82071.

Social Referencing and the Social Construction of Reality in Infancy, edited by Saul Feinman. Plenum Press, New York, 1992.

in the functioning of other realms of human relations (e.g., the comforting effect of another person's sheer physical presence).

Learning can be socially guided in two conceptually distinct ways, namely, through the provision of structure and through the provision of meaning (Feinman, 1991). One person can structure the environment and provide assistance in such a way that the other person will be able to engage individually in experiential learning. Thus, a parent could place several interesting toys in a 10-month-old's path—enough to be stimulating but not so many as to overwhelm—and then withdraw to let the infant discover and explore. In such guidance through structure, one person helps another discover experientially the nature and meaning of the situation. She does not directly contribute to the other's construction of that reality but, rather, does so indirectly instead.

A direct social contribution to reality construction is provided, however, in guidance through meaning, in which one individual offers to another interpretative information that defines the situation. If, for instance, the 10-month-old seems puzzled over how to feel and what to do with one of the toys, then the parent could come and sit on the floor near her, touch the toy and smile, and show her some possible ways to handle that object. In such a case, the parent is letting her child know how she feels about this referent object, and what she thinks might be done with it. Through the adult's conveyance of meaning, a direct and obvious contribution is being made here to the infant's construction of the reality of the toy.

Social referencing, as a process in which one person utilizes another person's interpretation of the situation to formulate her own interpretation of it (Feinman, 1982, 1985; Klinnert, Campos, Sorce, Emde, & Svejda, 1983), is founded upon this guidance through meaning modality. In referencing, one person serves as a base of information for another and, in so doing, facilitates the other's efforts to construct reality. For people generally, and for very young children in particular, such facilitation can help to reduce stress in everyday life (Lerner & East, 1984; Schachter, 1959), and is very much an expected and influential feature of routine social commerce (Farran & Margolis, 1987). In a social species, such as human beings, the availability of other conspecifics as a base of information is both comforting and essential, being one of the fundamental reasons for affiliation and sociality (Lenski & Lenski, 1982; Schachter, 1959).

It has long been accepted that adults make sense of the world around them, and their selves as well, through the assistance of interpretations which are proffered by other people, and which they can glean from what others say and do. That the individual's construction of reality is, in large part, a social enterprise is very much a stock-in-trade sociological assumption (Berger & Luckmann, 1966; Mead, 1934), and a well-accepted notion in social psychology (Festinger, 1954; Schachter, 1964). Put most plainly, the act of defining a situation is often a social act. The expectation that infants, in particular, participate in the social construction of reality is a hypothesis which has been in the air for some time (Orlansky, 1949; Sullivan, 1947). Nonetheless, it was not until fairly recently that the operation of this process during infancy has been the topic of systematic conceptual and empirical consideration. Indeed, an examination of textbooks, handbooks, and other treatises just a decade ago reveals the virtual absence of any mention of the role of social definition in infant cognition, and of the process of social referencing *per se*.

Beginning in the late 1970s, research and thinking about development generally, and about the development of very young children in particular, turned its attention to the role of social guidance in learning, and to a variety of processes within this broad phenomenon, one of which was social referencing. Upon retrospection, it seems that this time was a watershed from which flowed a new way of looking at infants and other young children—a "social world" zeitgeist (Feinman, 1991). Much of the research on infant perception and cognition, prior to this time, focused primarily upon how infants responded to stimuli either when alone or when their mothers (or other caregivers) were allowed to be present but had been asked not to initiate interaction or provide any definitional input to the child. This methodology made it virtually impossible to investigate just about any social influence that might otherwise have occurred, with the exception of the potentially comforting effect of the caregiver's mere presence. Instead, research focused on the question of how the infant, by herself, made sense of the physical world around her—in much the same way that research on animal learning, as Galef (1982) has noted, had long emphasized the individual acquisition of behavior (Thorndike, 1911). When present but noncommunicative, the caregiver could be thought of as stripped entirely of her function of a guide for learning, as well as much of her role as a source of comfort, support, and care, with the exception of being able to serve as a physical presence—somewhat like the dummy surrogate mothers used in social isolation studies of baby monkeys.

In such research, there was a significant interest in infants' perception of, and possible preference for, social stimuli (e.g., faces), but without a socialization or even a social emphasis. Research focused upon how infants made sense of social and nonsocial stimuli, but not upon how people influenced infants' cognitive functioning. In this perspective, the social environment was viewed more as something to be observed by infants than as a source of influence upon them. Furthermore, infants' reactions to people were often accounted for primarily as a function of the physical qualities of these "social stimuli," (e.g., contour, contrast, and complexity; Fantz, 1961; Koopman & Ames, 1968), thus invoking a form of "physical reductionism" in which people were conceptualized not as uniquely social beings but, rather, as perceptual objects within the infant's physical environment.

There was a great deal of investigation and thinking, during that time, about the infant's relationship with other people, and especially with attachment figures (Ainsworth, Blehar, Waters, & Wall, 1978). Nonetheless, it is important to note that, with rare exceptions (Stayton, Hogan, & Ainsworth, 1971), these relationships were looked at primarily in terms of their comforting and caring function, and with regard to the frequency and quality of interaction that transpired within them. In stark contrast, relatively little attention was paid to the socialization and guidance function that these relationships served (Feinman & Lewis, 1991). Such studies certainly did indicate that the infant had a place in the social world. But as for the ways in which very young children made sense of environmental events, the role of that social world in structuring, defining, interpreting, and guiding the child's learning was given little standing.

During the latter part of the 1970s, a new zeitgeist began to emerge— on a scale broader than the study of children or even human beings—a spirit expressed in the general notion that "nothing in nature can be understood apart from its ecological context" (Campos, 1983, p. 85). At about this time, some of Vygotsky's writings, which had been politically and linguistically inaccessible since the 1930s, became available and were taken to heart by developmental psychologists—writings which stressed the importance of social settings for individual development, and explicated the concept of the zone of proximal development in which individuals learned to perform tasks first with social assistance and only later by themselves (Vygotsky, 1978). At about this same time, interest resurfaced among developmentalists in Mead's sociological perspective on the influence of society upon mind and self, and in his view of thought as an essentially socially constructed process (Mead, 1934). In conjunction with the newly prevailing winds of the more general zeitgeist of ecological context, these views led to a paradigmatic shift in the study of young children—to the insistence, at least by some scholars, that their behavior and development, and particularly their cognition and construction of meaning, be investigated in the context of "social communicative processes" (Campos, 1983, p. 85). Thus, cognition and learning in young children came to be viewed within the context of their social worlds. This social world zeitgeist restored the social-guidance-of-learning function to the way in which young children's relationships with other people were understood.

In the climate of this zeitgeist, there was a blooming of excitement about how other people might influence, through both structure and meaning, the way that children make sense of their environments. This was reflected by interest in the manner in which young children first learned individual skills through the help of a guide, within Vygotsky's zone of proximal development (Rogoff & Wertsch, 1984); in the ways that adults arranged structures and sequences, and provided informational messages (Rogoff, Malkin, & Gilbride, 1984); and, generally, in the ways in which individuals became enculturated under the watchful eye and guiding hand of other people, in the context of an "apprenticeship in thinking" (Rogoff, 1990). Research on how adults "scaffolded" learning situations for young children, limiting and constructing what the child confronts so that she can be successful (Bruner, 1983; Ross & Lollis, 1987; Valsiner, 1985; Wood, Bruner, & Ross, 1976), flowed from this social world zeitgeist.

From this context emerged the hypothesis that infants utilize other persons' interpretations of situations to formulate their own definitions of these situations. Viewed from the new vantage point of ecological context, observations which, either had not meant very much at earlier times, or had been thought of as methodological problems, took on new meaning. The tendency of infants to turn to their caregivers when an unfamiliar adult entered the room, or a new object was encountered—actions which had long been noted in numerous investigations—came to be viewed, in the early light of the new paradigmatic dawn, as efforts to gather information from the caregiver about these referent stimuli. The cartoon image of a light bulb switching on is not an inappropriate metaphor for the way in which we came to see old data in new perspective. Out of the realization that infants might be gathering and utilizing information from other people to define reality emerged the initial studies of social referencing.

The first reports about infant social referencing were presented at the meetings of learned and professional societies in 1980 and 1981, and appeared in published form a few years later. By the mid-1980s, referencing's place in the infant's repertoire toward the end of the first year of life was established, and the subtleties of the process were beginning to be understood. By the end of the decade, theory and research about infant social referencing were accepted and integrated within the mainstream of thinking about infant development. Indeed, by this time, not only was the concept of social referencing during infancy mentioned in most child development textbooks (e.g., Mussen, Conger, Kagan, & Huston, 1990; Schickedanz, Hansen, & Forsyth, 1990), but its acceptance by the community of scholars and practitioners was reflected in that most awkward of compliments, namely, overuse and misuse. Indeed, by the mid-1980s, there was a need to be concerned that some person or another would cry "referencing!" every time an infant looked toward another person (a concern which led to the formulation of the operational distinctions between information-seeking looks and other forms of social looking; Clyman, Emde, Kempe, & Harmon, 1986; Hornik & Gunnar, 1988). A decade after it was first sighted, social referencing in infancy is a process whose existence is well founded empirically, and whose nuances are becoming understood.

In light of the progress which has been made in describing and understanding infant social referencing, it seems reasonable to pause, for a moment, for a critical look of this body of research. Typically, critical reviews and suggestions for new research directions are made by those who are active participants in the specific domain of investigation being put under the microscope. Although no one knows you as well as you know yourself, being too close to what you are examining often limits visual scope. At the very least, outsiders have a different perspective than insiders—as anthropologists have often noted with regard to making sense of cultural phenomena. In this perspective, our consideration of the current state, past history, and future directions of research and thinking about infant social referencing combines the efforts of some scholars who have been active in the study of this phenomenon with others who are interested in related but distinct phenomena and theoretical points of view. Furthermore, those individuals who have been active researchers of infant referencing were asked, for the purposes of this volume, to look at referencing from a somewhat different angle, to see it through new glasses, so to speak.

This approach is taken for another reason as well. As the discovery and construction of knowledge has expanded and become more specialized, especially during the past half century, scientific statements often have taken on a distinctly splintered and fractured appearance. Although we have come to know more about the particular parts, we have done so at the risk of understanding less about the whole. Even within particular disciplines or areas of study, such as that of infant behavior and development, it is remarkably easy for a specific topic of investigation to slide away from other research areas and develop in comparative isolation. The inclusion of scholars from outside as well as inside the particular niche of social referencing research gives us the benefit of seeing with our outer as well as our inner eye (Lee, 1990), and helps prevent the slide of social referencing into oblivious isolationism.

The study of referencing can gain from what other areas of substance and theory have to say, just as these areas may benefit from referencing's message. The determination of the state of the art of infant social referencing, and the laying out of new paths that future investigations might follow, is best done not in the insular and narrow canyon of this specialized area of study but, rather, within the broad valley which is home to a wide range of interconnected phenomena and theories. Furthermore, it is only within this expansive terrain that we can accurately map out the empirical and conceptual relationships between referencing and other phenomena.

Because referencing, as a process and as a field of study, lies at the intersection of the roads of developmental psychology, on the one hand, and social psychology and sociology, on the other, we have included in our midst scholars from each point of view, and some whose work proceeds from an interdisciplinary combination of both perspectives. Although it would seem reasonable to expect a veritable flood of back-and-forth conversation between these two areas, in truth one finds surprisingly little cross-talk between developmental psychology and social psychology (Feinman & Lewis, 1991). As Wertsch (1985, p. 1), in discussing disciplinary insularity, pointed out: "This intellectual isolation is nowhere more evident than in the division that separates studies of individual psychology from studies of the sociocultural environment in which individuals live." As a result of their derivation from rather dissimilar paradigmatic traditions, and their relative isolation from each other, it can be noted that the developmental and social psychological perspectives often view the same phenomena divergently, with these differences ranging from subtle shades of nuance to gross incongruities. Indeed, that social referencing occupies a place of convergence between these often divergent strains can be considered testimony to its centrality in the overall scheme of things. Because of the often striking contrasts which emerge when developmental and social psychology are juxtaposed, the inclusion of both developmental psychologists along with social psychologists and sociologists is essential if we are to do justice to our task.

Before getting to our examination of social referencing in infancy within a broad and integrative perspective, a review of the referencing literature *per se* is provided (Chapter 2). The lion's share of the book (Chapters 3 through 14) is devoted to drawing out the connections between referencing and other phenomena, or looking at referencing through different theoretical lenses. The chapters are divided heuristically into three major sections: Meaning and Understanding, Cognition and Information Processing, and Relationships and Interaction. These groupings reflect degrees of emphasis, rather than exclusive foci. Thus, chapters in each of these conceptual clusters overlap in the scope of what they consider, but vary with regard to the slant from which they look at referencing. Finally, Chapter 15 attempts to pull together major themes from the book into an integrated and broadly based assessment of the current state of our knowledge on referencing, and to offer some indications as to where new paths might be carved out for future research.

Four key thematic strands can be identified in the ways in which social referencing is examined here, falling roughly into the categories of skills, processes, relationships, and settings. First of all, a number of chapters examine the manner in which the skills that form the sociocognitive foundation of referencing can also be found in the operation of other phenomena. Thus, the role of intentional communication and intersubjectivity in a broad spectrum of phenomena in very early childhood—of which referencing is one—is discussed by Bretherton, by Rogoff, Mistry, Radziszewska, and Germond, and by Užgiris and Kruper. These chapters also discuss how the emergence of greater capacity for verbal expression and other conventionalized communication alters social referencing, a topic considered by Ainsworth, by Emde, and by Hornik-Parritz, Mangelsdorf, and Gunnar, as well. Clearly, the skills which are believed to underlie the emergence of referencing in the second semester of the first year, and the later developmental transformations in the second year and beyond, are capabilities whose expression can be seen in the initial appearance and later development of related processes as well.

Quite a few chapters deal with the ways in which the process of social referencing articulates with other phenomena in developmental and social psychology. Thus, Užgiris and Kruper analyze the connection between referencing and imitation, finding that there are contact points at which these two processes overlap, but noting that they typically operate through rather different mechanisms, a feature noted by Lewis and Feiring as well. The social cognitive conceptualization of referencing (Bretherton; Lewis & Feiring)—in contrast to a simpler contagion mechanism which can sometimes underlie imitation—is the starting point for Bandura's analysis of how referencing is governed by vicarious processes. Lewis and Feiring show us how referencing falls under the more general rubric of indirect effects and, as such, exhibits the hallmark characteristics of that broader phenomena. Hornik-Parritz and her colleagues help us to view social referencing through the wide-angle lens of the various mechanisms by which individuals predict and control threatening situations—a theme considered by Bandura as well. Finally, Gewirtz and Peláez-Nogueras show us how social referencing messages can influence the infant's interpretation of the situation through what is, in essence, a process of classical conditioning.

Through a more distinctly sociological eye, Webster and Foschi draw out the numerous parallel features between social referencing in infancy and the ways in which adults and older children are influenced by other people's evaluations. Their discussion includes consideration of the factors which underlie selectivity, that is, the processes through which an individual comes to be more receptive to input from some source persons than others—a topic also discussed in some depth by Bandura, and in my own chapter on referencing and conformity. The latter chapter aims, most generally, to delineate the similarities and divergences between referencing in infants versus conformity in older individuals, with special consideration for delineating the particular processes by which opinion is translated (or not) into action.

Referencing, much like any process, cannot exist in a vacuum; rather, it is well grounded in social relationships. Denzin's phenomenological analysis of referencing places it within the social context of the parent–infant relationship, where it changes and develops along with the relationship. The connections between attachment and referencing are delineated in intricate detail in Ainsworth's chapter, which touches upon (among other issues) the frequency at which infant requests for maternal information occur in the context of the mother–infant relationship. Both Emde, and Rogoff and her colleagues discuss the ways in which referencing becomes less of a one-way street and takes on a more mutual character as the infant's relationships with parents and other adults develop during the second year. Along this line, Ainsworth considers the way in which this more negotiated type of referencing might relate to the later progression of attachment relationships into goal-corrected partnerships.

Finally, several chapters examine the ways in which social referencing functions within the broader settings of family and society. Thus, Emde examines some of the issues involved in evaluating how well laboratory studies of referencing reflect the conditions under which this process operates in the young child's natural environment, and considers the ways in which referencing may serve as a socialization technique—an issue discussed by Ainsworth as well. Lewis and Feiring look at how referencing operates in the natural setting of families at dinner, finding that young children often have available to them information which may serve to help them construct reality. And, looking at referencing as it functions at the interface of the sometimes tense relationship between the individual and society, Denzin places referencing within the context of the social construction of reality that occurs in the infant's everyday encounters with other members of society.

In this book, we aim to shed some light on how social referencing in infancy is linked to other phenomena, both in young children in particular, and throughout the lifespan more generally. In so doing, we show how the cognitive and social skills which underlie referencing also can be found in cognate processes. Furthermore, because no process is disassociated from its context, the place of referencing within social relationships and the social settings of family and society are considered as well. From this analytical method emerges our commentary about the phenomenon of referencing, and our suggestions as to possible new directions for future empirical investigation and conceptual consideration, as well as our sense of where referencing fits into the broader scope of the way that reality is socially constructed within the context of human social relations.

REFERENCES

Ainsworth, M. D. S., Blehar, M. C., Waters, E., & Wall, S. (1978). *Patterns of attachment: A psychological study of the strange situation.* Hillsdale, NJ: Lawrence Erlbaum.

Berger, P. L., & Luckmann, T. (1966). *The social construction of reality.* Garden City, NY: Doubleday.

Bruner, J. (1983). *Child's talk: Learning to use language.* New York: Norton.

Campos, J. J. (1983). The importance of affective communication in social referencing: A commentary on Feinman. *Merrill-Palmer Quarterly, 29,* 83–87.

Clyman, R. B., Emde, R. N., Kempe, J. E., & Harmon, R. J. (1986). Social referencing and social looking among twelve-month-old infants. In T. B. Brazelton & M. W. Yogman (Eds.), *Affective development in infancy* (pp. 75–94). Norwood, NJ: Ablex.

Fantz, R. L. (1961). The origin of form perception. *Scientific American, 204,* 66–72.

Farran, D. C., & Margolis, L. H. (1987). The family economic environment as a context for children's development. In J. H. Lewko (Ed.), *How children and adolescents view the world of work* (pp. 69–87). San Francisco: Jossey-Bass.

Feinman, S. (1982). Social referencing in infancy. *Merrill-Palmer Quarterly, 28,* 445–470.

Feinman, S. (1985). Emotional expression, social referencing, and preparedness for learning in infancy—Mother knows best, but sometimes I know better. In G. Zivin (Ed.), *The development of expressive behavior: Biology–environment interactions* (pp. 291–318). New York: Academic Press.

Feinman, S. (1991). Bringing babies back into the social world. In M. Lewis & S. Feinman (Eds.), *Social influences and socialization in infancy* (pp. 281–325). New York: Plenum.

Feinman, S., & Lewis, M. (1991). Influence lost, influence regained. In M. Lewis & S. Feinman (Eds.), *Social influences and socialization in infancy* (pp. 1–19). New York: Plenum.

Festinger, L. (1954). A theory of social comparison processes. *Human Relations, 7,* 117–140.

Galef, B. G., Jr. (1982). Studies of social learning in Norway rats: A brief review. *Developmental Psychobiology, 15,* 279–295.

Hornik, R., & Gunnar, M. R. (1988). A descriptive analysis of infant social referencing. *Child Development, 59,* 626–634.

Klinnert, M. D., Campos, J. J., Sorce, J. F., Emde, R. N., & Svejda, M. (1983). Emotions as behavior regulators: Social referencing in infancy. In R. Plutchik & H. Kellerman (Eds.), *The emotions* (Vol. 2, pp. 57–86). New York: Academic Press.

Koopman, P. R., & Ames, E. W. (1968). Infants' preferences for facial arrangements: A failure to replicate. *Child Development, 39,* 481–487.

Lee, M. O. (1990). *Wagner's ring: Turning the sky round.* New York: Summit Books.

Lenski, G., & Lenski, J. (1982). *Human societies: An introduction to macrosociology* (4th ed.). New York: McGraw-Hill.

Lerner, R. M., & East, P. L. (1984). The role of temperament in stress, coping and socio-emotional functioning in early development. *Infant Mental Health Journal, 5,* 148–159.

Mead, G. H. (1934). *Mind, self and society.* Chicago: University of Chicago Press.

Mussen, P. H., Conger, J. J., Kagan, J., & Huston, A. C. (1990). *Child development & personality* (7th ed.). New York: Harper & Row.

Orlansky, H. (1949). Infant care and personality. *Psychological Bulletin, 46,* 1–48.

Rogoff, B. (1990). *Apprenticeship in thinking: Cognitive development in social context.* New York: Oxford University Press.

Rogoff, B., Malkin, C., & Gilbride, K. (1984). Interaction with babies as guidance in development. In B. Rogoff & J. V. Wertsch (Eds.), *Children's learning in the "zone of proximal development"* (pp. 31–44). San Francisco: Jossey-Bass.

Rogoff, B., & Wertsch, J. V. (Eds.), *Children's learning in the "zone of proximal development."* San Francisco: Jossey-Bass.

Ross, H. S., & Lollis, S. P. (1987). Communication within infant social games. *Developmental Psychology, 23,* 241–248.

Schachter, S. (1959). *The psychology of affiliation: Experimental studies of the sources of gregariousness.* Stanford, CA: Stanford University Press.

Schachter, S. (1964). The interaction of cognitive and physiological determinants of emotional state. In L. Berkowitz (Ed.), *Advances in experimental social psychology* (Vol. 1, pp. 49–80). New York: Academic Press.

Schickedanz, J. A., Hansen, K., & Forsyth, P. D. (1990). *Understanding children.* Mountain View, CA: Mayfield.

Stayton, D. J., Hogan, R., & Ainsworth, M. D. S. (1971). Infant obedience and maternal behavior: The origins of socialization reconsidered. *Child Development, 42,* 1057–1069.

Sullivan, H. S. (1947). *Conceptions of modern psychiatry.* New York: Norton.

Thorndike, E. L. (1911). *Animal intelligence: An experimental study of association processes in animals.* New York: Macmillan.

Valsiner, J. (1985). Parental organization of children's cognitive development within home environment. *Psychologia, 28,* 131–143.

Vygotsky, L. S. (1978). *Mind in society: The development of higher psychological processes.* Cambridge, MA: Harvard University Press.

Wertsch, J. V. (1985). *Vygotsky and the social formation of mind.* Cambridge, MA: Harvard University Press.

Wood, D., Bruner, J. S., & Ross, G. (1976). The role of tutoring in problem solving. *Journal of Child Psychology and Psychiatry, 17,* 89–100.

2

A Critical Review of Social Referencing in Infancy

Saul Feinman, Debra Roberts, Kuei-Fang Hsieh, Darby Sawyer, and Dee Swanson

One of the most common things that human beings do is gather information about the environment, and then utilize that information in formulating interpretation and action. In this information and action process, once the individual has become interested in some environmental event, she then becomes receptive to information about that event and pays attention to it when it is provided. Finally, this input is incorporated into the individual's understanding of the environmental event, and is the basis upon which action is founded (Feinman, 1986). This general sequence of informational receipt, reality construction, and action is what occurs when an infant first meets (face to face sometimes) the new puppy that mom and dad have brought home, when a teenager goes out on a blind date, and when an adult travels to a foreign country.

Variations on this information-and-action theme take many forms, which differ as to the extent to which information is provided by other people. Does the individual learn about the environment primarily

SAUL FEINMAN, DEBRA ROBERTS, KUEI-FANG HSIEH, DARBY SAWYER, AND DEE SWANSON • Child and Family Studies, Department of Home Economics, University of Wyoming, Laramie, Wyoming 82071.

Social Referencing and the Social Construction of Reality in Infancy, edited by Saul Feinman. Plenum Press, New York, 1992.

through direct experiential contact, or do social sources of information play a primary role in helping her make sense of the environment? Social referencing, a phenomenon in which other people serve as a base of information, clearly is a social process in which the definition of the situation is based largely on what other people think about that situation.

The notion that other people, and the broader societal context operating through the generalized other, have a significant impact upon the individual's construction of reality is a sociological commonplace, a basic tenet of the view that the world is a social place (Berger & Luckmann, 1966; Mead, 1934). From this microsociological point of view, the concept of social referencing is well within the mainstream of long-accepted beliefs about how society influences the individual, being related to theories about reference groups, social influence, conformity, and group processes. But it has only been during the past decade or so that we have begun to examine how reality construction is socially assisted in very young children. It is not the notion of social referencing *per se* but rather that of social referencing *in infancy* which has attracted our attention during this last decade.

THE INFLUENCE OF SOCIAL REFERENCING ON BEHAVIOR: THE REGULATORY FUNCTION OF REFERENCING

The most basic prediction about social referencing is that it will influence infants' interpretations of and responses to events, objects, and people. Over the last decade or so, considerable evidence has accumulated which provides consistent support for this hypothesis, indicating that information obtained through social referencing serves to regulate behavior. By the latter part of the first year, infants more readily accept and approach toys, strangers, and optical illusions after they have received positive referencing messages about these stimuli than after they have received neutral or negative messages. Thus, for example, when confronted with a modified visual cliff which presented the illusion of a 30-cm drop-off, none of the infants crossed over the deep side of the cliff when the mother displayed a fearful facial expression, but 74% crossed when she smiled (Sorce, Emde, Campos, & Klinnert, 1985). Similarly, infants and toddlers were more likely to approach and contact a toy about which the mother had spoken in a joyful tone of voice than one which appeared to frighten her (Walden & Baxter, 1989). Behavior to people as well as objects and illusions has also been found to be influenced by social referencing messages. Thus, behavior to unfamiliar adults is generally friendlier after receiving positive messages about the stranger (Feinman & Lewis, 1983).

Results similar to these have been noted in a considerable number of investigations, with no major contradictory findings reported. Generally, there is consistent support for the hypothesis that referencing messages have an impact upon the way that the infant understands and behaves with a variety of target stimuli.

Nature of the Referer, Referee, and Referent

In referencing, three essential components can be identified: referer (the person being influenced), referee (the person doing the influencing), and referent (the topic of the influencing message; Feinman, 1985). In studies of referencing's regulatory function, the infant typically is the referer—the individual who seeks and/or receives, and is influenced by the referencing message. We say "typically" here because, in some instances, older infants have been observed trying to influence the adult or to "negotiate" the construction of reality (Hirshberg, 1988; Hornik & Gunnar, 1988), that is, to reverse the roles. However, the infant has been the *intended* referer in all extent referencing studies. Most studies have recruited participants between the ages of 9 and 14 months, although two investigations have included 18-month-olds as well (Hornik & Gunnar, 1988; Klinnert, 1984), and two have examined a broader, continuous age spectrum from 6 to 22 months (Walden & Ogan, 1988) and from 6 to 40 months (Walden & Baxter, 1989). All studies have included infants of both genders and have drawn their samples from populations of North American (USA) children.

The referee is the individual who provides the message about the stimulus. In the earliest studies of social referencing's regulatory function (first reported at meetings during 1980–1982), the infant's mother was the referee (Garland, 1982; Klinnert, 1984; Sorce et al., 1985; Svejda & Campos, 1982) or either parent could serve in this role, although almost always (98% of the time) it was the mother (Feinman & Lewis, 1983). Although infants have been exposed to a wider range of referees in more recently conducted studies, it is still the mother who plays that role most often (Boccia & Campos, 1983; Feinman, Roberts, & Morissette, 1986; Gewirtz, Peláez-Nogueras, Diaz, & Villate, 1990; Gunnar & Stone, 1984; Hornik & Gunnar, 1988; Hornik, Risenhoover, & Gunnar, 1987). In two studies, when the parents were told that either the mother or the father could accompany the infant to be the referee, it was the mother who served in that capacity for four out of every five infants (Walden & Baxter, 1989; Walden & Ogan, 1988). Zarbatany and Lamb (1985) had either the mother or a familiarized stranger as the referee, while both served simultaneously as referees in Bradshaw, Goldsmith, and Campos' (1987) study. Mother and sibling together served as referees in one recent study (Feinman, Roberts, & Hsieh, 1988) as did mother and father in another (Hirshberg, 1988, 1990; Hirshberg & Svejda, 1990). In several studies, a familiarized stranger (experimenter) has provided the referencing message (Bingham, Emde, Landau, & Butterfield, 1988; Bradshaw, Campos, & Klinnert, 1986; Campos, Butterfield, & Klinnert, 1985; Klinnert, Emde, Butterfield, & Campos, 1986).

The referent—the topic or target of the referencing message—has most commonly been a novel toy or toylike object. In one study (Hornik & Gunnar, 1988), referencing communication was provided about a live (caged), large black rabbit, and in two others, about a reduced visual cliff (Bradshaw et al., 1987; Sorce et al., 1985). An adult female stranger has been the referent in four investigations (Boccia & Campos, 1983; Feinman & Lewis, 1983; Feinman et al., 1986; Garland, 1982). Although just about all of these experiments were performed in laboratory settings previously unfamiliar to the infants, it is noteworthy that the choice of both referents and referees reflects considerable ecological validity and mundane realism. New toys and unfamiliar persons are often encountered in the ordinary everyday world of infancy, and most infants, once they begin to get around, encounter surfaces and edges of varying depth. Although black rabbits are probably not within the worldly experience of the typical American infant, other small furry animals, that is, pets, certainly are. Thus, the referents utilized in the extant referencing studies have much in common with the objects and events that constitute the infant's life experiences.

Selecting mothers, fathers, siblings, and familiarized strangers to convey referencing messages indicates a further real-world connection in referencing research. Typically, American infants spend more time with nuclear family members than with anyone else (Feinman & Roberts, 1986); but contact with other individuals may also serve as a source of information input. The ecological relevance of the referees and referents studied facilitates the extrapolation of these experimental results to infant cognition and behavior outside of the laboratory.

Design of Studies of Referencing's Regulatory Function

Studies of the regulatory function of social referencing have all been experiments in which the content of the referencing message is manipulated as the key independent factor. These investigations have been performed in laboratory settings, although Walden's studies included familiar day-care as well as unfamiliar laboratory environments, and detected the expected behavior regulation effect in both settings (Walden & Baxter, 1989; Walden & Ogan, 1988). Significantly, there have been no studies of referencing's impact in the home.

In the prototypical methodology, each infant is randomly assigned to a referencing message condition, which is conveyed with regard to one or more referent stimuli. Thus, the infant received either a fear or a joy message about a toy spider in Zarbatany and Lamb's (1985) investigation, while in Hornik *et al.*'s (1987) study she received either a negative, neutral, or positive message about three toys. In a few studies, infants have been exposed to different messages for various stimulus objects, a technique which may confound the behavior regulation effect under some circumstances (Klinnert, 1981, 1984) but clearly does not interfere in others (Walden & Baxter, 1989; Walden & Ogan, 1988). Thus, Klinnert's (1984) subjects received (in a counterbalanced design) a joyful message for one toy, a neutral message for the second, and a fearful message for the third. Similarly, Gewirtz *et al.* (1990) systematically exposed 9- to 12-month-olds to positive cues for some objects, and negative cues for others.

It is standard operating procedure for the referee to present a consistent message about any one stimulus. Thus, mothers are not asked to pose joy and then fear with regard to a single referent. Likewise, they are not purposively requested to express disgust facially and pleasure vocally (although some incongruity could occur when the referee is urged to keep facial expression constant while manipulating tone of voice, such as in Svejda and Campos' 1982 study). In one study, however (Barrett, 1985), 10-month-olds were exposed to consistent versus inconsistent emotional messages. Inconsistent signals elicited more looking to the referee (probably in order to obtain further clarification) and had an inhibiting effect, as reflected in ambivalent responses to the stimulus toys. Consistent messages generate a clearer, more directed, behavior regulation effect.

Two or three message conditions are utilized in most studies, although five different emotions were posed in one investigation (Sorce *et al.*, 1985). There have been two studies, which do not utilize an experimental design in the strict sense, that involve only one message condition (a positive one) and either examine the impact of this communication on the infant in a more descriptive manner (Hornik & Gunnar, 1988), or investigate whether influence is greater when this message is provided by the mother versus a stranger (Feiring, Lewis, & Starr, 1984).

By far, the most common experimental design utilized in examining the impact of emotional referencing messages contrasts a positive with a negative message (e.g., Boccia & Campos, 1983). Some studies have compared neutral to positive messages (Feinman & Lewis, 1983), a few have contrasted negative with neutral messages (e.g., Bradshaw *et al.*, 1986), and others have examined the impact of positive, neutral and negative messages (e.g., Klinnert, 1984). Several investigations, which derive from an interest in discrete emotions theory, that is, the notion that particular emotions have particular effects (Hiatt, Campos, & Emde, 1979; Izard, 1977), have looked at the comparative impact of two or more negative emotions or two or more positive emotions. Other than the Sorce *et al.*,

(1985) study, which was able to compare joy with interest, discrete emotions referencing studies have focused on differentiating the effects of various negative messages (e.g., sadness vs. anger; Svejda & Campos, 1982).

Although some studies have utilized carefully controlled and comparatively "pure" signals conveyed through only one channel of communication—typically facial expression (e.g., Klinnert, 1984; Sorce et al., 1985)—others have used more freely flowing multichannel messages which include facial, vocal, and body language cues (e.g., Feinman & Lewis, 1983; Hornik et al., 1987). While much of the early research utilized one-channel messages, the use of multichannel message communication has become more common over time, although the ratio of strictly controlled versus more freely flowing message presentation has pretty much stayed the same. Perhaps, as Emde (chapter 4, this volume) has noted, the emphasis upon facial expression in quite a few referencing studies does not reflect what transpires in everyday life, in which more holistic multichannel expressions may be prototypical. In messages provided from a distance, especially if the infant is "outward bound," vocally conveyed communication may be especially common.

Typically, these messages are posed; the referee is asked to behave "as if" she is afraid, or sad, or joyful about the referent. Although there may be concern about the ecological validity of this practice, it is reasonable to assume that parents and other adult referees pose or "fake" referencing messages in everyday life as well. Thus, although a mother may, in truth, be amused by her infant's use of finger food to "draw" on the highchair tray, the knowledge that this behavior is socially undesirable leads her to suppress the smile and to pose facially expressed disgust while saying something like: "Yuck!! Food is not for drawing!" Similarly, adult referees outside of the laboratory may pose simple, "unblended" emotions when trying to get a referencing message across in a straightforward manner, perhaps using pure emotions more often in these instructional situations than in other ongoing interaction with babies. Although there is no denying the need for investigation of how referencing messages are conveyed in natural settings, it is also important to realize that the manipulated messages posed in the laboratory do bear some resemblance to the form that referencing conversations seem to take in everyday interaction.

There is also the question of how long and how often the message is given. Studies vary as to the frequency and duration of the referencing communication, but virtually all either repeat the message or present it for a continuous and substantial period of time. Repeated messages are provided intermittently over a period ranging from less than 30 seconds (Feinman & Lewis, 1983) to several minutes (Hornik et al., 1987; Walden & Baxter, 1989). Some facially expressed messages are exhibited continuously for as long as 2 minutes (Sorce *et al.*, 1985), but infants do not look at the display all that time. Messages which are expressed only vocally (Svejda & Campos, 1982), or vocally in combination with facial and/or gestural communication, are often given for much shorter bursts of time (e.g., Bradshaw *et al.*, 1986; Feinman *et al.*, 1986), but it is likely that the infant catches most if not all of the vocal component at least.

Especially in dealing with complex stimuli, infants appear interested in informational repetition (as noted by Hornik *et al.*, 1987). It is reasonable to assume that there is message repetition over minutes, hours, days, and even weeks of referencing communication in everyday life. Nonetheless, in the laboratory at least, brief messages do not seem to be proportionately less effective than longer ones. It may well be that infants are well equipped to learn a lot from briefly presented input. Such an orientation would be advantageous, generally, given that infants' "everyday interactions with stimuli in the world are often confined to brief glances" (Lamb & Bornstein, 1987, p. 215).

After the message has been communicated, and sometimes during its transmission as well, infant behavior with regard to the referent stimulus (e.g., the toy or the unfamiliar person) is examined to determine whether these responses differ systematically among message conditions. The most commonly used dependent measures are approach and contact variables, and hedonic response. Every study to date has utilized some measures of frequency, latency, or speed of approach, and/or amount and nature of contact with the target of the referencing message. Most have employed some indication of affective reaction to the stimulus, typically measured through facial expression. A small minority have included physical measures as well, such as activity level (Boccia & Campos, 1983; Klinnert, 1984; Zarbatany & Lamb, 1985) or physiological indicators, namely, heart rate (Boccia & Campos, 1983; Campos *et al.*, 1985). Overall, the measures used in the study of social referencing's regulatory function serve to tap variables which are important constituents of the infant's repertoire of response to environmental events.

INFORMATION GATHERING:
LEARNING ABOUT THE REFERENT

In addition to demonstrating that others' opinions can regulate infants' behavior to people and objects, referencing research has revealed that infants engage in behavior which can be interpreted as serving an "information-gathering" function. If the referee conveys the message through facial expression, then receipt of that information relies exclusively upon attending to the adult's face. That infants do look toward the referee when she provides exclusively facial messages about the referent has been noted in several studies (Bradshaw et al., 1987; Klinnert, 1984; Klinnert et al., 1986; Sorce et al., 1985; Zarbatany & Lamb, 1985). Unfortunately, information-acquisition behavior in such studies sometimes was operationally defined simply as looking to the referee, without more precisely limiting it to looking to the face in particular. Nonetheless, when looking to the face (vs. to other parts of the body) has been separately coded, it can be noted that looking to other than the face is rather rare, suggesting that most visual regard of the referee while she is conveying the message is directed to her face (Walden & Baxter, 1989; Walden & Ogan, 1988).

There is also evidence that infants look to the referee when referencing information is either imparted only through vocal communication or transmitted in a more naturalistic multichannel message which involves vocal, facial, and gestural cues (Boccia & Campos, 1983; Hornik & Gunnar, 1988; Svejda & Campos, 1982; Walden & Baxter, 1989; Walden & Ogan, 1988). Gestures conveyed through visually apparent body language obviously must be detected through looking, but vocal messages can be received without turning to look at the referee. That infants will turn to look to the person who is speaking to them (Svejda & Campos, 1982) suggests that they may be looking to see if there is additional information being conveyed through other channels. Orienting to the face of a person who is talking—a commonplace gesture in adulthood—has been noted in infancy as well (Clyman, Emde, Kempe, & Harmon, 1986).

Looking to the referee, interestingly enough, is a relatively low-frequency event in referencing studies. Several investigations of purely facially expressed messages found that infants looked to the referee about three to four times per minute (Klinnert, 1984; Klinnert et al., 1986; Sorce et al., 1985). When the message is conveyed through multiple channels, including a substantial vocal component, infants looked to the referee's face only about 10 seconds out of every 3 to 4 minutes (Walden & Baxter, 1989; Walden & Ogan, 1988). The brevity and infrequency of these looks suggests, as noted earlier, that infants learn a lot about the referent through brief glances.

Because looking can serve functions other than information gathering, some of the measures utilized, especially in earlier studies, may have been too crude to discriminate between referencing looks and looks which serve other purposes. Thus, a simple measure of whether the infant looks to the mother, or even to the mother's face, while she was transmitting information about the referent would not differentiate looking for the purpose of information gathering versus that for initiating social discourse, seeking comfort, or sharing affect. In an effort to remedy this situation, some investigations have developed specifically delineated criteria in which referencing looks are restricted to visual regard of the referee (or her face, in particular) which is preceded by orienting to the referent (Dickstein & Parke, 1988; Dickstein, Thompson, Estes, Malkin, & Lamb, 1984; Sorce, Emde, & Frank, 1982). Thus, the infant first looks at the referent, and then to the referee.

Even this refinement may not be specific enough. The sequence in which the infant orients to the referent, and then displays a strongly positive facial expression while looking to the adult may indicate that she likes the referent and wishes to share this pleasure with the adult. If the facial expression that accompanies the visual regard of the referee reflects strong distress, then possibly the infant has been frightened by the object and is looking to the adult not for information but, rather, for assistance and/or comfort. Looks which truly serve an information-gathering purpose are likely to be characterized by a quizzical, attentive, concerned, or worried (but not too worried) facial expression. The most sophisticated extant measures definitionally limit "referencing looking" to occasions in which the infant first glances at the referent and then looks toward the referee with an expression that indicates information seeking and/or acquisition (Clyman *et al.*, 1986; Hornik & Gunnar, 1988; Langhorst, 1983).

These tighter operational definitions have been utilized not only in investigating referencing's behavior-regulating influence (Hornik & Gunnar, 1988), but also in studies of its information-gathering function (Clyman *et al.*, 1986; Dickstein & Parke, 1988; Dickstein *et al.*, 1984; Langhorst, 1983; Sorce *et al.*, 1982). In these "looking studies," the adult typically does not communicate a prescribed message, and often conveys no message whatsoever. More often than not, the context of these investigations is a full or modified strange situation, in which the adult is asked to refrain from initiating interaction with the infant. The lower frequency of referencing looks in these studies (.5 to 2 looks per minute) as compared to behavior regulation studies (3 to 4 looks per minute) may very well reflect the difference in the referee's communication activity. One study had the referee first communicate only when the infant seemed to be requesting it, and then later offer such messages freely (Hornik & Gunnar, 1988). This study's finding of more social referencing looking to the mother when she was generous in providing information about a large caged black rabbit suggests that infants are more accustomed to, and comfortable with, active referees whose input does not have to be solicited.

No matter how it has been measured, referencing looking has been found to be a low-frequency behavior. Even when informational messages are being provided by an active referee, infants spend relatively little time visually attending to the adult. The scarcity of referencing looks in absolute terms is paralleled by its low relative frequency in comparison to other types of social looking. Thus, Hornik and Gunnar (1988) noted that referencing looks occurred less often than affect-sharing looks and "other" looks, although more frequently than glances/checks. Similarly, Clyman *et al.* (1986) found, in a modified strange situation procedure, that of five types of looks, social referencing occurred the least often. Even when the situation is structured so that information-gathering looking is likely to form a higher proportion of all social looking—as in some behavior regulation studies—the raw frequency of referencing looks still is low.

It has sometimes (Klinnert *et al.*, 1983) although not always (Feinman, 1985) been argued that referencing prototypically is a sequence which the infant initiates by actively soliciting information from others—usually through the special look-to-referent and then look-to-referee sequence during most of infancy, and later, by around 18 months, once she is more verbally proficient, through spoken requests (e.g., "what's that?"). It is toward this "ideal type" that definitions of referencing looking have gravitated, as they have been refined. In particular, they have been restricted in order to make sure that the look is one which requests information. This also is the rationale for designing experimental procedures (e.g., Klinnert, 1984) so that the referee makes no effort to "catch the gaze" of the infant (Langhorst, 1983) for the purpose of offering information about the referent. Instead, the infant is expected to come to the referee, and if she will not, the referee still does not come to her.

Perhaps this type of definition and procedure has served, inadvertently, to blind us to other aspects of information gathering in the referencing paradigm. Looking to the referee with a puzzled expression after making a referential gesture to the stimulus does indeed seem likely to be serving a solicitation function. But this look may persist for a while longer in order to take in the message which it has elicited. To gather other people's interpretations of a referent, the infant must attend to the messages—and not just solicit them. Furthermore, when these messages are volunteered by the referee (Svejda & Campos, 1982), or displayed continuously for several minutes after one brief soliciting look, then the infant simply needs to look at the referee and take it all in. In this perspective, looks such as glances/checks (Hornik & Gunnar, 1988) and orienting to voice or action (Clyman *et al.*, 1986) might be serving an information-gathering purpose.

There may be one other way in which infants learn about the situation through the referee's cues. Imagine that the infant performs an action with regard to the referent, and then turns to look at the referee, as if asking "does this action reflect a definition of the situation with which you agree?". Clyman *et al.'s* (1986) name for this sequence—"postaction reference"—suggests that it, indeed, does provide the infant with the referee's interpretation of the situation.

Similarly, Hornik and Gunnar (1988) have further suggested that social looks which are typically defined as affect sharing, in which the infant looks happily toward the mother (perhaps while concurrently vocalizing positively and babbling excitedly), may serve a postaction referencing function as well, especially if the infant has just made contact with the referent. Even if the infant is not trying, with this gesture, to ask a question, the mother's response may provide an answer anyway. Furthermore, the positive affect which accompanies this looking can be thought of as a coy, disarming way in which to ask a challenging question. Thus, Walden & Ogan (1988) interpreted the sequence, in which the toddler contacted the fear-defined toy and then turned to smile to her mother, as serving a negotiation of meaning function. It is interesting to note that the progression of act-first-and-ask-later is more common at 12 than 18 months (Hornik & Gunnar, 1988; Klinnert, 1984; Walden & Baxter, 1989; Walden & Ogan, 1988), while look-and-then-act becomes more readily observed in older toddlers.

It would seem that focusing the lion's share of our research efforts on soliciting looks *per se* when we are trying to understand how infants gather social information about referents may have some serious drawbacks. It makes good sense to be equally concerned about other forms of information gathering—those which involve simple observation of provided messages, and those in which the infant acts first and looks later. All of these looking mechanisms do occur in the course of acquiring information about how others define the situation, so why shouldn't all be considered? When they are investigated (Clyman *et al.*, 1986; Hornik & Gunnar, 1988), we are provided with a fuller and richer portrayal of what infants do when they gather social referencing information. Interestingly enough, even when all of these types of looks are considered, they still do not make up a large share of the infant's time and activity in referencing situations, thus further indicating that a lot is learned from a little, that brief glances can glean a wealth of information about the referee's interpretation of the referent.

VARIATIONS ON THE THEME

Asking and Getting: Requested and Offered Referencing Messages

Referencing studies vary as to whether the message is offered to the infant or withheld until she requests it. In what is sometimes termed "active" social referencing (Campos, 1983; Walden & Ogan, 1988), the message is not expressed by the referee until the infant looks toward her in a manner which seems to be soliciting information concerning the referent. In the Sorce *et al.* (1985) study, the infant had to look to the visual cliff and then to the mother to be considered to have requested input. Typically, studies which require that the infant appear to seek out and request the message are ones in which the referencing information is provided solely through facial expressions, with no vocal or tactile communication. Clearly, messages provided in this temporal sequence are likely to be contributing to reappraisal of the situation rather than to the initial appraisal. It is important to note, however, that although the infant is expected to solicit the referencing message in some studies, once she has done so, the message is offered continuously for 60 to 120 seconds without the need for renewing the request (Klinnert, 1984; Klinnert et al., 1986; Sorce et al., 1985; Zarbatany & Lamb, 1985).

Studies that restrict referencing to situations in which the infant engages in an active and purposeful search for information often suffer sizable subject losses, because infants who do not solicit information are excluded from the sample (17% in Klinnert et al., 1986; 19% in Klinnert, 1984; 21% in Sorce et al., 1985). If the referee had been permitted to attract the infant's attention, to "catch her gaze" and then offer the message, if information had been expressed vocally, or if the referee had been told to display the message (i.e., to make it available, even if the infant had not solicited it), then subject loss would certainly have been reduced. Along this line, in cases where the infant did not, on her own, look to the mother's face, Gewirtz and his colleagues (1990) asked the mother to act in ways which would elicit the infant's attention. Of course, however, if the message was displayed exclusively through visually accessible cues, then any infant who never looked could not have received social referencing information.

Other studies offer referencing information whether or not it is requested. For example, in Feinman et al.'s (1988) study of referencing in triadic situations, as soon as the stimulus toy (a robot) was revealed, the mother provided either a joyful or disgusted message to her infant and the infant's older sibling. Similarly, in Bingham et al. (1988) and Campos et al. (1985), the emotional message is provided right after the stimulus event (a doll's leg falling off) occurs. When the message is provided in this immediate manner, it probably contributes to the infant's initial appraisal of the referent, since, in all likelihood, it is offered before the infant can form a first impression of the event. In a variation on this theme, referee input is triggered by the infant's initial approach to the stimulus (Bradshaw et al., 1986; Svejda & Campos, 1982). In this variant, it appears that the infant has made an initial appraisal of the referent (a somewhat favorable one, given that she has started to approach it); therefore, the referencing message serves a reappraisal function.

Despite earlier definitional disagreements as to whether "true" referencing must be characterized by active search for information about the referent—with the narrower definition arguing in favor of this restriction (Campos, 1983) and the broader definition arguing against (Feinman, 1983a)—the impact of offered as well as solicited messages has been examined in referencing research. There seem to be somewhat more investigations of offered than requested referencing; and one study, by design, examined both (Hornik & Gunnar, 1988). It is noteworthy that the results from the requested and offered studies are essentially the same. However, Hornik and Gunnar (1988) did note a greater impact of the referencing communication when the mother actively provided information compared to when she did so only when it was solicited by the child.

How could offered messages have come to be excluded from the restricted conceptualization of referencing (Campos, 1983; Klinnert *et al.*, 1983)? Social referencing research emerged as part of a broader paradigmatic shift which challenged the validity of the "self-sufficiency" perspective for the study of infancy (Feinman, 1991). In that earlier paradigm, although the presence of the social context was acknowledged, most studies of infants' cognitive functioning arranged for the baby to respond on her own, without any social input. Although social referencing was viewed and accepted as part of the new "social world" zeitgeist in which the infant's cognitive functioning is viewed in its social context, it may be instructive to note that referencing remains more individualistic and self-reliant when it is requested than when it is offered. Offered referencing requires that we take one further step away from the self-reliant individualistic view (Feinman, 1991).

Another possible reason for the emphasis upon the requested form of referencing is that the word "refer" implies an active seeking for information. In everyday lexicon, when we "refer" to someone or something, we are engaging in purposeful, active searching for information. For this semantic reason, it is understandable why referencing was considered by some to be prototypically defined as involving active search. Nonetheless, the term "social referencing" itself derived from the sociological concept of reference group (Feinman, 1982) which is simply the "set of significant others with whom the individual may compare his attitudes, beliefs and behaviors" (Webster, 1975, p. 115). The reference group concept in no way implies that comparison and guidance must be *sought*. Despite the linguistic implication of activity with which the word "refer" is imbued, the conceptual origins of social referencing imply a broader phenomenon— one in which the key focus is on the importance of comparative guidance from others, regardless of whether such guidance is imposed, offered, made available, or requested.

In recent years, there seems to be more definitional acceptance of the place of offered messages within the phenomenon of referencing. Referring to the requested form of the phenomenon as "active" referencing (rather than as referencing, plain and simple) implies that the impact of unsolicited messages is not beyond the pale of definitional borders. While perhaps viewing referencing through active search as the prototypical or most strongly motivated form of the phenomenon, this conceptualization does not restrict referencing to only this "active" form. The prevalence of studies in which messages are offered, and the similarity of results from offered and requested message investigations—suggesting that these two variants serve the same function—further reinforces this definitional shift. In addition, as was discussed earlier, the finding that the "prototypical" requested form of referencing does not occur frequently (Clyman *et al.*, 1986; Hornik & Gunnar, 1988; also see Ainsworth, Chapter 14, this volume) raises some doubts about the validity of definitionally restricting the phenomenon to active search conditions only. Rather than referencing being most often and most powerfully effected through the active solicitation of information, it seems much more likely that it operates in a wider variety of ways. Given the manner in which infants behave when referees are noncommunicative, it may very well be that the prototypical case, if indeed there is such a beast, is reflected more in situations where the referee offers and makes available referencing messages. The safest approach, in light of what we currently know about infant social referencing, would be to investigate the ways in which information can be gathered both by requesting it and by having it volunteered.

How to Feel and What to Do: Emotional and Instrumental Referencing

Almost all of the investigations which have delved into the regulatory function of infant referencing have focused on the impact of emotional messages, which define "how to feel," rather than instrumental messages, which define "what to do" (see Hornik & Gunnar, 1988, for an exception). Typically, the referee is asked to pose an emotional reaction to the stimulus, rather than demonstrate how to deal with it. Similarly, the focus on infants' emotional expressions in response to the stimulus, and to broad approach–avoidance behavioral measures, reflects an interest in how the infant has come to feel about the event, and pays little attention to what she does in dealing with it.

Generally, the distinction between emotional and instrumental referencing reflects the nature of the input message more than that of the outcome effects. It is possible that a message which indicates how to feel about a toy can result in differences not only in basic affective response and approach–avoidance, but in specific instrumental actions as well. Thus, Klinnert *et al.* (1986) noted that infants touched the robot by patting or kissing it if they had received the joy message, but by swatting it or knocking it over in the fear condition. It is likely that an emotional message will have instrumental as well as emotional outcomes, since instrumental actions are often emotion linked (e.g., you do not hit a robot that you like or offer a toy to an adult you dislike). Instrumental input, in contrast, could result solely in instrumental outcomes, particularly if the message is communicated only after the emotional definition of the referent has been established. Nonetheless, it is possible, as Hornik and Gunnar (1988) have noted, to modify the affective valence of the stimulus through the provision of instrumental guidance about how to contact and cope with it.

Thus, in general, although it is possible to distinguish between emotional versus instrumental messages, emotional and instrumental outcomes tend to covary. It is most probably only because studies of the impact of emotional messages tend to focus primarily or exclusively on emotional and broad approach–avoidance behavioral tendencies that we do not see the specific instrumental consequences of messages which help the infant determine "how to feel."

Why has emotional referencing been highlighted to the almost complete exclusion of instrumental influence? Probably the major source of this bias was the emergence of interest in emotions and emotional development in the late 1970s (Lewis & Rosenblum, 1978; Plutchik & Kellerman, 1983), which was one of the major perspectives that converged to create the concept of social referencing. Within the framework of emotional communication, social referencing was conceptualized as functioning primarily if not exclusively through emotionally expressed messages, and was seen as one of several important forms of emotional exchange (Campos, 1983; Campos & Stenberg, 1981; Klinnert, Campos, Sorce, Emde, & Svejda, 1983). In the restricted definition, referencing was presumed to include emotional but not instrumental influence (Campos, 1983). Within the broad conceptualization of referencing, however, the scope of the phenomenon extends to influence on what to do as well as how to feel (Feinman, 1982, 1983a, 1985). The definitional range of referencing has been debated (Bretherton, 1984; Campos, 1983; Feinman, 1982, 1983a), and although most studies have continued to focus primarily upon the impact of emotional messages, there seems to be more acceptance in recent years of a more spacious conceptualization which includes instrumental as well as emotional referencing (e.g., Dickstein & Parke, 1988; Hornik et al., 1987; Walden & Baxter, 1989). Furthermore, Hornik and Gunnar's (1988) study of how mothers can influence not only how their 12- and 18-month-olds feel about a caged black rabbit but also how they attempt to touch or otherwise interact with the rabbit has served to more firmly establish, in empirical as well as conceptual firmament, the broader idea that referencing provides instrumental as well as emotional guidance.

But the accentuation of emotional referencing, especially in the earlier studies, has been much more than a matter of definitional perspective. Even those who viewed referencing as incorporating instrumental as well as emotional counsel hypothesized that emotional referencing was of prior interest and was, perhaps, the more elemental of the two forms, mainly because it was assumed that learning how to feel about an environmental event possessed temporal precedence over learning what to do when interacting with that event (Feinman, 1985). The presumption that infants (as well as more mature individuals) first defined the situation emotionally, and only later figured out how to cope with it instrumentally, easily led, even for those who defined referencing broadly, to the emphasis upon emotional referencing. Hornik and Gunnar's (1988) suggestion that instrumental referencing may actually be the more potent force, and the idea that it is only by learning how to interact with a stimulus that one can reduce fear about approaching it (Bandura, Chapter 8, this volume; Hornik-Parritz, Mangelsdorf, & Gunnar, Chapter 9, this volume), reflects a possible shift in our thinking about the relative importance and functions of instrumental versus emotional referencing. The implication of more recent work is that learning what to do about a referent can, in turn, serve to modify how to feel about it. Furthermore, the finding that infants' behavior to unfamiliar objects can be shaped by cues that have no inherent emotional meaning, but which can be utilized to predict the consequences of contact with these objects (Gewirtz *et al.*, 1990), implies that an exclusive emphasis upon the role of affective signals in the operation of social referencing may needlessly blind us to the full scope of the pathways through which this phenomenon proceeds, as well as to the nature of the functions which it serves.

PROCESS AND POWER IN SOCIAL REFERENCING

The Cognitive Nature of the Behavior Regulation Effect

Social referencing is hypothesized to be a sophisticated social cognitive process in which the infant comprehends the nature of the referee's message and understands that this message applies specifically to the particular referent. Thus, if the mother speaks happily to the infant about a novel toy, the infant must realize that this positive definition refers particularly to that toy—not to any other toy in the room, not to the experimental situation generally, not to the mother's mood, and not to the state of the world at large. For an infant to meet this requirement, she must be able to accomplish at least three social cognitive tasks (see Feinman, 1982, 1985, and Klinnert *et al.*, 1983, for reviews of the social cognitive prerequisites for referencing).

First of all, she must understand the content of the message. Thus, if the father provides a fearful message about the visual cliff, the infant must recognize these facial, vocal, and kinesthetic cues as reflective of fear, rather than of joy or interest. There is a fair amount of evidence indicating that, by about 6 months, infants can do this, that is, they are able to discriminate among and respond appropriately to others' expressed emotions. Second, infants need to be in an appraisal and evaluation mode when they are processing information about environmental events. In other words, they must be constructing the reality of the situation, and not just responding to it in a prewired fashion. There is evidence that cognitive processing which reflects appraisal, which suggests that the infant is evaluating likely consequences before responding, becomes more solidly established during the second semester of the first year, typically by around 9 months. Third, the infant must be able to identify the particular referent that is the topic of the referee's communication. Providing a message, especially an emotional message, about a specific referent to an infant who is not using such cues in a referential manner will fail to generate a social referencing effect. Evidence from research concerning infants' expressive and receptive understanding of referential gestures, such as the following of another person's pointing or line of vision, suggests that this skill is not established in most infants until the end of the first year.

Communication from adult to infant can serve several distinct purposes and mean quite a number of things. It could be an overture to interaction, it could signal the adult's intended actions or reactions to the infant, it could be requesting information from the infant, or it could be conveying social referencing information about an environmental event. Discriminating among these various functions is a lifelong issue in any socially communicative species. Thus, Frijda (1969) indicates that communication from one conspecific to another could provide information either about the signaler's intentions (anticipation of action) or about some environmental event (situational reference). As Smith (1981, p. 1273) has noted, communication can indicate "what [the signaler] may be doing or [is] about to do, aspects of its internal state, and things or events other than itself." Social referencing cannot occur unless the infant not only understands the content of the message, and is in appraisal mode, but also is able to determine whether the communication is indeed referential, and if it is, to identify the particular referent. These are ordinary and routine tasks for adults and even for preschool children, but often lie right on the cutting edge of what infants in the second semester of the first year can do.

The finding, for instance, that infants respond in a friendlier manner to an unfamiliar adult after the mother speaks joyfully rather than neutrally about that stranger is consistent with the behavior regulation prediction of social referencing. But it could also reflect a simpler, less sophisticated and more biological mechanism of contagion, emotional resonance, or "mood modification" (Feinman, 1982; Feinman & Lewis, 1983). In this more primitive process, the mother's emotional message is taken as a reflection of her mood, and is not interpreted by the infant as having anything particularly to do with the stranger. If the infant "catches" the mother's joyful mood, then she will likely not only be friendly to the stranger, but also behave more positively to other elements in the environment. To demonstrate that the infant has engaged in social referencing *per se* rather than mood modification, it must be shown that the impact of the message is specific to the intended referent. Thus, in this example, we would need to see the infant being friendlier to the stranger but not to other objects and people as the result of the mother's positive message. When the referee defines a particular toy as one to be feared, we would need to see a pattern in which the infant shows avoidance of that toy, but not of others.

The first analytical step in looking at data from studies which investigate the behavior regulation function of referencing is to determine whether actions toward the intended referent are consistent with the conveyed message. If that effect cannot be found, then we cease our efforts, and conclude that referencing has not occurred. But even if this effect is detected, we still must demonstrate that this pattern does not generalize to other aspects of the situation. Those studies which have tested for specificity have reported that, beginning at about 10 months, infants engage in specific learning about the particular referent. Thus, Hornik *et al.* (1987) and Feinman *et al.* (1988) reported that the effect of the mother's emotional message upon infant behavior to the referent toy did not extend to the infant's contact with other toys in the laboratory room. Walden and Ogan (1988) found that infants who received a positive message about one toy and a fearful one about another had more positive contact with the joy-defined toy than with the fear-defined toy in a subsequent free-play session. In studies where a referencing message is provided about a stranger (Feinman & Lewis, 1983; Feinman *et al.*, 1986), it has been noted that infants are friendlier to the stranger in the positive than the neutral condition but that no significant differences in behavior to the mother are displayed. Overall, there is a fair amount of evidence for the theorized specificity of the referencing effect.

Toward the end of the first year, it appears that infants are able to engage in specific learning about particular referents through social referencing. Nonetheless, this is a complex cognitive and social event in which the infant must attend to and interrelate several critical elements. First of all, she needs to grasp the substantive content of the referee's message. Second, she must comprehend its referential nature. And, concurrently, she must attend to the referent, especially if it is on the move, such as an approaching stranger (e.g., Boccia & Campos, 1983) or a mobile mechanical toy (e.g., Zarbatany & Lamb, 1985).

It is quite reasonable to expect that, in this complex juggling act, the infant could easily be "thrown off" by the manner in which the adult provides the message, as well as by the adult's general demeanor. It may be that a significant portion of individual variation in the degree to which infants are influenced by the referencing message is due to such factors. Thus, when the mother touched her baby while conveying an affective message about a stranger, the infant displayed a pattern which more resembled mood modification than referencing (Feinman, 1983b). Perhaps the mother's touch draws the infant's attention away from the connection between the message and the referent.

Furthermore, if an adult communicates joyfully to an infant about a referent, it is possible that this signal could be misinterpreted as an overture to interact. This "error" is distinctly different from the mood modification error just discussed above. In mood modification, the infant perceives the communication as an indication of the adult's overall feeling. But in the "invitation-to-interact" mechanism, the message is viewed as a request for social interaction, or more generally as an indication of how the referee feels about the infant. If the infant perceives it in this manner, then we would expect to see more favorable behavior by the infant to the referee, but not to any other feature of the environment. Analogously, if the adult has expressed a negative emotion which the infant interprets as directed at her specifically, then we can expect to see the infant become more upset and uncomfortable with the adult. Generally, the invitation (rejection)-to-interact process has not been observed in social referencing studies. Even when referees display anger in response to a referent, infants do not exhibit discomfort in their subsequent commerce with that adult (Bingham *et al.*, 1988)—which suggests that they do not take the referee's message "personally" but, rather, see it as information about the target event. Such findings are consistent with reports that prohibitions of actions (e.g., "No!" "Stop!") are taken not as a rejection of the infant but, rather, as a communication of danger. That such prohibitions are likely to be internalized (Stayton, Hogan, & Ainsworth, 1971; Ainsworth, Chapter 14, this volume; Emde, Chapter 4, this volume) indicates that the message is not interpreted as an indication of how the adult feels about the child. Indeed, if all messages about environmental events' danger or attractiveness were "taken personally," socialization would indeed be an exceptionally difficult if not an impossible task in infancy and toddlerhood.

One circumstance under which the infant does seem to take the referencing message personally is when a primary caregiver demonstrates her positive interpretation of a stranger through a friendly greeting. This indirect conveyance of the referencing message is interpreted by children and even older infants transitively (i.e., "I like and trust my mother, she likes the stranger, so I guess I like the stranger too"). Indeed, this seems to be what occurs when 15-month-olds observe their mothers interacting positively with a stranger (Feiring et al., 1984). But the 10-month-old seems to interpret her mother's friendly greeting of the stranger as an indication that the mother will spend time with the unfamiliar adult (a good assumption), in which case the mother–infant interaction might suffer (Feinman & Lewis, 1983). In this condition, 10-month-olds' behavior to the stranger does not differ as a function of whether the mother demonstrated a positive or neutral greeting to the stranger. Rather, these 10-month-olds are less friendly to their mothers if the mother communicated positively with the stranger than if she did so neutrally. Perhaps the salience and formative character of the attachment relationship at this age biases the child to view the indirect referencing message not as input about the stranger but, rather, as data about the mother's availability in the near future. It could be that the 10-month-old does interpret the valence of the mother's greeting as information which emotionally defines the stranger, but this aspect of the situation is overshadowed by the concern about the attachment relationship.

Generally, there is strong and consistent evidence that infants can and do engage in social referencing by about 10 months. All studies of infants 10 months or older have found basic evidence for social referencing, and tests for specificity have been positive. With infants younger than 10 months, we find either a lack of discriminatory behavior to the referent (Walden & Baxter, 1989), or equivocal evidence and/or a delayed effect (Walden & Ogan, 1988), or a pattern which better resembles emotional resonance than specificity (Boccia & Campos, 1983). In this latter study, 8.5-month-olds were friendlier to mother as well as to stranger when the mother expressed positive rather than negative emotion with regard to the stranger. Svejda and Campos (1982) reported a referencing effect for their sample of 8- and 11-month-olds and did not find any significant age differences. The lack of any testing for specificity may explain this finding. Generally, it appears that 10 months is the best estimate for the natural emergence of social referencing. Mood modification and other less cognitively sophisticated processes can be seen to emerge earlier.

As young children make the transition from infancy to toddlerhood, the character of referencing seems to change. It is not a radical change; referencing effects can still be detected later in the second year (Hornik & Gunnar, 1988; Walden & Baxter, 1989; Walden & Ogan, 1988) and on into the third and fourth years (Walden & Baxter, 1989). Nevertheless, there are some differences. Walden and Ogan (1988) noted that infants aged 14 to 22 months displayed a degree of what seems to be rebellion, touching the fearfully defined toy more than the joyfully defined one. In contrast, behavior between 10 and 13 months is more clearly consistent with the feeling definitions provided by parents. In the second year, especially as children acquire proficiency in expressive language, we seem to see a more two-sided, mutual and negotiated character to referencing. The child is clearly interested in what the adult has to say, but there seems to be a certain degree of "backtalk"—discussion and questioning about the definition of the stimulus. Hornik and Gunnar (1988), in noting that part of the instrumental referencing found in their black rabbit study involved labeling the rabbit (in what Brown, 1986, calls "The Great Word Game"), provided this particular account: "one 18-month-old said 'doggy?' repeatedly until her mother said ' no, bunny,' at which point the child switched to an assertive 'doggy!'" (p. 632). Walden and Ogan noted, similarly, that when 13- to 22-month-olds touched the fear-defined toy, and then turned to smile at their mothers, it seemed that they were trying to discuss their parent's interpretation of the toy through a "negotiation of meaning" (Walden & Ogan, 1988). This negotiated quality has been noted as early as 12 months (Hirshberg, 1988). It seems that not all that long after infants acquire the capacity to engage in referencing, they become more active in negotiating and discussing situational definitions with other people.

Magnitude, Potency, and Endurance of the Behavior Regulation Effect

The size of the behavior regulation effect in most referencing studies is, on average, best described as moderate. Typically, the mean impact of the message is powerful enough to be felt, but not so authoritative that it overshadows all other sources of variation. What are probably the largest and the smallest effects were both found in two of the earliest referencing studies. The differences in behavior to stimulus toys among the emotional message conditions of fear, neutral, and joy were comparatively small in the Klinnert (1984) investigation, possibly because of difficulties that sometimes occur in utilizing repeated-measures designs in which different emotional messages are given for different stimuli, or because the critically important measures of amount and nature of contact with the stimuli were not included in the analysis. In contrast, dramatic differences were found in Sorce et al.'s (1985) modified visual cliff study. Three-fourths of the infants who received either a joy or interest message crossed the deep side of the surface, while none of those who were exposed to a fear message crossed. More typical of the average magnitude of the behavior regulation effect in referencing studies is Klinnert et al.'s (1986) finding that infants in the fear group spent an average of 11 seconds touching the robot stimulus toy, while those in the smile group did so for a mean of 42 seconds (68% of those who received the smile signal approached and touched the robot, compared to 42% in the fear condition). Similarly, Feinman and Lewis (1983) found that infants were about five times more likely to smile at the stranger and twice as likely to offer a toy to the stranger in the positive than in the neutral condition. Through the use of repeated exposure to the referencing message, in which infants were conditioned to a response criterion, Gewirtz and his colleagues (1990) were able to shape infants' behavior so that they reached for the positive-cue stimulus more than 75% of the time, and for the negative-cue stimulus less than 25% of the time—an effect somewhat more powerful than that typically found in referencing studies.

With rare exceptions, these central tendencies usually are surrounded by considerable individual variation. Not all infants receive and accept the referencing message. Thus, although 74% of the infants who received the smile message crossed the reduced visual step in the Sorce et al. (1985) study, it must be remembered that the remaining 26% did not. Similarly, in the Klinnert et al. (1986) investigation, 32% of those infants in the smile signal condition did not touch the robot. In our study of social referencing in the infant–sibling–mother triad, there was considerable variation as to how infants and their older siblings dealt with the mother's favorable or negative reaction to the robot (Feinman et al., 1988), including one infant who, despite the mother's negative message about the robot and a deluge of additional unfavorable communication about it from her sibling, maintained a self-reliant determination to have contact with this toy.

Relatively little among-subjects variation in social referencing studies has yet been accounted for. With only one exception, no gender differences in referencing's behavior regulation function have been reported. Bradshaw et al. (1986), however, did find that the predicted difference in behavior to attractive toys was significant for girls but not for boys, primarily due to the greater impact of the negative messages on female babies. Examination of the correlation between infant temperament and the impact of referencing messages has yielded equivocal results. Using the Revised Infant Temperament Questionnaire (RITQ; Carey & McDevitt, 1978), one study found that referencing effects are more powerful for easier than for more difficult 10-month-olds (Feinman & Lewis, 1983), while no differences were noted in an investigation of 12-month-olds using a similar methodology (Feinman et al., 1986). Similarly, the use of Rothbart's (1981) Infant Behavior Questionnaire (IBQ) has also yielded inconsistent results. While Hirshberg (1988) found a correlation between IBQ subscales and receptivity to referencing messages about new toys, Bradshaw et al. (1987) failed to detect any correlation between the affect factor in the IBQ and infants' willingness to cross the visual "step" after receiving a smile message from mother. The source of these discrepancies is not at all clear. The almost complete absence of gender differences and the inconsistency of temperament effects further reinforce the general lack of understanding of the sources of individual variation in infants' responses to referencing messages.

Although it seems reasonable to expect that a more powerful behavior regulation effect will be found in comparing negative to positive signal conditions, than when comparing positive to neutral conditions, this does not seem to be born out in the extant studies. The effects found in two investigations which provided neutral versus positive messages about a stranger (Feinman & Lewis, 1983; Feinman et al., 1986) did not produce smaller effects than stranger studies which utilized positive versus negative messages (Boccia & Campos, 1983; Garland, 1982). The small differences between the positive and neutral conditions in Gunnar's studies (Gunnar & Stone, 1984; Hornik et al., 1987) may be due to the operationalization of the "neutral" condition as a control condition (in which the referee provides no input).

In interpreting these small "neutral" (control) versus positive signal differences, it is instructive to note that when Feinman and Lewis (1983) utilized positive, control, and true neutral message conditions (in the neutral condition, the mother spoke to the infant in a bland and nonpartisan manner about the stranger; in the control condition, no message was given), infant behavior to the stranger in the control condition was intermediate to that in the positive and neutral conditions. Thus, use of what is actually a control or no-input condition as the "neutral" message produces an artifactually small apparent positive versus neutral difference. Truly neutral messages actually can have a fairly sobering impact upon a 1-year-old. Klinnert (1981) has noted that neutral expressions have a flat affective tone to them that can be quite alarming and upsetting to some infants. In the Feinman and Lewis (1983) study, the finding that infants' behavior to the stranger was less friendly in the neutral than in the control condition suggests that perhaps infants interpret neutral messages somewhat more negatively than positively.

Gunnar and her colleagues have suggested that negative-affect messages have an especially powerful and immediate regulatory impact (Hornik et al., 1987). Negative emotional signals elicit more infant looking in some studies (Svejda & Campos, 1982; Zarbatany & Lamb, 1985), but not in others (Klinnert, 1984; Klinnert et al., 1986; Sorce et al., 1985). Walden and her colleagues have found that while children in the second year do look more often to negative than to positive parental signals (Walden & Baxter, 1989; Walden & Ogan, 1988), no such difference is found in the third and fourth year (Walden & Baxter, 1989). In contrast, more attention to positive than negative signals was noted for infants in the second semester of the first year in one study (Walden & Baxter, 1989), and from 6 to 9 months in another (Walden & Ogan, 1988), Thus, evidence concerning differential attention to negative messages is mixed, and it varies by age.

The finding that all infants went along with a fear message about the reduced visual cliff, while one-fourth did not behave in accordance with the smile message (Sorce *et al.*, 1985) does support the proposition that negative messages are more potent, although it may well be subject to alternative interpretations. The method of choice, however, for evaluating this hypothesis calls for experimental designs which utilize three emotional message conditions—positive, neutral, and negative. Unfortunately, only two studies satisfy this requirement: Hornik *et al.* (1987) and Klinnert (1984). If negative messages are more potent, then we can reasonably expect to find that the difference between the negative and neutral conditions will be larger than that between neutral and positive. No such pattern was noted by Klinnert (1984), but it was reflected in Hornik *et al.*'s (1987) results: infants' play and proximity to the stimulus toys in the positive and neutral conditions were more similar to each other than either were to the negative condition. Nevertheless, caution must be exercised in interpreting these results because, as noted above, the "neutral" message in that particular study was really a silent, control condition. Perhaps silence is taken as an implicit mildly positive statement, as an indication that "all is well," and therefore would be expected to generate an effect more similar to the positive than to the negative message. Nonetheless, especially in light of the saliency of negative messages as natural clues to danger (Bowlby, 1969) and the finding that infants sometimes look more at negative communications, it would seem profitable to further investigate the hypothesized greater regulatory power of negative messages.

While referencing research has consistently indicated that broad categories of emotional messages (i.e., positive vs. negative or neutral) have a differential impact upon infant behavior to the referent, there is little evidence that discrete emotions within these broad categories generate distinct effects, with the exception of the impact of sadness. Interest and joy had virtually the same impact upon infants' crossing behavior on the modified visual cliff (Sorce *et al.*, 1985). There were no significant or major differences between fear and anger (Sorce *et al.*, 1985; Svejda & Campos, 1982) or between anger and disgust (Bradshaw *et al.*, 1986). But while infants in the fear condition never crossed the visual "step" and 11% crossed in the anger condition, 33% crossed when the mother expressed sadness. It may be that 12-month-olds (as well as adults) find sadness to be a somewhat confusing and mixed signal with regard to potential danger, while fear is considerably more contextually appropriate. The discrete effects of sadness versus fear were most clearly demonstrated by Campos *et al.* (1985). Those 14-month-olds who received a sadness message from the experimenter after the doll's leg fell off attempted to comfort the doll, but they did not avoid it. In contrast, when a fear response was displayed by the referee in reaction to the doll's accident, these toddlers played less with that doll than with other toys in the room. Thus, fear generated avoidance while sadness led to consolation of the injured doll.

How long does the behavior regulation effect last? Endurance of the regulatory effect is best measured by determining how long it can be detected after the referencing communication has ceased. The extant referencing studies are remarkably unsuited to address this issue of endurance, because they typically last only a few minutes. There are no reports that the referencing effect wanes as the experimental session proceeds, indicating that it can be found for at least several minutes after the message has ceased. In one study of the impact of referencing on response to strangers (Feinman *et al.*, 1986), it was noted that the power of the message seemed to be greater later on in the procedure, but this, alternatively, could have been due to the fact that the stranger was instructed to become more interactive as the session proceeded. In the only investigation designed to look at whether the impact of the referencing message could still be detected some time later, Bradshaw *et al.* (1986) found that 15-month-olds but not 10-month-olds still exhibited the behavior regulation effect 30 minutes later. If, as noted above, infants can learn from brief contacts with their environment, it is possible that even one quick referencing message could, under some circumstances, have a lasting impact. On the other hand, message reinforcement and repetition probably are provided in everyday interactions, and may be efficacious in producing an enduring and deeply rooted effect upon behavior. Clearly, the question of how long and at what strength the behavior regulation effect persists is a highly significant issue which, unfortunately, has received very little attention in referencing research.

POSTULATES OF SOCIAL REFERENCING THEORY

The Ambiguity of the Referent

The hypothesis that referencing has an especially profound impact upon the interpretation of ambiguous referents, which emerged early in the study of this phenomenon (Campos & Stenberg, 1981; Feinman, 1982), can be termed the "ambiguity postulate." It makes good intuitive sense to predict that infants—much like human beings throughout the lifespan—will be more easily influenced by other people in defining unstructured, confusing situations than in making sense of events which possess clear structure and meaning. Indeed, it has even been suggested that the role of ambiguity is so powerful as to constitute a biological boundary upon the power of referencing, that is, that there is a biological, prewired disposition to resist influence from others in clear-cut situations (Feinman, 1985).

The ambiguity postulate suggests not only that referencing will be enhanced in situations which are experienced as unclear by most infants, but also that, for any given stimulus, infants who are uncertain will be more receptive to referencing messages. Thus, *subjective* uncertainty as well as *situational* uncertainty is expected to heighten the impact of other people's definitions of the situation. Despite the obvious conceptual and heuristic value of distinguishing subjective from situational uncertainty, it would seem that it is the subjective aspect of ambiguity which is the higher-order concept. Events which are situationally uncertain are ones in which most if not all individuals feel unsure of how to respond. It is the subjective meaning, or *verstehen*, which the individual experiences in the situation that makes her receptive to social influence. When situational and subjective uncertainty do not coincide—such as when an infant can barely be restrained from eagerly approaching a toy which elicits uncertainty in all of her peers—it is the subjective feeling rather than the "objective reality" which predicts her response.

Studies that have not aimed to expose infants to stimuli whose situational clarity varies have, however, usually selected referents which were assumed, typically on the basis of face validity, to be ambiguous. Strangers, black rabbits, and unusual toys (especially those that move on their own) seem likely to possess a less than obvious meaning. However, it is noteworthy that these studies typically have not actually established through pretesting the situational ambiguity of these events. To a large extent, this concern for using what were identified as ambiguous referents derived from the assumption that the ambiguity postulate was correct, and that the largest effects would be found with such stimuli. Along this line, it is interesting to note that in attempting to account for the relatively weak effects found in her study, Klinnert (1981, 1984) pointed out that, although the stimuli she utilized were designed to be ambiguous, they might have produced fear, which would have reduced the impact of referencing. Thus, there seems to have been implicit faith in ambiguity's power to heighten referencing's impact.

Nonetheless, even if the referents in these various studies can be taken at their face value of apparent ambiguity, the finding of a behavior regulation effect does not necessarily mean that referencing is enhanced in situational uncertainty. Rather, it merely indicates that the behavior regulating function of referencing has occurred. It is in studies where the cognitive clarity of the referents is varied systematically that we can best evaluate the ambiguity postulate. And, in line with what was expected, the first studies relevant to the ambiguity postulate did, in fact, support this proposition. This early evidence, in combination with the obvious intuitive appeal of the idea, lead to its ready acceptance (Feinman, 1985; Klinnert et al., 1983). Probably the major exhibit in support of this postulate came from research that varied the apparent drop-off of a visual cliff. Although it was found that the infant's behavior on a reduced visual cliff (an apparent 30-cm drop-off) was powerfully influenced by the mother's message, referencing did not affect response to a surface with no depth cues (Sorce et al., 1985)—a stimulus which is clearly unambiguous. Furthermore, very few infants displayed any interest in receiving social input in this situation (17 of 23 did not look to the mother for referencing input), and those few who did still crossed the surface even when their mothers displayed fear. Similarly, pretesting had indicated negligible receptiveness to referencing information when the cliff was restored to its full 40-inch depth illusion (Campos, personal communication, 1981); instead, infants displayed the usual strong aversive response found in earlier visual cliff studies (Walk & Gibson, 1961). Pretesting had also indicated that the 30-cm apparent drop induced a state of ambiguity in the absence of referencing signals, eliciting pausing at the edge and frequent looking to the mother, but yet no obvious fear of the drop-off.

These results became well known early in the course of social referencing research (they were first presented at the 1981 meeting of the Society for Research in Child Development), and served as appealing and compelling evidence that referencing was, indeed, more influential when the referent was ambiguous—as indicated in the enthusiasm with which the ambiguity postulate was embraced then (Feinman, 1982; Klinnert et al., 1983). Previous findings from research on depth perception—that, by 10 months, infants would not cross the full visual cliff, even using the accepted procedure of having the mother try to "coax" her baby across, but that some infants could be lured across illusions of lesser depth (Walk & Gibson, 1961)—further reinforced the belief that social referencing was of greater potency in situational uncertainty.

Soon after, Gunnar and Stone (1984) reported that a significant difference between positive and neutral messages was found in infant response to an ambiguous toy but not for either a pleasant or an aversive toy (these toys were pretested). Furthermore, in a post hoc analysis of individual differences, Zarbatany and Lamb (1985) found that infants who were initially fearful of a toy spider were less affected by the referee's message than were infants who were initially uncertain about it. Overall, the initial evidence concerning the enhancing impact of situational and subjective uncertainty on referencing was consistently supportive of the validity of the ambiguity postulate, and this conclusion was reflected in critical assessments of the literature at that time (Feinman, 1985).

In contrast, however, later evidence has not been nearly as supportive. First of all, the formidable effects which demonstrated the powerful impact of social referencing upon behavior on the reduced visual cliff (Sorce et al., 1985) were not evident in a partial replication of that procedure (Bradshaw *et al.*, 1987). The replication used the same visual cliff apparatus, although adjusted to a slightly shallower drop-off (26 rather than 30 cm), in the same laboratory room utilized in the earlier investigation. The infant subjects were of the same age (12 months) in both studies. The replication study utilized the smile message condition from the Sorce *et al.* (1985) procedure, but had a familiarized stranger as well as the mother standing across the deep side of the apparatus, with both adults smiling continuously once the infant reached the midline of the surface. In addition, unlike the original study, in which the visual cliff session was performed as the sole procedure to which the infant was subjected, in the replication this episode followed soon after the infant had been exposed to stimuli which may have made her wary, as Bradshaw *et al.* (1987) have noted. Furthermore, it appears that while the original study retained in the sample only those infants who had appeared to request referencing information, the replication did not make any such stipulation. Whether or not these differences can explain the discrepancy, the facts are that, when infants were exposed to a smile message, the replication study found that only 37% crossed the deep side, while the corresponding figure for the original investigation was 74%. Perhaps including only infants whom it could be ascertained had actually looked to the referee in the Sorce *et al.* (1985) study can account for their finding of twice as much crossing. It is hard to imagine that the 4-cm reduction in depth could have significantly altered the ambiguity of the stimulus, but that possibility must be considered. Unexplained, the Bradshaw *et al.* (1987) study does cast a bit of a shadow on the special power of referencing in particularly ambiguous situations.

Further questions about the salience of ambiguity were raised by the results of an expanded replication of Gunnar and Stone's (1984) investigation. Hornik *et al.* (1987) extended the earlier methodology to include a negative message condition as well as the positive and "neutral" (silent control) conditions previously utilized. They used the same pretested aversive, ambiguous, and pleasant toys, and their subjects were of the same age as in the earlier study (12–13 months). Unlike Gunnar and Stone's (1984) report that a significant difference between the positive and neutral conditions was found only for the ambiguous toy, the expanded replication found that the behavior regulation effect for the ambiguous toy was not any different than that for the obviously aversive or pleasant toys.

It has been suggested that the attachment of plastic "bugs" to the stimulus toys in all of the message conditions of the Hornik *et al.* (1987) study—done to help the mothers express the negative message—might have overshadowed the ambiguity differences among the toys (Feinman, 1986). Nonetheless, it must be noted that overall differences in infants' responses to these toys were consistent with the pretested nature of these stimuli: infants played most with the pleasant toy and least with the aversive one (Hornik *et al.*, 1987), which indicates that the lack of an ambiguity effect cannot be readily attributed to bugs. The proposal that the saliency of the negative message condition may have overshadowed any impact of ambiguity (Hornik *et al.*, 1987) also does not fit exceptionally well with the results: the impact of the positive message across the three toys parallels that of the negative message. Thus, we are left with evidence, from a well-designed and carefully executed study, which does not support the ambiguity postulate.

Zarbatany and Lamb's (1985) report that subjectively uncertain infants were more influenced by the referencing message does not seem to be supported by Hornik and Gunnar's (1988) black rabbit study. Based on their behavior in the initial segments of the procedure, infants were classified as either "bold" or "wary"—with the latter group viewed as being more uncertain about the rabbit. Although the wary infants did engage in more initial referencing looking than their bold counterparts, this difference did not hold up over the duration of the procedure, and there was no apparent indication that the mother had more of an influence upon the wary infants' behavior to the rabbit.

With regard both to toys and depth illusions, the evidence as to whether social referencing's behavior regulation function is enhanced by situational ambiguity must be considered to be mixed, as are the findings concerning subjective uncertainty. Indeed, the lack of consistency among the results of these studies has, in recent years, been noted (Walden & Ogan, 1988). While there may be an understandable reason why the discrepancy exists in the visual cliff studies, it is more difficult to make sense of the differences among the toy studies. Overall, then, extant studies of the ambiguity postulate are not consistent among themselves as to the validity of this hypothesis, although they seem to be somewhat more supportive than not.

The possibility, suggested by this ambivalent evidence, that ambiguity may not have an enhancing impact upon referencing, has implications for the inclusion of uncertainty in the definition *per se* of the phenomenon of referencing (Klinnert *et al.*, 1983). Defining referencing as something that is done to resolve situational uncertainty suggests that informational messages will regulate behavior *only* for events which are ambiguous. This goes one step beyond the ambiguity postulate, which argues that, although referencing *can* influence reality construction in more clear-cut situations, it is *maximally* effective in ambiguous circumstances (Campos & Stenberg, 1981; Feinman, 1982). The incorporation of uncertainty into the definition of referencing calls for more extreme patterns of behavior regulation than those predicted by the ambiguity postulate. Perhaps because of the lack of such evidence, more recent commentary has become skeptical of the hypothesis that referencing occurs exclusively in situations which are characterized by uncertainty. As Klinnert *et al.* (1986, p. 431) have noted: "Although they [referencing effects] may be clearest when events are maximally uncertain (e.g., Gunnar & Stone, 1984), social referencing effects are not restricted to conditions of uncertainty." The finding of mixed evidence with regard to the ambiguity postulate, and the indication that referencing may have an impact even when infants can construct an initial appraisal on their own (e.g., Klinnert *et al.*, 1986; Svejda & Campos, 1982), strongly contraindicates the utilization of situational uncertainty as a definitional parameter of referencing.

Selectivity and the Relationship with the Referee

Early in the investigation of referencing, it was suggested that infants would be selectively more receptive to some referees than others. It was the referee's credibility—a multiplicative function of trustworthiness and expertise—which was predicted to be the most basic feature according to which receptivity would vary (Feinman, 1982). A similar but even more restrictive position was reflected in the portrayal of referencing as something that infants did specifically with regard to their mothers (Campos & Stenberg, 1981). The former, more modest formulation of the selectivity postulate implies that infants may utilize a wide range of social sources of interpretation, but that they will prefer some over others. A more radical position suggests that only mothers—or generically, only primary caregivers—will be accepted as referees, which implies that a powerful relationship exists between attachment and referencing, between being a base of security and being a base of information. This sentiment has been echoed, although in a more tempered manner, in Ainsworth's (Chapter 14, this volume) suggestion that emotional referencing may be confined to trusted attachment figures.

Most studies of referencing's behavior regulation function have utilized only one referee, usually the mother. A few investigations, however, provide data which are pertinent to the selectivity postulate. Referencing messages have been found to be just as effective whether they come from father or mother (Hirshberg & Svejda, 1990). With both mother and father present, infants received a fear message about a toy from one parent (with the other parent remaining noncommunicative and emotionally unavailable) and then, in counterbalanced order, a joy message about a different toy from the other parent. Regardless of which parent gave which message about which toy, the infants were just as interested in and influenced by the referencing communication from father as from mother. The equal potency of paternal versus maternal referencing input is further demonstrated when the infant is given, in the same study, a fear message from one parent and a joy message from the other about the same toy. Generally, infants were upset by the contradiction between mother's and father's message, and reduced their activity with the toy, suggesting that they were caught between two equally powerful messages. In fact, infants played less with the toy in the contradictory message condition than they did in the single parent fear message (Hirshberg, 1990). The finding of no difference in the amount of attention paid to mother versus father when they provide messages (Hirshberg & Svejda, 1990) is paralleled by the absence of any difference in looking to the two parents when they are not actively communicating to the infant, as in a modified strange situation (Dickstein & Parke, 1988).

How does the relationship with a caregiver impact upon referencing processes and outcomes? It makes sense to expect that a close and sensitive relationship with the caregiver will enhance the infant's trust in that person as a referee. Furthermore, more expressive caregivers may be better providers of interpretative information. These questions have been considered only minimally in behavior regulation studies. Bradshaw *et al.* (1987) found no association of attachment scales with acceptance of a positive referencing message about a reduced visual cliff or a fearful message about a novel toy. That referencing patterns may reflect the adult's attitude to the child is suggested by the finding that when 20-month-olds were upset by a robot which was introduced when their backs were turned, all adult mothers offered support and explained the robot, in contrast to only 71% of adolescent mothers who offered support and 41% who offered explanation (J. Osofsky & A. Eberhart-Wright, personal communication, May, 1987).

Differences in looking to the caregiver have been examined in several studies in which the mother was present but, because of the experimenter's instructions, was not communicating freely and fully. No association of information seeking and acquisition with attachment was detected by Bradshaw *et al.* (1987). In contrast, Dickstein *et al.* (1984) found more looking to the mother in resistant–insecure infants than in avoidant–insecure infants, with securely attached infants falling in between these two extremes. Because the coding procedures did not specify that the referencing look must involve a puzzled, mildly concerned, or bland attentive facial expression, these results could alternatively be interpreted as attachment differences in affect sharing or comfort seeking. That the attachment differences were heightened when the mother spoke in a friendly manner with a stranger further suggests that these looks reflected the use of the mother as a base of security rather than as a base of information. Similarly, the finding that infants, whose fathers were experiencing higher levels of marital satisfaction, looked more to both parents (Dickstein & Parke, 1988) also is subject to various interpretations because the operational definition of referencing looking was not specific enough. Generally, thus far, findings concerning the association between referencing looking and relationship variables have been difficult to interpret.

Are infants more likely to be influenced by referencing messages from intimate caregivers than other people? Zarbatany and Lamb (1985) found that while infants displayed the predicted behavior regulation pattern with respect to a large toylike spider when their mothers displayed either joy or fear, messages from a familiarized stranger had no effect. However, no selectivity in looking to mother versus stranger was found in that study, or in Bradshaw et al. (1987). Feiring et al. (1984) reported that observing the mother talking positively with a stranger was more likely to result in later sociability toward the stranger than when the infant saw another adult talking positively with the stranger. Furthermore, infants paid more attention when the referee was the mother. These investigations are subject to alternative methodological explanations: that the mother's absence had so profound an effect that it distracted the infant from the stranger's referencing message (Zarbatany & Lamb, 1985), and that rather than learn about the stranger through the process of watching mother interact with her, the infant's attention had been drawn to the mother and since the stranger was right next to her, the infant had more direct visual experience of the stranger in that condition (Feiring et al., 1984). Assuming that the results can be taken at face value, however, both of these studies indicate that infants are more accepting of referencing messages from their mothers than from adults whom they have just met in the laboratory.

In several investigations, infants came in contact with a new toy or event while with their mothers, and received an emotional message about the referent from an experimenter. In these investigations, the mother, although physically present, was asked either to act puzzled (Klinnert et al., 1986) or to be noncommunicative (Bingham et al., 1988; Bradshaw et al., 1986), that is, to act in a manner which has been referred to as emotional unavailability (Sorce & Emde, 1981) or functional absence (Feinman, 1991). Infants were affected by the experimenter's message, as reflected in lower latency to touch and more time in contact with the stimulus. Klinnert et al. (1986) noted, as well, that there was more looking to the stranger than to the mother (although it must be noted that those infants who never looked to the stranger (8 of 46) were not included in the data analysis sample). Similarly, when a stranger played with the infant in a modified strange situation, more looking to the stranger than to the mother with regard to ambiguous toys was noted (Clyman et al., 1986).

Generally, these results suggest that referencing input from individuals who appear to be "in charge" and knowledgeable about an unfamiliar environment (the laboratory) and its contents (the toys) will be accepted, particularly when the mother, although physically present, does not provide any definition of the situation. It seems that preference for referencing input from caregivers does not go so far as to preclude accepting input from an informed stranger when the trusted caregiver is silent. The experimenter may have been the more credible referee, inasmuch as the mother, although trusted, showed a manifest lack of expertise.

Overall, the extant evidence indicates that infants are equally influenced by referencing from intimate caregivers, but selectively more receptive to guidance from a parent than from a familiarized stranger. Nonetheless (caveat emptor!), communicative, confident strangers who may be perceived as being "in the know" with regard to the laboratory situation are able to regulate the infant's behavior toward referent toys when the mother is not communicating or appears puzzled. Perhaps the infant is capable of sensing who would be the more expert referee in particular situations. Thus, in the experimenter's domain of the lab, even a communicative mother might not be the preferred referee. Analogously, the parent would be the preferentially selected base of information at home, and the day-care provider in the child care center.

In addition to attributing expertise on the basis of domain, infants may also be guided by the referee's apparent knowledgeability, as reflected in their willingness to express an opinion and in the confidence with which they do so. A confounding of the factors of domain expertise and apparent knowledgeability seems to be operating in the studies where the experimenter provides a message while the mother is either silent or puzzled. The relative salience of each of these variables cannot be addressed in the extant research, but could be investigated in studies which completely cross these factors. Investigations which present the infant with conflicting signals from mother versus experimenter in the laboratory and home settings would be especially useful in putting selectivity to its most extreme test.

Furthermore, although infants seem to be more receptive to referencing influence from parents than from strangers, we do not know how they might respond to messages from someone who is neither parent nor stranger. There is some preliminary evidence that siblings' definitions of situations are as readily accepted, and sometimes even more so, than those of mothers (Feinman et al., 1988). Also, infants do have considerable social contact with other relatives and with friends of the family (Feinman & Roberts, 1986), and seem to form meaningful relationships, perhaps even attachments, with such people (Myers, Jarvis, & Creasey, 1987). It seems likely that these individuals would be accepted as referees.

AN ACCOUNT OF PROGRESS AND AN AGENDA FOR THE FUTURE

Evidence accumulated over the past decade, from a considerable number of studies, has indicated that social referencing does regulate infants' behavior to a variety of referent people, objects, and events. That this influence takes the form of specific learning about particular referents, rather than a more generalized and biological mechanism of contagion, is convincingly indicated by referencing investigations. Although further investigation of the developmental history of referencing is needed, studies in recent years, especially the work of Walden and her colleagues, have considerably expanded our knowledge about the onset and further course of referencing in the first years of life.

On the other hand, what we know about the processes through which referencing operates is more limited. Clearly, a good deal has been discovered about how infants gather information from other people, about how they seek out and take in the messages that others provide about situations. Nevertheless, many important questions remain unanswered. Nothing is known about how tactile and kinesthetic cues from others might function in referencing, and little is known about how infants attend to vocally provided cues, despite the obvious impact of these cues in regulating behavior. And, despite the considerable effort that has been devoted to studying visual attention, it is not yet evident how it is that infants are able to derive considerable knowledge from relatively brief messages.

Further investigation of process questions would benefit greatly from consideration of developmental issues. Although there is reasonably consistent evidence concerning the onset of referencing, and the age at which it takes on a more negotiated, mutual character, there has been virtually no documentation of the social and cognitive skills which, one must assume, accompany and underlie this developmental progression. Can it be demonstrated that developments in information-gathering capacity, in referential communication, and in appraisal skills actually do form the foundation for the emergence of referencing? What are the social and cognitive capabilities which underlie the shift of referencing from a unidirectional process in which the adult influences the infant, to a mutual process in which meaning is negotiated?

The centrality of the ambiguity postulate in referencing theory makes it imperative that we come to a more definitive determination of its confirmation status. The inconsistency of the evidence concerning ambiguity's impact upon referencing suggests that uncertainty may indeed boost referencing's power, but only under some conditions. Specific delineation of these circumstances will help in sorting out the tangled strands that currently exist in the empirical consideration of this aspect of the referencing process.

Although the evidence concerning the selectivity postulate is fairly consistent, we still need to determine what it is about the selected referee that leads her to be preferred by the infant as a source of information.

Infants, like adults, appear to select sources on the basis of their trustworthiness and expertise, but it is not clear how they appraise individuals with regard to these qualities. Does setting make a difference, that is, do infants prefer a referee specifically within the particular domains in which they appear to have expert knowledge, or is this selection process more general?

The selection of bases of information may be just as important in infant development as the selection of bases of security. Just as the emergence of emotional well-being relies upon responsive and sensitive attachment figures, so does enculturation into the environments of home and family, community, and society depend upon informed, communicative, and trustworthy referencing figures. It may well be that referencing relationships vary in the confidence and dependability which they bring into the young child's life, much in the way that attachment relationships vary in the degree of security and sensitivity which they provide for the infant. Future research efforts would do well to dig deeper into the critical issue of how the infant goes about selecting referencing figures who will guide her interpretation of the world in which she lives.

One striking feature of extant social referencing research is its restriction, with only rare exceptions, to laboratory situations. The finding that referencing regulates infant behavior in a more natural setting—the child care center—suggests that what we have seen in the laboratory can be extrapolated to the everyday world in which the infant resides. The reasonably high mundane realism of the referents and referees in extant studies further reinforces the extrapolability of these findings. Nonetheless, it must be ascertained, through investigations in the home and other natural environments, just how referencing actually functions in the infant's everyday life.

The behavior regulation effects noted in experimental studies of referencing appear to be ones which would play a key role in infant socialization. Nonetheless, there is no extant systematic evidence as to how this process actually does function in socialization and enculturation. Although there is good reason to suspect that it does serve this purpose (e.g., Farran & Margolis, 1987), we still must demonstrate that this is so, that is, that referencing does indeed play the role which we suspect it does in socializing the young child. Despite what is already known about the effects and operating mechanisms of referencing, there still is a pressing need for unobtrusive observation of referencing within the infant's ongoing social commerce with caregivers, family, and other people, so that we can examine the role that this process actually does play in her life.

The generalizability of referencing research may be limited by the exclusive focus of reported and published studies on infants in the United States. What we have seen in American infants seems likely, more or less, to occur in infants within other societies as well. Nevertheless, there are some specific reasons to suspect that, although the basic parameters are probably similar across societal and cultural boundaries, particular features may vary. The suggestion that social interaction in Japan is characterized by extreme sensitivity to nonverbal affective cues implies that referencing, especially emotional referencing, may be even more powerful there than in the United States (Campos, personal communication, September, 1983). Societal differences in expressivity, and in the volume and nature of communication, either generally or in infant–caregiver relationships particularly, might also result in some cross-national differences. If infants receive little communication from other people, especially about environmental events, then they may be less interested in and influenced by referencing. Furthermore, the possibility that parental teaching styles may vary among societies (e.g., American parents seem to be especially concerned about reducing uncertainty, Azuma, 1979) could have implications for the cross-cultural patterning of the impact of ambiguity on referencing. Most generally, in light of the findings of national differences in adult conformity (e.g., Milgram, 1961), it is worth wondering whether the culture in which infants grow up has an effect upon their receptivity to referencing influence.

These suggestions for future research reflect the progress that has been made in social referencing research as much as they indicate its limitations. The basic regulatory function of referencing has been sufficiently demonstrated, and we are reasonably confident that this result is achieved through a process of specific learning. We have learned a good deal about the manner in which infants gather information about referees' definitions of the situation, and about how they are affected by particular types of messages provided in various ways. The basic developmental history of referencing over the first few years, especially the first year, has been outlined. Referencing research has indicated that ambiguity may be a factor under some conditions, although perhaps less of a factor than was originally suspected. And while we knew virtually nothing a decade ago about how infants choose their referees, we can now draw at least a sketch of the structure of selectivity.

The early years of research and thinking about referencing were characterized by considerable discussion about definition and scope (e.g., Campos, 1983; Feinman, 1982, 1983a; Klinnert *et al.*, 1983). Research since then has indicated that the parametric restrictions of the narrower definition are not necessarily supported by the empirical evidence. The belief that uncertainty has a monopoly on referencing cannot be justified when there is evidence of a behavior regulation impact on clear-cut stimuli, and when even the ambiguity postulate, which predicts that referencing will be more potent in ambiguous situations, is in question. In light of this evidence, it would be sensible to refrain from utilizing uncertainty as a defining parameter of referencing.

Similarly, limiting the phenomenon by definition to emotional referencing is more difficult to justify now that there is evidence of instrumental influence as well, and in light of the suggestion that referencing may have even more of an impact on learning what to do than on learning what to feel. There is no conceptual reason to focus exclusively on the emotional aspects of reality construction and ignore the instrumental. That the emotional definition of the referent implies particular ways of interacting with it indicates that the emotional and instrumental functions of referencing are intimately connected. The possibility that learning how to cope with a novel stimulus can shape emotional responses to it further reinforces this connection. These intimate links between learning from others what to do and how to feel about a situation indicate that even those scholars, researchers, and practitioners who are most interested in the emotional aspects of the phenomenon cannot ignore its instrumental side.

The definitional disagreement, over whether referencing is restricted to situations in which the infant solicits the informational messages, is addressed by some of the results of referencing research. The finding that the behavior regulation effect is essentially the same, regardless of whether messages are volunteered or requested, suggests that a more inclusive definitional approach be taken. Perhaps even more convincing is the finding that the "prototypical" case of referencing, in which the infant requests information, examines it, and then acts, is a relatively rare occurrence during infancy. It is difficult to justify the construction of definitional boundaries around a rare and questionable hypothetical prototype.

Theorizing about referencing has, from the beginning, viewed this phenomenon in a lifespan perspective, often noting that the same fundamental process can be seen to be operating throughout life. It we wish to maintain such a view, then it is important to think about how this process has been conceptualized beyond infancy. It has long been recognized that, in adulthood, the definition of the situation includes the construction of instrumental as well as emotional reality. Recent evidence in referencing research indicates that infants, much like adults, are influenced instrumentally as well as emotionally by the guidance which they receive from other people. Similarly, concepts such as reference group and the like, have not assumed that the individual must seek out influence from others, but only that social input, however evoked, is relevant to the individual's definition of the situation. Studies of referencing in infancy indicate that infants, like adults, can be influenced by other people even when they have not sought this influence. The finding that infants' responses to clear-cut stimuli can sometimes be regulated is consistent with what we know about influence among adults, for whom cognitive clarity typically reduces but does not eliminate the impact of what other people think. It has long been known that referencing processes influence adults' feelings, thoughts, and actions in the broadest conceivable way, and in the widest imaginable range of circumstances. The evidence from studies of social referencing in infancy indicates that this is true for infants as well. Despite developmental differences, the social construction of reality operates in infancy in very much the way that it does throughout the rest of the human lifespan— broadly, powerfully, and significantly.

REFERENCES

Azuma, H. (1979). Culture-education interaction and the problem of a changing society. In S. Doxiadis (Ed.), *The child in the world of tomorrow: A window into the future* (pp. 251–254). New York: Pergamon.

Barrett, K. C. (1985). Infants' use of conflicting emotion signals. (Doctoral dissertation, University of Denver, 1984). *Dissertation Abstracts International, 46,* 321B–322B.

Berger, P. L., & Luckmann, T. (1966). *The social construction of reality.* Garden City, NY: Doubleday.

Bingham, R. D., Emde, R. N., Landau, R., & Butterfield, P. (1988, April). *Regulation of social behavior in infants following sad, anger, and interest expressions.* Paper presented at the Sixth International Conference on Infant Studies, Washington, DC.

Boccia, M. L., & Campos, J. J. (1983, April). *Maternal emotional signals and infants' reactions to strangers.* Paper presented at the biennial meeting of the Society for Research in Child Development, Detroit.

Bowlby, J. (1969). *Attachment.* New York: Basic Books.

Bradshaw, D. L., Campos, J. J., & Klinnert, M. D. (1986, April). *Emotional expressions as determinants of infants' immediate and delayed responses to prohibitions.* Paper presented at the Fifth International Conference on Infant Studies, Los Angeles.

Bradshaw, D. L., Goldsmith, H. H., & Campos, J. J. (1987). Attachment, temperament, and social referencing: Interrelationships among three domains of infant affective behavior. *Infant Behavior and Development, 10,* 223–231.

Bretherton, I. (1984). Social referencing and the interfacing of minds: A commentary on the views of Feinman and Campos. *Merrill-Palmer Quarterly, 30,* 419–427.

Brown, R. (1986). *Social psychology* (2nd ed.). New York: Free Press.

Campos, J. J. (1983). The importance of affective communication in social referencing: A commentary on Feinman. *Merrill-Palmer Quarterly, 29,* 83–87.

Campos, J. J., Butterfield, P., & Klinnert, M. D. (1985, April). *Cardiac and behavioral differentiation of negative emotional signals: An individual differences perspective.* Paper presented at the biennial meeting of the Society for Research in Child Development, Toronto.

Campos, J. J., & Stenberg, C. (1981). Perception, appraisal, and emotion: The onset of social referencing. In M. Lamb & L. Sherrod (Eds.). *Infant social cognition* (pp. 273–314). Hillsdale, NJ: Erlbaum.

Carey, W. B., & McDevitt, S. C. (1978). Revision of the Infant Temperament Questionnaire. *Pediatrics, 61,* 735–739.

Clyman, R. B., Emde, R. N., Kempe, J. E., & Harmon, R. J. (1986). Social referencing and social looking among twelve-month-old infants. In T. B. Brazelton & M. W. Yogman (Eds.), *Affective development in infancy* (pp. 75–94). Norwood, NJ: Ablex.

Dickstein, S., & Parke, R. D. (1988). Social referencing in infancy: A glance at fathers and marriage. *Child Development, 59,* 506–511.

Dickstein, S., Thompson, R. A., Estes, D., Malkin, C., & Lamb, M. E. (1984). Social referencing and the security of attachment. *Infant Behavior and Development, 7*, 507–516.

Farran, D. C., & Margolis, L. H. (1987). The family economic environment as a context for children's development. In J. H. Lewko (Ed.), *How children and adolescents view the world of work* (pp. 69–87). San Francisco: Jossey-Bass.

Feinman, S. (1982). Social referencing in infancy. *Merrill-Palmer Quarterly, 28*, 445–470.

Feinman, S. (1983a). How does baby socially refer? Two views of social referencing: A reply to Campos. *Merrill-Palmer Quarterly, 29*, 467–471.

Feinman, S. (1983b, April). The role of maternal touching in infant social referencing. In C. Saarni (Chair), *Processes in the socialization of affect*. Symposium conducted at the biennial meeting of the Society for Research in Child Development, Detroit.

Feinman, S. (1985). Emotional expression, social referencing, and preparedness for learning in infancy—Mother knows best, but sometimes I know better. In G. Zivin (Ed.), *The development of expressive behavior: Biology–environment interactions* (pp. 291–318). New York: Academic Press.

Feinman, S. (1986, July). Social referencing as social attention. In M. L. Boccia (Chair), *Social attentional processes in human and nonhuman primates*. Symposium conducted at the XIth Congress of the International Primatological Society, Gottingen, Germany.

Feinman, S. (1991). Bringing babies back into the social world. In M. Lewis & S. Feinman (Eds.), *Social influences and socialization in infancy* (pp. 281–325). New York: Plenum.

Feinman, S., & Lewis, M. (1983). Social referencing at ten months: A second-order effect on infants' responses to strangers. *Child Development, 54*, 878–887.

Feinman, S., & Roberts, D. (1986, April). *Frequency and duration of social contact during the first year: Basic patterns, age effects, and infant temperament differences*. Paper presented at the Fifth International Conference on Infant Studies, Los Angeles.

Feinman, S., Roberts, D., & Hsieh, K. (1988, April). *Social referencing within the context of the infant–sibling–mother triad*. Paper presented at the Sixth International Conference on Infant Studies, Washington, DC.

Feinman, S., Roberts, D., & Morissette, P. L. (1986, April). *The effect of social referencing on 12-month-olds' responses to a stranger's attempts to "make friends."* Paper presented at the Fifth International Conference on Infant Studies, Los Angeles.

Feiring, C., Lewis, M., & Starr, M. D. (1984). Indirect effects and infants' reaction to strangers. *Developmental Psychology, 20*, 485–491.

Frijda, N. H. (1969). Recognition of emotion. In L. Berkowitz (Ed.), *Advances in experimental social psychology* (Vol. 4, pp. 167–223). New York: Academic Press.

Garland, J. B. (1982, March). *Social referencing and self-produced locomotion*. Paper presented at the Third International Conference on Infant Studies, Austin, TX.

Gewirtz, J. L., Peláez-Nogueras, M., Diaz, L., & Villate, M. (1990, August). *Infant social referencing as an instrumental conditioned process*. Paper presented at the annual meeting of the American Psychological Association, Boston.

Gunnar, M. R., & Stone, C. (1984). The effects of positive maternal affect on infant responses to pleasant, ambiguous and fear-provoking toys. *Child Development, 55*, 1231–1236.

Hiatt, S., Campos, J., & Emde, R. N. (1979). Facial patterning and infant emotional expression: Happiness, surprise and fear. *Child Development, 50*, 1020–1035.

Hirshberg, L. M. (1988, April). *Patterns of coping with conflict in infancy: 12 month olds' response to conflicting parental emotional signals*. Paper presented at the Sixth International Conference on Infant Studies, Washington, DC.

Hirshberg, L. (1990). When infants look to their parents: II. Twelve-month-olds' response to conflicting parental emotional signals. *Child Development, 61*, 1187–1191.

Hirshberg, L. M., & Svejda, M. (1990). When infants look to their parents: I. Infants' social referencing of mothers compared to fathers. *Child Development, 61*, 1175–1186.

Hornik, R., & Gunnar, M. (1988). A descriptive analysis of infant social referencing. *Child Development, 59,* 626–634.

Hornik, R., Risenhoover, N., & Gunnar, M. (1987). The effects of maternal positive, neutral, and negative affective communications on infant responses to new toys. *Child Development, 58,* 937–944.

Izard, C. (1977). *Human emotions.* New York: Plenum.

Klinnert, M. D. (1981). *The regulation of infant behavior by maternal facial expression.* Unpublished doctoral dissertation, University of Denver, Denver.

Klinnert, M. D. (1984). The regulation of infant behavior by maternal facial expression. *Infant Behavior and Development, 7,* 447–465.

Klinnert, M. D., Campos, J. J., Sorce, J. F., Emde, R. N., & Svejda, M. (1983). Emotions as behavior regulators: Social referencing in infancy. In R. Plutchik & H. Kellerman (Eds.), *The emotions* (Vol. 2, pp. 57–86). New York: Academic Press.

Klinnert, M. D., Emde, R. N., Butterfield, P., & Campos, J. J. (1986). Social referencing: The infant's use of emotional signals from a friendly adult with mother present. *Developmental Psychology, 22,* 427–432.

Lamb, M. E., & Bornstein, M. H. (1987). *Development in infancy* (2nd ed.). New York: McGraw-Hill.

Langhorst, B. H. (1983, April). *Early antecedents of affect referencing.* Paper presented at the biennial meeting of the Society for Research in Child Development, Detroit.

Lewis, M., & Rosenblum, L. A. (Eds.). (1978). *The development of affect.* New York: Plenum.

Mead, G. H. (1934). *Mind, self and society.* Chicago: University of Chicago Press.

Milgram, S. (1961). Nationality and conformity. *Scientific American, 205* (6), 45–51.

Myers, B. J., Jarvis, P. A., & Creasey, G. L. (1987). Infants' behavior with their mothers and grandmothers. *Infant Behavior and Development, 10,* 245–259.

Plutchik, R., & Kellerman, H. (Eds.). (1983). *The emotions* (Vol. 2). New York: Academic Press.

Rothbart, M. K. (1981). Measurement of temperament in infancy. *Child Development, 52,* 569–578.

Smith, W. J. (1981). Referents of animal communication. *Animal Behaviour, 29,* 1273–1275.

Sorce, J. F., & Emde, R. N. (1981). Mother's presence is not enough: Effect of emotional availability on infant exploration. *Developmental Psychology, 17,* 737–745.

Sorce, J. F., Emde, R. N., Campos, J. J., & Klinnert, M. D. (1985). Maternal emotional signaling: Its effect on the visual cliff behavior of 1-year-olds. *Developmental Psychology, 21,* 195–200.

Sorce, J. F., Emde, R. N., & Frank, M. (1982). Maternal referencing in normal and Down's syndrome infants: A longitudinal analysis. In R. N. Emde & R. J. Harmon (Eds.), *The development of attachment and affiliative systems* (pp. 281–292). New York: Plenum.

Stayton, D. J., Hogan, R., & Ainsworth, M. D. S. (1971). Infant obedience and maternal behavior: The origins of socialization reconsidered. *Child Development, 42,* 1057–1069.

Svejda, M. J., & Campos, J. J. (1982, March). *Mother's vocal expression of emotion as a behavior regulator.* Paper presented at the Third International Conference on Infant Studies, Austin, TX.

Walden, T. A., & Baxter, A. (1989). The effect of context and age on social referencing. *Child Development, 60,* 1511–1518.

Walden, T. A., & Ogan, T. A. (1988). The development of social referencing. *Child Development, 59,* 1230–1240.

Walk, R., & Gibson, E. (1961). A comparative and analytical study of visual depth perception. *Psychological Monographs, 75*(15, Whole No. 519).

Webster, M. (1975). *Actions and actors: Principles of social psychology.* Cambridge, MA: Winthrop.

Zarbatany, L., & Lamb, M. E. (1985). Social referencing as a function of information source: Mothers versus strangers. *Infant Behavior and Development, 8,* 25–33.

II
Meaning and Understanding

3

Social Referencing, Intentional Communication, and the Interfacing of Minds in Infancy

Inge Bretherton

Infant researchers have defined social referencing in a number of ways. Feinman (1982), who approaches the field from a sociological perspective, uses a very broad definition. Any situation in which infants rely on another person's cognitive and/or emotional appraisal to form their own understanding of a situation qualifies as social referencing. The information can be actively solicited, casually observed, or actively imparted by another person, and referencing can be affective (whether to feel positively or negatively about a situation), instrumental (how to behave in or cope with a situation), or both. Feinman's broad definition of social referencing is based on the concept of reference group, which has a venerable history in sociology and social psychology. A *reference group* is a "set of significant others with whom the individual may compare his attitudes, beliefs and behaviors" (Webster, 1975, p. 446). By contrast, Campos and his colleagues (Campos, 1983; Klinnert, Campos, Sorce, Emde, & Svejda, 1983) restrict the term social referencing to those situations in which an infant *actively seeks*

INGE BRETHERTON ● Child Development and Family Studies, School of Family Resources and Consumer Sciences, University of Wisconsin, Madison, Wisconsin 53706.

Social Referencing and the Social Construction of Reality in Infancy, edited by Saul Feinman. Plenum Press, New York, 1992.

an adult's *emotional* expression to help interpret an *ambiguous* situation, thus excluding situations in which the relevant information is instrumental, and not actively solicited. The differences between the broad and narrow definitions of social referencing are important, but should not obscure what both have in common: the astounding claim that infants as young as 10 months can make deliberate and specific use of another person's judgment to form their own appraisal of a situation.

SOCIAL REFERENCING OR MOOD MODIFICATION?

Does it make sense to assume that a 10-month-old infant is aware that mother's affective expression directed toward a novel and somewhat peculiar object refers to that object? Are we dealing with social referencing when an infant recoils from a remote-controlled robot after having referenced mother's fearful face, or is the infant's behavior more accurately interpreted as due to mood modification? Feinman and Campos both argue that their findings are not consonant with the mood modification hypothesis. In a study conducted by Feinman & Lewis (1983), 10-month-old infants behaved differentially toward a stranger, depending on whether the mother talked to the infant about the stranger with positive or neutral affect. Yet, the infant's behavior to the mother herself was not influenced by the experimental manipulation of her speech. In a more recent study, Walden and Ogan (1988) reported that when they received a positive message about one toy and a negative one about a different toy, infants' subsequent free play with these toys reflected the specificity of these communications. Similarly, Klinnert, Emde, Butterfield, and Campos (1986) found that a stranger's negative response to a robot did not influence 12-month-olds' behavior toward the stranger, although it did apparently deter the infants from approaching the robot. Finally, Hornik, Risenhoover, and Gunnar (1987) discovered that mothers' messages about stimulus toys affected the infants' behavior to these particular toys, but not to other available toys.

If Feinman and Campos are correct in rejecting the mood modification hypothesis and espousing the social cognitive hypothesis (i.e., assuming that infants can understand and use another person's judgment of a situation in order to form their own interpretation), we must credit 10-month-old infants with more advanced levels of social cognition than has traditionally been the case. Unfortunately, evidence against the mood modification hypothesis, though suggestive, falls short of being conclusive. It is therefore important to note that strong convergent evidence for the social cognitive hypothesis comes from many studies of communicative and language development.

In what follows, I present a detailed review of research on infant communicative development to make the point that social referencing can be understood as one aspect of the infant's ability to "interface minds" through intentional communication. Studies of intentional communication between 9 and 12 months demonstrate the infant's ability to recruit and guide a partner's attention through well-timed gestures. This period coincides with the onset of social referencing and will be discussed first. I then consider further developments during the second year when verbal components play an increasing role in infants' communicative interchanges with others. This literature provides further persuasive corroboration for Feinman's (1982) and Campos's (1983) social cognitive interpretation of social referencing. Finally, I discuss future directions in the study of social referencing in the narrow and broad sense. There is a clear need for further studies that are specifically designed to clearly demonstrate that the infant's seeking of emotional information from the adult is deliberate. Techniques used in the study of gestural communication might be useful in the pursuit of this goal. In addition, social referencing research could shed further light on the development of intentional emotional signaling, which has been neglected by students of early communication and language acquisition. As regards future investigations of infant social referencing in the broad sense, I favor an approach that explicitly examines links between the behavior of both partners in social referencing situations and individual differences in the young child's construction (or misconstruction) of social reality. True, the evidence against the mood modification hypothesis of social referencing is still somewhat circumstantial. I believe, however, that the corroborating evidence from the study of early communicative development presented in this chapter clearly justifies the assumption that infants around 1 year of age can begin to use another person's appraisal to interpret a new or puzzling situation for themselves. This allows us to move beyond studies demonstrating that social referencing occurs, and permits us to pursue the long-term implications of social referencing for the development of individual differences in the construction of social reality.

INTERFACING OF MINDS DURING THE
PREVERBAL PERIOD

A number of investigators have noticed striking changes in how infants interact with their mothers during the period around 9 months, that is, around the time when social referencing phenomena seem to emerge. Scaife and Bruner (1975) showed that 9-month-olds have the ability to establish a joint topic of attention with mother. Whereas 4-month-olds *occasionally* followed their mothers' line of regard, this behavior became reliable and common only around 8 to 9 months. The interpretation of shared reference (Scaife and Bruner's term) as intentional search for the target of another person's gaze was supported by Butterworth's (1979, cited in Bruner, 1980) subsequent observation that 12-month-old infants turned to follow mother's line of regard only once her gaze had settled upon a particular location, but then turned to check her face if her gaze was directed at a blank space (i.e., when "shared referencing" yielded no referent). It was as if the infants were asking mother "why are you looking up there?" Other studies show that infants can follow mother's pointing gestures as well as her line of regard, although this ability is still fairly limited at 9 months (Murphy & Messer, 1977). Nine-month-olds sitting next to their mothers were able to follow mother's pointing when it was directed to a location ahead or to the side, but they did not respond correctly when mother pointed across the infant's body. By 14 months, infants understood pointing gestures directed across their bodies as well.

Not only did infants between 9 and 12 months of age understand maternal attempts to establish joint reference or a common focus of attention, they were also able to actively produce shared reference through a variety of gestures. The use of gestures with communicative intent has been documented by, among others, Bates, Camaioni, and Volterra (1975), Bruner (1975), and Lock (1980), where communicative intent is defined as the sender's prior awareness of the effect which a message is designed to have on the addressee. According to Bates (1979), the communicative intent of infant gestures can be inferred on the basis of three behavioral indices:

1. *Gaze alternation.* In pointing or reaching toward desired objects infants will often turn to the addressee as if to check that the message is being received.
2. *Repair of failed messages.* If the addressee does not respond in the intended manner, infants frequently augment the intensity of the communicative behavior or substitute a new gesture for the first, as if to clarify the message.
3. *Ritualization of previously instrumental gestures.* Behaviors that previously served purely instrumental functions are now transformed into ritualized signals. For example, infants may ask for an object with empty-handed grasping motions directed toward the object instead of peremptorily taking it from another person's hand.

Bates' (1979) claim that gaze alternation, repair of failed messages, and ritualization of instrumental gestures index an emerging ability to engage in intentional communication is supported by a variety of other studies, and these indices are among the factors associated with mother's understanding of infant communication (Golinkoff & Gordon, 1988). Sugarman-Bell (1978) pointed out that gaze alternation enables an infant to integrate intentional behavior toward an object (topic) with intentional behavior directed toward a social partner (comment). Harding and Golinkoff (1979) showed that what appears to underlie this coordination is an understanding of physical causality. With respect to the repair of failed messages, Golinkoff (1983) found that such attempts increased during the preverbal stage. Message repetitions were most common initially, while message augmentations and signal substitutions became frequent during the later preverbal stage.

Studies of mother–infant play have independently described behaviors fulfilling the same three criteria of communicative intent. Trevarthen and Hubley (1979) reported that infants under 9 months of age could not yet coordinate person and object attention (reminiscent of Sugarman-Bell's [1978] findings regarding gestural requests). A dramatic shift occurred at 9 months, when infants began to look up from object to mother during joint play, and to invite mother's participation by offering and giving objects. What is more, the infants began to understand the instructive intention of maternal behavior. For example, when the mother pointed from a peg to the hole into which it fitted, 9-month-olds did not slavishly imitate her incomplete demonstration. Instead, they displayed their understanding of the instruction by placing the peg in the hole. It is interesting to note that !Kung San infants (in northwestern Botswana) begin to engage in actions such as object offers, which call for coordination between object and person, around the same age (Bakeman, Adamson, Konner, & Barr, 1990). In addition to demonstrating the emergence of gaze alternation, studies of infant–adult play have also documented infant attempts to repair failed messages. Ross and Kay (1980) found that, in turn-taking games with an unfamiliar adult companion, 12-month-olds employed a variety of strategies for reviving reciprocal games. In the Ross and Kay paradigm the adult "stopped playing the game" for 10 seconds after smooth turn-taking had been established. Infants responded to this interruption by looking back and forth from adult to toy, by partially or fully retaking their own turn and then waiting, or by holding up their hands to invite a turn from the adult (in object exchange games). These signals occurred almost exclusively during game interruptions. The infants also watched the adult playmate's face more during interruptions, whereas they looked more at her hands and at game-related objects during the normal phases of the game. Inspection of the data provided by Ross (1980) revealed that all infants had several of these strategies at their disposal. Ross concluded that the infants knew that it was now the partner's turn to act, and that they understood the structure which controlled the interaction. In view of the variety of behaviors infants used to reinstitute interrupted games, it also seems plausible to assume that the infants expected the partner to understand their signals. Similar findings and interpretations can be noted in the more recent Ross and Lollis (1987) study.

Two especially instructive examples provide a more vivid illustration of intentional acts of communication in preverbal infants. In the first, an infant aged 14 months used gaze alternation as well as two ritualized behaviors (vestigial crying and lip smacking) to communicate with each of two adults in turn:

> Mother enters the room holding a cup of tea. Paul turns from his playpen in her direction and obviously sees it. (i) He *cries vestigially* and so attracts his mother's attention; immediately he *points toward her* and *smacks his lips* concurrently (Paul's way of asking for food or drink). Mother: No, you can't have this one, it's Andy's. Mother gives me (the observer) the cup of tea, and I put it on the mantelpiece to cool. Paul crawls across to me and grasps my knees. (ii) I turn to look at him; he *looks toward the mantelpiece and points, turns back to me, continues to point,* and *smacks his lips.* (Lock, 1980, pp. 95–96; clarification in parentheses and italics added)

This communicative interchange can be interpreted as follows: the child indicated a desire by vestigial (ritual) crying; he then focused the partner's attention on the object of his desire (by lip smacking and pointing). When the addressee refused the child's request, passing the desired tea to someone else, the child turned toward the new "owner" of the tea (gaze alternation). This occurred despite the fact that the tea was now resting on the mantelpiece, at a distance from both adult conversants. Note the precise timing and directionality of the communicative signals, in addition to the ritualization of instrumental behaviors in the service of conveying an intentional message.

The second example illustrates the successful negotiation of an initially ambiguous message between a 14-month-old preverbal infant and his mother at lunchtime:

1. JORDAN: Vocalizes repeatedly until his mother turns around.
2. MOTHER: Turns around to look at him.
3. JORDAN: Points to one of the objects on the counter.
4. MOTHER: "Do you want this?" (holds up milk container).
5. JORDAN: Shakes his head "no," continues to point.
6. MOTHER: "Do you want this?" (holds up jelly jar).
7. JORDAN: Shakes his head "no," continues to point.
8. 9. 10. 11. Two more offer–rejection pairs.
12. MOTHER: "This?" (picks up sponge).
13. JORDAN: Leans back in highchair, puts arm down, tension leaves body.
14. MOTHER: Hands Jordan sponge.
(Golinkoff, 1983, pp. 58–59)

The mother interpreted the infant's initial pointing as a request, but was uncertain of the desired object's identity. By holding up a series of possible targets, she was actually helping the child to repair the failed message, but the child was an equally active participant by persistently giving the required feedback. The process worked only because the mother assumed that the child was communicating about a specific goal, and because the child appeared to assume that the mother was attempting to discover his goal.

Like Trevarthen (1988; Trevarthen & Hubley, 1978), Bruner (1975), and Stern (1985), I interpret the preverbal infant's ability to produce and understand intentional gestures as evidence for the emergence of inter-subjective understanding. Bruner (1975) used the term *intersubjectivity* to describe the child's dawning understanding of reciprocal intentions. Trevarthen and Hubley (1978) use the same term in two distinct senses. Primary intersubjectivity characterizes early mother–child interactions that have no topic other than the interaction itself: the partners are affectively resonating to each other (see also Stern, 1977, 1985). Secondary inter-subjectivity refers to interactions in which both partners are intentionally exchanging messages about a common topic. Bretherton and Bates (1979) argue that secondary intersubjectivity implies two emerging abilities: (1) the infant is beginning to understand others as psychological beings, and (2) the infant has an emergent realization that minds can be deliberately interfaced through intentional signals.

Why use fancy terms like intersubjectivity or interfacing of minds when it might be more parsimonious to credit the infant with intention-ality pure and simple (see Shatz, 1983). After all, the acquisition of inten-tional gestures seems to coincide with an emerging understanding of physical means–end relations and physical causality (see Bates *et al.*, 1975; Bates, Benigni, Bretherton, Camaioni, & Volterra, 1979; Harding & Golink-off, 1979). My objection to an explanation couched purely in terms of understanding physical relations is that it fails to take into account the infant's budding ability to specify messages for the addressee. The infant's communicative behaviors appear designed to attract and direct the ad-dressee's attention to topics of mutual interest. The most parsimonious explanation is therefore one that assumes that, by the end of the first year, infants have acquired a rudimentary "theory of mind" or ability to impute mental states to self and other (Astington, Harris, & Olson, 1988; Hala, Chandler, & Fritz, 1991; Lewis & Osborne, 1990; Premack & Woodruff, 1978), and further, that they have begun to understand that one mind can be interfaced with another through conventional or mutually compre-hensible signals (Bretherton & Bates, 1979; Bretherton & Beeghly, 1982; Bretherton, McNew, & Beeghly-Smith, 1981).

Other evidence also argues in favor of this interpretation. For example, during the period when infants acquire the ability to engage in intentional communication, they become able to reverse roles in social games (Ratner & Bruner, 1978), to engage in deliberate imitation of another person's facial movements (Piaget, 1961), and somewhat later to take the maternal role in play with dolls (Nicolich, 1977; Wolf, 1982) and to comfort victims of distress (Cummings, Hollenbeck, Iannotti, Radke-Yarrow, & Zahn-Waxler, 1986; Harris, 1989; Zahn-Waxler, Radke-Yarrow, & King, 1979).

Let me add some qualifications at this point. I do not mean to suggest that 1-year-old infants can reflect on their own theory of mind. What I do want to argue is that they can operate with it, in the same way that 3-year-olds operate with grammatical rules that they cannot state verbally. Nor do I presume to claim that 1-year-olds are mind–body dualists who make a clear distinction between inner states and outward behavior. Indeed, before humans can understand that outward expressions do not always reflect inner feelings and goals, they must discover that a person's inner states and expressive behaviors are, for the most part, *concordant* and therefore interpretable (Bretherton, Fritz, Zahn-Waxler, & Ridgeway, 1986). Along the same lines, Rommetveit (1979a, p. 96) claimed that "intersubjectivity has to be in some sense taken for granted for it to be achieved. It is based on mutual faith in a shared world."

I suggest that studies of gestural communication provide convincing evidence that infants begin to take intersubjectivity for granted during the last part of the first year. Results from these studies hence strengthen the circumstantial evidence against a mood modification explanation of the social referencing hypothesis offered by Feinman (1982) and Campos (1983), and support the social cognitive hypothesis.

INTERFACING OF MINDS DURING THE ONE-WORD STAGE

With the onset of language, evidence for a capacity to interface minds becomes even stronger, although the attention-getting and -directing signals from the preverbal stage continue to play a crucial role. Single words tend to be inserted into ever-more complex message structures (Bretherton, 1988). Indeed, infants' one-word utterances are comprehensible only because some of the referents are present to view *and* because the child is skillful at obtaining and then directing the partner's attention through gestures. Take, for example, the following anecdote from Greenfield (1988), about a child whose mother was unable to attend to him immediately because she was in charge of a swimming class:

The child goes towards his mother, whining "shoes, shoes" (he only has socks on). He comes back towards me and gets his blue sandals. I try to help him while standing up, but cannot do it. So I sit down with one shoe, put him on my lap, and put his shoe on. Then I put him down, not saying anything. He walks straight to his other shoe, picks it up and comes back to me. I put him on my lap and put his other shoe on. He then runs towards his mother still talking, saying "shoe, shoe" in an excited voice. He lifts his foot to show her. When she attends, he points to me. She understands, saying something like "The lady put your shoes on". Both are very excited. (p. 275)

This fairly sophisticated message is primarily conveyed through well-timed and well-directed gestures. The child holds up his foot until mother attends. Only then does he point to the person who helped him put on his shoes. Although the mention of shoes initially helps to clarify the topic, this message could have been transmitted by nonverbal signals alone. The following example, also from Greenfield (1980), illustrates, the negotiation of an unclear message in one-word speech. Note the similarity between this anecdote and the earlier gestural example, cited from Golinkoff (1983):

(Matthew's sister Lauren had gone out of the room).
MATTHEW: Lara (Lauren)
MOTHER: Yeah. Lauren. What happened to Lauren?
MATTHEW: Oh (or ou, two transcribers disagreed)
MOTHER: Oh?
MATTHEW: No
MOTHER: Hoe?
MATTHEW: Ou
MOTHER: Out?
MATTHEW: Yeah, Yaya (Lauren).
(Greenfield, 1980, p. 271)

Like the child Jordan in Golinkoff's (1983) report, Matthew repeated his message with slight variations until the mother guessed the correct answer. Without patience on her part, his communication could not have succeeded, but without Jordan's acknowledgment of the correct answer his mother would not have been certain that she had understood his intent.

In studying further developments during the single-word stage, investigators have distinguished between the acquisition of two classes of words: nouns and relational words (e.g., Bloom, 1973). For the purposes of this chapter, the acquisition of relational words is of special interest. Relational words include terms such as "allgone," "up," "no," and "uh-oh." In contrast to nouns, relational words do not make reference to objects or particular actions. They take on specific meaning only in the context of relationships among agents, objects, and actions that are either present or established through naming or pointing. Bloom (1973) argued that one-word utterances consisting of relational words are often more readily interpretable than one-word utterances formed with names or nouns because the intended relationships among objects and agents may be more difficult to infer from gestures and context than the objects to which the relationships apply. For example, if mother and child are emptying containers filled with blocks, the utterance "allgone" as the child looks into the container is relatively unambiguous. By contrast, the utterance "block" in the same context is more difficult to interpret. We know that the topic is block, but we do not know what the child is trying to say about the block.

Bloom (1973), in her detailed case study, reports that her daughter Allison used relational words in a variety of situations that had to do with notions of appearance, disappearance, absence, and recurrence of objects and actions. Allison said "gone" when looking into an empty container, while her mother was drinking juice from a cup, as a soap bubble popped, and while she was searching for a missing object. She used "more" initially to request more food, more tickling, and more reading of a book. Somewhat later "more" served to point out several instances of the same category. Allison began to use "uh-oh" when she dropped or spilled something, later she commented with "uh-oh" when her mother caused a mishap. Finally, she seemed to be teasing her mother by announcing "uh-oh" before she inverted an almost empty cup to spill some more liquid on the floor. McCune-Nicolich (1981) corroborated and amplified Bloom's (1973) findings. In both studies (Bloom, 1973; McCune-Nicolich, 1981) the children appeared to expect their mothers to use the shared context in order to understand the relationship on which they were commenting. The children's mothers, conversely, seemed to be able to live up to these expectations. Both partners relied on their experience of a shared here-and-now reality to effectively convey and understand meanings.

INTERFACING OF MINDS THROUGH SIMPLE TOPIC–COMMENT CONSTRUCTIONS

From the communicative standpoint, Bloom's (1973) distinction between relational words and nouns becomes even more interesting once the child has mastered a variety of both, for now we can examine under what conditions a toddler chooses to use one or the other. In a detailed case study, Greenfield and Smith (1976) noticed that when their subjects, Matthew and Nicky, communicated about an object (topic) that was already the focus of joint attention, the children chose to comment on the action component of the situation with a relational word. By contrast, when the focus of attention was uncertain, the children would verbally establish the topic rather than comment on it with a relational word. Hence, the object was frequently named in issuing a demand, but the relational word "no" was generally used in refusals where the joint topic was already known or obvious. For example, in drawing attention to events, one of the children always mentioned the record player (topic) before commenting that it was "ong." The other child named toy cars he was *not* holding or cars that were passing by outside, but mentioned the action of a toy car ("allgone"), if he was already playing with it. Likewise, when mother established the topic of conversation by asking what the car outside was doing, the child answered with the comment "bye-bye." On reanalyzing utterances in their own and in Bloom's (1973) case studies, Greenfield and Smith (1976) discovered that in almost every instance the child referred first to the object if a joint topic of attention had not yet been established, but mentioned an activity first if the topic of conversation was clear.

Greenfield (Greenfield, 1979; Greenfield & Smith, 1976) used the concept of informativeness (relative certainty) to explain toddlers' choices of object versus relational words. An object is said to be relatively certain when it is in the child's hands, but uncertain when not in the child's possession. The child's tendency is to mention the uncertain aspect of the situation. But who is experiencing uncertainty? Greenfield (1979) claimed that the child was labeling the most informative (most uncertain or unclear) aspect of the situation for himself. Yet it seems that it was the listener not the child who had cause to be uncertain about the topic (for further discussion of this point, see Ninio & Snow, 1984). Greenfield rejected this interpretation, presumably because tailoring a message to listener needs is supposed to be beyond a toddler's capacity. But is it? Since we have discovered that even 1-year-olds can understand and nonverbally establish topics of joint attention through pointing and looking, it seems reasonable to assume that young children in the one-word stage know that establishment of a joint topic through word or gesture is a prerequisite for verbal comment about the topic. Moreover, the data support such an assumption.

Scollon (1979) coined the term *vertical construction* for those topic–comment propositions that are continued across several speaker turns (as opposed to horizontal constructions in which topic and comment are contained in the same utterance). He identified four levels of vertical construction. The earliest form contains many repetitions and requires the intervention of a conversational partner, as illustrated by the following example (Scollon, 1979, p. 217):

BRENDA: f ĕ î, f a.
MOTHER: Hm?
BRENDA: f ǽ.
MOTHER: Bathroom?
BRENDA: fañi, faî.

MOTHER: Fan. Yeah.
BRENDA: k^{h}u.
MOTHER: Cool, yeah. Fan makes you cool.

As children's phonology improves, the need for repetitions declines, and the adult partner's intervention is no longer necessary. Finally, children learn to comment on topics provided by a parent, the beginning of true discourse. For example, in a game format (playing at eating toes), Matthew's father said "toe, toe" and Matthew replied "eat" (Greenfield & Smith, 1976). The father's previously established topic of "toe" is presupposed in Matthew's subsequent comment "eat."

Note that, in order to draw conclusions about a child's communicative intentions it is crucial that the transcriptions take into account all aspects of the communicative situation: the timing and directedness of a child's gestures and words, as well as the responses of the partner. An example from Atkinson (1979) illustrates the power of such contextual analyses especially well:

> ... consider the following situation which I have observed with my own son. His mother has been out for several minutes, and he approaches me saying *mummy* with no signs of distress or special intonation to indicate that he might be asking a question. It is clearly difficult to gloss his utterance as a statement. *That's mummy* and similar candidates just do not make sense, and what happened next is interesting. My response to the child was *mummy?* using marked question intonation to which the child immediately responds with *gone*. ... for the moment I merely want to suggest that a plausible candidate for the function of the initial *mummy* is that of drawing the father's attention to that individual, and only when the child gets some feedback to indicate that his addressee is suitably attending does he go on and predicate something of mummy. (pp. 235–236)

Atkinson's anecdote is an instance of Scollon's (1979) vertical topic–comment construction with adult help, clarified here by the addition of vital contextual information: the child goes on to elaborate on the topic only once the father has signaled its uptake. On the basis of this, and other detailed examples, Atkinson suggests that adult inattentiveness (in addition to phonological problems) may often be the reason for the topic repetition noted by Scollon (1979). Such findings *lend further support to the hypothesis that children still in the one-word stage attempt to use their limited linguistic capacity so as to guide the adult's understanding.*

The examples cited above are limited to communication about topics that were at hand, or at least perceptible in some way. In the course of further communicative development during the second year, children begin to converse about absent topics. Take, for example, the following instructive conversation recorded by Bloom (1973, p. 227) when her daughter Allison was almost 21 months old, and just beginning to use topic–comment constructions in successive single word utterances. Mother and child are playing together in a laboratory playroom. The child mentions a bathtub:

MOTHER: Bathtub? I don't see a bathtub.
ALLISON: (*turns, pointing but not looking*) Home.
MOTHER: Home. Home.
ALLISON: Home.
MOTHER: What do we do in the bathtub?
ALLISON: Bath/bath.
MOTHER: We take a bath.
ALLISON: Mommy/shower.
MOTHER: Mommy shower. Mommy takes a shower.
ALLISON: Nudie.
MOTHER: Nudie. Yes.
ALLISON: (*touching her head*) Hat/on.
MOTHER: "With a hat on, yes" (shower cap).

I suggest that without their shared life history and hence an extensive shared knowledge base, such conversations between mother and child would be impossible. Yet a few judicious words can go a long way when so much can be jointly presupposed or taken for granted. Indeed, similar "conversations" might be studied in social referencing situations during the second year of life.

INTERFACING OF MINDS: SIMILARITIES BETWEEN INFANT AND ADULT COMMUNICATION

It is obvious that infants' one-word utterances depend heavily on shared presuppositions and contextual information. To draw conclusions about infants' ability to interface minds, the timing, direction, and sequence of message components must be studied in detail. It is less obvious that, throughout the lifespan, verbal and nonverbal communication can never be totally divorced from the social context. Intentional acts of communication and comprehension are always based on presuppositions about what knowledge can be taken for granted, and what new information must be added by the speaker or message sender. Infants are less different from adults in this respect than we tend to assume.

For example, when an adult cries out "magnificent" after the last bars of a rousing symphony performance, the addressee must use the timing and context of the utterance to conclude that "magnificent" referred to the symphony. Some linguists take such adult one-word utterances as an elliptical version of the more complete underlying statement, "The concert was magnificent," from which other constituents have been deleted (Holz-man, 1971). Others (Rommetveit, 1979a) argue that an adult's one-word utterance can be understood only if it is complemented by presupposed knowledge implicitly shared by speaker and listener. The technique of "rich interpretation" used by developmental psycholinguists to infer the communicative intent of a toddler's message similarly depends on shared presuppositions. Seen through Rommetveit's eyes, it becomes evident that rich interpretation is not just a technique applicable to young and in-experienced communicators; it is the sine qua non for the production and comprehension of intentional communicative acts, whatever the age of the communicator. Hence, in deciding whether or not infants are capable of understanding that minds can be interfaced, we must be careful not to apply stricter standards of explicitness to infants than to adults.

Rommetveit's writings on the architecture of intersubjectivity (1971, 1972, 1979a, 1979b, 1985) may be especially helpful in shedding further light on these issues. He contends that intentional communication be-comes possible only when partners are able to establish jointly negotiated spatiotemporal intersubjective coordinates. The conversants (you and I) must agree on what constitutes here and now (versus the there and then) in the present dialogue (Rommetveit, 1972). The primary problem of com-munication is *what is made known and how it is made known in a shared social reality* (Rommetveit, 1971). Grammatically incomplete utterances (ellipsis) are the norm under conditions of trust and a shared social world. Only what is new need be explicitly mentioned. When an adult speaker encodes a message, he is therefore always monitoring it from the listener's perspec-tive (anticipatory decoding), taking into account what is and what is not jointly known. The listener's task is to reconstruct the intended message from the verbal and nonverbal message components. If much is shared, much less needs to be explicitly encoded.

What I wish to claim here is that 1-year-olds already have a rudimen-tary version of later adult strategies for establishing a shared intersubjec-tive framework with a partner. Beginning around 9 months of age, infants can set up intersubjective coordinates through pointing, gaze direction, and other gestures. At the same time, they begin to understand inter-subjective coordinates set up by adults. They do not always succeed in making themselves understood, but they frequently help their conversa-tional partners by using well-timed gestures, and by persisting or repeat-ing when the partner signals that the message has not been understood (repair of failed messages). This could not be achieved without the infant's assumption of a shared mental world, and without some primitive ability to take the role of the other (Mead, 1934). Even 10-month-olds seem to make some attempt at constructing communicative acts with some atten-tion to listener needs, and, as social referencing studies show, assume that a partner can convey important information about the environment to them.

Around the end of the first year, children begin to notice and acquire complex conventional meaning-exchange systems used by adults in their environment (whether these be verbal or manual languages, conventional emotion expressions, or gestures). We still do not know all the factors that contribute to this developmental shift, but the available evidence suggests that it is not only the acquisition of sensorimotor notions of objects, means–end relations, and causality that makes the interfacing of minds possible. The realization that persons can share understandings (that minds can be interfaced) does not follow after, but is a prerequisite for, learning to engage in deliberate meaning exchange. A creature without the potential for developing a theory of interfacing minds could not acquire and would not be motivated to learn complex message-making strategies. Such a creature could also not engage in social referencing as understood by Feinman (1982) and Campos (1983). To quote Rommetveit (1979b, p. 161) again: "We must naively and unreflectingly take the possibility of perfect intersubjectivity for granted in order to achieve partial intersubjectivity in real life discourse with our fellow men." It appears that this naive and unreflecting assumption seems to emerge around 9 months, leading to a developmental shift of enormous significance.

FUTURE DIRECTIONS FOR THE STUDY OF SOCIAL REFERENCING

The many intriguing findings concerning infants' ability to interface minds through intentional communication are consonant with and strongly support the social cognitive interpretation of social referencing offered by Feinman (1982) and Campos (1983): namely, that infants can seek and understand another person's interpretations of a situation. Viewed in this light, an infant's ability to solicit and accept another person's judgment about what to do (instrumental referencing) and how to feel (emotional referencing) in a situation come to be seen as part of the wider ability to engage in reciprocal intentional communication. This raises the question of what is to be gained by continuing to study infant social referencing as a separate domain.

Regarding studies of social referencing in the narrow sense, much still needs to be discovered about developmental changes in the second year. Does social referencing behavior become more complex? Could we find the beginnings of social referencing "conversations" in which the partners help each other to clarify the meaning of their emotional messages? What modalities are used to construct and comprehend multilayered emotional signals? I suggest that such studies are especially important because developmental psycholinguists have tended not to include emotional signaling in their investigations.

Regarding studies of social referencing in the broad sense, I believe that a change of emphasis is in order. The time has come to shift our major focus from showing *that* infants engage in referencing to more explicitly examining *the role* of social referencing in the child's construction of social reality (Feinman, 1982). The corroboration of the social cognitive hypothesis of social referencing by research on early communicative development justifies this shift.

Through emotional and instrumental messages from older partners, infants and toddlers learn how to respond to situations they have not encountered before. Therefore, processes like modeling, persuasion, observation, and social comparison (all related to social referencing) play an important role in how infants come to interpret the world. Specifically, through social referencing processes, adult models influence an infant's or child's interpretation of events as dangerous, amusing, annoying, exciting, or desirable. Through social referencing processes infants and children also acquire new coping responses from their caregivers. In pointing to one thing but ignoring something else, in expressing a particular emotion about an action or event but masking another, a parent highlights that thing or that emotion as either relevant and important or irrelevant and unimportant. Thus, a capacity for social referencing obviates the need for inexperienced individuals to always engage in their own, sometimes dangerous, trial-and-error appraisal of the environment. As Bowlby points out in his 1973 volume, *Separation*, the ability to acquire culturally transmissible clues to danger through social referencing has obvious survival value.

However, parental interpretations in social referencing situations offer infants and toddlers not only a *basis*, but also a *bias* for the construction of social reality. Recent work on maternal affect attunement (Stern, 1985) shows such processes at work in infancy. Stern noticed that mothers of 9-month-olds began to engage in a new form of affect sharing. Before 9 months, mothers often imitated or mirrored the infant's behavior as a way of "being with" the infant. In affect attunement (after 9 months), mothers no longer imitated the infant's behavior *per se*, but matched the behavior's temporal beat, intensity contour, duration, and/or spatial shape. In other words, in response to an infant's joyful sound the mother resonated not with a similar sound but with a joyful movement that matched the rhythm and intensity contour of the infant's vocalization.

Stern (1985) believes that maternal affect attunement focuses the infant's attention on the shared affect rather than the shared behavior. This has two important consequences. On the one hand, affect attunement comes to play a vital role in the infant's developing ability to recognize that feeling states can be shared with others. On the other hand, affect attunement teaches the infant what may and what may not be shared. When mothers consistently "underattune" or "overattune" to their infants' expressions, or when they choose not to attune to certain expressions at all, they convey information about how the child should feel in specific situations. Stern contends that consistent parental misattunements may undermine infants' ability to adequately appraise their own inner states. Moreover, states to which the caregiver does not attune may later be experienced alone, isolated from the interpersonal context. Interestingly, mothers of depressed or preterm infants seem to be less in tune with their children than do those of "normal" infants (Field, Healy, Goldstein, & Guthertz, 1990; Stevenson, Roach, ver Hoeve, & Leavitt, 1990).

What Stern claims with regard to behavioral misattunements also holds true of other forms of miscommunication. When a parent's verbal interpretation is very incongruent with what the child experienced, the child may find it difficult or impossible to construct a coherent social reality. Bowlby (1973, 1980) and Stern (1985) suggest that in such cases the child's own appraisal of the situation may be defensively excluded from awareness, but continue to lead an underground existence.

Whereas the adaptive function of social referencing is to provide vicarious instrumental and emotional information to inexperienced individuals, it appears that this propensity also has its dangers. First, the referenced partner may intentionally or unintentionally convey deceptive or biased information, and as social referencing experiments show (Campos & Stenberg, 1981; Feinman & Lewis, 1983; Klinnert et al., 1983), infants' ability to see through deceitful communications is not well developed. Second, even older children, who understand that outward appearances are not necessarily veridical (Selman, 1981), do not appear to submit all messages to the acid test of trustworthiness. This is especially true if the message senders are attachment figures, teachers, or friends (see Bretherton et al., 1986, for further discussion). Thus, as Bowlby (1973, 1980) has poignantly documented, in cases where an attachment figure communicates inappropriate, misleading, or contradictory interpretations of events to a child in social referencing situations, the reality constructed on the basis of such secondhand appraisals may be confusing and maladaptive. Where the parent also forbids the child to mentally review and reinterpret such distorted social constructions, psychopathology may ensue. In sum, infants' normally adaptive and useful disposition to engage in social referencing also has its darker side. The study of social referencing would be greatly enriched if we examined how referencing phenomena relate to individual differences in infants' and children's developing constructions of social reality.

Acknowledgments: While writing this chapter, I received support from the John D. and Catherine T. MacArthur Foundation Network for the Transition from Infancy to Early Childhood.

REFERENCES

Astington, J. W., Harris, P. L., & Olson, D. R. (Eds.). (1988). *Developing theories of mind*. New York: Cambridge University Press.

Atkinson, M. (1979). Prerequisites for reference. In E. Ochs & B. B. Schieffelin (Eds.), *Developmental pragmatics* (pp. 215–247). New York: Academic Press.

Bakeman, R., Adamson, L. B., Konner, M., & Barr, R. G. (1990). !Kung infancy: The social context of object exploration. *Child Development, 61,* 794–809.

Bates, E. (1979). Intentions, conventions and symbols. In E. Bates, L. Benigni, I. Bretherton, L. Camaioni, & V. Volterra (Eds.), *The emergence of symbols* (pp. 33–42). New York: Academic Press.

Bates, E., Benigni, L., Bretherton, I., Camoioni, L., & Volterra, V. (1979). Cognition and communication from 9–13 months: Correlational findings. In E. Bates, L. Benigni, I. Bretherton, L. Camaioni, & V. Volterra (Eds.), *The emergence of symbols* (pp. 69–140). New York: Academic Press.

Bates, E., Camaioni, L., & Volterra, V. (1975). The acquisition of performatives prior to speech. *Merrill-Palmer Quarterly, 21,* 205–226.

Bloom, L. (1973). *One word at a time*. The Hague: Mouton.

Bowlby, J. (1973). *Attachment and loss. Vol. 2: Separation*. New York: Basic Books.

Bowlby, J. (1980). *Attachment and loss. Vol. 3: Loss*. New York: Basic Books.

Bretherton, I. (1988). How to do things with one word: The ontogenesis of intentional message making in infancy. In M. D. Smith & J. L. Locke (Eds.) *The emergent lexicon* (pp. 225–260). Orlando, FL: Academic Press.

Bretherton, I., & Bates, E. (1979). The emergence of intentional communication. In I. Uzgiris (Ed.), *New directions for child development* (Vol. 4, pp. 81–100). San Francisco: Jossey-Bass.

Bretherton, I., & Beeghly, M. (1982). Talking about internal states: The acquisition of an explicit theory of mind. *Developmental Psychology, 18,* 906–921.

Bretherton, I., Fritz, J., Zahn-Waxler, C., & Ridgeway, D. (1986). Learning to talk about emotions: A functionalist perspective. *Child Development, 57,* 529–548.

Bretherton, I., McNew, S., & Beeghly-Smith, M. (1981). Early person knowledge as expressed in gestural and verbal communication: When do infants acquire a "theory of mind"? In M. E. Lamb, & L. R. Sherrod (Eds.), *Infant social cognition* (pp. 333–373). Hillsdale, NJ: Erlbaum.

Bruner, J. (1975). The ontogenesis of speech acts. *Journal of Child Language, 2,* 1–19.

Bruner, J. (1980). Afterword. In D. R. Olson (Ed.), *The social foundations of language and thought* (pp. 376–386). New York: Norton.

Butterworth, G. (1979, September). *What minds have in common is space: A perceptual mechanism for joint reference in infancy*. Paper presented to the Developmental Section, British Psychological Society, Southampton.

Campos, J. J. (1983). The importance of affective communication in social referencing: A commentary on Feinman. *Merrill-Palmer Quarterly, 28,* 445–470.

Campos, J. J., & Stenberg, C. R. (1981). Perception, appraisal and emotion: The onset of social referencing. In M. E. Lamb & L. R. Sherrod (Eds.), *Infant social cognition* (pp. 273–314). Hillsdale, NJ: Erlbaum.

Cummings, E. M., Hollenbeck, B., Iannotti, R., Radke-Yarrow, M., & Zahn-Waxler, C. (1986). The early organization of individual differences in aggression and altruism. In C. Zahn-Waxler, E. M. Cummings, & R. Iannotti (Eds.), *Altruism and aggression* (pp. 165–188). New York: Cambridge University Press.

Feinman, S. (1982). Social referencing in infancy. *Merrill-Palmer Quarterly, 28*, 445–470.

Feinman, S., & Lewis, M. (1983). Social referencing at 10 months: A second-order effect on infants' responses to strangers. *Child Development, 54*, 878–887.

Field, T., Healy, B., Goldstein, S., & Guthertz, M. (1990). Behavior-state matching and synchrony in mother–infant interactions of nondepressed versus depressed dyads. *Developmental Psychology, 26*, 7–14.

Golinkoff, R. M. (1983). The preverbal negotiation of failed messages. In R. M. Golinkoff (Ed.), *The transition from prelinguistic to linguistic communication* (pp. 57–78). Hillsdale, NJ: Erlbaum.

Golinkoff, R. M., & Gordon, L. (1988). What makes communication run? Characteristics of immediate successes. *First Language, 8*, 103–124.

Greenfield, P. M. (1979). Informativeness, presupposition, and semantic choice in single-word utterances. In E. Ochs and B. B. Schieffelin (Eds.), *Developmental pragmatics* (pp. 159–166). New York: Academic Press.

Greenfield, P. M. (1980). Toward an operational and logical analysis of intentionality: The use of discourse in early child language. In D. R. Olson (Ed.), *The social foundations of language and thought* (pp. 254–279). New York: Norton.

Greenfield, P. M., & Smith, J. (1976). *The structure of communication in early language development*. New York: Academic Press.

Hala, S., Chandler, M., & Fritz, A. S. (1991). Fledgling theories of mind: Deception as a marker of three-year-olds' understanding of false belief. *Child Development, 62*, 83–97.

Harding, C. G., & Golinkoff, R. M. (1979). The origins of intentional vocalizations in prelinguistic infants. *Child Development, 50*, 33–40.

Harris, P. L. (1989). *Children and emotion: The development of psychological understanding*. Oxford and New York: Basil Blackwell.

Holzman, M. S. (1971). Ellipsis in discourse: Implications for linguistic analysis by computer, the child's acquisition of language, and semantic theory. *Language and Speech, 14*, 86–98.

Hornik, R., Risenhoover, N., & Gunnar, M. R. (1987). The effects of maternal positive, neutral, and negative affective communications on infant responses to new toys. *Child Development, 58*, 937–944.

Klinnert, M., Campos, J., Sorce, J., Emde, R., & Svejda, M. (1983). Emotions as behavior regulators: Social referencing in infancy. In R. Plutchik & H. Kellerman (Eds.), *Emotions in early development (Vol. 2): The emotions* (pp. 57–86). New York: Academic Press.

Klinnert, M., Emde, R. N., Butterfield, P., & Campos, J. J. (1986). Social referencing: The infant's use of emotional signals from a friendly adult with mother present. *Developmental Psychology, 22*, 427–432.

Lewis, C., & Osborne, A. (1990). Three-year-olds' problems with false belief: Conceptual deficit or linguistic artifact. *Child Development, 61*, 1514–1519.

Lock, A. (1980). *The guided reinvention of language*. New York: Academic Press.

McCune-Nicolich, L. (1981). The cognitive bases of relational words in the single word period. *Journal of Child Language, 8*, 15–34.

Mead, G. H. (1934). *Mind, self and society*. Chicago: University of Chicago Press.

Murphy, D. J., & Messer, D. J. (1977). Mothers, infants and pointing: A study of a gesture. In H. R. Schaffer (Ed.), *Studies in mother–infant interaction* (pp. 323–354). New York: Academic Press.

Nicolich, L. (1977). Beyond sensorimotor intelligence: Assessment of symbolic maturity through analysis of pretend play. *Merrill-Palmer Quarterly, 23*, 88–99.

Ninio, A., & Snow, C. (1984). *Language acquisition through language use.* Unpublished manuscript, Hebrew University, Israel.

Piaget, J. (1962). *Play, dreams and imitation in childhood.* New York: Norton.

Premack, D., & Woodruff, G. (1978). Does the chimpanzee have a "theory of mind"? *The Brain and Behavioral Sciences, 1,* 515–526.

Ratner, N., & Bruner, J. (1978). Games, social exchange, and the acquisition of language. *Journal of Child Language, 5,* 391–401.

Rommetveit, R. (1971). Words, context and verbal message transmission. In A. E. Carswell & R. Rommetveit (Eds.), *Social context of messages* (pp. 13–26). New York: Academic Press.

Rommetveit, R. (1972). Language games, syntactic structures and hermeneutics. In J. Israel and H. Tajfel (Eds.), *The context of social psychology* (pp. 212–267). New York: Academic Press.

Rommetveit, R. (1979a). On the architecture of intersubjectivity. In R. Rommetveit & R. M. Blakar (Eds.), *Studies of language, thought and verbal communication* (pp. 93–107). New York: Academic Press.

Rommetveit, R. (1979b). On negative rationalism in scholarly studies of verbal communication and dynamic residuals in the construction of human intersubjectivity. In R. Rommetveit and R. M. Blakar (Eds.), *Studies of language, thought and verbal communication* (pp. 147–161).

Rommetveit, R. (1985). Language acquisition as increasing linguistic structuring of experience and symbolic behavior control. In J. V. Wertsch (Ed.), *Culture, communication, and cognition: Vygotskian perspectives.* Cambridge: Cambridge University Press.

Ross, H. S. (1980, April). *Infants' use of turn alternation signals in games.* Paper presented at the International Conference on Infant Studies, New Haven, CT.

Ross, H. S., & Kay, D. A. (1980). The origins of social games. In K. Rubin (Ed.), *Children's play* (pp. 17–32). San Francisco: Jossey-Bass.

Ross, H. S., & Lollis, S. P. (1987). Communication within infant social games. *Developmental Psychology, 23,* 241–248.

Scaife, M., & Bruner, J. (1975). The capacity for joint visual attention in the infant. *Nature, 253,* 265–266.

Scollon, R. (1979). An unzippered condensation of a dissertation on child language. In E. Ochs & B. B. Schieffelin (Eds.), *Developmental pragmatics* (pp. 215–227). New York: Academic Press.

Selman, R. L. (1981). What children understand of the intrapsychic processes. In E. K. Shapiro & E. Weber (Eds.), *Cognitive and affective growth* (pp. 187–215). Hillsdale, NJ: Erlbaum.

Shatz, M. (1983). Communication. In J. H. Flavell & E. M. Markman (Eds.), *Handbook of child psychology. Vol. 3: Cognitive development* (pp. 841–889). New York: Wiley.

Stern, D. (1977). *The first relationship.* Cambridge, MA: Harvard University Press.

Stern, D. (1985). *The interpersonal world of the infant.* New York: Basic Books.

Stevenson, M. B., Roach, M. A., ver Hoeve, J. N., & Leavitt, L. A. (1990). Rhythms in the dialogue of infant feeding: Preterm and term infants. *Infant Behavior and Development, 13,* 51–70.

Sugarman-Bell, S. (1978). Some organized aspects of preverbal communication. In I. Markova (Ed.), *The social context of language* (pp. 49–66). London: Wiley.

Trevarthen, C. (1988). Universal co-operative motives: How infants begin to know the language and culture of their parents. In G. Jahoda & I. M. Lewis (Eds.), *Acquiring culture: Cross cultural studies in child development* (pp. 37–90). London: Croom Helm.

Trevarthen, C., & Hubley, P. (1979). Secondary intersubjectivity: Confidence, confiding, and acts of meaning in the first year. In A. Lock (Ed.), *Action, gesture and symbol* (pp. 183–229). New York: Academic Press.

Walden, T. A., & Ogan, T. A. (1988). The development of social referencing. *Child Development, 59,* 1230–1240.

Webster, M. (1975). *Actions and actors: Principles of social psychology.* Cambridge, MA: Winthrop.

Wolf, D. (1982). Understanding others: A longitudinal case study of the concept of independent agency. In G. Forman (Ed.), *Action and thought: From sensorimotor schemes to symbol use* (pp. 297–327). New York: Academic Press.

Zahn-Waxler, C., Radke-Yarrow, M., & King, R. (1979). Childrearing and children's prosocial initiations towards victims of distress. *Child Development, 50,* 319–330.

4

Social Referencing Research
Uncertainty, Self, and the
Search for Meaning

Robert N. Emde

This chapter considers the prospects of social referencing research as we move from experimental to more naturalistic and clinical settings. Five topics of theoretical importance are highlighted. These include (1) fundamental strategic issues, (2) early self-development, (3) early moral development, (4) emotional availability and its development, and (5) individual differences and psychopathology.

STRATEGIC ISSUES

Definition

Our Colorado group has chosen to define social referencing in infancy as a form of active emotional communication. Thus, social referencing is thought to mediate behavior when the infant is confronted by a situation of uncertainty; when the infant is observed to seek out emotional information from another (usually by looking at another's face); and when the infant modifies his or her patterned behavior as a result. As Feinman

ROBERT N. EMDE • Department of Psychiatry, University of Colorado Health Sciences Center, Denver, CO 80262.

Social Referencing and the Social Construction of Reality in Infancy, edited by Saul Feinman. Plenum Press, New York, 1992.

points out (Feinman, 1982), this kind of definition of social referencing is a restricted one. We have adopted such a definition for both strategic and theoretical reasons. Rather than considering social referencing as a broader influence, we have found it strategic to consider it an aspect of emotional signaling in which there is an active search; thus, we have been able to manipulate emotional signals as independent variables and we have been able to use our observation of the infant's search behavior as a clear experimental marker preceding behavioral regulation. But our theoretical reasons for concentrating on emotions are equally important. We view emotions as active, ongoing, and adaptive processes—processes which are biologically patterned with a similar organization throughout the lifespan. Our emotions provide us with a sense of constancy and what might be considered an "affective core" for our self-experience (Emde, 1983). They allow us, therefore, to know we are the same in spite of the many ways we change. The biological patterning of emotions throughout the human species provides the basis for a form of communication, and, in early development, it allows the infant to find a sense of constancy in repeated patterns of emotional experiences with a caregiver. From a theoretical standpoint, therefore, defining social referencing as an active form of emotional communication seems promising for understanding self-development and socialization prior to language.

A final comment about definition. Considering the lifespan, Bandura points out (Chapter 8, this volume) that social referencing processes can be typed as either affective or instrumental. The contributions of this volume focus on infancy and concern the affective type. This probably reflects the special salience of affective social referencing in infancy. Whether this type of social referencing is as influential in later development is a matter for research.

Other Looking, Other Channels

As we move to the arena of naturalistic studies, we encounter complexities which are not apparent in our isolated experimental settings. In a more free-running environment, we are faced with the questions as to how we delimit an uncertain situation and how we mark the infant's seeking of emotional information. Further, we discover that social referencing involves only one form of social looking. In one "semi-naturalistic" study, done in our laboratory by Clyman, Emde, Kempe, and Harmon (1986), it was necessary to establish a descriptive typology of social looking. One of eight types of looks occurred whenever an infant looked at an adult's face. These included (1) orient to a voice, (2) orient to an action, (3) social reference, (4) postaction reference, (5) bid for social interaction with pause (long bid), (6) bid for social interaction without pause (short bid), (7) watching others communicate, and (8) gaze aversion. These looks imply different degrees of social interaction between the infant and adult and varying amounts of information processing on the part of the infant. In a study of 52 twelve-month-old infants who had been videotaped in a modified strange situation, social referencing occurred infrequently and was difficult to separate from other types of social looks. Contributing to unreliability in a free-running situation was the dilemma of determining when uncertainty occurs and judging what constitutes the necessary event for social referencing.

As we consider studies of social referencing in the home, we are reminded that emotional communication involves more than vision. How other channels (e.g., voice and gesture) amplify, modify, or substitute for one another is not known. Certainly vocal signaling (wherein the infant does not have to engage in visual search) would seem especially important in the home, a fact which our preliminary observations confirm. Indeed, social referencing of the sort we have studied in the laboratory may be infrequent in the home, as our preliminary observations and Judy Dunn's more systematic observations would indicate (Dunn, 1988). In any event, in a more naturalistic study we need to analyze the available signals offered to the infant—their abundance, their strength, and their clarity. Beyond this, we need to know what kind of information is usually signaled in the midst of social referencing. Will parents typically respond with instructive signals, such as showing how something works or by offering emotional guidance through indicating a new toy is fun or safe? Furthermore, what will be the effects of social referencing beyond the immediate behavior of the infant? Home studies will lead us to questions related to the circumstances under which a child will look to an adult. What are the acquired rules which come to govern who is referenced under what circumstances?

The Experience of the Other

There is another area of strategic issues needing study as we move into naturalistic and clinical settings. This concerns the experience of the one who is being referenced. Typically, when I show our videotapes of social referencing experiments to a clinical audience, a question arises about deception. Is it possible, some ask, that the infant responds differently to mother's "faked emotion" of fear as compared with what might be a spontaneous emotion? This kind of question is even more relevant now that we have the provocative results of Ekman, Levinson, and Friesen (1983) linking precise facial patterning of discrete emotions with feeling states. Twelve-month-olds seem to respond in predictable ways to our manipulations in social referencing studies, but at what age does the experience of the person who is signaling make a difference? In other words, at what age can toddlers discern subtle aspects of deception? A related issue concerns the role of mixed messages and "blends" of discrete emotion signals and the role of low-intensity emotional signals. In a longitudinal study of emotional signaling among toddlers and their mothers and fathers, we have observed that clear, extreme, discrete emotional signals are the exception rather than the rule; instead, lower-intensity signals, mixed signals, and blends are considerably more common. Similarly, our longitudinal observations remind us that we need to study the consequences of the adult's experience of being referenced. Under some circumstances, parents feel gratified, affirmed, or amused; under other circumstances, parents may feel interrupted or may not even take notice. Different signals and different parental action sequences are likely to accompany these various states of mind.

An anecdote from the early days of our visual cliff social referencing work may be instructive. At one point, we found that mothers' fear faces were not having the expected effect on their infants; a number of infants began laughing instead of retreating. Examination of the videotapes was revealing: as the mothers in question started to see their infants influenced by the fear face, they were amused and subtly altered their fear expression by relaxing brows or by slightly raising the corners of the mouth. Infants seemed remarkably perceptive of this shift in expression, as if fear had changed to surprise and as if the meaning of the signal changed to indicate an all-too-familiar surprise game. Once we understood this confound in mother's emotional signal, we removed the problem by changing her experience in a simple but profound way. We placed a wireless microphone in mother's ear so that the experimenter, from another room, could narrate observations of the infant's and the mother's activities. It seemed as if the hearing of an outside observer "inside one's own head" altered the experience in a critical way—for mother and, consequently, also for infant.

The Caregiver's Social Referencing of the Infant

The experience of the other, the "referee" in infant social referencing, leads us to consider another omission from our research enterprise. We have been attending to social referencing as a communicative process, and, curiously, we have neglected social referencing on the part of caregivers. Mothers use their infants' changing and complex affective expressions to resolve uncertainty. Mothers seek out emotional information from their infants in order to guide caregiver action.

As we consider caregiver social referencing, it is important to realize that mothers engage in such an infant-referencing process, not just to respond to physiological-homeostatic needs, but also to respond to needs and intentions related to protection, play, exploration, and learning. Regarding the latter, it might be said that mothers rely on their infant's affective expressions to discover those windows of time and states when learning and exploration can take place. Thus, in a fundamental way, a form of caregiver social referencing serves to reduce uncertainty about developmental systems. In some instances, affective information from the infant tells the mother the system is open and capable of expansion; in other instances, different affective information conveys that the system needs restitution.

Perhaps we have neglected social referencing from the caregiver's point of view because the referencing process has been a subject of so much research from the infant's side. Still, both sides should be included in consideration of social referencing processes in early development. Observations of caregiver conditions for social referencing may contribute to further knowledge concerning individual differences with respect to such concepts as maternal sensitivity and caregiver emotional response. Such observations might in turn also contribute to a better understanding of environmental predisposing to early childhood disorder.

Social Referencing and Negotiation: A Dyadic Progression in Infancy

Hinde (1985) has emphasized that emotional signals in animals vary on a continuum from expression to negotiation. Threat signals, for example, express what the animal's motivational state is, but they are also a signal to another animal, and the response of the other will determine what the first animal will do. Beyond this, there is apt to be negotiation, even "duels" involving emotional signals (instead of actions) between animals. This dynamic aspect of emotional signals may explain why most naturally occurring emotion displays tend to be *graded and blended*, rather than full or simple. In social encounters, it is probably adaptive to create some ambiguity or uncertainty so that negotiation can take place with social referencing.

Such considerations lead me to think of a dyadic progression of social referencing in infancy. The earliest phase (the first 6 months) is that of *maternal social referencing*. The infant presents emotional expressions of need states, and mother references the infant in order to decrease her uncertainty about caregiving regulations and guides her behavior accordingly. She looks to the infant and meets the infant's expressed need. The infant has a clear or marked signal. During the next phase of this dyadic progression (beginning during the second half of the first year), there is the addition of *infant social referencing*. The infant encounters uncertain situations and seeks out clear emotional expressions from the significant other (usually mother) to resolve the uncertainty. This is the level of social referencing which has been the focus of most referencing research. The third dyadic progression of social referencing, beginning in the second year, is *social referencing in negotiation.* In this situation, there is back and forth emotional signaling in a situation of dyadic uncertainty. The uncertainty concerns the expectations with respect to the response of the other in relation to one's need or intention. Modifications of expectations and intentions occur during the course of the social interaction. Here we see the increasing use of instrumental emotional expressions, which are not necessarily related to simple motivational states.

The concept of social referencing is broadened when we consider it from the perspective of negotiation. As such, it seems appropriate as a framework for research during the second and third years, when we must consider the infant's new world of uncertainties regarding standards, rules, prohibitions, intentions, and counterintentions (Emde, 1988). This perspective also seems appropriate as a framework for understanding early language exchange.

EARLY SELF-DEVELOPMENT

Social referencing research should contribute substantially to our knowledge of early self-development. Although parametric studies have not been done, it would seem that social referencing begins in the third quarter of the first year, in the midst of the biobehavioral shift in development which includes the onset of crawling, fearfulness, intentionality (sensorimotor Stage IV), and focused attachment (Emde, Gaensbauer, & Harmon, 1976; Klinnert, Campos, Sorce, Emde, & Svejda, 1983). Although the infant probably has some sense of agency before this age (Papousek & Papousek, 1979; Stern, 1985), there is now a shift such that the infant has targeted expectations and goals in relation to both people and things. Now, *shared meaning* becomes possible with its components of (1) shared memories, (2) shared appreciation of the current context, and (3) shared expectations or goals. In other words, social referencing must be seen as a part of a larger process of shared attention, shared intentions, and shared feelings in the context of the infant–caregiver relationship (see Bretherton, McNew, & Beeghly-Smith, 1981; Kaye, 1982; Sameroff & Emde, 1989; Scaife & Brunner, 1975; Stern, 1985; Trevarthen & Hubley, 1979).

Let us look at this development in another way. The 8-month-old infant's new competencies in the motor, affective, cognitive, and social domains bring on a new world of uncertainty. The need for emotional information and, more specifically, the need for the emotional availability of a caregiver who can provide the uncertain, actively moving infant with such information is major. One would assume that the infant at this age encounters many circumstances where there is a need for the signaling of security or containment by the caregiver who now matters especially. The extent of the infant's world of uncertainty is further dramatized when we realize that self-awareness and self-recognition is probably not established for another year or so (Amsterdam, 1972; Kagan, 1981; Lewis & Brooks-Gunn, 1979; Schulman & Kaplowitz, 1977; and see review in Emde, 1983). Thus we might hypothesize that social referencing, in terms of the infant's pausing and looking for emotional information from another, emerges and becomes especially salient in the period between 6 and 18 months because of broad adaptive reasons. Not only does social referencing allow for the infant's learning about "a third event" from another but it also facilitates the process of self-development. Social referencing can be thought of as a mediator of the three aspects of such a process: (1) the differentiation of the experience of self, (2) the differentiation of the experience of other, and (3) the differentiation of the experience of "self-with-other" (see the roots of these developmental aspects in works of Klein, 1976; Kohut, 1971, 1977; Winnicott, 1971; as well as an explicit statement about all three aspects in Stern, 1985). One is reminded of observations of "checking back" and of "emotional refueling" of Mahler and her colleagues (Mahler, Pine, & Bergman, 1975), of Ainsworth's concept of "using the mother as a secure base for exploration" (Ainsworth, Blehar, Waters, & Wall, 1978), and of a number of experimental studies which have demonstrated a connection between the infant's ability to look at mother's face and the level of exploration and play (Carr, Dabbs, & Carr, 1975; Sorce & Emde, 1981).

In such a process, social referencing reminds us of certain writings of philosophers (e.g., Sartre, 1956) who wrote of the development of self "under the eyes of the other." Through repeated experiences with social referencing, "working models" of self, other, and of self-with-other (the relationship) emerge. It remains a fascinating question for individual differences research in naturalistic and clinical settings to test intriguing hypotheses which emerge from this. Some examples would be: To what extent are early social referencing experiences related to subsequent outcomes in the quality of self-awareness development? To what extent are they related to differential outcomes in self-esteem development? Can early individual differences in social referencing predict the later quality of attachment (working model of self-with-other)?

EARLY MORAL DEVELOPMENT

Around the time of the first birthday, parents begin to hold their toddlers accountable for some actions; discipline becomes a parental concern in addition to nurturing. Over the course of the second year, the toddler experiences many prohibitions from parents on a daily basis and comes to internalize important aspects of restraints.

Our longitudinal home and playroom-laboratory observations have convinced us that social referencing has an important mediating role in this process. One might say that in the second year, situations of prohibition are among the most salient ones involving uncertainty. The infant seems uncertain about the shared meaning of the prohibition and about its consequences, and looks to the parent's face by way of checking for more information. Social referencing in this sense may occur at the onset of the prohibition (which is usually vocal), it may occur as the infant begins a prohibitive act, or it may occur when the infant completes a prohibited act and checks by looking to the face of the parent. In the middle of the second year, corresponding to what we believe is the time of emergence of self-awareness, there is an enhanced self-conscious quality to this checking process; the associated infant expression may have a positive affective tone (sometimes interpreted as "pride") or a negative affective tone (sometimes interpreted as "shame" or a "hurt-feelings look").

Certain emotions which appear in the context of prohibitions and which involve social referencing might be considered "moral emotions." Such emotions have the following qualities: they are more complex than discrete emotions, with no simple correspondence to face, voice, or gesture; they are based on relationships with a past history shared with particular individuals in particular contexts; they are based on a sense of struggle, dilemma, or conflict; and they are anticipatory or "signal emotions." Interestingly, the earliest form of such an emotion may be that of "positive affect sharing," which occurs early in the second year, with great individual variation, and which involves the infant's seeking to amplify an expression of joy or interested excitement with one or more social partners. The infant actively engages another and persists until there is an acknowledgment and a sharing of affect.

In a longitudinal study, we found that by 24 months all of our infants presented evidence of internalized rules for "don't's" as well as for "do's" *as long as parents were present and could be referenced* (Emde, Johnson, & Easterbrooks, 1987). In the context of rules about what to do, referencing seemed to occur with the 2-year-old sharing positive affect and occasionally displaying behavior which looked like pride with mastery pleasure (this occurred, for example, after a child engaged in a dusting gesture with a tissue or after a child put a toy back on a table). This seemed to be a natural continuation of an earlier developmental manifestation of what we took to be social referencing in the midst of the child's internalized sense of rules about where things belonged and to whom they belonged. We found that when a toy robot approached them in our playroom-laboratory,

12-month-old infants looked to a familiarized adult (the tester) even more than they did to mother in order to get emotional information (Klinnert, Emde, Butterfield, & Campos, 1986). It was as if infants at this earlier age were saying to the tester: "I know this is your playroom–you are the one who can tell me if it is safe to go to this strange toy or not." Thus, social referencing seemed to be used selectively to checkout the uncertain consequences of internalized rules about what was right under the circumstances. We might say that in the realm of the "do's" of moral development, social referencing is used to check for the consequences of internalized standards about what is expectable or appropriate. But now back to the "dont's" in the course of the child's second year. We found the internalization of "don't's" involved what might be considered social referencing in a number of phases.

A suggested sequence is presented in Table 1. Throughout, social referencing seemed to have the function of confirming shared intentions. After self-awareness and self-consciousness, it seemed to have a different quality and was often accompanied by words or pointing. Most of the observations represented in the table were made in our playroom during family visits at 6-month intervals. Mother, father, and toddler were engaged in various activities and several objects were placed in the playroom

Table 1. Responses to Prohibitions during the Second Year: A Suggested Sequence Occurring "under the Eyes of the Caregiver"

1. No inhibition with a prohibition—there may be a pause with an orienting response, often with the child seeming to respond to anger in the mother's voice. Looking to the mother is in the context of orienting.
2. The above occurs but there is now increased social referencing with hesitation.
3. The child approaches the prohibitive object and pauses, then looks to parent as if for "reassurance of the correctness of the act."
4. There is now restraint with internalization of the don't being more stable. The parent does not have to repeat the "no." The child may repeat "no, no" and may engage in head shaking. Sometimes the child will point or bring the object with a concerned expression as if needing reassurance. There may also be a variety of negative affects. There may be aggression after the prohibition (a seeming displacement activity like banging or throwing another object), a "hurt-feelings look" or, in some contexts, a shame expression.
5. The child generalizes the internalized restraint. We observe evidence of this with pointing and often with words. The child may look to the parent while pointing and say "no" to a new prohibitive object. Another observation revealed the child's moving toward an empty chair, pausing, and saying to the parent, "It's the doctor's"—after an earlier prohibition of the tape recorder had been issued with "It's the doctor's" from mother.

to function as possible "prohibitives" (a box with tissues, a small tape recorder on a low table, a plastic vase with dried flowers).

Formulations about the role of social referencing in early moral development now remain to be systematized and tested by research. Will individual differences in the amount and quality of social referencing be related to later differences in the amount and quality of internalized prohibitions? Are there clinical problems which influence parental emotional availability, emotional signaling, and social referencing, and thereby put the child at risk for later disorder of morality or conduct?

Further Developmental Levels of Social Referencing

Thus far, we have enumerated two developmental levels at which the child's social referencing is used to deal with different kinds of uncertainty. First, in infancy, there are *uncertainties of self and safety*. A broad adaptive purpose of social referencing was proposed having to do with facilitating the development of self-awareness, the differentiation of self and other, and the development of "we-awareness." Second, in toddlerhood, there were *uncertainties of standards, rules, and prohibitions*. The broad adaptive functions here are concerned with facilitating early moral development. A third developmental level may have to do with *uncertainties of roles and relationships*. As the child begins to expand social interaction with peer play in the third and fourth years, social referencing may again have a significant place at a still higher level of development. Research observations of Nachman (personal communication) in a preschool play environment would seem to indicate this. Children often look to caregivers when encountering new peers, seemingly seeking reassurance and emotional information. One would assume that familiar peers soon become sources of reference as well. Such preliminary observations need systematic study.

One also wonders about social referencing with language. Our focus thus far has been on nonverbal social referencing, wherein shared meaning has been a matter of shared nonverbal presuppositions between the child and the other. As these presuppositions become increasingly complex, linked to different contexts, and hierarchically, I assume such nonverbal functions will increasingly be taken over by language. In thinking about higher developmental levels of social referencing, it is important to bear in mind that symbolic activity not only occurs in the form of direct interchanges with another; it also occurs in the form of internal dialogue and fantasy. As the child gets older, social referencing will occur predominantly with evoked images. There will be imagined dialogues with representations of significant others—or "reference figures."

When does this internalized form of social referencing begin, using mental dialogues with reference figures instead of overt looks and other behavioral exchanges with others? From a developmental standpoint, the beginning is likely to be a process with a gradual onset, rather than a sudden shift concomitant with the emergence of language. In Chapter 3 (this volume), Bretherton implies a form of social referencing during the prolonged one-word stage, which is in accordance with this idea. Stern (1985) discusses the likely emergence of "evoked companions" in later infancy. From the clinical and observational evidence at hand, one would probably guess that social referencing through language and internal dialogues with evoked companions does not become convincing until the third year.

EMOTIONAL AVAILABILITY AND ITS DEVELOPMENT

Defining social referencing as a form of emotional signaling presupposes the availability of an active, nonverbal communication system within the context of the infant–caregiver relationship. The enduring nature of this system and its adaptive importance is indicated by our concept of "emotional availability." The gist of this section is as follows:

1. Emotional availability is a vital aspect of the infant–caregiver relationship before the onset of social referencing.
2. After its development, social referencing serves to expand emotional availability by introducing a sense of shared meaning about events.
3. Social referencing, within the context of emotional availability, not only contributes to the developing awareness of that inner executive we conceptualize as "self" or "ego," but it also contributes to another inner executive we might conceptualize as "self-with-other" (Stern, 1985), or "we-go" (Klein, 1976).

Let me elaborate. Before the developmental onset of social referencing, the infant's patterned emotional expressions signal a variety of need states to caregivers. Over time, the infant comes to rely on expectable caregiving responsiveness to these expressions. Erikson (1950) has portrayed this well, indicating how the infant comes to develop a sense of "basic trust," an expectation that good things will happen with the parent. It should be emphasized that parental emotional responsiveness includes more than the relief of distress leading to satisfaction of homeostatic needs. It also includes the provision of interesting, surprising, and pleasurable exchanges—leading to the expansion of the child's experiential world. Indeed, there is now considerable evidence linking maternal emotional sensitivity and responsiveness, rated in early infancy, to the child's security of attachment observed at 1 year (Bretherton, 1985).

But now to social referencing. With its onset, the infant benefits from the emotional availability of the parent according to a profound new dimension—that of shared meaning. Social referencing serves shared meaning in the immediate sense of enabling attention and a joint affective understanding about a "third event" (i.e., beyond the two communicating individuals). But it goes beyond the immediate, for in repeated social referencing experiences within the caregiver–infant relationship, there will be shared memories and shared expectations as well as shared aspects of understanding the current contexts for events. The coherence of these repeated experiences will presumably lead to knowledge structures, or internal working models, of shared meaning. Thus, to some extent, emotional availability will become internalized. There will then be an internal guide for actions and for support—along with an available sense of the "we."

INDIVIDUAL DIFFERENCES AND PSYCHOPATHOLOGY

Could individual differences in infant social referencing be important for later psychopathology? I believe it could. The reason for this is that social referencing, as a form of emotional communication, is a mediator of relationship information. In the context of the caregiver's emotional availability and responsiveness, social referencing can mediate effects on the child's (1) mood and emotional balance, (2) developing sense of self and self-esteem, and (3) moral standards. Let us review the process in somewhat more detail.

In infancy, before there is a coherent awareness of self, the child knows and validates himself or herself through the other. An important component of this occurs through day-to-day experiences in resolving uncertainty about his or her intended actions through social referencing of the caregiver. The infant comes to count on repeated emotional communication from the caregiver which can guide his or her actions. Furthermore, in the course of such activity, the infant "exercises" his or her own emotions which are found to be reciprocal or to some extent in synchrony with those of the caregiver. There are increasing experiences which involve shared meaning (in the sense of shared referencing to external events), shared feelings, and shared expectations. Eventually, the infant comes to experience a sense of trust and security in the midst of the caregiver's presence which enhances exploration and play. During the second year, social referencing mediates the child's learning of prohibitions and rules about "don't's" (what should not be done) as well as "do's" (what should be done). This can be considered the beginning of moral development, for what was external conflict (conflicting intentions between child and parent) becomes internalized (conflicting intentions within the child). The key feature of this process, from our point of view, is that it occurs "under the eyes of the caregiver." By the end of the second year children can show evidence of this internalization, providing the caregiver is available to be referenced. In other words, it would seem that this early form of morality is dependent on the presence of the parent (and by implication, upon a particular shared history of experiences within the context of the parent–infant relationship).

As we move toward more explicit clinical considerations, it seems important to again emphasize that social referencing is a mediator. Individual differences in social referencing should reflect individual differences in more fundamental aspects of the quality of the parent–infant relationship and its underpinnings in the emotional availability of the parent. This becomes especially important in the infancy period because before there is a coherent sense of self, it is difficult to speak of disorder as residing within the infant. Instead, emotional disorders of infancy are "relationship disorders"; there is a regulatory problem within the context of the caregiving relationship.[1]

What then are the implications for clinical research? First of all, thinking of social referencing as a mediator directs the clinician's attention to the fact that its disturbances would be an indicator of a problem in social regulation, but not the problem itself. In other words, features of social referencing could provide a "barometer" of adaptive functions; as such, they may sensitize the clinician to look further. Second, there are two ways that individual differences in social referencing might relate to clinical problems. One way concerns its possible indicator role for relationship disorders. Unusual patterns of social referencing might alert the clinician to infancy syndromes of abuse/neglect, failure to thrive, and other regulatory disorders involving sleep, feeding, security, separation, and oppositional interactions. The other way concerns the possible indicator role of social referencing for risk of later-developing psychopathology. Adverse situations known to be associated with such risk might be discovered so that clinical follow-up and intervention could occur. Thus, unusual patterns of social referencing might alert the clinician to a number of well-known risk situations, including depression in

---

[1] A developmental model of infancy and early childhood which forms the basis for considering early relationship disorders can now be reviewed in the volume edited by Sameroff and Emde (1989). The model results from a Special Projects Group on "Developmental Processes in Psychopathology" at the Center for Advanced Study in the Behavioral Sciences during 1984–85. Members of the group were Drs. Thomas Anders, Robert N. Edme, Herbert Leiderman, Arthur H. Parmelee, David Reiss, Arnold Sameroff, L. Alan Sroufe, and Daniel Stern.

a parent, anxiety in a parent, negative or hostile parental attitudes, marital dysfunction (pronounced conflict and hostility between parents) and disorganization in the macro-environment, including situations of poverty and social isolation.

In conclusion, it seems there is considerable promise for clinical research involving individual differences in social referencing. Our experimental research programs, which have viewed social referencing as a form of emotional communication, have led us not only to a variety of normative developmental questions, but also to questions of meaning. In these considerations, I am reminded that the clinical perspective, like the developmental perspective, goes beyond classification, beyond the "objective" and "logical." Social referencing sharpens our focus on what is meaningful—on what is emotionally important and can be shared; it also directs us to what is individual and unique. We can therefore communicate with another in an intimate way and share experience. Even if it is only for a few moments, we can get in touch with another's affective core of self.

Acknowledgments: This work was supported by NIMH project grant #MH22803 and Research Scientist Award #5 K02 MH36808. During the year this was written, Dr. Emde was a Fellow at the Center for Advanced Study in the Behavioral Sciences and received partial support from the John D. and Catherine T. MacArthur Foundation.

REFERENCES

Ainsworth, M. D. S., Blehar, M., Waters, E., & Wall, S. (1978). *Patterns of attachment.* Hillsdale, NJ: Erlbaum.

Amsterdam, B. K. (1972). Mirror self-image reactions before age two. *Developmental Psychology, 5,* 297–305.

Bretherton, I. (1985). Attachment theory: Retrospect and prospect. In I. Bretherton & E. Waters (Eds.), Growing points of attachment theory and research. *Monographs of the Society for Research in Child Development, 50*(1-2, Serial No. 209).

Bretherton, I., McNew, S., & Beeghly-Smith, M. (1981). Early person-knowledge as expressed in gestural and verbal communication: When do infants acquire a "theory of mind"? In M. Lamb & L. Sherrod (Eds.), *Infant social cognition* (pp. 333–373). Hillsdale, NJ: Erlbaum.

Carr, S. J., Dabbs, J. M., & Carr, T. S. (1975). Mother–infant attachment: The importance of the mother's visual field. *Child Development, 46,* 331–338.

Clyman, R. B., Emde, R. N., Kempe, J. E., & Harmon, R. J. (1986). Social referencing and social looking among twelve-month-old infants. In T. B. Brazelton & M. Yogman (Eds.), *Affective development in infancy* (pp. 75–93). Norwood, NJ: Ablex.

Dunn, J. (1988). *The beginnings of social understanding.* Cambridge, MA: Harvard University Press.

Ekman, P., Levinson, R. W., & Friesen, W. V. (1983). Autonomic nervous system activity distinguishes among emotions. *Science, 221,* 1208–1210.

Emde, R. N. (1983). The prepresentational self and its affective core. *The Psychoanalytic Study of the Child, 38,* 165–192.

Emde, R. N. (1988). Development terminable and interminable: I. Innate and motivational factors from infancy. *International Journal of Psycho-Analysis, 69,* 23–42.

Emde, R. N., Gaensbauer, T., & Harmon, R. J. (1976). Emotional expression in infancy: a biobehavioral study. *Psychological Issues, A Monograph Series, Inc. 10*(37). New York: International Universities Press.

Emde, R. N., Johnson, W. F., & Easterbrooks, M. A. (1987). The do's and don't's of early moral development: Psychoanalytic tradition and current research. In J. Kagan & S. Lamb (Eds.), *The emergence of morality in young children* (pp. 245–276). Chicago: University of Chicago Press.

Erikson, E. (1950). *Childhood and society.* New York: Norton.

Feinman, S. (1982). Social referencing in infancy. *Merrill-Palmer Quarterly, 28,* 445–470.

Hinde, R. A. (1985). Expression and negotiation. In G. Zivin (Ed.), *The development of expressive behavior: biology–environment interactions* (pp. 103–116). Orlando, FL: Academic Press.

Kagan, J. (1981). *The second year: The emergence of self-awareness.* Cambridge: Harvard University Press.

Kaye, K. (1982). *The mental and social life of babies: How parents create persons.* Chicago: University of Chicago Press.

Klein, G. S. (1976). The resolution of experienced incompatibility in psychological development. In G. S. Klein (Ed.), *Psychoanalytic theory: An exploration of essentials* (pp. 163–209). New York: International University Press.

Klinnert, M. D., Campos, J. J., Sorce, J. F., Emde, R. N., & Svejda, M. (1983). Social referencing: Emotional expressions as behavior regulators. In R. Plutchik & H. Kellerman (Eds.), *Emotion: Theory, research and experience. Vol. 2: Emotions in early development* (pp. 57–86). Orlando, FL: Academic Press.

Klinnert, M. D., Emde, R. N., Butterfield, P., & Campos, J. J. (1986). Social referencing: The infant's use of emotional signals from a friendly adult with mother present. *Developmental Psychology, 22,* 427–432.

Kohut, H. (1971). *The analysis of the self.* New York: International Universities Press.

Kohut, H. (1977). *The restoration of the self.* New York: International Universities Press.

Lewis, M., & Brooks-Gunn, J. (1979). *Social cognition and the acquisition of self.* New York: Plenum.

Mahler, M. S., Pine, E., & Bergman, A. (1975). *The psychological birth of the human infant.* New York: Basic Books.

Papousek, H., & Papousek, M. (1979). Early ontogeny of human social interaction: Its biological roots and social dimensions. In M. von Cranach, K. Foppa, W. Lepines, & D. Ploog (Eds.), *Human ethology: Claims and limits of a new discipline* (pp. 456–478). Cambridge: Cambridge University Press.

Sameroff, A., & Emde, R. N. (Eds.). (1989). *Relationship disturbances in early childhood: A developmental approach.* New York: Basic Books.

Sartre, J. P. (1956). *Being and nothingness: An essay on phenomenological ontology.* Translated and with an introduction by Hazel E. Barnes. New York: Philosophical Library.

Scaife, M., & Bruner, J. S. (1975). The capacity for joint visual attention in the infant. *Nature, 253,* 265–266.

Schulman, A. H., & Kaplowitz, C. (1977). Mirror-image response during the first two years of life. *Developmental Psychobiology, 10,* 133–142.

Sorce, J. & Emde, R. N. (1981). Mother's presence is not enough: Effect of emotional availability on infant exploration. *Developmental Psychology, 17,* 737–745.

Stern, D. N. (1985). *The interpersonal world of the infant.* New York: Basic Books.

Trevarthen, C., & Hubley, P. (1979). Secondary intersubjectivity: Confidence, confiding, and acts of meaning in the first year. In A. Lock (Ed.), *Action, gesture and symbol* (pp. 183–229). New York: Academic Press.

Winnicott, D. O. (1971). *Playing and reality.* New York: Basic Books.

5

A Phenomenological Analysis of Social Referencing

Norman K. Denzin

My intention is to offer a phenomenological analysis of the process of social referencing, as this phenomenon has been observed in the interactions that occur between young children (6–15 months) and their mothers in the "visual cliff," the unusual toy, and the stranger situations (Feinman, 1985). A phenomenological analysis (Heidegger, 1982; Husserl, 1913/1931) dictates that I (1) "deconstruct" (Derrida, 1978) the concept of social referencing by untangling the theoretical, methodological, and conceptual problematics that are embedded within it; (2) analyze the structures of social referencing as the phenomenon is experienced in the social situation; (3) locate social referencing within the caregiver–child social relationship; and (4) describe social referencing as lived experience, offering, in the process, a proposed ontogenesis of social referencing in early childhood. It will be necessary to discuss, in terms of points 3 and 4, the psychoanalytic and linguistic theories of the mother–child relationship that Jacques Lacan (1956/1968, 1977c, 1973/1978, 1982; Bowie, 1987; Grosz, 1990) has developed. Indeed, at one level, this chapter may be read as a "Lacanian interpretation of social referencing."

NORMAN K. DENZIN • Department of Sociology, University of Illinois at Urbana-Champaign, Urbana, IL 61801.

Social Referencing and the Social Construction of Reality in Infancy, edited by Saul Feinman. Plenum Press, New York, 1992.

SOCIAL REFERENCING:
A DECONSTRUCTION AND CRITIQUE

A "deconstructive" reading (Derrida, 1978; Parker & Shotter, 1990) of the central literature on social referencing (see Feinman, Roberts, Hsieh, Sawyer, & Swanson, Chapter 2, this volume, for a review) must reveal the underlying conceptual, rhetorical, and empirical structures that are at work in these texts. This requires an analysis of the key terms and processes that are assumed to operate in social referencing. These terms must be taken back to their original meanings and sources so that any preconceptions that might be embedded in the term "social referencing" can be disclosed (see Kuhn, 1964, and Schmitt, 1972, pp. 14–38, for reviews of the "reference group" literature that the social referencing perspective draws upon; and Feinman, 1982, p. 446).

Conceptual Issues

Social referencing is defined by Feinman (1982) as that process by which individuals utilize another's interpretation of a situation as they form their own interpretation of the situation. Social referencing involves two essential features: (1) mental activity by which interpretation is formed from sensation through an appraisal and evaluation process (Feinman, 1985), and (2) the interpretations provided by other persons. The person who seeks another's interpretation is termed the *referer*, and the person whose influence is sought, the *referee*. The situation, object, or event that is the focus of the information provided by the referer is the *referent* (Feinman, 1985). The interpretation that is utilized by the referer may be sought, or offered. It may be verbal or nonverbal, and it may be direct or indirect. The information that is provided may be affective ("how to feel"), or instrumental ("what to do") (Feinman, 1985).

There are several problematics in the above formulations. First, the abstract, or general, concept of social referencing does not make explicit reference to the social relationship that obtains between the referer and the referee (Schmitt, 1972). Is the relationship symmetric or asymmetric, primary or secondary, global or specific, same or different sex, age stratified or age equivalent? If the referer is a child and the referee is a caregiver, a mother or a father, then a phenomenology of the mother–child–father relationship must be inserted into the referer–referee relationship. Such a model is absent in the social referencing literature.

Second, *how* does the referer interpret the interpretations offered by the referee. Does a process of role taking, or taking the attitude of the other, as Mead (1934) argued, operate? Does the process of a looking-glass self

(Cooley, 1902/1956) structure this interpretive process, or are other processes assumed to be at work? That is, what mental processes structure this activity? Third, how does the referer interpret these interpretations of the referee and where do the interpretations of the referee come from (Bateson, 1972; Goffman, 1974; James, 1890; Schutz, 1964; Thomas, 1923)? That is, under what circumstances does the referer construct definitions of the situation which are counter to, or in conflict with, the interpretations of the referee? Furthermore, from what interpretive frames do these interpretations flow? And, how does the relationship (historical, personal, ideological) between the referer and the referee structure and shape these interpretations. Fourth, how are affective and instrumental to be understood? How are these processes separated in the interactions that unfold and interweave between a referer and a referee? What forms of affect (verbal, nonverbal, sincere, insincere, spurious, infectious, shared, not shared) are experienced in the social referencing relationship (See Denzin, 1984, pp. 105–159)?

These problematics, embedded as they are in the concept of social referencing, must be clarified. More attention, of a historical, personal, and biographical nature, must be given to the place of power, conflict, and competing interpretations of the situation as these processes are stitched into the mother–child relationship.

Empirical Issues

Feinman (1985) describes the optimal experimental design for the study of infant social referencing. It requires

> the deliberate variation of the affective or instrumental message that is provided to the infant by another person. For example, upon encountering a new toy, some infants in such a study would hear their mothers speaking happily about the toy while others would hear their mothers speak fearfully about the toy. The central data analysis would consider whether happy-message and fearful-message infants differ in consequent reaction to the toy. (p. 302)

Locating the preferred study of social referencing in the laboratory, not in the natural social situation, Feinman proceeds to review recent investigations of infants (6–15 months) and their mothers in situations where the visual cliff, a novel toy, or a stranger were present. In general, the patterns of infant behavior observed in these studies confirm the social referencing hypothesis. The hypothesis predicts that when the infant is confronted with a new toy, a stranger, or placed in the visual cliff situation, she will respond to the mother's facial expressions of fear, joy, or neutrality and/or to her verbal statements of a positive or neutral nature regarding the toy, stranger, or visual cliff. If the mother expresses fear in regard to the object, the infant is less likely to move toward a novel toy, or cross the apparent 12-inch drop in the visual cliff situation. If the mother speaks positively to the child about a stranger, the infant is more likely to engage in friendly behavior with the stranger. The infant's reactions to a relevant object appear to be correlated with the mother's emotional expressions (Feinman, 1985).

The recent literature has suggested three counterhypotheses to the social referencing predictions. The first is the hypothesis of mood modification, which argues that as the mother modifies her expressed mood toward the referent object, the child commits an error of either (1) judging the referent of the mother's affective communication to be her mood, and not the referent object, or (2) fails to recognize that the communication is in fact referential (Campos, 1983; Feinman , 1985; Klinnert, Campos, Sorce, Emde & Svejda, 1983). The empirical materials bearing on the mood modification hypothesis are less than clear cut (Feinman, 1985; Walden & Ogan, 1988).

The second counterhypothesis raises the question of whether infants in the indirect referencing condition with strangers associate the mother's affective message as a perceived threat to her emotional availability, and not as a message regarding the stranger. If the mother appears to be friendly to a stranger, the infant may feel that she will be ignored by the mother. Infants in this situation were less friendly to their mothers than when she spoke neutrally to the stranger. Feinman (1985, p. 308) suggests that perhaps the "salience of the attachment relationship with the mother prepares the 10-month-old to be biased to utilize the mother's communication to the stranger as information about maternal availability rather than as information about the intended referent, the stranger."

The third counterhypothesis concerns uncertainty and the infant's conduct in the visual cliff situation. Recent evidence (Sorce, Emde, Campos, & Klinnert, 1985; see Feinman, 1985, for a review) reveals that there are conditions under which the infant's conduct is not influenced by the mother's affective interpretations of the situation. When the full visual cliff with its apparent drop of 3½ feet was revealed, infants did not follow their mother's request to cross over the cliff. When the cliff apparatus was covered with a cloth so that depth clues were not visible, the mother's facial expression did not have an impact on whether the infant crossed over the surface.

Feinman (1985) speaks to the first of these two situations, where the infant does not follow the mother's interpretation, but not to the second. He argues that it would be maladaptive for "locomoting infants to be convinced by their mothers that a fall of 3½ feet is anything but dangerous"

(Feinman, 1985). In this situation the infant acts as if she in fact knows better than her mother what her conduct should be.

There are, then, three situations in which the social referencing hypotheses appear to require modification. They all turn on affect, or emotionality, the infant's relationship with the mother, and conduct in uncertain situations. They each speak to the acutely sensitive emotional relationship the infant has with the mother. They each suggest that the infant is deeply bonded, emotionally and cognitively, to the mother, in what Wiley (1979, p. 94) has called (modifying Schutz) the "we experience." That is, the infant senses and experiences herself through the mother's "looks, smiles, caresses, embraces . . . and body language" (Wiley, 1979, p. 94). A "flood of mutual warmth," to use Wiley's phrase, joins the mother and child in an exchange of shared meanings that brings them closely together. The infant defines herself in and through the emotional conduct of the mother. Social referencing becomes, in light of the three situations outlined above, emotional referencing. Thus Feinman's basic hypothesis requires a theory of mother–child interaction that locates emotionality at the center of the social referencing process (see Campos, 1983; Feinman, 1983; Klinnert *et al.*, 1983).

Review of Problematics

An examination of the theoretical and empirical issues involved in the social referencing studies has revealed a number of problematics. They may be stated in summary fashion as: (1) a phenomenology of the mother–child relationship, as that relationship structures the social referencing process, is needed; (2) the interpretive process that underlies social referencing is not given in the social referencing literature; (3) the emotional foundations of social referencing remain unclearly stated; (4) the operation of the social referencing hypothesis in natural social situations needs to be studied; that is, do the laboratory findings generalize to the world of lived experiences? (5) the three counterhypotheses that have been identified need to be integrated into a broader social referencing model. I turn now to a consideration of the basic structures of social referencing.

THE STRUCTURES OF SOCIAL REFERENCING

Six interactional structures underlie the social referencing process. These are self, temporality, other, the social situation, emotionality, and the lived-body. I briefly speak to each of these structures for they stand at the center of the interaction process that unfolds when an infant interprets the conduct of a mother in a social referencing situation.

Self and Temporality

A theory of infant selfhood and temporality is not given in the social referencing literature. Wiley (1979, pp. 87–105) has outlined such a theory. Drawing insightfully upon the work of James, Mead, Erikson, Durkheim, Kant, Sartre, Scheler, Winnicott, Wynne, and Laing, he argues that there are three stages in the genesis of the self in the first year of life. The infant's sense of self-awareness emerges first in the "me" stage when she defines herself through her mother. This stage flows into the second, the "we experience" in which mother and child merge in a field of shared social intersubjectivity. The third stage, the "I," develops when the infant can turn back on her behavior from the standpoint of the "me" and the "we experience" and see herself as a "psychological I." She lives in the knife-edge temporality of the present, as well as within a band of spread-out time that reaches forward and backward alongside the present. She is able, in the "I" phase of self-genesis, to temporally and interactionally reflect upon her own conduct from the double standpoint of her's and her mother's point of view in the social situation. She is able, that is, to take her own attitude as well as the attitude of her mother toward her own emerging line of action. Her mother has gotten inside her social experience.

Other and Situation

The mother and the father are the others who structure the infant's conduct. They act as mediating "third parties" who intervene in the social situation, structuring the child's conduct as present and absent others. Structurally the other appears thusly: other–child–other–social situation. As hovering interactional presences, mother and father supply the emotional and cognitive directions the child requires when conduct becomes problematic. A theory of the other in early childhood is needed. The other is the one from whom the child must detach, if selfhood is to be accomplished. Yet the other is the one who shapes that selfhood. Hence, to study the infant in the social referencing situation is to study the other as the self that stands behind the infant's emerging self-defined actions. The mother is the other who mirrors the infant's conduct. But the infant mediates that mirror image the mother gives her, through her self-conversations and self-indications. This is the key finding from the "visual cliff" studies.

Every situation the child confronts is unique, for each situation, as Sartre (1943/1956) reminds us, is imminently personal and concrete. In the social situation the child carves out a line of action that is solely hers, for as she moves in and through her situations she creates meaning that only she could produce. But while her situations are solely hers, they are shared, as well, by her mother and her father, for as structuring third parties these others give her meaning and direction as she acts. That is, the infant never acts alone; even when her mother is absent, she acts in ways to call her mother to her. Thus the infant's situations are social constructions.

Consider the "Fort/Da" game discussed by Freud in *Beyond the Pleasure Principle* (1920/1961) and Lacan in *Speech and Language in Psychoanalysis* (1956/1968). In the "Fort/Da" game, Freud observed the infant's apparent obsessive repetition of presence and absence in a game of throwing a toy from a cot and repeating "Fort" ("there it goes"), and "Da" ("here it comes") when it was returned by the mother. Each time the mother returned with the toy, the infant said "Da." What was coming back was the mother-with-the-toy. Linguistically the child controlled the mother's actions. More deeply, the infant constructs a social situation which joins herself with the toy and the mother, and the words "Fort/Da" (see also Grosz, 1990, pp. 60–61).

In the social referencing experiments, a variation on the classic "Fort/Da" game is played. That is, the mother makes an indication to the child to "Do this." The child connects the mother's indication to the thing indicated and acts, and then presumably looks to the mother to see if she has in fact acted correctly. However, the variation that is played out involves the mother throwing out a line of action to the child. "Da," "here it comes," is the interpretation she offers for the child. Her first look, "Da," is "there it is," this is how you should act. When the child refuses to move across the deep cliff in the visual cliff situation she is saying "No!," I will not follow your look.

A clash of interpretations is produced. A new game is being played. This is a game in which the child asserts her authority over the mother's. She has dared her mother, and will not cross the line her mother has asked her to cross. Like the "Fort/Da" game, the infant has taken control away from the mother. By refusing to cross the line she asserts her own self-authority in the social situation. While the visual cliff game is nonverbal, and the "Fort/Da" game verbal, similar processes are operating in both. The infant is learning how to deal with self-authority in a problematic situation that has been socially constructed.

Emotionality and the Lived-Body

The pivotal place of emotionality in the social referencing process has been indicated. What needs to be elaborated is the importance of the child's lived-body for emotional experiences. Elsewhere (Denzin, 1984) I have suggested four levels of emotional experience. These are (1) bodily sensations, (2) feelings of the lived-body, (3) feelings of the self, (4) and intentional value feelings. Sensible feelings are given in particular parts of the lived-body. Feelings of the lived-body are given as part of bodily self-awareness. Self-feelings originate in the inner stream of consciousness of the person. Intentional value feelings are given independent of specific feelings of self, or the lived-body. They are embodied in such terms as grief, or joy, and are typically located in social situations where they are expected feelings (e.g., grief at a funeral).

In any given social referencing situation these four levels of emotionality are potentially experienced by the infant. She sees her mother's smile and applies it to herself (a bodily sensation and a feeling of the lived-body). She interiorizes that smile as a self-feeling and she interprets that smile as an intentional value feeling regarding how she should feel and act in the social situation at hand (i.e., crossing the cliff). Emotionality, as self-feeling, mediates self-referencing. The lived-body of the infant becomes the instrument for the self-enactment of emotional feelings. Indeed, the lived-body of the infant is the instrument of social referencing. Accordingly, a theory of social referencing must involve a theory of the infant's lived-body as the locus and instrument of feeling and referencing conduct. Such would also include a theory of self, temporality, the other, and the social situation. I turn now to social relationships and social referencing.

SOCIAL RELATIONSHIPS AND SOCIAL REFERENCING

I have suggested that the mother–child relationship is the key to social referencing. Seven interactional stages structure the social referencing process in infancy. These seven stages overlap with the three stages of self-genesis that Wiley has identified. The first, borrowing Piaget's (1953) phrase, is the sensorimotor phase; the second is the "splitting phase;" the third is the "mirror phase" (Lacan, 1949/1977), which emerges by the age of 6 months and may continue to 18 months; the fourth is the "acquisition of pronouns" phase; the fifth is the "emergence of subjectivity" phase; the sixth is the loss of subjectivity phase; and the seventh is the phase of "identity crisis," which is different for male and female children. In the main, I shall follow Lacan's (1949/1977a, 1956/1968, 1977c, 1973/1978, 1982) arguments regarding the emergence and structuring of these phases.

Sensorimotor Phase

In this stage the infant is like a "homolette," a little man, spreading without hindrance or interference in all directions (Coward & Ellis, 1977, p. 101). As the infant locomotes in its spatial and temporal environment, its actions are framed within an interactional dyadic context, which is the mother–child relationship. In this phase a sense of "oneness" with the mother is experienced. The infant is held, carried, rocked, sung to, caressed, changed, and moved around by the mother. It experiences its lived-body and its sensations through the interpretations the mother offers, and it moves with the mother's body, as if in patterned synchronicity.

Splitting Phase

In this phase the infant begins to make a distinction between "inner" and "outer" bodily experiences. It senses, through its hands, objects external to its body. Toilet training produces a distinction between objects in and outside the body. At the same time the infant feels a oneness with the presence and absence of the mother, although a detachment from the mother, as seen in the "Fort/Da" game, is evidenced. In this phase the mother is still the recipient of all the demands the infant makes and she is the source of all satisfactions. She is also the object of the infant's desires. In the splitting phase a global division between self and world is experienced, yet the infant's body remains the stable point of reference in the environment. At the same time the mother is the posturing "third party" who mediates between the child, its body, and the world (see Coward & Ellis, 1977, pp. 102–103). The emerging sense of prelinguistic self-awareness that the infant evidences (which may be as early as 3 months; see Field, 1979, and Martin & Clark, 1982, for evidence of neonate "self" awareness at 1 day of age) is carved out in the space that separates it from its surroundings.

The Mirror Phase

In the mirror stage the infant, seeing her own image in the mirror's reflection, forms an ideal image of self. This image refutes the "split" sense of self and body experienced in the splitting phase. This ideal image gives the infant a false sense of wholeness and unity. It produces an "imaginary" sense of self and a conflict within the emerging conceptual structures of the infant. That is, the infant becomes a being who can only imagine herself when she is mirrored back to herself from the position of another who is not she.

The mother becomes a stand-in for the mirror, and the infant sees herself in the actions the mother takes toward her. The infant becomes, in her own eyes, a representation and extension of the mother. But because the mother is the source of attention and satisfaction for her, the split between self and world that was experienced earlier is exaggerated even more. The infant experiences an alienation from herself that is coded and interpreted within the emerging primary (as opposed to secondary) cognitive and emotional processes in her consciousness. The "Fort/Da" game symbolizes this process.

Lacan (1949/1977a) argues that in the mirror phase the infant assumes an "Ideal" image of self, or "I." This "I" situates the self in a fictional direction, for it is not real. It gives a false sense of exteriority to the infant, yet it brings her to the threshold of the visible, external world. She appears to herself as a double, yet this relationship is unstable and uneasy, for it can dissolve at any moment. She is unable, that is, to locate herself within a stable linguistic system, including her own name. Such linguistic identifications would stabilize, if only momentarily, this "Ideal I" she is experiencing.

The mirror phase (see Anderson, 1984, for a review of recent literature on self-recognition and infants' responses to their reflections in mirrors), Lacan (1949/1977a, p. 2) argues, situates the agency of the infant's ego in an imaginary world of reflections. Thus the specular image (Merleau-Ponty, 1960/1964, p. 135) produces for the infant a sense of jubilation. Lacan (1949/1977a) describes this process:

> Unable as yet to walk, or even to stand up, and held tightly as he is by some support, human or artificial (what, in France, we call a 'trotte-bébé'), he nevertheless overcomes in a flutter of jubilant activity, the obstructions of his support and, fixing his attitude in a slightly leaning-forward position, in order to hold it in his gaze, brings an instantaneous aspect of the image.
>
> This jubilant assumption of his specular image by the child at the *infans* stage, still sunk in his motor incapacity and nursling dependence, would seen to exhibit in an exemplary situation the symbolic matrix in which the I is precipitated in a primordial form, before it is objectified in the dialectic of identification with the other, and before language restores it, in the universal, its function as subject. (pp. 1–2)

In the mirror phase the child's contact with the world is based, Lacan (1949/1977a, p. 6) contends, on *méconnaissance*, or "misconstruction," including a failure to recognize that the image that is perceived is imaginary and false. For Lacan knowledge, *connaissance*, "is inextricably bound up with *méconnaissance*" (Sheridan, 1977, p. xi). This point is central to all of Lacan's formulations regarding the mirror and subsequent stages of development. Because the "I" of the infant is ushered in under imaginary circumstances, the underlying social foundations of the imaginary "I," the social "I," and the sexual "I" or identity of the infant are unstable, and fragmented. This genesis of self and self-referencing that Lacan locates in the mirror stage prefigures alienation, narcissism, aggressivity, neurosis, and madness (Lacan, 1949/1977a, p. 7) in later life. For Lacan there is no firm, steady, inner center to the self. In infancy *méconnaissance* facilitates the construction of a succession of fantasies, including a belief that the mirror image of the infant's body is in fact the body as it is lived. This fallacious assumption which locates the "Ideal I" in the image leads to a future alienation in identity. When the infant locates herself in language she finds that the pronoun "I" does not in fact refer to her mother, or to her "Ideal I" as given in the mirror. The self and social referencing process that underlies these early mother–infant interactions thus rest on a misinterpretation of identity. The infant confuses herself with her mother, and she blurs her image of her body with her nascent image of who she is. These points have not been adequately addressed in the social referencing literature.

Stages Four, Five, and Six: Language and Subjectivity

Lacan contends (1949/1977a, p. 2) that the child emerges as a subject, constructed out of language, when the pronoun "I" is acquired. The "I" of language is a false ego ideal, for this "I" has no real permanence in the child's world. The subjectivity of the child appears with the acquisition of speech and language. Lacan's theory of language draws on the work of Saussure (1959), Benveniste (1971), Levi-Strauss (1949), Jakobson (1962), and to a certain extent Althusser's (1969).

Following Saussure (1959), language is conceptualized as a system of signs, a sign being divided into two parts: signified and signifier. The signified portion of a sign refers to the concept that is embedded in a word, for example, *tree*. The signifier refers to the sound-image that is produced when the signifier is spoken. With the word *tree* this would be the image of a tree. This may be given as follows (Saussure, 1959, pp. 66–67):

$$\text{Sign:} \quad \frac{\text{Signifier}}{\text{Signified}} \qquad \text{Tree:} \quad \frac{\text{Image of tree}}{\text{Word } tree}$$

The process of using signs in ordinary language is termed signification. The meanings that are given in any sign are assumed to be arbitrary and to be established through a system of differences. Thus the word *cat* becomes *cot*, when the letter *a* is replaced by the letter *o*. The letters *a* and *o* intervene between the letters *c* and *t* to establish the meanings of two different words.

In his reformulations of the Saussure model of the sign, Lacan (1957/1977b, p. 151) introduces the following division:

implying with it that all speaking subjects must align themselves along the axis of sexuality. By doubling the noun sign , Lacan extends the scope of the Saussurian signifier, suggesting a chain of signifiers referenced by a single term, man, or human. In this fashion he shows how the signifier enters the realm of the signified, and questions, in the process, the place of the signified in reality. Meaning, then, is not strictly given in what the sign signifies (through the signified), but is located instead in the chain of signifiers that are evoked, as in the rings of a necklace, when a word such as man, mother, or infant is spoken. Language is seen by Lacan "as having the dizzying effects of a dictionary: each word, definition by definition, refers to the others by a series of equivalents . . . language results in a tautology, without at any moment having been able to 'hook onto' any signified at all" (Coward & Ellis, 1977, p. 97). The signified slides under the signifier. There is no permanent one-to-one relationship between signified and signifier. The image of many different types of trees is evoked with the word tree, for example (see also Denzin, 1988).

Lacan (1957/1977b, p. 154) introduces the phrase *"points de caption"* (anchoring points) to reference those "privileged points at which the direction of the signifying chain is established" (Coward & Ellis, 1977, p. 97). Every signifying chain has "a whole articulation of relevant contexts suspended 'vertically', as it were, from that point" (Lacan, 1957/1977b, p. 154). These anchoring points in the signifying chain locate meaning. One can say: "Plant the tree so that it can be climbed by my grandchildren." In this context specific acts toward the tree are called forth and different meanings of the word tree are produced. The chain of signifiers leads the speaker to imagine a giant oak some day being climbed by his as yet unborn grandchildren.

In the above move Lacan has complicated the Saussurian concept of sign. His next step is to suggest that for the infant, in the mirror stage, the original signifier/signified relationship is: mother/child. The mother is the ideal ego of the child and the child is the ego ideal that is sought in the mother. The sign of the mirror reflects this doubling relationship between child and mother.

The infant must find a place for herself in language. This place is first given with the pronoun "I." However, the pronoun "I" is a slider; it is a signified that can refer to many different individuals, not just the infant. Lacan locates the infant in the following relationship to the sign:

$$\text{Child} \quad \frac{\text{Signifier (Mother)}}{\text{Signified ("I" Infant)}}$$

He places the infant simultaneously in and alongside language. However, as indicated, Lacan enters the child into language as a "sexed" subject. Hence, she must align and be aligned within one of two opposing sexual categories: male/female. By placing the mother in the position of the signifier to the infant, the signified, Lacan inserts the other as a witness to the infant's acts.

The mirror stage has given the child two imaginary relationships which are now restructured in and through language. First, she has imagined herself as she sees her mother seeing her. Second, she has attached herself to the image of herself she sees reflected in the mirror. Both of these relationships are imaginary. They have no firm foundation in reality. Her original ideal ego is the ideal of another self, the mother. Lacan now argues that in the realm of the signifier two signifying chains exist alongside each other: the imaginary and the symbolic. The imaginary references the two realms just noted. The symbolic references language, the personal pronouns, the moral understandings, and the codes and laws of the society that the infant is born into. For Lacan, society, in the form of the other, is identical with language. The subjectivity of the infant is thereby situated in the signified/signifier axis of language.

In order for the infant to discover her subjectivity she must submit to the mother, the signifier, finding therein that her sexuality is regulated, both symbolically and interactionally. She is produced as a female, through her language and the gestures and actions her mother takes toward her.

If the mirror stage reflected the infant to herself as a unified subject, language separates her from herself. The pronoun "I," as a shifter, is attached to no particular subjectivity. The "I" can shift and take different places in language because it only refers to who uses it. Hence, with language, a false subjectivity is acquired, and the infant is once again split from herself. She is only able to conceptualize herself when she is mirrored back to herself from the position of another (the mother), or from the standpoint of language ("I"). Her identity, however, is constructed in language. This language speaks to, or references, the loss of subjectivity that is felt when the infant discovers that she is neither *in* language, or *in* the reflections from the mirror, or the mother. She is, rather, located in the chain of signifiers that branch out from the emerging subjectivity, or sense of self, that she is acquiring. Her consciousness is structured in terms of metaphor and metonymy, or similarity and contiguity and difference (i.e., male/female). The infant must be able to represent herself to herself from the standpoint of another who is like her, but not like her, who is sexed, but of the same, or different sex.

As these emerging differences appear in her consciousness, the realms of the imaginary and the symbolic collide, while existing alongside each other. The realm of the real, which for Lacan reflects the intersection of the imaginary and the symbolic, is always dislocated from the subject's "real" location in the world. The real is structured, then, like a language. The infant exists in and through the discourse of the other (the mother) who is conceptualized only within the realm of the imaginary. Because the mother cannot fill all of the infant's desires and wants, a sense of lack, or absence, is experienced. This lack, and the fear and the anxiety that surround it, stands at the core of the infant's existence. To be separated from the mother, or to be threatened by her absence, produces a threat to the infant's sense of being in the world.

Stage Seven: Crisis of Subjectivity and Identity

As the infant is detached from the mother and finds her signifying place in language, a second discovery occurs. She is unable to identity herself with the ideal type of her sex. She is not her mother, but she is a sexed individual. In the triadic family drama with the mother and father the child experiences what Lacan, following Freud, terms the "castration complex." The male child cannot use his penis to express his desire for his mother. The female child is deprived of a penis, as is her mother, and she experiences herself as lack, or absence. Sexual desire is thus repressed. The child is forced to submit to language and the symbolic order wherein human subjectivity and human sexuality is regulated. This is only possible through the interiorization of the other and through language.

Without using the concept "castration complex," it is possible to argue that an identity crisis indeed occurs and this crisis centers on the infant's relationship to herself, her mother, and her father. Because no single individuality can ever fulfill all of the desires the infant and young child experiences, there is never universal satisfaction. Loss is always experienced. Consciousness, accordingly, restructures need/demand/desire within the repressive, distorting structures of language. Hence, Lacan's image of the infant is one that suggests an inner anxiety, and narcissistic dependence upon the mother. It suggests, as well, that there are fundamentally different modes of sexual alignment toward the mother and the father that are experienced by males and females. A theory of social referencing in infancy must accord with these differences.

SOCIAL REFERENCING AS LIVED EXPERIENCE

Gender, sexuality, and personal biography structure the social referencing process. The morality and emotionality of male–female, mother–child relationships align male-to-male and female-to-female interactions along the axis of value and mood (Stone, 1962), or instrumental detachment and emotional attachment (Gilligan, 1982, pp. 8–9). Male infants define their masculinity through the achievement of detachment from the mother, female infants through a process of emotional identification with the mother.

Two moral codes (Erikson, 1950; Kohlberg, 1981) are thus evidenced: one masculine, the other feminine. These codes turn on instrumentality versus emotionality, on abstract rules versus specific interactional understandings and agreements. The primary and secondary socializing situations (Berger & Luckmann, 1967) that male and female infants and young children encounter structure identity formation along these two dimensions, producing, then, two distinct interactional orders in the social world: male and female. These two orders are mediated by language and the other, who for young infants is the mother.

As the self of the infant emerges and stabilizes, within language and interaction, it becomes a structure that mediates the referencing process. That structure of inner and outer experiences is connected to the emerging sense of a *generalized* and *specific interactional other* (Mead, 1934) that is distinctly different for males and females (Gilligan, 1982; Lever, 1978).

The study of social referencing as a lived process must, then, take into account the following factors:

1. Who is the generalized and specific interactional other for the child in *this* situation?
2. How is this situation defined by the referencing other and the infant (e.g., fearfully, without fear, etc.)?
3. What is the sex of the infant and the referring agent in this interactional situation?
4. What is the nature of this relationship, historically, biographically, and interactionally?
5. What experiences have the infant and the agent had in previous interactional situations that are like the present situation; that is, do they bring a shared biographical history to the current situation? Or, is it a completely novel situation for both of them?
6. How do value and mood structure the referencing process?
7. What place does the infant's lived-body occupy in the referencing act? For example, in the visual cliff situation, the infant must crawl across a space; in the novel toy situation a toy is played with. These are two entirely different interactional contexts.
8. How is the referencing process structured linguistically? What words are spoken, and how is the infant's subjectivity referenced?

These questions, or problematic issues, flow from the above considerations of Lacan's theory of self in infancy. More specific questions and predictions can be formulated.

1. Social referencing should vary by the gender and sexuality of the infant and the referring agent.
2. Loss, or fear, or frightened emotionality should be greater for female–mother dyads than for male–female, or male–male referencing dyads.
3. The visual cliff and the stranger experimental situations should produce the greatest amount of negative emotionality for both sexes. This is because the loss of the mother as a source of interactional support is greatest in these contexts. However, this fear should be less for males than for females. (But see the argument above concerning the "dare" in this situation).
4. The referent of the referring agent's actions must be located within a chain of signifying acts (Perinbanayagam, 1985) that refer *not only* to the agent's mood, to the referent, and to the infant. They refer, as well, to past associations, understood metaphorically and metonymically by the infant. In this chain of signifiers, past situations are evoked, as are the infant's understandings of his relationship to the mother, or the father.
5. In the referencing act, presence and absence is experienced by the infant. That is, as the infant is separated from the mother, that absence is experienced as an emotional loss that can be filled in by actions that will bring the mother back to her. Hence, when the infant complies with the mother's directions she is seeking attachment once again to the mother. Her conduct has meaning, then, primarily in relationship to the mother, not the referent object, event, or person.
6. Finally, what is referenced is not the object, but the actions of the child in relationship to herself in the social situation. The self—imaginary, symbolic, and real—mediates and structures the referencing process. But the self, as Lacan argues, rests upon the "otherness" of the other, and the omnipresence of language, in the form of signifying chains of meaning. By placing the infant in a situation of potential mother loss (with a stranger, or the cliff), social referencing investigators have studied, perhaps unwittingly, the most basic of socializing processes. They have, that is, uncovered experimentally the pivotal place of the mother in the emerging self and action repertoires of young infants.

CONCLUSIONS

The ontogenesis of social referencing in infancy proceeds through the stages which I have termed sensorimotor, splitting, mirror, language acquisition, emergence of subjectivity, loss of subjectivity, and identity crisis. The "me–we–I" structures of self–other relating that Wiley (1979) has identified overlie these seven phases. The infants that have been studied in the social referencing literature have ranged from 6–15 months of age. As a consequence all of these phases have been operating in these studies. In the main, however, the mirror phase of development predominates. Consequently, these studies have examined infants in that stage where a false sense of self-unity is experienced. The cliff and stranger studies shatter that unity, for they produce a situation where the infant is symbolically and physically separated from the mother. Thus it is not surprising that in these settings the infant was least likely to comply with the mother's direction. To do so would place a wedge between infant and child that is too self-threatening. It would symbolize, that is, the infant's autonomy from the mother, and that is precisely what the infant does not want at this stage of development. But a conflict in perspective is produced in this situation, for the infant is divided between autonomy and detachment.

I have argued for the study of gender differences in social referencing studies. And, I have suggested that a theory of self, the other, and language must be incorporated into an understanding of how emotionality differentially organizes and gives meaning to the referencing process. Referencing is more complex than the current literature suggests. In particular, Lacan's theory of the sign, of the signifier and the signified, must be inserted into the referer, referee, referent relationship. Lacan argues that the infant's subjectivity, as given in the pronoun "I," slides underneath a chain of signifiers which metaphorically and metonymically extend, like an umbrella, above and beyond a single "signed" object. When the mother refers and the child acts, a drama is produced. That drama cuts to the core of who the infant is. Here, in her actions, the infant dramatizes all that she sees herself as being, in her eyes, and in her mother's eyes. And, if the infant is male, a great deal more is occurring, for a separation (not an attachment) from the mothering one is attempted.

Social referencing studies, to conclude, bring us to the edge of society, as society is constructed in early childhood. On this edge, as we peer in, we see the primordial infant–parent dyad being constructed. In that social construction all that a society needs in terms of sexed subjectivities, social control through language, and meaning grounded in emotionality is given. The social referencing studies are, then, mirrors to the emergence of society as society is created and recreated in the interaction rituals of infancy.[1]

Acknowledgments: I would like to thank Norbert Wiley for his helpful comments and suggestions concerning this chapter.

REFERENCES

Althusser, L. (1969). *For Marx* (B. Brewster, Trans.). Hammondsworth, England: Penguin.

Anderson, J. R. (1984). The development of self-recognition: A review. *Developmental Psychobiology, 17,* 35–49.

Bateson, G. (1972). *Steps to an ecology of mind.* San Francisco: Chandler.

Benveniste, E. (1971). *Problems in general linguistics.* Miami: University of Miami Press.

Berger, P., & Luckmann, T. (1967). *The social construction of reality.* New York: Doubleday.

Bowie, M. (1987). *Freud, Proust and Lacan: Theory as fiction.* Cambridge: Cambridge University Press.

Campos, J. J. (1983). The importance of affective communication in social referencing: A commentary on Feinman. *Merrill-Palmer Quarterly, 29,* 83–87.

Cooley, C. H. (1956). *The two major works of Charles H. Cooley: Social organization and human nature and the social order.* Glencoe, IL: Free Press. (Original work published 1902, 1909, 1922)

Coward, R., & Ellis, J. (1977). *Language and materialism: Developments in semiology and the theory of the subject.* London: Rutledge, Kegan Paul.

Denzin, N. K. (1984). *On understanding emotion.* San Francisco: Jossey-Bass.

Denzin, N. K. (1988). Act, language, and self in symbolic interactionist thought. In N. K. Denzin (Ed.), *Studies in symbolic interaction. Vol. 9* (pp. 51–80). Greenwich, CT: JAI Press.

Derrida, J. (1978). *Writings and difference.* Chicago: University of Chicago Press.

Erikson, E. H. (1950). *Childhood and society.* New York: Norton.

Feinman, S. (1982). Social referencing in infancy. *Merrill-Palmer Quarterly, 28,* 445–470.

---

[1]Lacan's theory of language—the subject, the "I," the other, and the realms of the imaginary, the symbolic, and the real—speaks directly to Mead's theory of the "I" and the "me" in social interaction. His position "de-stabilizes" Mead's self, making the "I," rather than an interpretive response to the "me," an unstable, sliding structure of signifiers, with no firm referent in the world of immediate interaction. The "I" of the sexed subject is itself an unsteady signified structure. The "me," in the form of the other, is always coded and interpreted through symbolic and imaginary relations, which serve to distort the "direct" message that is received, and then interpreted by the "I." Mead's significant symbols, which call out meaningful gestures on the part of the speaker and the hearer, appear overly simplistic, when placed inside Lacan's (and Saussure's) theories of the sign and language. In particular, Lacan's views on the signifier having no direct and immediate relationship to signified suggest that Mead's symbol, and the referential theory of meaning it rests upon, are inappropriate. Meaning is lodged in the crabgrass-like network of signifiers any sign (symbol) evokes when uttered. Meaning is not immediately and directly connected to the referent of a sign, or the referent of an act. A thorough working out of the relationship between Lacan and Mead's theories is called for. If Mead's theory is to survive, it must incorporate Lacan's understandings of the individual, the subject, the self, and language.

Feinman, S. (1983). How does baby socially refer? Two views of social referencing: A reply to Campos. *Merrill-Palmer Quarterly, 29,* 467–471.

Feinman, S. (1985). Emotional expression, social referencing, and preparedness for learning in infancy—Mother knows best, but sometimes I know better. In G. Zivin (Ed.), *The development of expressive behavior: Biology–environment interactions* (pp. 291–318). Orlando, FL: Academic Press.

Field, T. (1979). Differential behavioral and cardiac responses of 3-month-old infants to a mirror and peer. *Infant Behavior & Development, 2,* 179–184.

Freud, S. (1961). Beyond the pleasure principle. In J. Strachey (Ed. and Trans.), *The standard edition of the complete psychological works of Sigmund Freud* (Vol. 18, pp. 1–64). London: Hogarth Press. (Original work published 1920)

Gilligan, C. (1982). *In a different voice: Psychological theory and women's development.* Cambridge: Harvard University Press.

Goffman, E. (1974). *Frame analysis: An essay on the organization of experience.* Cambridge, MA: Harvard University Press.

Grosz, E. (1990). *Jacques Lacan: A feminist introduction.* London: Routledge.

Heidegger, M. (1982). *The basic problems in phenomenology.* Bloomington, IN: Indiana University Press.

Husserl, E. (1931). *Ideas: General introduction to pure phenomenology.* New York: Collier Books. (Original work published 1913)

Jakobson, R. (1962). *Selected writings.* The Hague: Mouton.

James, W. (1890). *The principles of psychology.* New York: Dover.

Klinnert, M. D., Campos, J. J., Sorce, J. F., Emde, R. N., & Svejda, M. (1983). Emotions as behavior regulators: Social referencing in infancy. In R. Plutchik & H. Kellerman (Eds.), *Emotion: Theory, research, and experience: Vol. 2, Emotions in early development* (pp. 57–86). New York: Academic Press.

Kohlberg, L. (1981). *The philosophy of moral development.* San Francisco: Harper and Row.

Kuhn, M. (1964). The reference group reconsidered. *Sociological Quarterly, 5,* 5–24.

Lacan, J. (1968). *Speech and language in psychoanalysis* (A. Wilden, Trans.). Baltimore: Johns Hopkins University Press. (Original work published 1956)

Lacan, J. (1977a). The mirror stage as formative of the function of the I as revealed in psychoanalytic experience. In J. Lacan, *Ecrits: A selection* (A. Sheridan, Trans.) (pp. 1–7). New York: Norton. (Original work published 1949)

Lacan, J. (1977b). The agency of the letter in the unconscious or reason since Freud. In J. Lacan, *Ecrits: A selection* (A. Sheridan, Trans.) (pp. 146–178). New York: W. W. Norton. (Original work published 1957)

Lacan, J. (1977c). *Ecrits: A selection* (A. Sheridan, Trans.). New York: W. W. Norton.

Lacan, J. (1978). *The four fundamental concepts of psycho-analysis* (J. A. Miller, Ed.; A. Sheridan, Trans.). New York: Norton. (Original work published 1973)

Lacan, J. (1982). *Feminine sexuality* (J. Mitchell & J. Rose, Eds.; J. Rose, Trans.). New York: Norton.

Lever, J. (1978). Sex differences in the complexity of children's play and games. *American Sociological Review, 43,* 471–483.

Martin, G. B., & Clark, R. D. (1982). Distress crying in neonates: Species and peer specificity. *Developmental Psychology, 18,* 3–9.

Mead, G. H. (1934). *Mind, self and society.* Chicago: University of Chicago Press.

Merleau-Ponty, M. (1964). *The primacy of perception* (J. M. Edie, Ed.; W. Cobb and others, Trans.). Evanston, IL: Northwestern University Press. (Original work published 1960)

Parker, I., & Shotter, J. (Eds.). (1990). *Deconstructing social psychology.* London: Routledge.

Perinbanayagam, R. (1985). *Signifying acts.* Carbondale, IL: Southern Illinois University Press.

Piaget, J. (1953). *Logic and psychology.* Manchester: Manchester University Press.

Sartre, J. P. (1956). *Being and nothingness* (H. E. Barnes, Trans.). New York: Philosophical library. (Original work published 1943)

Saussure, F. de (1959). *The course in general linguistics.* New York: McGraw-Hill.

Schmitt, R. L. (1972). *The reference other orientation: An extension of the reference group concept.* Carbondale, IL: Southern Illinois University Press.

Schutz, A. (1964). *Collected papers. Vol. 2: Studies in social theory.* The Hague: Martinus Nijhoff.

Sheridan, A. (1977). Translator's note. In J. Lacan, *Ecrits: A selection* (A. Sheridan, Trans.) (pp. vii–xii). New York: Norton.

Sorce, J. F., Emde, R. N., Campos, J. J., & Klinnert, M. D. (1985). Maternal emotional signaling: Its effect on the visual cliff behavior of 1-year-olds. *Developmental Psychology, 21,* 195–200.

Stone, G. P. (1962). Appearance and the self. In A. Rose (Ed.), *Human behavior and social-processes* (pp. 86–144). Boston: Houghton Mifflin.

Thomas, W. I. (1923). *The unadjusted girl.* Boston: Little Brown.

Walden, T. A., & Ogan, T. A. (1988). The development of social referencing. *Child Development, 59,* 1230–1240.

Wiley, N. (1979). Notes on self genesis: From me to we to I. In N. K. Denzin (Ed.), *Studies in symbolic interaction, Vol. 2* (pp. 87–105). Greenwich, CT: JAI Press.

6

The Links between Imitation and Social Referencing

Ina Č. Užgiris and Jan C. Kruper

Two directions stand out in the current rethinking of development during infancy; one emphasizes the biologically given abilities and inclinations of the infant as a foundation for development, while the other stresses the infant's social orientation and involvement from the earliest days of life. These two directions converge in studies of preverbal communication. The earliest communicative exchanges between infants and their adult partners are thought to rely on the sensitivity of both partners to certain aspects of human action, which seem to have biologically given significance. In the course of social exchanges, however, an infant's developing understanding of reality is influenced by the meanings and interpretations given to actions and events by those interacting with the infant. Thus, the cultural understanding of the world soon begins to be reflected in various facets of infant activities.

As applied to infancy, the notion of social referencing highlights the reliance of infants on their caregivers for guidance during interactions with the world. We think that social referencing presumes some means of communication between caregivers and infants. Feinman (1982) has defined social referencing as "a process characterized by the use of one's perception of other persons' interpretations of the situation to form one's

INA Č. UŽGIRIS AND JAN C. KRUPER • Department of Psychology, Clark University, Worcester, Massachusetts 01610.

Social Referencing and the Social Construction of Reality in Infancy, edited by Saul Feinman. Plenum Press, New York, 1992.

own understanding of that situation" (p. 445). In his view, the formation of an understanding of a given situation on the basis of information gleaned from the actions of others is central. By referencing the adult, the infant obtains direction for interpreting the situation and how to act in it. Campos (1983; Campos & Stenberg, 1981), on the other hand, has stressed the direct effect of an emotional reaction by a significant other in controlling activity. The adult's own emotional reaction defines the situation and influences the infant's response to it. This suggests that a cognitive construction of an event may follow rather than precede the infant's actions in a situation. Although a communicative exchange between the infant and adult is more clearly implied in Feinman's conception of social referencing, both views require that the expressions and actions of the adult be meaningful to the infant at some level in order to affect how the infant relates to the situation.

Understanding of others' actions is also involved in imitation, but the relation of imitation to social referencing is not simple. If, for purposes of discussion, imitation is defined as the reproduction of another person's actions after exposure to them, an area of overlap between imitation and social referencing becomes apparent. When another's actions not only communicate about an object or event, but also model how to behave with respect to it, social referencing and imitation may coincide. However, as has been pointed out by Feinman (1982), social referencing need not lead to imitation. The other's actions may influence the observer's understanding of the situation, but the specific actions pursued by the observer may differ. Similarly, imitation can occur outside the context of social referencing.

Even where social referencing and imitation coincide, different aspects of the interaction are important to the two perspectives. From the social referencing perspective, the importance of the modeled behavior lies in the information that it provides about the situation and not in the specifics of the modeled expressive or instrumental actions. Adoption by the observer of the modeled course of action rather than reproduction of particular acts is of interest. In contrast, from the perspective of imitation, the similarity of action is important. The degree to which the model's actions help to define the situation for the observer is less central, but the information they entail about how to carry out such expressive or instrumental acts is crucial. Hence, only when imitation of another's actions helps to interpret a situation or when the modeling of an action contributes to uncertainty in the observer and a felt need for guidance do imitation and social referencing become closely intertwined.

Nevertheless, both imitation and social referencing point to channels of social influence during development. In both contexts, infants are provided with information which has to be interpreted and integrated into their subsequent activities. Because both imitation and social referencing exchanges involve communication, it seems to us that links between imitation and social referencing can be best understood within the framework of infant–adult communication. In this chapter, we first consider social referencing as a form of communicative exchange and then examine the types of modeling and imitation that may occur in the context of social referencing. We specifically discuss the dimensions of uncertainty and of selection of a source for guidance as they apply to imitation and social referencing during infancy. In the final section of the chapter, we take a developmental perspective and discuss some achievements that may support increasing competence in both imitation and social referencing.

SOCIAL REFERENCING IN THE FRAMEWORK OF COMMUNICATION

In a prototypical social referencing situation, infants receive some information about a problematic event or object from another and use this information to guide their own subsequent actions. As in any communication situation, infants must understand the meaning of the other's acts and must identify the appropriate referent of the other's message. Therefore, as infants' communicative abilities develop, changes in the nature of infants' participation in social referencing exchanges can be expected to occur as well.

The existing literature on social referencing in infancy suggests that infants begin to seek and to be receptive to evaluations of problematic situations from others in the third quarter of the first year of life (Feinman, 1982; Klinnert, Campos, Sorce, Emde, & Svejda, 1983; Lewis & Michalson, 1983). This age period corresponds to the time when infants begin to include objects in their interactions with caregivers. Such object-oriented interactions often involve identical or reciprocal actions performed in alternation and appear to facilitate the construction of shared understandings about the potentialities and uses of objects (e.g., Bruner, 1978; Newson, 1979; Schaffer, 1979). An ability to communicate about a mutual focus of interest with another seems necessary for using the other's acts as a guide for either an affective evaluation or a cognitive understanding of a problematic object or event.

In addition to development with respect to the focus of communication, there are also changes between the first and second years of life in the means used for communication and in the range of partners with whom an infant readily communicates. For communication to be effective, the infant must be able to interpret the meaning of the other's acts appropriately. Limitations of the infant's communicative abilities may affect not only the type of message that can be understood, but also alter the range of persons with whom the infant can communicate. With respect to means, the earliest communications depend largely on affective expressions; then, in the second half of the first year of life, some portions of play routines and some gestures become elements of a communication lexicon (e.g., Bates, Camaioni, & Volterra, 1975; Bates, Benigni, Bretherton, Camaioni, & Volterra, 1977). At this level, however, effective communication depends to a considerable extent on a shared history of joint participation in such play routines. Only the acquisition of conventional gestures opens the way to communication with a wider range of partners. The learning of conventional forms for expressing particular meanings may be related to participation in modeling–imitation exchanges during play (Užgiris, 1991). These developments in communication can be expected to affect social referencing situations both in terms of who can provide relevant interpretations for the infant and what kind of information those interpretations can convey.

Aspects of the Social Referencing Situation

To place social referencing within the framework of communication, we distinguish six aspects of the social referencing situation. We acknowledge that these six aspects are not equally important to all investigators of social referencing. Our aim is not to prescribe a definition for social referencing (for a discussion of definitional issues, see Feinman, Chapter 2, this volume), but to delineate dimensions along which social referencing makes contact with other phenomena of social interaction. Therefore, we take a situation in which all six aspects are present as prototypical of social referencing, but view a number of variants of the prototypical case as falling within the realm of social referencing.

Let us consider a situation with an infant, an adult, and some feature of the situation attended to by both infant and adult. In a prototypical case of social referencing, we presume an interaction in which the infant directs a communication to the adult source of guidance (the referee), making clear that the request pertains to a feature of the situation about which the infant is experiencing some uncertainty. The referee, in turn, directs a communication to the infant pertaining to the same feature of the situation. The infant then uses the information provided by the referee to construct a course of action in the situation. Although there can be many variants on the prototypical case, its main aspects include a focus for the experience of uncertainty, a communicative exchange between the actor and the referee, the presence of a significant other to serve as the referee, and interest on the part of the actor to select or construct a course of action with respect to the focal object or event. A more extensive discussion of these aspects of social referencing provides a basis for understanding the links between social referencing and imitation within the framework of communication.

The Occurrence of Uncertainty.   The presence of ambiguity leading to uncertainty for the actor has been taken to be a condition for the occurrence of social referencing (e.g., Emde, Chapter 4, this volume; Klinnert *et al.*, 1983) or at least to increase the likelihood of social referencing (e.g. Campos & Stenberg, 1981; Feinman, 1982). There has been less discussion on what features of a situation can engender uncertainty. In our view, some uncertainty must be an aspect of social referencing, but it can occur with respect to several features of a situation. First, there may be uncertainty about the nature of the situation itself. In this case, an infant may seek a global evaluation of the situation from a significant other. Or, the infant may be uncertain about a specific object or event within a situation. For example, when confronted with a novel toy, an infant may be unsure whether to be frightened or interested and whether to approach it or not. The adult's facial expression and verbal statements can communicate to the infant information about the adult's view of the toy.

However, there may be many instances in which the infant has no uncertainty about a situation (e.g., play at home) and no uncertainty about the nature of an object (e.g., a familiar toy), but may still be uncertain about what to do with the object in a particular action context. In such cases, the infant may seek guidance from another on *how* to interact with the object, not *whether* to interact with it. The infant may be uncertain either about which action to select from several possible ones or about how to carry out a specific action. In these cases, the adult may communicate the choice of action by modeling the action or by symbolically indicating the appropriate one. Here, modeling and imitation may become parts of the information exchange leading to a reduction of uncertainty and producing evidence of influence by the adult. In addition, uncertainty may concern the type of interaction expected by another person even when the interaction as such is not problematic. In this case, again, modeling and imitation may serve to clarify the nature of the expected interaction for the infant. Because uncertainty can pertain to different aspects of a situation, the determination of when an infant is experiencing uncertainty remains an important problem for empirical research.

The Type of Communication.   During social interaction, adults offer interpretations to the infant from the first days of life; however, these interpretations are not requested by the infant and it is not clear which of their aspects are meaningful to the infant. For example, studies of mother–infant interaction indicate that mothers often match the facial expressions and "echo" the moods of their infants (Malatesta & Haviland, 1982; Papoušek & Papoušek, 1977; Trevarthen, 1979). These actions reflect a mother's understanding of her infant's state and also vividly demonstrate the various expressive components of such a state for the infant. In addition to bodily expressing the state, the mother often provides appropriate vocal or verbal accompaniment as well.

To the extent that young infants' states are somewhat indistinct and labile, such reflection by the mother can pull the infant toward specific states. Kaye (1979) has described how a mother may modulate an infant's negative state or lead the infant into a more positive mood by reflecting the desired mood to the infant in a stepwise fashion. It has been noted also that mothers tend to be more responsive to clear than to indistinct expressions of their infants (Malatesta & Haviland, 1982), suggesting that selective responsivity may influence the development of affect expression (Malatesta, Grigoryev, Lamb, Albin, & Culver, 1986).

The verbal statements made by both mothers and fathers during interaction with their infants in the first year of life contain many interpretations of the infant's mood, state, or interest (Kruper, 1984; Kruper & Užgiris, 1987). Although the verbal statements are not meaningful to young infants, the accompanying paralinguistic features and expressive movements may convey to the infant something of the parent's understanding of the situation. It is of interest that the greatest number of such interpretations are offered to young infants (between 2 and 4 months of age), which is a time when infants are least able to clearly express their own feelings or desires. Similarly, when interacting with toys, mothers demonstrate conventionally appropriate play actions from the earliest months of life, offering the infant a demonstration of the function of various objects in relation to culturally meaningful activities (Užgiris, Benson, Kruper, & Vasek, 1989; Užgiris, Benson, & Vasek, 1983). These demonstrations are given in response to some act by the infant (minimally, a visual orientation to the parent), so they can be viewed as interpretations of the object for the infant, which at the same time model a conventionally understood action in relation to the object.

In these instances, parental interpretations are offered without a specific request, but they are not unlike those that may be offered upon a specific request from the infant. It can be argued that the requested interpretations are meaningful to infants toward the end of the first year of life precisely because of the history of interaction in which parental interpretations have been offered in conjunction with various states and interests being experienced by the infant.

Nonsolicited interpretations continue to be offered to infants and older children even when they become quite capable of requesting opinions and information from others. Feinman (1985) has argued for including such imposed interpretations among social referencing phenomena. In our view, some indication of a need or desire for guidance on the part of the actor is an aspect of a prototypical social referencing situation. The presence of subjective uncertainty is the basis for an openness to interpretation and guidance. This openness need not take the form of an explicit request for guidance, and, therefore, may not be easy to discern in some situations, but it must not be contradicted by resistance to the other's message. Empirical studies are needed on the effects of solicited and nonsolicited interpretations at different developmental levels to help determine the importance of making this distinction with respect to social referencing.

The Directness of Communication.   A related aspect of social referencing concerns the means by which an infant obtains an interpretation from another. When an infant turns to another for guidance, the other usually responds to the request and communicates an interpretation to the infant. Such a directed communication presumes the existence of some mutually understood code for communicating the interpretation. The message conveyed, however, need not coincide with the feeling state or activity of the person giving the interpretation.

For example, wishing to discourage the mouthing of incidentally encountered crumbs or scraps, a mother may express disgust in her face and tone of voice in order to communicate a negative evaluation of such objects to her infant, while not feeling particularly disgusted with them herself. Or, because of a wish to encourage motor agility in her daughter, a mother may smile and offer encouraging verbal statements when her daughter turns to her upon approaching a playground ladder, even though she may be quite fearful of heights herself. Similarly, when in experimental studies mothers pose facial expressions requested by the experimenter, they attempt to communicate a specific message to the infant rather than to express their own feeling states of the moment. As these instances illustrate, the referee's response is a communication which takes a different form from the action that it suggests. Only rarely might a communication also include a demonstration of an action to be imitated by the child. Thus, in the first instance cited, the mother might not so much express disgust as emphatically demonstrate the depositing of such crumbs and scraps in a wastebasket, thereby communicating that such objects are to be discarded, as well as providing an action for the infant to imitate.

In situations where the other does not perceive or recognize the infant's request for an interpretation and, therefore, does not give a directed message, the ongoing actions and expressions of the other might still guide the infant's view of the situation. If, in our above example, the mother did not notice her daughter's glance and implicit request for an evaluation, but in her demeanor did reveal her tenseness arising from being around climbing children, the daughter might still use her mother's expression to form a negative view of climbing activity. Here, we can consider the communication nondirected, in parallel with the nonsolicited communications mentioned previously. Such instances may be considered variants of social referencing in which the probability of error is increased, because the observed expression of the referee, not being directed to the infant, may in fact pertain to a different aspect of the situation than the one focal for the infant. Indeed, there are many problematic situations in which infants and

young children do not receive directed communications, but have an opportunity to observe the expressions and actions of others. In such instances, it is more likely that infants would use the others' actions as a model for
their own behavior, because these actions would be relevant to the situation in question, and imitation would be a part of social referencing.

The Focus of Communication.   A fourth aspect of social referencing pertains to the feature of the situation requiring interpretation. When
an interpretation is specifically requested, the referent of the request must
be indicated. In turn, the communication from the other must show that it
pertains to the same referent. In the previously discussed interaction situations in which a mother offers an interpretation of the infant's state or even
of her own action directed to the infant, there is no referent besides the
participants and the flow of the interaction. In contrast, when the infant
references the mother upon encountering a new toy, the mother can show
pleasure or demonstrate an action and indicate that it relates to the toy. The
ability to include an external object in the interaction and to refer to this
object through gaze direction, pointing, or some other means of indication
is necessary for prototypical social referencing. Although an aspect of the
interaction itself could always be a focus of referencing (e.g., during a
conversation, a frown by the listener may elicit a query from the speaker
about the clarity of her statement), making such features the specific focus
of a referencing communication seems to require greater communicative
and cognitive abilities than are possessed by infants.

In cases where the interpretation is not specifically communicated to
the infant, but is only noted by the infant, the establishment of a common
referent is particularly problematic. Feinman and Lewis (1983) have right-
ly noted the need to distinguish instances where the other's expressions or
actions have a direct effect on the infant (as in mood modification) from
those where these actions are taken as communications about an un-
certainty-inducing feature of the situation. The effects of parental interpretations and reflections during early dyadic interactions are likely to be
direct, rather than ensuing from a change in the infant's perception of the
interaction. Similarly, when another person's actions in some situations are
observed by a young infant, it seems likely that such observations have a
direct effect, because the young infant may not be able to relate these
actions to an object other than the self. Thus, the need to establish mutual
agreement on an object of communication may set a limit on the developmental level for engaging in social referencing.

The Referee.   A fifth aspect of social referencing that needs to be
considered is who may serve as an appropriate referee for an infant. The
broader literature on social influence suggests that attraction to reference
persons and attribution of expertise to them affect their influence (see

Feinman, Chapter 10, this volume). This implies that attachment figures would be the most likely referees for infants and, in fact, most studies of social referencing have used the mother as the available referee. It seems to us that the ability to communicate with another may be the most important variable in restricting the range of possible referees for infants. To the extent that infants are able to communicate with friendly adults from an early age, they may be able to use them as referees as well.

Because social referencing requires infants to communicate their query about an event or object and to interpret the referee's response, it is likely that young infants would be best able to exchange information with a familiar person. Infants under 1 year of age may be less likely to reference an unfamiliar adult not only because of a lack of attachment to the adult, but also because of difficulties in conveying their requests for information. Even when they do look to an unfamiliar adult for clarification, they may not be able to interpret the adult's message. As infants learn to communicate by means of conventional codes such as gestures and words, they become better able to direct their requests for information as well as to interpret the referee's responses. This may contribute to an increase in social referencing during the second year of life.

The greater range of partners with whom infants can communicate during the second year is likely to increase the number of acceptable persons for social referencing. For example, within the family context, infants may begin to reference siblings as well as parents. Moreover, infants may begin to have preferences for different referees in particular situations. A perception of expertise may then begin to influence the choice of referee. However, with the expansion of the range of referees, the possibilities for miscommunication also increase. Because communication depends to a considerable extent on shared understanding of emotional expressions, gestures, and intonations, the child's lesser familiarity with the typical expressive styles of some persons used as referees may lead to confusing or misunderstood messages. In addition, the child's willingness to rely on different referees may outstrip her ability to consider the referee's perspective and to appreciate the context of the message being conveyed.

The Effect of Communication.   A final aspect of the social referencing situation to be mentioned pertains to the message that is communicated. In most cases, the interpretation that is offered facilitates a choice between alternative constructions of an uncertainty-producing object or situation. Once a particular construction is made, the actions to be taken follow from the construction. For example, when confronted with a novel object, the infant may be unsure whether to be frightened or interested, whether to treat it as a plaything or not. The adult's happy face and encouraging verbalization may communicate a positive evaluation and lead the infant to explore the object. Having picked it up, the infant may play with it in different ways without further hesitation.

However, there may be other situations in which the infant has a positive evaluation of an object, but does not know the actions needed to make use of it. In those instances, the infant may also seek guidance from an adult. Request for or acceptance of demonstration and guidance may be construed as instances of social referencing in that another's cultural understanding and knowledge are communicated to the infant and change the infant's understanding or feeling about an object or event. The role of modeling and imitation is particularly important in these instances. For example, by observing the actions of adults, infants may learn the culturally appropriate ways for dealing with their worlds: that strangers are to be feared or welcomed, that tools and utensils are to be used in particular ways, that some plants may be pulled and trampled, while others are to be smelled and admired. Such learning may take place through observation of the actions of others in situations of uncertainty or through more direct instruction, which may also involve modeling and imitation. Bandura (1986; Chapter 8, this volume) has described learning from observing others as vicarious acquisition. We think that when there is some felt uncertainty and openness to be guided by the actions of others, learning through observation does become a part of social referencing.

Development in Social Referencing during Infancy

In summary, when viewed within a communication framework, the prototypical social referencing situation involves clear instances of communication between one person and another about a clearly indicated object or situation, which is producing some uncertainty for the actor. There is openness to an interpretation from the other, the object of reference is indicated, and the communication from the other entails a message suggesting the construction to be placed on the object of reference. The choice of referee reflects the goals and judgments of the actor. We think it would not be productive to restrict the notion of social referencing to such prototypical situations, however, because this would preclude appreciation of the existence of links between the different ways in which the social construction of reality proceeds, especially during infancy. On the other hand, we think it would not be desirable to make social referencing just a new term for all of social interaction that brings about some change in one of the participants. Consequently, we think it is useful to keep the prototypical social referencing situation in mind when discussing its variants.

There are many instances of social interaction in which one person exerts some influence on another's construction of a situation or event, but in which one or more aspects of the prototypical social referencing situation are different or absent. The variants that we have already discussed include instances where the interpretation is given without being requested, where cues or signals about the other's reaction offer guidance without being specifically directed to the actor, where a referent for the reactions is not specifically indicated, and where the other's guidance is needed not so much for an evaluation of the situation as for the construction of an effective course of action. In the following section, we discuss those variants in which modeling and imitation play some part.

During infancy, social referencing seems to be less clearly differentiated from other types of social interaction, possibly because of the infant's limited cognitive, communicative, and interpersonal skills. For several aspects of prototypical social referencing, it seems possible to delineate a developmental progression and thereby to suggest development in social referencing itself. Table 1 presents an outline of possible progressions for three main aspects of the social referencing situation: the referent, the means used to communicate about the referent, and the referee. Development in these aspects would change the observed form of social referencing. This suggests that links between what we described as prototypical social referencing and related phenomena may also differ in the course of development.

IMITATION IN RELATION TO SOCIAL REFERENCING

It is impressive that a major increment in infant imitation occurs at about the same age as does clear evidence for social referencing. This congruence, however, is likely to be due to shared dependence on the same cognitive and communicative abilities and not to a direct link between the two phenomena. Furthermore, modeling and imitation may be a means for clarifying the meaning of exchanges in social interaction and may facilitate

Table 1. Developmental Progression in Three Aspects of Social Referencing during the First Three Years of Life

Referent	Referee (Significant other)
Dyad	Familiar caregiver
Object being acted on	Familiar person
Object present in the situation	Knowledgeable person
Object not present in the situation	Target of identification

Means of Communication
Expressions of emotion
Idiosyncratic actions
Conventional gestures or actions
Linguistic forms

the development of communicative skills required for social referencing. Our discussion of imitation in relation to social referencing includes the previously mentioned variants of the prototypical situation as instances of social referencing.

A direct link between imitation and social referencing may be most evident in situations in which the infant experiences uncertainty regarding the social situation itself. However, in studies of imitation, the social aspects of the modeling situation have been largely neglected. The infant's communications with the mother, who is usually present during testing for imitation, have not been examined. In the second half of the first year of life, when faced with a stranger in a typical imitation study, the infant may experience uncertainty about the nature of the social encounter. Usually, there is an object present, but it may be in the possession of the experimenter. It seems likely that the infant may consider the model's action on the object as a communication concerning the play that is to take place. At this point, the infant may even reference the mother and she may encourage the infant to interact with the experimenter, but this exchange usually goes unrecorded. The infant may view the demonstrations as communications about how to act in the situation, because if the infant does not immediately imitate the model, the demonstration is repeated. More importantly, even when the infant does imitate the model's action, the demonstration is also repeated, because most studies provide more than one trial for each modeling. The resulting imitative exchange may be taken by the infant as communication about the way to interact with the experimenter.

There is no direct evidence for this proposition, but an argument can be made to support it. During the first year, infants are much more likely to imitate well-known rather than novel actions (e.g., Abravanel, Levan-Goldschmidt, & Stevenson, 1976; Killen & Užgiris, 1981; Masur, 1988; Poulson, Nunes, & Warren, 1989; Rodgon & Kurdek, 1977; Užgiris 1972). Infants are not using the demonstrations to learn a new way of playing with a toy, but are selecting from their repertoire of actions one that matches the model's action. Even when they begin to imitate relatively novel actions, their imitation of well-known actions does not decline (Užgiris, 1981). Thus, their imitations seem less an attempt to understand the model's demonstrations than to carry on a social interaction in which the model's actions indicate to the infant that "this is an imitation game." The observation from the play literature that infants often use the beginning actions in a game to communicate their desire to engage another in that game (e.g., Bruner & Sherwood, 1976; Eckerman & Stein, 1990) suggests that action imitations may be understood as communications by infants.

Although the mother is usually present, social referencing to the mother during laboratory studies of imitation has not been studied. Some observations indicate, however, that older infants perceive the model as the person who defines the nature of the social situation and direct their gaze to the model both before and after acting on a toy (e.g., McCabe & Užgiris, 1983). Informal observations also suggest that some infants in the second year of life really "catch on" to the nature of the "game"; their imitation increases during the course of the session and they may even model actions for the experimenter to imitate. In these instances, the modeling can be viewed as a communication about the nature of the interaction which happens to demand the same actions from the two participants.

A different type of link between imitation and social referencing may exist in situations in which the infant is uncertain about an object as well as about the action to be directed toward the object. In these instances, an affective communication directed to the infant with respect to the object may influence the infant's view of the object, but still leave the infant unprepared to deal with it. For example, when first exposed to a moving mechanical toy, the infant may reference the parent to determine how to evaluate this novel object. If the parent communicates a positive evaluation of the toy, the infant may approach it, but then realize that he does not know how to activate the toy. The infant is again likely to reference the parent, even bring the toy to the parent, and request its activation (Sexton, 1983). The modeling–imitation interaction that may follow can be viewed as part of the referencing sequence, in which the infant is guided to construct an appropriate action toward the toy. In fact, some social referencing studies have considered modeling of appropriate actions toward the uncertainty arousing object as instrumental information for the infant and have added it to the affective expressions presented by the referee (Hornik & Gunnar, 1988).

A similar interpretation may be given to some exchanges that take place during early language learning. Upon encountering an interesting object or event, the infant often seeks some communication from the parent about it. Although in such situations parents usually label the object, they also often provide an affective interpretation through their tone of voice and other expressive behaviors. For example, the naming is likely to be accompanied by a different affective message if the infant happens to point to a flower than to a dirty rag. In either case, if the infant makes an attempt to imitate the label provided, a modeling–imitation exchange may follow during which the infant practices the label for the object. Because these instructional exchanges proceed from instances of social referencing, they may be viewed as extensions of referencing to the realm of action toward encountered objects or events.

There are almost no studies of imitation in infancy in which the infant would have the opportunity to observe another person modeling an action without the modeling being directed to the infant. It may be that actions appropriate for infants and for adults differ so much that it appears strange to have an adult engage in an instrumental action seemingly for its own sake and then have the action performed by the infant. However, everyday observations show that infants do pick up adult mannerisms and action styles even though they are not directly demonstrated for them. At least by the second year of life, infants seem capable of imitating observed activities. One study (Hay, Murray, Cecire, & Nash, 1985) has shown that 18-month-old infants can imitate actions which they observe being directed to another person and select this same person as a target for their own imitations; however, the frequency of such imitations is not very high. The actions of the model in observational learning situations can be construed as nondirected communications about how to act toward the target object or person, which may then influence the infant's understanding of the situation.

Thus, some observational learning may be viewed as related to the phenomenon of referencing. Similarly, studies of deferred imitation may be seen as instances in which the actions of another observed at an earlier time are used to guide one's actions when faced with the same situation at a later time. There are few controlled studies of deferred imitation in infancy, but the existing ones indicate its occurrence by the beginning of the second year of life (e.g., McCall, Parke, & Kavanaugh, 1977; Meltzoff, 1985; 1988). A presumption of felt uncertainty on the part of the infant concerning the target object or person underlies the suggested tie of both observational learning and deferred imitation to social referencing.

If imposed interpretations are considered to be variants of social referencing, then additional modeling situations may be viewed as linked to it. From earliest infancy, adults model affective as well as instrumental behaviors during social interactions. To the extent that these demonstrations are tied to infant actions or interests, they may be taken as interpretations offered to the infant. When a young infant orients to the adult and the adult then starts a greeting routine, the adult's action may be seen as an interpretation of their encounter. Similarly, when an infant focuses on an object and the adult hands the object to the infant, this action may be seen as an interpretation of the infant's signal. A number of theorists have suggested that the treatment of infant actions as intentional and meaningful allows infants to acquire such communicative actions (e.g., Clark, 1978; Kaye, 1982; Newson, 1974). Through their own actions, adults offer an interpretation of the interaction to the infant; in addition, through selectivity in responding to infant signals, they also convey an evaluation of different kinds of signals. It remains unclear whether infants take these actions as communications about the interaction and use them to guide their own subsequent actions or whether they are directly influenced by such adult behaviors.

Imitation of another's actions during a social encounter may also be viewed as a check on one's interpretation of the other's actions or a request for clarification. The establishment of congruence through imitation of the other's preceding action indicates mutuality of feeling or understanding

(Užgiris, 1984). Imitations of routine and familiar actions do not seem to have a cognitive base in uncertainty, but to constitute a primitive means for expressing commonality with the other. Both maternal and infant matching of the other's actions has been observed during mother–infant interaction throughout the first year of life (e.g., Pawlby, 1977; Užgiris *et al.*, 1983). Performance of the same action as the other's also seems to be a frequent way to begin and to maintain early peer interactions (e.g., Abramovitch & Grusec, 1978; Eckerman, Davis, & Didow, 1989; Nadel-Brulfert & Baudonniere, 1982). Serving as communications, these imitations reduce uncertainty about the relation to the other and about the interaction. The performance of a distinct action in such situations may be viewed as a request for a validation of one's understanding of the exchange and an imitation of this action by the other as such a validation.

As the preceding discussion indicates, some instances of modeling and imitation during social interaction may communicate an interpretation about some aspect of the situation or about the interaction itself. Although it might be useful to differentiate instances which are initiated by a clear request for guidance from those in which an indication of a desire for an interpretation is less clear, this differentiation is not easy to make. As Feinman (1985) has pointed out, a look to the other is not an incontrovertible indication of a request for an interpretation. In any case, imitation does not seem to link up exclusively with either requested or directed communications during social referencing.

In delineating the prototypical social referencing situation, we have proposed that the existence of uncertainty, either about the situation itself or about an object and the action to be directed toward that object, is an inherent aspect of social referencing. In so far as imitation may be a way to resolve uncertainty, focus on the resolution of uncertainty suggests one relation between social referencing and imitation.

Manipulation of Uncertainty in Studies of Imitation

Studies of social referencing seem to support a connection between uncertainty and social referencing. That is, when confronted with an ambiguous set of circumstances, infants are more inclined to look to others for guidance than in situations in which they are better able to assess the conditions for themselves. For example, a study of infants' responses on the visual cliff (Sorce, Emde, Campos, & Klinnert, 1985) showed that year-old infants were most influenced by their mothers' posed facial expressions when the perceived depth of the cliff was neither great enough to produce strong avoidance nor shallow enough to lead to no hesitancy in crossing. Similarly, in a study of the influence of maternal expressions on 12- and 13-month-old infants' responses to different toys (Gunnar & Stone, 1984), it was found that mothers' expressions were most influential in the ambiguous toy condition. The expressions of positive or neutral affect had no effect on infants' reactions to a clearly pleasant or a clearly aversive toy; only when faced with the ambiguous toy were infants more likely to approach the toy when their mothers showed positive affect.

If infants are seen as capable of making independent evaluations of different situations, then social referencing, like imitation, may be a strategy employed most often under conditions of medium arousal, when infants' cognitive involvement is not dominated by emotional responses. A number of theorists have claimed that moderate discrepancy from expectation (i.e., moderate uncertainty) produces moderate arousal and leads to greatest interest and cognitive involvement (McCall & McGhee, 1977). To the extent that referencing involves cognitive effort in forming an understanding of a situation, it can be expected to be most likely during moderate arousal accompanying moderate uncertainty. A clear emotional response can help to conceptualize events and organize behavior (e.g., Campos, Barrett, Lamb, Goldsmith, & Stenberg, 1983; Sroufe, 1979), thereby reducing the need for information gathering about the situation.

Imitation also is most likely when there is moderate arousal. Piaget (1945/1962) proposed that the greatest interest is produced by models that are within the infant's range of comprehension but are not understood completely. When a model can be partially assimilated to an already functioning scheme, the scheme will accommodate and imitation will be an overt expression of the accommodation. In contrast, when the model can be assimilated without effort or when the model is so discrepant that no available scheme is appropriate, imitation is unlikely. Therefore, it can be expected that infants will imitate those models which they do not understand completely, that is, those that arouse moderate uncertainty for the infant.

Infants' greater facility in imitating relatively novel models during the second year of life has been viewed as an indication of the greater accommodative capacity of sensorimotor schemes at higher developmental levels (Užgiris, 1979). Since it is difficult to determine the novelty of specific models, some studies have attempted to manipulate uncertainty by presenting infants with atypical action–object combination models. Actions that use an atypical object (e.g., a spoon for hair brushing) have been called counterconventional, and actions that use an ambiguous object (e.g., an odd-shaped piece of wood for the same purpose) have been called neutral. Imitation of both types of models can be viewed as an attempt to cope with the uncertainty they engender for infants who can assimilate a part of the model, but not its totality.

In a study by Killen and Užgiris (1981), infants at 7.5, 10, 16, and 22 months of age were presented with simple, conventional, and counterconventional actions for imitation. The effectiveness of these models was expected to vary with the age of the infants, because they were expected to be differentially understandable to the four groups of infants. The youngest group of infants did not imitate the counterconventional actions; their imitations consisted mostly of the simple actions. The two middle groups of infants imitated the conventional actions significantly more often than the counterconventional ones. Only the oldest group of infants imitated the conventional and the counterconventional actions equally. Taken together, these results suggest that infants tend to imitate actions that present a challenge to their cognitive understanding, actions that engender some uncertainty.

Similar results were obtained in a study by McCabe and Užgiris (1983), in which infants at 12, 17, and 22 months of age were presented with conventional, counterconventional, and neutral actions for imitation. The youngest group imitated the conventional actions significantly more often than the other types, while the middle age group imitated both conventional and neutral actions. All three kinds of actions were imitated about equally by the oldest group of infants. The imitation of neutral and counterconventional actions by the oldest group of infants fits the grounding of imitation in uncertainty, but the equivalent imitation of conventional actions does not. The continued imitation of well-known actions by older children has been interpreted as implying a social interactive function for imitation (Užgiris, 1981).

The greater challenge of actions requiring the use of atypical (or "abstract") objects compared to typical objects has been observed also during evaluation of infants' comprehension of verbal symbols (Bretherton et al., 1981). Moreover, in studies of symbolic play, infants have been observed to progress from using typical objects to being able to use neutral objects (e.g., Fein, 1975; Watson & Fischer, 1977). These findings suggest that a moderate level of uncertainty arouses greatest interest and efforts to understand the nature of the uncertainty-arousing objects or events.

Although the empirical base is quite limited, the data are consistent in pointing to a similarity between imitation and social referencing: both are most likely when moderate uncertainty prompts the infant to attempt to cope with the problematic situation. The two phenomena seem most closely linked in situations where imitation occurs as a result of a selection of a course of action from several options in the context of social referencing.

Manipulation of Selectivity in Studies of Imitation

Given a situation of uncertainty, infants are expected to reference individuals whom they trust to provide appropriate guidance. This expectation has been examined empirically by comparing the influence of expressions posed by mothers and expressions posed by strangers on infants' approach to a toy. In a study by Zarbatany and Lamb (1985), infants between 13 and 15 months of age were found to rely more on information provided by their mothers. The basis of this effect is not completely clear. It may be that attachment figures are trusted more to provide appropriate guidance. However, several recent studies (Dickstein & Parke, 1988; Hirshberg & Svejda, 1990) have shown that infants reference fathers as well as mothers in situations of uncertainty and even seek information from familiar caregivers, especially if they are highly expressive (Camras & Sachs, 1991). Moreover, when faced with an unexpressive parent and an expressive friendly stranger, one-year-old infants reference the stranger at least as much as they reference the parent in a condition where the parent is expressive and the stranger is not (Cirillo, 1990). It is possible that preverbal infants find communication with familiar partners easier and use the information provided by caregivers when it is available because they find it more meaningful.

In the literature on imitation, it has also been suggested that infants might tend to imitate persons with whom they have an affective relationship because the similarity attained through imitation would be more rewarding. In several studies of infants, however, imitation has not been found to be selective with respect to the identity of the model.

In a majority of the controlled laboratory studies of imitation, the models have been adults unfamiliar to the infants. The findings of more frequent and more varied imitation with increasing age during infancy pertain to imitation of unfamiliar models. It has even been argued that a lack of prior contact with the model is necessary for obtaining interest and imitation from very young infants (Meltzoff & Moore, 1983). Older infants, however, may be sensitive to certain model characteristics. McCall *et al.* (1977) found that children in the second year of life are more likely to imitate actions directed to objects than actions requiring direct social interaction with an unfamiliar experimenter. Moreover, during the same age period, live models were attended to and imitated more than televised models, and, among the live models, one particular experimenter was consistently more successful in obtaining imitation than were the other two. Thus, older infants can be selective in imitating different models.

There have been very few studies in which the imitation of a familiar and an unfamiliar person has been compared directly. In one study (McCabe & Užgiris, 1983), the responses of 12-, 17-, and 22-month-old infants to actions modeled by their own mothers and by an unfamiliar female experimenter were observed. There were no significant differences in the imitation of the two models, but infants' attention was consistently higher during modeling by the experimenter than by the mother. In addition, the infants' imitation correlated with their degree of attention when mothers modeled neutral or counterconventional actions. It may be that the heightened attention to the mother when she performs the more unusual actions indicates some uncertainty on the part of the infant, which is accommodated through imitation.

A similar lack of a model effect was found in a study of 10- and 12-month-old infants (Užgiris, 1983). In this study, several actions and gestures were presented to infants by both their mothers and an unfamiliar female experimenter during play. Some of the actions were similar to ones used in typical imitation studies, and others (e.g., pointing) were meant to elicit a reciprocal rather than an imitative response. Infants responded more often to actions calling for reciprocation than to those calling for imitation, but there was no overall model effect. The only finding involving the identity of the model was a significant order effect for reciprocal actions; infants who had their mother as the first model were more responsive to the presentation of reciprocal actions (see Table 2). It is possible that the meaning of these actions was easier to comprehend for these relatively young infants when the actions were first presented by their mothers.

In accord with these findings is the report that 18-month-old children imitate social acts modeled by their mothers or by an unfamiliar experimenter about equally (Hay et al., 1985). In that study, some of the acts were directed to the infants themselves, while others were directed to another unfamiliar person. Even in the latter case, modeling by the child's mother did not lead to greater imitation.

In all of the above studies, infants were given an opportunity to imitate both their mothers and the unfamiliar adult. It is possible that different processes account for the similar levels of imitation of the two models. We also have some results from a study in which infants had to make a choice between imitating an action modeled by their mothers and one modeled by an unfamiliar adult (Squadron & Užgiris, 1985). Twenty-four infants were studied, with the infants equally divided between 14- and 20-month-old groups. Some of the modeled actions were conventional toy manipulations and were expected to be familiar to the infants; other actions involved either relatively novel objects (e.g., a slinky) or relatively novel manipulations of an object (e.g., wrapping a scarf around one's

Table 2. Mean Number of Reciprocal Responses to Each Model's Reciprocal Acts

Order	Model	
	Mother	Experimenter
Mother first, experimenter second	3.00	2.83
Experimenter first, mother second	2.25	2.00

Note. Total number of actions presented by each model = 4.

wrist). Two actions were associated with each of the six familiar and six novel presentations. During each object's presentation, a different action was modeled by the experimenter and by the infant's mother. After the first model performed an action, she gave the object to the second model, who performed a different action and then gave the object to the infant. The assignment of actions to models and the order of the models was counterbalanced across infants.

Imitation was evaluated by assigning a score of 1 for each partial imitation and a score of 2 for each complete imitation during each of the 12 presentations. These scores were analyzed by a four-way ANOVA with age, type of presentation, identity of model, and order of model as factors. In terms of frequency of imitation, we found that infants imitated both their mothers and the experimenter more during the familiar presentations ($F(1, 22) = 7.81$, $p < .05$).

There was also a significant interaction between the identity of the model, the order of the model, and the age of the infant ($F(1, 22) = 26.26$, $p < .01$). At both ages, infants imitated their mothers more often when the mothers were the second model rather than the first model. In contrast, for the experimenter, older infants imitated her more frequently when she was the second model, but younger infants imitated her more frequently when she was the first model (see Table 3). Therefore, the triple interaction resulted from the fact that model order was differentiated by older infants, but model identity was differentiated by younger infants. Some sensitivity to the identity of the model among 14-month-old infants was suggested by this finding.

In the empirical literature on social referencing, a look to another person, especially following a look at the focal object, has been treated as indicating a request for interpretation. We examined who the infants looked at first upon being given the object and, also, the total number of

Table 3. Mean Imitation Scores Combined for Familiar and Novel Presentations

	Model			
	Mother		Experimenter	
Order	14 months	20 months	14 months	20 months
Mother first, experimenter second	4.83	4.58	3.08	7.67
Experimenter first, mother second	5.00	6.08	5.00	3.83

times they looked at both the mother and the experimenter while playing with each object. As shown in Table 4, a somewhat greater number of the first looks were directed to the person who had modeled second in the sequence and had presented the object to the infant. Moreover, a significantly greater number of first looks were directed toward the experimenter rather than toward the mother, irrespective of the sequence in which they modeled ($F(1, 22) = 16.61$, $p < .01$).

In terms of total looks, infants of both ages looked significantly more often to the experimenter ($F(1, 22) = 21.43$ $p < .01$). There was also an interaction between the identity of the model and the type of presentation ($F(1, 22) = 7.08$, $p < .05$). Although infants looked most often to the experimenter in both presentations, they were especially likely to do so during the familiar one. The proportion of looks to the mother and the experimenter are shown in Table 5. These results suggest that infants check on the reactions of others to their actions and are aware of the identity of persons serving as models for their actions during imitation tasks, but the model's identity combines with other factors in affecting imitation.

In a subsequent study (Ramirez & Užgiris, 1990), we examined social referencing by one-year-old infants during the presentation of a series of actions for imitation. Six conventional and six counterconventional actions on objects were modeled by the experimenter in the presence of the mother both at home and in the laboratory. The order of the tasks and of the environmental contexts was counterbalanced. In keeping with previous studies, infants imitated the conventional actions more, but there was an interaction with environmental context and the order of contexts. Infants imitated the conventional actions more in the laboratory, particularly when presentation in the laboratory followed presentation of the actions at home.

Social referencing looks were differentiated from general looks at a

Table 4. Mean Number of First Looks to the Two Models

	Model			
	Mother		Experimenter	
Order	14 months	20 months	14 months	20 months
Mother first, experimenter second	1.92	1.33	3.67	3.92
Experimenter first, mother second	3.42	2.08	2.58	3.75

Table 5. Mean Proportion of Total Looks
to the Two Models

	Age Group	
Model	14 Months	20 Months
Mother	.35	.39
Experimenter	.65	.61

person in the present study. The results for social referencing looks were comparable in both environmental contexts, irrespective of their order. During the modeling of both types of actions, infants referenced the experimenter more than the mother. In addition, infants referenced more at the beginning of each session than at the end. These results highlight the role of uncertainty for imitation as well as for social referencing and suggest that infants seek information from persons other than their parents during imitation tasks.

Taken together, these results from the various studies cited suggest that selectivity with respect to the source of information plays a somewhat different role in imitation than it does in social referencing. In social referencing, trust and ability to understand the other's message may be more important because the infant experiences sufficient uncertainty to solicit guidance. In contrast, when the infant attempts to imitate, the degree of uncertainty may be less and imitation itself may offer a way for resolving it. Therefore, there may be less selectivity with respect to models in typical imitation contexts than there is with respect to referees in more ambiguous situations.

THE ROOTS OF IMITATION AND SOCIAL REFERENCING IN EARLY INTERACTION

In much of the literature on social referencing, the cognitive capacities necessary for engaging in social referencing have been emphasized (Bretherton, 1984; Campos & Stenberg, 1981). A similar emphasis on cognitive aspects has been prevalent in the work on infant imitation. More recently, however, it has been pointed out that imitation is also an interpersonal event and needs to be studied in the context of an ongoing interaction (Kaye, 1982; Užgiris, 1981, 1984). In so far as social referencing, like imitation, involves the communication of information between persons, the roots of both phenomena may be traced to early interactions between infants and their adult partners.

Establishment of Joint Attention

For an infant to be able to understand an adult's communication about an object (in whatever form it is expressed), the infant must first be able to determine to which object the adult is referring. Similarly, infants must learn to indicate their own focus of interest in order to communicate about it with others. Interaction with adults helps in the acquisition of these skills.

In interactions between very young infants and adults, the focus of the interaction is on the dyad itself. The partners spend a majority of time in states characterized by mutual monitoring (e.g., Fafouti-Milenković & Užgiris, 1979; Trevarthen & Hubley, 1978; Tronick, Als, & Brazelton, 1980). Later in the first year, a higher proportion of time is spent in joint attention to the same object or in joint involvement in a common activity. Thus, the focus of the interaction expands to include a shared referent as in play with an object (e.g., Bakeman & Adamson, 1984; Bruner, 1977; Fafouti-Milen-ković, 1980; Sugarman-Bell, 1978; Trevarthen & Hubley, 1978).

One of the earliest means that parents and infants use to identify the object of the other's interest is following the partner's line of gaze. Collis and Schaffer (1975) found that when presented with a number of attractive toys, mothers and infants between 5 and 12 months of age spent much time looking at the toys. Typically, mothers looked at the same toys as their infants. These results suggest that early coordination of attention between mothers and infants may derive from the mother's identification of the object of her infant's interest through matching of her infant's line of gaze. A study by Scaife and Bruner (1975) demonstrates the increasing contribution of the infant to the establishment of joint attention in the second half of the first year of life. Although only a third of the infants between 2 and 7 months of age followed their mothers' gaze, the proportion was doubled for infants between 8 and 10 months of age. All infants between the ages of 11 and 14 months were able to follow their mothers' line of regard. Thus, both partners are soon able to contribute to the maintenance of joint attention.

In the second half of the first year of life another nonverbal method for establishing joint attention begins to be used—the pointing gesture (Bates et al., 1975). Infants begin to use pointing at around 9 months of age and at about the same time mothers also increase their pointing to and verbal labeling of indicated objects (Murphy, 1978). By looking back and forth between the object at which they are pointing and the infant, mothers provide cues to help the infant identify external referents (Murphy & Messer, 1977).

As infants approach their first birthday, they show a marked increase in the ability to follow their mothers' pointing gesture (Leung & Rhein-gold, 1981; Murphy & Messer, 1977). While pointing themselves, infants also begin to vocalize and to look at their mothers. Infants' looking to the other after gesturing has been interpreted as an indication of an intent to communicate with the other (e.g., Harding & Golinkoff, 1979). Thus, the ability to coordinate visual gaze and to identify the focus of interest by means of gestures such as pointing (seen toward the end of the first year of life), provides a basis for communicative exchanges about a referent external to the dyad. Once the focus of communication extends beyond the activities of the dyad, the referents in social referencing situations and imitative exchanges can begin to include events and objects in the larger situational context.

Construction of Shared Meanings of Acts

For an infant to be able to correctly interpret an adult's communication about an object or event, she must understand the meaning of the adult's actions. Several investigators have suggested that the infant and adult construct such shared meanings in their interaction with each other (e.g., Bullowa, 1979; Schaffer, 1979). Others have also suggested that a critical component in this construction of meaning is adults' imputing of meaning and intentionality to some of young infants' actions (e.g., Newson, 1974).

In early infancy, the establishment of shared meaning for affective expressions may be of particular importance. During social interactions, young infants do show various expressions of affect (e.g., Gaensbauer & Hiatt, 1984; Trevarthen, 1979) and soon appear able to discriminate the expressions of others (e.g., Field & Walden, 1982). The ability of infants, even neonates, to discriminate among some facial expressions of others is indicated by reports of imitation of such expressions (Abravanel & De-Yong, 1991; Field et al., 1983; Kaitz, Meschulach-Sarfaty, Auerbach, & Eidelman, 1988) although additional studies on this issue are needed.

During social interaction, young infants seem to have some general expectations about the actions and affective displays of their adult partners, although they may not have a sophisticated understanding of the meaning of the adults' expressions of affect. Intriguing evidence comes from studies in which mothers have been asked to deviate from their normal interaction patterns by remaining "still-faced" (Gusella, Muir, & Tronick, 1988; Tronick, Als, & Adamson, 1979; Tronick, Als, Adamson, Wise, & Brazelton, 1978) or by simulating depression (Cohn & Tronick, 1983). As their mothers became less active and more unresponsive, infants were observed first to attempt to reestablish the usual patterns of interaction through increased smiling and vocalizing. Only after several failures to entice their mothers into interaction did they appear to withdraw and show signs of depression as well.

Thus, although young infants show affective expressions and seem able to respond to some expressions of others, they do not seem to interpret the information conveyed through facial expression as pertaining to anything beyond the interaction until the second half of the first year (Klinnert *et al.*, 1983). Only at that age do infants begin to actively monitor the facial expressions of parents in order to use them to guide their own actions. For example, Walden and Ogan (1988) found that, during a presentation of toys designed to provoke uncertainty, infants between the ages of 14 and 22 months looked primarily at their parents' faces, whereas younger infants looked equally as often at other parts of their parents' bodies. The authors interpret these findings as indicating that older infants are specifically seeking information about the nature of the toys rather than general reassurance from their parents.

It may be that shared meanings for facial expressions are constructed in the context of interaction through parental imputation of meaning to infant behaviors, parental matching of infant expressions, and parental modeling of exaggerated expressions corresponding to infant states. A number of investigators have noted that mothers often mirror the emotional states of their young infants (e.g., Papoušek & Papoušek, 1977, 1987; Trevarthen, 1977) and attempt to channel their infants' expressions in specific directions (e.g., Kaye, 1979; Malatesta & Haviland, 1982). Thus, infants may learn not only the meaning of specific expressions, but also the culture-specific rules regarding their display. The verbal labeling of specific affective states by parents may also influence the process of meaning construction (Lewis & Michalson, 1983). The infant's ability to correctly interpret adults' affective expressions, whether or not these expressions are part of a message directed to the infant, is clearly important in situations in which the infant looks to others for guidance about how to interpret the situation and how to feel about it.

Along with an understanding of affect expressions, infants construct shared meanings for various acts and gestures with the assistance of their adult partners. One way for infants to learn about the nature of different objects is to look to others for guidance on how to act and then to imitate the others' actions. Near the end of the first year, infants begin to use social gestures such as pointing and showing (Bates *et al.*, 1975). These gestures often initiate exchanges with others during which shared understanding of those objects is established. Through participation in games, they gain a shared understanding of various game actions and of the overall structure of games (e.g., Bruner & Sherwood, 1976; Hodapp, Goldfield, & Boyatzis, 1984; Ratner & Bruner, 1978; Ross & Kay, 1980; Ross & Lollis, 1987). Through participation in joint play with objects, infants also gain a shared understanding of conventional play actions (e.g., Killen & Užgiris, 1981; Užgiris *et al.*, 1989). During the second year of life, some infants and parents adopt a shared lexicon of iconic gestures to communicate about common experiences (Acredolo & Goodwyn, 1985, 1988). The achievement of shared meaning for expressions and actions allows communication prior to language acquisition by the child.

Once communication skills increase, infants can more readily seek and obtain information about specific aspects of their environment. Facility in communication may be especially important in situations where uncertainty is produced by a specific object or event, rather than by the situation as a whole. It is on these occasions that social referencing may also involve imitation of the referee's actions toward the focal object or event. In addition, attainment of more conventional communication skills permits the infant to seek information and guidance from a greater number of referees.

Achievement of Cooperation in Task Performance

An important component in the understanding of another's actions is a recognition that the other is a person like the self, capable of conscious, intentional behavior. This recognition has been called secondary inter-subjectivity by Trevarthen (Trevarthen & Hubley, 1978) and has been discussed as the interfacing of minds by Bretherton (Bretherton & Bates, 1979; Bretherton, McNew, & Beeghly-Smith, 1981; Bretherton, Chapter 3, this volume). Although intentional actions are shown in the first year of life, the coordination of intentions with others seems to be achieved only around the beginning of the second. Achievement of the recognition of the other's intentions permits the evaluation of the other's messages in relation to one's own goals in a situation.

During the second half of the first year, game routines become more frequent in interactions between infants and their mothers. In cooperative games such as peek-a-boo or giving and taking, adults initially structure the turn-taking exchanges by helping the infant to take a turn and by providing both verbal and nonverbal signals when it is the infant's turn to act (Bruner, 1977). Around the end of the first year, infants show evidence of understanding the roles of both participants; they attempt to elicit appropriate actions from their partner if the partner fails to cooperate in the middle of a game (Ross & Kay, 1980; Ross & Lollis, 1987). They also become able to change roles with their partner and to adopt more varied ways of carrying out each role (e.g., Bruner & Sherwood, 1976). Infants' increasing ability to initiate as well as participate in imitative exchanges toward the end of the first year of life has been documented (e.g., Užgiris et al., 1983), but infants' abilities to assume both roles in social referencing situations are just beginning to be investigated (Rogoff, Mistry, Radzis-zewska, & Germond, Chapter 13, this volume).

Hubley and Trevarthen (1979) have specifically studied cooperation in the performance of simple tasks by infants and their mothers. They observed that 9-month-old infants often initiated sequences in which they gained their mothers' attention and engaged them in interaction over an object. Mother–infant pairs were also observed to engage in sequences in which the mother attempted to instruct the infant in the performance of some act with objects. However, only around 1 year of age did the infants seem to understand maternal actions as attempts to influence their own actions. As a result, they were able to use their mothers' demonstrations more effectively and to cooperate with their mothers' goals.

The ability to select among different courses of action may be especially important in social referencing and imitation. For example, when confronted with a new situation, an infant may act independently or may engage in social referencing and attempt to obtain guidance from the reactions of others. Having checked with a trusted other, the infant may or may not incorporate the other's interpretation of the situation in selecting a course of action. In some situations, the other's actions may be a model of how to behave in the situation. The ability to relate not only one's own actions but also the actions of others to specific goals makes true cooperation possible, but also opens the way to manipulation and deceit (Bretherton, 1984; Chandler, Fritz, & Hala, 1989; Leslie, 1987; Lewis, Stanger, & Sullivan, 1989).

Development of Self-Understanding

The development of self-understanding is intimately tied to the development of understanding of others. Both are in turn dependent upon direct interaction with other persons and observation of the behaviors of the self and others (Mead, 1934). A critical achievement for the understanding of self and others is the differentiation of the self from others. The infant must come to recognize that he or she is an agent and that others are also separate agents (Brownell & Kopp, 1991; Lewis, 1990; Lewis & Brooks-Gunn, 1979). Subsequently, the infant must establish categories for the self in terms of how he is like others and in terms of how he differs from specific others.

The initial differentiation of self from other is critical for distinguishing those affective expressions and actions of another that are directed toward an external object from those that are directed toward the infant. This distinction may be essential for engaging in social referencing; it may be equally important for the imitation of others' actions on objects. Seeing the actions of another as related to an object (distinct from the self) may allow the infant to use the other's actions as a model of how to act with that object.

·Although the knowledge that the self is separate from the other is critical for the development of self-understanding, awareness of similarity between oneself and others is equally important. The awareness of similarities may be particularly relevant to observational learning and the use of observation for guiding one's own actions. The infant must be able to see himself as like the other in order to expect that similar relations hold between actions and consequences for them both. It may be expected that infants would begin to imitate actions which they observe others perform (in contrast to actions which are directly demonstrated for them) and to show selectivity among models when they begin to categorize the self in relation to others.

CONCLUDING SUMMARY

Throughout this chapter, we have taken a developmental perspective in discussing both social referencing and imitation. Specifically, we have examined the transmission of information entailed in modeling and imitation and construed this factor as providing a major link between imitation and social referencing. Imitation changes in the course of development not only in terms of frequency and accuracy, but also in terms of what actions in what contexts are imitated by which children. We think that some of the questions with respect to social referencing can be better handled if social referencing is also viewed as changing in the course of development.

As infants' communicative abilities develop, their participation in and understanding of imitative and social referencing situations change as well. Both imitation and social referencing depend upon the achievement of joint attention, shared understanding of acts, and progress in the understanding of the self and others as intentional beings. With development in these domains, different types of communication become possible. Whereas affective communication seems to characterize the early months of infancy, communication about actions and intentions can be seen by the middle of the second year of life. Moreover, the communicative actions of others first seem to have a direct effect on the infant, and then come to be treated as messages about other objects or events. These communications seem to be understood without being specifically directed to the infant later still. Furthermore, the earliest communication seems to rely upon biologically shaped patterns of action, while acts having conventional meaning and symbolic acts begin to appear only in the latter part of infancy. The communicative aspects of social referencing may not be problematic in later childhood and adulthood, but they seem of paramount importance during infancy.

We have previously outlined possible developmental progressions in several aspects of social referencing including the referent, the referee, and the means of communication between the participants in the situation. We could have also suggested changes in other aspects, such as the source of uncertainty. As infants' abilities to apprehend different features in various contexts develop, it follows that the occurrence of uncertainty and its potential sources will change as well. We have included uncertainty within our prototypical social referencing situation because we consider it important for distinguishing social referencing from other types of social interaction in which information exchange may occur. Infants and their adult partners communicate about a variety of topics. However, in only some of these information exchanges does the infant seek or pay attention to the adult's interpretations of the situation. From our perspective, when the infant experiences some subjective uncertainty about how to feel or how to act and looks for guidance from the adult, social referencing can most clearly be inferred.

In some instances uncertainty may arise from the actions of others. When affiliative concerns are not highly central, instead of referencing a significant other, the child might attempt to reproduce the observed actions and attempt to cope with uncertainty through knowledge and mastery. Once children begin to engage in deferred imitation, a situation of uncertainty also offers the option of applying a previously observed mode of action as well as seeking guidance from others who are present in the situation on how to deal with it. The issue of what motive determines the manner of coping with uncertainty remains to be clarified for the period of infancy and early childhood.

In this discussion, we have attempted to define as explicitly as possible what we take to be some main aspects of the prototypical social referencing situation. We fully recognize that not all researchers are in agreement as to what does or does not constitute social referencing. We do not advocate restricting the notion of social referencing to the prototypical situation that we described, because consideration of links between different modes of social interaction can suggest new and important issues for research. For example, it would be interesting to contrast retention of actions imitated within a social referencing versus an instructional context. In addition, recognition of variation around the prototypical situation in terms of certain aspects (e.g., whether information is solicited, whether interpretation is directed, whether action is required from the actor) suggests important comparisons requiring further investigation. At the same time, we would like to see social referencing designate a distinctive mode of social interaction rather than come to encompass all forms of social influence. Consequently, in discussing the relation of imitation to social referencing, we have tried to point out differences as well as points of contact between the two phenomena.

REFERENCES

Abramovitch, R., & Grusec, J. E. (1978). Peer imitation in a natural setting. *Child Development,* *49,* 60–65.

Abravanel, E. & DeYong, N. (1991). Does object modeling elicit imitative-like gestures from young infants? *Journal of Experimental Child Psychology, 52,* 22–40.

Abravanel, E., Levan-Goldschmidt, E., & Stevenson, M. B. (1976). Action imitation: The early phase of infancy. *Child Development, 47,* 1032–1044.

Acredolo, L. P., & Goodwyn, S. W. (1985). Symbolic gesturing in language development. *Human Development, 28,* 40–49.

Acredolo, L. & Goodwyn, S. (1988). Symoblic gesturing in normal infants. *Child Development, 59,* 450–466.

Bakeman, R. & Adamson, L. B. (1984). Coordination attention to people and objects in mother–infant and peer–infant interaction. *Child Development, 55,* 1278–1289.

Bandura, A. (1986). *Social foundations of thought and action: A social cognitive theory.* Englewood Cliffs, NJ: Prentice-Hall.

Bates, E., Benigni, L., Bretherton, I., Camaioni, L., & Volterra, V. (1977). From gesture to the first word: On cognitive and social prerequisites. In M. Lewis & L. Rosenblum (Eds.), *Interaction, conversation, and the development of language* (pp. 247–307). New York: John Wiley & Sons.

Bates, E., Camaioni, L., & Volterra, V. (1975). The acquisition of performatives prior to speech. *Merrill-Palmer Quarterly, 21,* 205–226.

Bretherton, I. (1984). Social referencing and the interfacing of minds: A commentary on the views of Feinman and Campos. *Merrill-Palmer Quarterly, 30,* 419–427.

Bretherton, I., & Bates, E. (1979). The emergence of intentional communication. In I. Č. Užgiris (Ed.), *Social interaction and communication during infancy* (pp. 81–100). San Francisco: Jossey-Bass.

Bretherton, I., Bates, E., McNew, S., Shore, C., Williamson, C., & Beeghly-Smith, M. (1981). Comprehension and production of symbols in infancy: An experimental study. *Developmental Psychology, 17,* 728–736.

Bretherton, I., McNew, S., & Beeghly-Smith, M. (1981). Early person knowledge as expressed in gestural and verbal communication: When do infants acquire a "theory of mind"? In M. E. Lamb & L. R. Sherrod (Eds.), *Infant social cognition* (pp. 333–373). Hillsdale, NJ: Lawrence Erlbaum.

Brownell, C. A. & Kopp, C. B. (1991). Common threads, diverse solutions: Concluding commentary. *Developmental Review, 11,* 288–303.

Bruner, J. S. (1977). Early social interaction and language acquisition. In H. R. Schaffer (Ed.), *Studies in mother–infant interaction* (pp. 271–289). New York: Academic Press.

Bruner, J. S. (1978). Learning how to do things with words. In J. S. Bruner & A. Garton (Eds.), *Human growth and development* (pp. 62–84). Oxford: Clarendon Press.

Bruner, J. S., & Sherwood, V. (1976). Peek-a-boo and the learning of rule structures. In J. Bruner, A. Jolly, & K. Sylva (Eds.), *Play—Its role in development and evolution* (pp. 277–285). New York: Basic Books.

Bullowa, M. (Ed.). (1979). *Before speech.* New York: Cambridge University Press.

Campos, J. J. (1983). The importance of affective communication in social referencing: A commentary on Feinman. *Merrill-Palmer Quarterly, 29,* 83–87.

Campos, J. J., Barrett, K. C., Lamb, M. E., Goldsmith, H. H., & Stenberg, C. (1983). Socioemotional development. In P. H. Mussen (Ed.), *Handbook of child psychology* (Vol. 2, pp. 783–915). New York: Wiley.

Campos, J. J., & Stenberg, C. R. (1981). Perception, appraisal and emotion: The onset of social referencing. In M. E. Lamb & L. R. Sherrod (Eds.), *Infant social cognition* (pp. 273–314). Hillsdale, NJ: Lawrence Erlbaum.

Camras, L. A. & Sachs, V. B. (1991). Social referencing and caretaker expressive behavior in a day care setting. *Infant Behavior and Development, 14,* 27–36.

Chandler, M., Fritz, A. S., & Hala, S. M. (1989). Small-scale deceit: Deception as a marker of two-, three- and four-year-olds' early theories of mind. *Child Development, 60,* 1263–1277.

Cirillo, A. (1990). *Selectivity in affective and instrumental infant social referencing.* Unpublished Honors Thesis, Clark University.

Clark, R. A. (1978). The transition from action to gesture. In A. Lock (Ed.), *Action, gesture and symbol* (pp. 231–257). New York: Academic Press.

Cohn, J. F., & Tronick, E. Z. (1983). Three-month-old infants' reaction to simulated maternal depression. *Child Development, 54,* 185–193.

Collis, G., & Schaffer, H. R. (1975). Synchronization of visual attention in mother–infant pairs. *Journal of Child Psychology and Psychiatry, 16,* 315–320.

Dickstein, S. & Parke, R. D. (1988). Social referencing in infancy: A glance at fathers and marriage. *Child Development, 59,* 506–511.

Eckerman, C. O., Davis, C. C., & Didow, S. M. (1989). Toddlers' emerging ways of achieving social coordinations with a peer. *Child Development, 60,* 440–453.

Eckerman, C. O., & Stein, M. R. (1990). How imitation begets imitation and toddlers' generation of games. *Developmental Psychology, 26,* 370–378.

Fafouti-Milenković, M. (1980). *Communicative exchanges between mothers and infants in early infancy.* Unpublished doctoral thesis, Clark University, Worcester, MA.

Fafouti-Milenković, M., & Užgiris, I. Č. (1979). The mother–infant communication system. In I. Č. Užgiris (Ed.), *Social interaction and communication during infancy* (pp. 41–56). San Francisco: Jossey-Bass.

Fein, G. G. (1975). A transformational analysis of pretending. *Developmental Psychology, 11,* 291–296.

Feinman, S. (1982). Social referencing in infancy. *Merrill-Palmer Quarterly, 28,* 445–470.

Feinman, S. (1985). Mother knows best—but sometimes I know better: Emotional expression, social referencing and preparedness for learning in infancy. In G. Zivin (Ed.), *The development of expressive behavior: Biology–environment interactions* (pp. 291–318). New York: Academic Press.

Feinman, S., & Lewis, M. (1983). Social referencing at ten months: A second-order effect on infants' responses to strangers. *Child Development, 54,* 878–887.

Field, T. M., & Walden, T. A. (1982). Production and perception of facial expressions in infancy and early childhood. In H. Reese & L. P. Lipsitt (Eds.), *Advances in child development and behavior* (Vol. 16, pp. 169–211). New York: Academic Press.

Field, T. M., Woodson, R., Cohen, D., Greenberg, R., Garcia, R., & Collins, K. (1983). Discrimination and imitation of facial expressions by term and preterm neonates. *Infant Behavior and Development, 6,* 485–489.

Gaensbauer, T. J., & Hiatt, S. (1984). Facial communication of emotion in early infancy. In N. A. Fox & R. J. Davidson (Eds.), *The psychobiology of affective development* (pp. 207–229). Hillsdale, NJ: Lawrence Erlbaum.

Gunnar, M. R., & Stone, C. (1984). The effects of positive maternal affect on infant responses to pleasant, ambiguous, and fear-provoking toys. *Child Development, 55,* 1231–1236.

Gusella, J. L., Muir, D., & Tronick, E. Z. (1988). The effect of manipulating maternal behavior during an interaction on three- and six-month-olds' affect and attention. *Child Development, 59,* 1111–1124.

Harding, C. G., & Golinkoff, R. M. (1979). The origins of intentional vocalizations in prelinguistic infants. *Child Development, 50,* 33–40.

Hay, D. F., Murray, P., Cecire, S., & Nash, A. (1985). Social learning of behavior in early life. *Child Development, 56,* 43–57.

Hirshberg, L. M. & Svejda, M. (1990). When infants look to their parents: I. Infants' social referencing of mothers compared to fathers. *Child Development, 61,* 1175–1186.

Hodapp, R. M., Goldfield, E. C., & Boyatzis, C. J. (1984). The use and effectiveness of maternal scaffolding in mother–infant games. *Child Development, 55,* 772–781.

Hubley, P., & Trevarthen, C. (1979). Sharing a task in infancy. In I. Č. Užgiris (Ed.), *Social interaction and communication during infancy* (pp. 57–80). San Francisco: Jossey-Bass.

Kaitz, M., Meschulach-Sarfaty, O., Auerbach, J., & Eidelman, A. (1988). A reexamination of newborns' ability to imitate facial expressions. *Developmental Psychology, 24,* 3–7.

Kaye, K. (1979). Thickening thin data: The maternal role in developing communication and language. In M. Bullowa (Ed.), *Before speech* (pp. 191–206). New York: Cambridge University Press.

Kaye, K. (1982). *The mental and social life of babies.* Chicago: University of Chicago Press.

Killen, M., & Užgiris, I. Č. (1981). Imitation of actions with objects: The role of social meaning. *Journal of Genetic Psychology, 138,* 219–229.

Klinnert, M. D., Campos, J. J., Sorce, J. F., Emde, R. N., & Svejda, M. J. (1983). Emotions as behavior regulators: Social referencing in infancy. In R. Plutchik & H. Kellerman (Eds.), *Emotion: Theory, research, and experience: Vol. 2. Emotions in early development* (pp. 57–86). New York: Academic Press.

Kruper, J. C., & Užgiris, I. Č. (1984, April). *Maternal speech to infants in the first year of life.* Poster presented at the International Conference on Infant Studies, New York.

Kruper, J. C. & Užgiris, I. Č. (1987). Fathers' and mothers' speech to young infants. *Journal of Psycholinguistic Research, 16,* 597–614.

Leslie, A. M. (1987). Pretense and representation: The origins of "theory of mind." *Psychological Review, 94,* 412–426.

Leung, E. H. L., & Rheingold, H. L. (1981). Development of pointing as social gesture. *Developmental Psychology, 17,* 215–220.

Lewis, M. (1990). Social knowledge and social development. *Merrill Palmer Quarterly, 36,* 93–116.

Lewis, M., & Brooks-Gunn, J. (1979). Toward a theory of social cognition: The development of self. In I. Č. Užgiris (Ed.), *Social interaction and communication during infancy* (pp. 1–20). San Francisco: Jossey-Bass.

Lewis, M., & Michalson, L. (1983). *Children's emotions and moods: Developmental theory and measurement.* New York: Plenum.

Lewis, M., Stanger, C., & Sullivan, M. W. (1989). Deception in 3-year-olds. *Developmental Psychology, 25,* 439–443.

Malatesta, C. Z.,Grigoryev, P., Lamb, C., Albin, M., & Culver, C. (1986). Emotion socialization and expressive development in preterm and full-term infants. *Child Development. 57,* 316–330.

Malatesta, C. Z., & Haviland, J. M. (1982). Learning display rules: The socialization of emotion expression in infancy. *Child Development, 53,* 991–1003.

Masur, E. F. (1988). Infants' imitation of novel and familiar behaviors. In T. R. Zentall & B. G. Galef (Eds.), *Social learning: Psychological and biological perspectives* (pp. 301–318). Hillsdale, NJ: Erlbaum.

McCabe, M., & Užgiris, I. Č. (1983). Effects of model and action on imitation in infancy. *Merrill-Palmer Quarterly, 29,* 69–82.

McCall, R. B., & McGhee, P. E. (1977). The discrepancy hypothesis of attention and affect in infants. In I. Č. Užgiris & F. Weizmann (Eds.), *The structuring of experience* (pp. 179–210). New York: Plenum.

McCall, R. B., Parke, R. D., & Kavanaugh, R. D. (1977). Imitation of live and televised models by children 1–3 years of age. *Monographs of the Society for Research and Child Development, 42,* (5, Serial No. 173).

Mead, G. H. (1934). *Mind, self and society.* Chicago: University of Chicago Press.

Meltzoff, A. N. (1985). Immediate and deferred imitation in fourteen and twenty-four-month-old infants. *Child Development, 56,* 62–72.

Meltzoff, A. N. (1988). Infant imitation after a 1-week delay: Long-term memory for novel acts and multiple stimuli. *Developmental Psychology, 24,* 470–476.

Meltzoff, A. N., & Moore, M. K. (1983). The origins of imitation in infancy: Paradigm, phenomena, and theories. In L. P. Lipsitt (Ed.), *Advances in infancy research* (Vol. 2, pp. 263–300). Norwood, NJ: Ablex Press.

Murphy, C. M. (1978). Pointing in the context of a shared activity. *Child Development, 49,* 371–380.

Murphy, C. M., & Messer, D. J. (1977). Mothers, infants and pointing: A study of gesture. In H. R. Schaffer (Ed.), *Studies in mother–infant interaction* (pp. 325–354). London: Academic Press.

Nadel-Brulfert, J., & Baudonniere, P. M. (1982). The social function of reciprocal imitation in 2-year-old peers. *International Journal of Behavioral Development, 5,* 95–109.

Newson, J. (1974). Towards a theory of infant understanding. *Bulletin of the British Psychological Society, 27,* 251–257.

Newson, J. (1979). Intentional behavior in the young infant. In D. Shaffer & J. Dunn (Eds.), *The first year of life* (pp. 91–96). New York: John Wiley & Sons.

Papoušek, H., & Papoušek, M. (1977). Mothering and the cognitive headstart: Psychobiological considerations. In H. R. Schaffer (Ed.), *Studies in mother–infant interaction* (pp. 63–85). New York: Academic Press.

Papoušek, H., & Papoušek, M. (1987). Intuitive parenting: A dialectic counterpart of the infants' integrative competence. In J. D. Osofsky (Ed.), *Handbook of infant development* (2nd ed.). New York: Wiley.

Pawlby, S. J. (1977). Imitative interaction. In H. R. Schaffer (Ed.), *Studies in mother–infant interaction* (pp. 203–224). New York: Academic Press.

Piaget, J. (1962). *Play, dreams and imitation in childhood* (C. Gattego & F. M. Hodgson, Trans.). New York: Norton. (Original work published 1945)

Poulson, C. L., Nunes, L. R. P., & Warren S. F. (1989). Imitation in infancy: A critical review. In H. W. Reese (Ed.), *Advances in child development and behavior. Vol. 22* (pp. 271–298). San Diego, CA: Academic Press.

Ramirez, C. & Užgiris, I. Č. (1990, April). *Social referencing during imitation.* Poster presented at the International Conference of Infant Studies, Montreal, Canada.

Ratner, N., & Bruner, J. S. (1978). Games, social exchange, and the acquisition of language. *Journal of Child Language, 5,* 391–401.

Rodgon, M. M., & Kurdek, L. A. (1977). Vocal and gestural imitation in 8-, 14-, and 20-month-old children. *Journal of Genetic Psychology, 131,* 115–123.

Ross, H. S., & Kay, D. A. (1980). The origins of social games. K. Rubin (Ed.), *Children's play* (pp. 17–31). San Francisco: Jossey-Bass.

Ross, H. S., & Lollis, S. P. (1987). Communication within infant social games. *Developmental Psychology, 23,* 241–248.

Scaife, M., & Bruner, J. S. (1975). The capacity for joint visual attention in the infant. *Nature, 253,* 265–266.

Schaffer, H. R. (1979). Acquiring the concept of the dialogue. In M. Bornstein & W. Kessen (Eds.), *Psychological development from infancy: Image to intention* (pp. 279–305). Hillsdale, NJ: Lawrence Erlbaum.

Sexton, M. E. (1983). The development of the understanding of causality in infancy. *Infant Behavior and Development, 6,* 201–210.

Sorce, J. F., Emde, R. N., Campos, J., & Klinnert, M. D. (1985). Maternal emotional signaling: Its effect on the visual cliff behavior of 1-year-olds. *Developmental Psychology, 21,* 195–200.

Squadron, D., & Užgiris, I. Č. (1985). *Imitation of alternatives offered by mother and stranger.* Unpublished manuscript, Clark University, Worcester, MA.

Sroufe, L. A. (1979). Socioemotional development. In J. D. Osofsky (Ed.), *Handbook of infant development* (pp. 462–516). New York: Wiley.

Sugarman-Bell, S. (1978). Some organizational aspects of preverbal communication. In I. Markova (Ed.), *The social context of language* (pp. 49–66). New York: John Wiley & Sons.

Trevarthen, C. (1977). Descriptive analyses of infant communicative behavior. In H. R.

Schaffer (Ed.), *Studies in mother–infant interaction* (pp. 227–270). New York: Academic Press.

Trevarthen, C. (1979). Communication and cooperation in early infancy: A description of primary intersubjectivity. In M. Bullowa (Ed.), *Before speech* (pp. 321–347). New York: Cambridge University Press.

Trevarthen, C., & Hubley, P. (1978). Secondary intersubjectivity: Confidence, confiding, and acts of meaning in the first year. In A. Lock (Ed.), *Action, gesture and symbol* (pp. 183–257). New York: Academic Press.

Tronick, E., Als, H., & Adamson, L. (1979). Structure of early face-to-face communicative interactions. In M. Bullowa (Ed.), *Before speech* (pp. 349–370). New York: Cambridge University Press.

Tronick, E., Als, H., Adamson, L., Wise, S., Brazelton, T. B. (1978). The infant's response to entrapment between contradictory messages in face-to-face interaction. *Journal of Child Psychiatry, 17,* 1–13.

Tronick, E., Als, H., & Brazelton, T. B. (1980). Monadic phases: A structural analysis of infant–mother face-to-face interaction. *Merrill-Palmer Quarterly, 26,* 3–24.

Užgiris, I. Č. (1972). Patterns of vocal and gestural imitation in infants. In F. J. Monks, W. W. Hartup, & J. de Witt (Eds.), *Determinants of behavioral development* (pp. 467–471). New York: Academic Press.

Užgiris, I. Č. (1979). Die Mannigfaltigkeit der Imitation in der Frühen Kindheit [The many faces of imitation in infancy]. In L. Montada (Ed.), *Brennpunkte der Entwicklungspsychologie* [Focal issues in developmental psychology]. Stuttgart: Verlag W. Kohlhammer.

Užgiris, I. Č. (1981). Two functions of imitation during infancy. *International Journal of Behavioral Development, 4,* 1–12.

Užgiris, I. Č. (1983). *The role of imitation in pre-verbal communication.* Final Report to the Spencer Foundation (7-1-1981–7-31-1983).

Užgiris, I. Č. (1984). Imitation in infancy: Its interpersonal aspects. In M. Perlmutter (Ed.), *The Minnesota Symposia on Child Psychology,* vol. 17: *Parent–child interactions and parent–child relations in child development* (pp. 1–32). Hillsdale, NJ: Lawrence Erlbaum.

Užgiris, I. Č. (1991). The social context of infant imitation. In M. Lewis & S. Feinman (Eds.), *Social influences and socialization in infancy* (pp. 215–251). New York: Plenum.

Užgiris, I. Č., Benson, J. B., Kruper, J. C., & Vasek, M. (1989). Contextual influences on imitative interactions between mothers and infants. In J. J. Lockman & N. L. Hazen (Eds.), *Action in social context: Perspectives on early development* (pp. 103–127). New York: Plenum.

Užgiris, I. Č., Benson, J. B., Vasek, M. (1983, April). *Matching behavior in mother–infant interaction.* Paper presented at the biennial meeting of the Society for Research in Child Development, Detroit.

Walden, T. A., & Ogan, T. A. (1988). The development of social referencing. *Child Development, 59,* 1230–1240.

Watson, M. W., & Fischer, K. W. (1977). A developmental sequence of agent use in late infancy. *Child Development, 48,* 828–836.

Zarbatany, L., & Lamb, M. E. (1985). Social referencing as a function of information source: Mothers versus strangers. *Infant Behavior and Development, 8,* 25–33.

III

Cognition and
Information Processing

7

Social Referencing as a Learned Process

Jacob L. Gewirtz and Martha Peláez-Nogueras

INTRODUCTION

Social referencing has been conceived as the process whereby, in the fourth quarter of their first year, human infants seek out and use information in the facial (but also vocal and/or gestural) emotional expressions of others (most often the mother) to cue/guide their responding in contexts of uncertainty or ambiguity (Campos & Stenberg, 1981; Klinnert, Campos, Sorce, Emde, & Svejda, 1983). Social referencing also has been characterized as infants' perception and use of other persons' interpretations of a situation to form their own understanding of that situation (Feinman, 1982; Feinman & Lewis, 1983). Up to now, the infant social referencing literature has devoted almost total emphasis to describing and delineating this phenomenon, and to emphasizing the feature of affective communication between mother and infant (Campos & Stenberg, 1981; Feinman, 1983, 1985; Gunnar & Stone, 1984; Hornik & Gunnar, 1988; Klinnert, Emde, Butterfield, & Campos, 1986; Walden & Ogan, 1988; Zarbatany & Lamb, 1985). To date, the main etiological theory in the literature has been pre-

JACOB L. GEWIRTZ AND MARTHA PELÁEZ-NOGUERAS • Department of Psychology, Florida International University, Miami, Florida 33199.

Social Referencing and the Social Construction of Reality in Infancy, edited by Saul Feinman. Plenum Press, New York, 1992.

formationist, that infant social referencing involves prewired responses and perceptions, a "prewired communication process" (Campos, 1983).

An alternative to that nativist theory is proposed here (and in Peláez-Nogueras, 1992), that social referencing can result from the infant's *learning* in contexts of uncertainty that maternal-expressive cues, consequent upon its referencing looking response, can predict reliably positive or aversive consequences for its actions. The results of a paradigmatic study that supports such an operant-learning model of social referencing are presented in this chapter. The reported research demonstrates that the differential cue value (meanings) of originally meaningless maternal facial expressions contingent upon infant referencing-looks can be conditioned readily, depending on the predictive utility of those maternal facial-expressive cues for infant responding in ambiguous contexts. Finally, we emphasize that the maternal expressive cues in social referencing need not relate to conceptions of emotion or affect.

PREFORMATIONISM AND INFANT SOCIAL REFERENCING

Few theories have been advanced to explain how infant social referencing and the maternal facial-expressive and other (e.g., vocal) cues controlling the referencing response come into being, what maintains referencing, and what the nature of the underlying process is. Campos (1983) has proposed that " . . . social referencing is biologically adaptive and involves prewired responses and perceptions . . . [and] serves as an occasion for the operation of much more fundamental processes . . . [such as involve] emotional communication" (p. 85). Elsewhere, in a major handbook chapter on socioemotional development, Campos, Barrett, Lamb, Goldsmith, and Stenberg (1983) assert that

> . . . unlike language or cognition, *the basic emotions*—which we believe include joy, anger, disgust, surprise, fear, sadness, sexual ardor, affection, and possibly others–*utilize a noncodified, prewired communication process*, a process now known to require no social learning either for the *reception* of at least some facial and gestural signals . . . or for the *production* of such. (p. 785)

From this preformationist conception it follows that, early in life, the human infant will perceive/understand the meanings of its mother's emotional facial expressions (with or without vocal or gestural accompaniment) via social referencing. That is, the position assumes that, on an unlearned basis, the mother's facial expression will communicate the meaning of her "emotion" to her infant, and that such a meaning will help the infant to regulate its behavior in ambiguous contexts. Campos *et al.* (1983) have cited three research reports as the basis for their assertion that the human mother's facial expression will, on an unconditioned basis, communicate her emotional response's meaning to her infant. However, for the reasons detailed, it is not apparent how those reports can support a preformationist assumption.[1]

It is axiomatic that researchers must remain open-minded about whether or not, on an unlearned basis, human infants can perceive the meanings of their mothers' emotional-expressive patterns. Hence, given equivocal macaque data and an absence of definitive human infant supporting data, it is remarkable that Campos (1983) and Campos *et al.* (1983) have advanced their strong assertions that one-year-old human infants—in whom the social referencing phenomenon has been identified—are born with this unlearned ability. Indeed, one can conceive diverse scenarios in the evolutionary history of *Homo sapiens* that involve contingencies of survival and adaptations to ecological demands. Nevertheless, given

---

[1]In comment, we note the following: First, those three studies (Kenney, Mason, & Hill, 1979; Mendelson, Haith, & Goldman-Rakic, 1982; Sackett, 1966) all investigated rhesus macaque (*Macaca mulatta*) infant and postinfant monkeys, a species with a different evolutionary history than *Homo sapiens*, to which Campos *et al.* generalized the purported findings of those studies. Second, none of the three studies dealt in macaques with infant and postinfant reactions to maternal expressive facial reactions, much less in the humans to which Campos *et al.* generalized the purported findings. Third, Sackett's (1966) presentations of the threatening-macaque infant slide generated, in the observer macaques, not only a relatively high mean incidence of behavior denoting disturbance, but also relatively high mean incidences of vocalizations, play, and exploration, behaviors that do not ordinarily denote disturbance. This result pattern necessarily complicates/dilutes an interpretation that a macaque-threat slide stimulus is a releaser of behavior denoting disturbance. Further, Sackett's threatening-macaque slide presentations evoked more mean vocalizing, behavior denoting disturbance, and play behavior than did the fearful-expression monkey slide which, in turn, did not differ in eliciting mean behaviors than such slides as those showing a macaque infant, or monkey play, withdrawal, or exploration. These mean-result patterns make Sackett's (1966) findings equivocal with regard to innate recognition mechanisms in infant and postinfant (a few days to 9 months post partum) macaques, much less for infant humans showing innate recognition of maternal facial expressions. This is because it is not obvious that presentations of macaque facial-threat slides (or even fear-face slides) "release" an inborn fear response unconfounded by vocalization, play, and exploration behavior in monkeys reared in isolation for most of their lives post partum. Fourth, we note that Kenney, Mason, and Hill (1979) tested macaques for their lip-smacking and grimacing reactions to their own mirror images, or to a human face, during the first 12 weeks of life, and compared mean responses for groups reared with (1) both monkeys and people, (2) only one monkey, or (3) neither monkeys nor people. Their design does not impact on the question of the unlearned versus the learned basis of communication of the meaning of the mother's emotional facial reaction to her infant. Finally, we note that the Mendelson, Haith, and Goldman-Rakic (1982) study of infant macaque gaze aversion and fixation found that infants looked more at the eyes of pictured monkey faces "looking back" than at faces "looking away." Again, it is difficult to see how these findings bear directly on the issue of whether or not the macaque or human mother's emotional facial reaction has innate meaning for her infant.

that newborns and infants of an altricial species such as humans remain helpless and incapable of locomotion for an extensive period, it is difficult to imagine an evolutionary scenario in which the human species would survive better, or be more advanced in its ecological niche, by its infants having the ability from birth on an unconditioned basis to discriminate the meanings of diverse maternal emotional expressions.

Indeed, what the young human does seem to have acquired via evolutionary adaptation is the specialized capacity to *learn*, that is, to adapt readily to changing circumstances in its ecological niche early and late in ontogeny (Petrovich & Gewirtz, 1984, 1985). In this connection, it may be more reasonable to assume that the actual consequences for infant responses in the presence of maternal facial-emotional expressions, rather than a preprogrammed stimulus–response connection, is what comes to determine the infant's approach or avoidance to ambiguous objects. There is ample evidence in newborns and in infants in the first months of life that they can be trained readily to discriminate between stimuli (visual, auditory, tactile) that cue responses leading to differing consequences (reinforcing or nonreinforcing) by responding differentially to them, very much like what is involved in the social referencing phenomenon (Ling, 1941; Munn, 1965; Peláez-Nogueras & Gewirtz, 1990; Simmons & Lipsitt, 1961; Siqueland & Lipsitt, 1966; Staples, 1932).

Further, there are illustrations in several research realms of the influence of very early, even prenatal, experiential factors that, when overlooked, could imply innate/preformed capacities. A nonhuman example based on research with mallard hens and hatchlings can be instructive. Early work on *imprinting* in precocial fowl had concluded that imprinting was a prewired response of the hatchling based on simple visual exposure of the hatchling to a moving and vocalizing model of the hen, and that there was a critical period for this imprinting (Gottlieb, 1971, 1973; Hess, 1973; Hess & Petrovich, 1973). Subsequent research found relevant to the explanation of imprinting the fact that the hatchling exhibits auditory capacity and organized motor patterns after it breaks into the egg's air space, which can occur as early as 72 hours before hatching. In the egg's air space the hatchling hears the hen's calls, vocalizes, and the hen vocalizes apparently in response, to the point where the hen may vocalize as often as 45 times per minute during the last phase before hatching. The hen's calls heard by the hatchling are the same as the calls she will emit some 48 hours later, when she signals to her brood the move to a new ecological setting, such as a nearby body of water. Experience with the hen's call and preference for it were seen to have an important role in the process of imprinting.

Post hatching, the earlier experience with the hen's call was found to have a significant role in the imprinting process. The duckling will typically orient to and follow—that is, imprint—its moving and vocalizing hen mother whose calls are familiar, even in contexts where several hens are in the vicinity. This example from imprinting research can illustrate a process that, in early work, involved strong assumptions that imprinting was prewired and limited by a critical period. In later work, those strong assumptions were seen to be unwarranted as an explanation of the imprinting process, for imprinting was seen significantly to involve systematic prior-to-hatching vocal interaction between hen and hatchling. This pattern of prehatching experience led the duckling to exhibit post hatching, a filial pattern of differential orientation to, and preference for, its mother's call. Thus, in the absence of prehatching data, imprinting was considered by some to be entirely preformed, and to result only from exposure to a moving and vocalizing hen model during a critical period (see also Petrovich & Gewirtz, 1991).

A similar instructive case involving human neonates is provided by DeCasper and Spence (1986), who demonstrated that, 3 days post partum, neonates manifested differential preferences (determined via operant preference procedures) for the acoustic patterns of 600-word stories that were read to them, as fetuses, by their mothers 67 times on average during the last 6 weeks of gestation. Preferences were determined via an operant reinforcement procedure wherein the differential-reinforcing value for operant nonnutritive sucking of the earlier maternally read passage and control passages were compared. (This finding indicates that, in the last 6 weeks of gestation, human fetuses can discriminate vocal auditory signals that they must have received in attenuated form through the amniotic fluid which, subsequently, as 3-day-old neonates, they were able to compare to nonattenuated signals.)

These reports exemplify how preformationist assumptions about "prewired" unconditioned processes can be problematic even in the newborn, and much more so in the 1-year old infant who has served as the typical subject of social referencing studies. In the absence of information about systematic prenatal experience with a parent, the newborn duckling's filial response to the first moving and vocalizing object it sees and the human neonate's differential preference for acoustic patterns of stories read by their mothers, could be assumed incorrectly to have been due to preformation rather than to exposure learning. In any case, an empirical question remains at issue at the proximal level of analysis, one that in principle can be answered only by systematic observation and experimentation. In this context, with so little of the required research done, it is puzzling that researcher–theorists of social referencing phenomena and early communication, like Campos and his associates, so readily have assumed that infants of a species so highly adaptable and sensitive to environmental contingencies as *Homo sapiens* operate in a prewired manner.[2] Human evolution reflects an unusual capacity to modify and extend phenotype characteristics as the result of particular experiences (denoting learning). As the Gottlieb, Hess and Petrovich, and DeCasper and Spence analyses have illustrated (and as our analysis assumes), via exposure-learning processes very early in ontogeny, systematic environmental stimulation can influence cued-response patterns of communication between mother and infant, patterns that might otherwise appear unconditioned/prewired to those unfamiliar with the specific behavior and its fetal or early postnatal environmental history.

SOCIAL REFERENCING AS A LEARNED PROCESS

Absent from the social-referencing literature is a conception that is proposed here (and in Gewirtz, 1991) as an alternative to preformationistic/nativistic hypotheses, like the one Campos (1983) and Campos *et al.* (1983) have advanced to explain the social referencing detected in infants during the last quarter of the first year.[3] This alternative is that, early in the first year, social referencing can result from the infant's *learning* that, in contexts of uncertainty, maternal facial-expressive cues (that we assume are originally neutral in value) can come reliably to predict positive or aversive consequences for the infant's actions in those ambiguous contexts or to those ambiguous objects. Specifically, in contexts of uncertainty infant responses such as reaching for or approaching, or avoiding, objects or

[2]At first glance, it could appear that all preformation versus all learning determinants of social referencing are being counterposed. Hence, a comment is in order about how genetic and environmental factors interact in a developmental learning analysis. All learning must occur in a genetic (genotype) frame, where dispositions to learn are inflected by environmental demands for behavioral change (In this sense, behavior is neither innate nor learned.) The genotype provides the template or blueprint basis for development, organizing the processes that enable the organism to employ particular responses—responses that can have environmental consequences. The genetic template must be realized in a real environment. The development of all behaviors, including learned behaviors, " . . . requires the interaction of environmental and genetic inputs at every stage of the developmental [learning] process" (Fantino & Logan, 1979, p. 475).

[3]In an as yet unpublished work (Peláez-Nogueras & Gewirtz, 1992) we have found in our laboratory that infants as young as 4 months referenced-looked at their mothers' faces in ambiguous contexts. However, during a pretreatment assessment, after their mothers' contingent fearful or joyful emotional expressions were referenced, no differential responding of those 4-month-old infants to the ambiguous objects was found. In contrast, after conditioning, those infants responded differentially to a joyful and a fearful maternal expression.

activities are seen as conditionable instrumental responses that are cued by maternal/caregiver expressions and shaped and maintained by the ensuing consequences (in the form of reinforcing or aversive stimulus events).

Thus, our thesis in this chapter is twofold: First, on the assumption that maternal facial emotional expressions initially have no (unconditioned) cue value when an infant references her mother's face and that the cue value of what appear to be intrinsically meaningful emotional expressions could have been conditioned via experiential learning, our thesis is that the effectiveness of the maternal expressions in cuing the infant's responses in uncertain contexts would depend on support from the pattern of experienced consequences contingent on the infant's behaviors cued, that is, the *predictive* function of social referencing. Among the relevant conditioning details are how consistently responsive the mother is in providing those cues, the degree of concordance between the cued responses and their consequences, the contextual variables involved such as the degree of object ambiguity, and the effectiveness of the consequences for the cued responses on which they are provided systematically contingent. In particular, infants are likely to reference (look at) the faces of adults who provide valid information cues about behavior consequences, and *not* to reference—or to discount—the facial (or vocal) cues of caregivers who provide invalid or inconsistent information about behavior consequences. Second, our thesis is that emotional components can be involved in the maternal facial cues (with or without verbalizations or gestures), but that emotions or affect are incidental and not a required feature of the social referencing process. That is, communication in the form of social referencing does not uniquely require facial emotional expressions for cues to function effectively in guiding infants' responses in ambiguous contexts. Therefore, it is thought that gestural-facial cues, that in no way can be considered to be emotional expressions (like originally meaningless expressions used in the study we report in this chapter), can serve the same predictive function for infant behavior in uncertain contexts as typically do maternal emotional facial, vocal, and/or gestural expressions.

The social referencing phenomenon has been classified in the literature (Feinman, 1982; Hornik & Gunnar, 1988) under two headings: *affective* social referencing refers to the infant's (unlearned) use of facial emotional expressions of others to determine how to feel about an ambiguous event (Campos, 1983; Klinnert, Campos, Sorce, Emde, & Svejda, 1983); *instrumental* social referencing involves the infant's use of cues from others' interpretations of events as indicators of how to act in the uncertain situation, or in the presence of strangers (Feinman, 1983; Feinman & Lewis, 1983). In our view, this distinction between affective and instrumental social referencing is artificial and misleading, as the two social referencing usages appear to be features/outcomes of the very same conditioning process. That is, at the same time as they convey affective components, the messages conveyed in emotional facial expressions also contain instrumental information, functioning as discriminative cues that can come to control instrumental infant behavior by predicting consequences for that behavior in such uncertain/unknown contexts. Thus, maternal affective expressions can come to be instrumental once they acquire distinct *cue value* for the infant's responses. In this frame, we consider the findings obtained via the experimental paradigm underlying the research reported in this chapter relevant to social referencing phenomena within the entire range, regardless of whether they are termed affective or instrumental.

In the section that follows, an experiment is reported and discussed (Gewirtz, Peláez-Nogueras, Díaz, & Villate, 1990). The experiment was mounted to evaluate the assumption that maternal affective expressive cues contingent on the infant social referencing response can acquire informational value as a result of operant conditioning, resulting from patterns of contingent consequences for infant responses cued by the maternal expressions in interaction in ambiguous settings during the first year. To this end, we explored whether or not originally meaningless (neutral) hand-to-face "facial expressions" could come to function as maternal cues for infant social referencing. One maternal hand-to-face "expression" was to predict for the infant that an approach to each of a series of ambiguous objects would lead to *positive* consequences, and a second hand-to-face "expression" was to predict for the infant that an approach to each of a series of ambiguous objects would lead to *aversive* consequences. The unfamiliar objects were made ambiguous by their being covered by a towel at the beginning of each of their presentations to the infant.

In discrimination-learning training, a stimulus (S+) that is correlated with positive contingencies (i.e., reinforcement) sets the occasion for responding, providing information about the availability of reinforcement for that responding. A stimulus (S−) that is correlated with aversive consequences cues nonresponding, providing information about the availability of aversive contingencies for responding. Once the subject responds differentially in the presence of S+ and S− (by an increase or decrease in frequency or in some other attribute of the response), the behavior is said to be under *discriminative control* (see Figure 1). Obtaining a differential rate of infant reaching-for-the-object responses following each of the two maternal hand-to-face "expressive" cues used in this study would evidence that social referencing, the maternal facial cues, and the ensuing approach or avoidance responses can result from a discrimination-learning process. In the section that follows, we report the study on the conditioning of maternal "expressive" cues that maintain the infant's reference-looking response and determine the infant's subsequent differential responding to each of a series of ambiguous events.

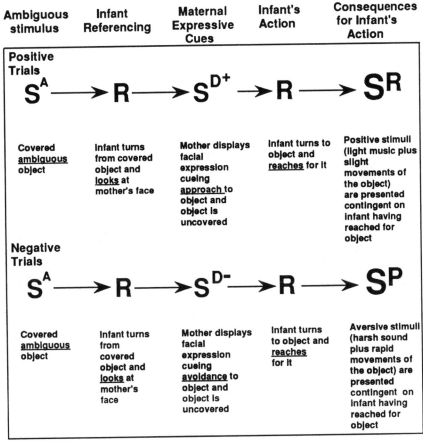

Figure 1. Elements of the social referencing paradigm underlying the experiment being reported. The diagram gives the sequential detail of the social referencing process. The terminal consequences of the positive and the negative trials support the elements and operation of the stimulus–response chains involved.

THE CONDITIONING OF MATERNAL "EXPRESSIVE" CUES FOR INFANT RESPONDING IN AMBIGUOUS CONTEXTS: A PARADIGMATIC EXPERIMENT

Method

As detailed in Gewirtz, Peláez-Nogueras, Diaz, and Villate (1990), the procedure of the experiment being presented and discussed in this chapter involved bringing 20 middle-class infant–mother pairs into the laboratory for 8 to 13 successive weekday training sessions. Mothers brought their infants to the laboratory daily, provided the infant was not ill and on its regular schedule. These normal, healthy infants included 12 males and 8 females, ranging in age from 9 to 12 months at the start of the experiment. The behavior of the mothers was under the earphone control of an experimenter observing both infant and mother on a split-screen TV monitor in an adjacent room. Mother–infant dyads were assigned randomly to one of two conditions, to counterbalance for the cue value of the particular positive and negative maternal facial cues used and to balance gender in each condition. Beginning in the second treatment session, each of the 20 infants was exposed concurrently (within the same treatment session) to both positive and negative maternal cues.

In the center of the laboratory stood a table on which there was a puppet theater. The infant subject sat in a booster chair attached to the table facing this puppet theater. Out of sight, next to the experimenter behind the puppet theater there were eight covered boxes, each containing a set of eight objects. A total of 64 objects were rotated across all sessions for all subjects. Objects were selected to be unfamiliar to infants of the developmental level of the subjects, and their unfamiliarity was confirmed with each infant's mother before the first session. At the beginning of a session, a mother was asked to choose a box number that had not been previously used with that infant (this cycle was repeated after the eighth session.) In random order during the eight trials of a session, eight objects were presented to the infant by an experimenter through the puppet theater. There were four positive and four negative trials per session (on the third and subsequent treatment sessions). At the beginning of every trial, the object presented was covered by a white cloth that was removed following the infant's turning back to the covered object after referencing (looking at) the mother's face (see Figure 2). By their being covered at the beginning of a trial, the objects were made ambiguous/unpredictable for the infant.

Maternal Cues, Infant Responses, Contingencies, and Sessions. Before the experiment began, mothers were trained to pose the two maternal facial-expressive cues that were later employed (see Figures 3 and 4). These two maternal response-provided cues (i.e., conditioned discriminative stimuli) denoted for the infant that either a pleasant or an aversive consequence would follow the infant's reaching for the ambiguous object. Between presentation of the cues, mothers maintained a natural but unexpressive face (no maternal vocal or gestural expressions-of-emotion cues were emitted to preclude confounding with the facial-expressive cues used in the experiment). For half the subjects, a palms-to-both-cheeks cue of the mother communicated a pleasant consequence for infant reaching (Figure 4), and a maternal fist-to-nose cue communicated an aversive consequence

Figure 2. The infant references its mother's face, in response to which the mother displays her facial expression. The covered ambiguous object is directly in front of the infant.

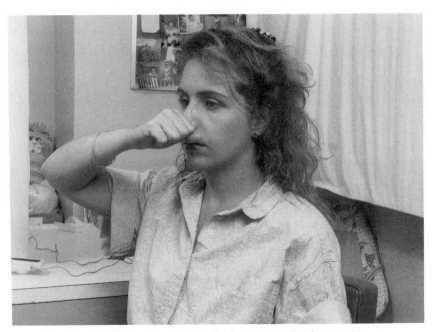

Figure 3. A mother displays the first-on-nose facial expression.

for infant reaching (Figure 3). For the other half of the subjects, a maternal fist-to-nose cue communicated a pleasant consequence for infant reaching, and a palms-to-both-cheeks cue communicated an aversive consequence for infant reaching. Thus, the valence of the cues (positive or negative) was counterbalanced between the two halves of the sample. Once the ambiguous (covered) object was introduced, the mother displayed one of these facial-expressive cues immediately after her infant turned to look directly at her face. When the infant turned back to look at the object, the object's cover had been removed and it was pushed forward into the radius of the infant's reach (about 10 inches from the infant's trunk). The dependent variable was the proportion of positive or negative trials of a session on which the infant reached for the ambiguous object (Figure 5).

For trials on which a maternal facial cue predicted a positive, pleasant consequence for infant reaching to the ambiguous object, the pleasant stimulus was provided by the activation, up to 3 seconds in duration, of a taped musical baby melody accompanied by four slow metronome-like movements of the uncovered object. For trials on which a maternal facial cue predicted an aversive consequence for infant reaching for the ambiguous object, the aversive stimulus was provided by the activation, up to .5

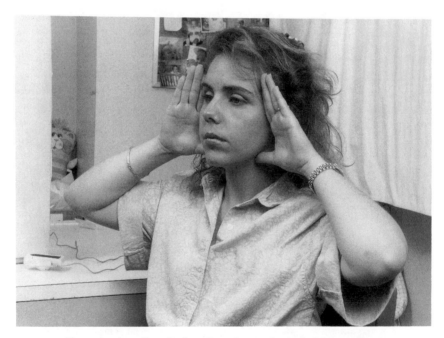

Figure 4. A mother displays the palms-to-cheeks facial expression.

Figure 5. After looking at the mother's face and registering the positive cue in the mother's facial expression, the infant turns to the formerly ambiguous object, now uncovered, and reaches for it.

second in duration, of one of three alternating stimuli (often heard around the home): a harsh door buzzer, a taped sound of a concrete drill, or a food blender. The loudness of these brief aversive sounds did not exceed 82 decibels at the source, some 2.5 feet from the infant. These three alternating sounds, accompanied by four rapid metronome-like movements of the uncovered object, were aversive insofar as they would subsequently be found to be effective in inhibiting infant reaching responses. (Although mothers were consulted routinely on the qualities of the positive and the aversive events, not once did a mother complain that a stimulus intended to be positive or aversive was inappropriate or too harsh for her baby.)

Order of Trials for Cues–Consequences.   After the second treatment session, on four of the eight session trials following the mother's positive cue to the infant's referencing response, positive consequences were provided contingent on the infant's reaching for the object. On the other four interspersed trials, following the mother's aversive cue to the infant's referencing response, aversive consequences were presented contingent on the infant's reaching for the object. The conditioning treatment sessions continued for subjects until a predetermined joint reaching-response criterion was attained, determining the final treatment session.

That joint response criterion was that more than 75% of the positive-cue trials, and less than 25% of the negative-cue trials, included infant reaching responses. The range of total number of daily conditioning sessions for this responding criterion to be attained by all 20 subjects was 6 to 12, with a median of 6.5.

In order to minimize the possibility that infants would break down crying and/or that they or their mothers would refuse to continue as subjects, due to the everyday aversive consequences, a sliding scale of increase in the number of aversive trials across sessions was implemented: the proportion of aversive trials was .00 on the first treatment session (day), .25 on the second treatment session, and .50 on all subsequent weekday sessions until the joint response criterion was attained. In an eight-trial session, the order of positive- and aversive-cue consequence trials was random, with the constraint implemented that an aversive-consequence trial was never the first in a session, and that no more than two successive aversive trials occurred. (In retrospect, this procedure, implemented to insure that the infant subjects would continue participating across all trials in a session, was too cautious.)

The Training Procedure

Mothers sat 2 feet to their infant's right, slightly behind the infant and away from the puppet theater, in order to insure the salience of the social referencing response, during which the infant had to turn her head and make eye contact with the mother. Hidden behind the puppet theater, Experimenter A, on each trial, manipulated the ambiguous object (i.e., pushed it forward outside the infant's reach before the infant reference-glanced, and then, after the look, uncovered it and pushed it within the infant's reach) and, as programmed, presented either the positive or the negative stimulus consequence (the independent variable) contingent upon the infant's postreferencing response of reaching for the object (the basis of the dependent variable). From the adjacent room, Experimenter B observed the mother–infant interaction while instructing the mother (via earphones) on how and when to present her facial-expressive cues contingent on her infant's referencing response. Experimenter B also instructed Experimenter A on when to present the positive or aversive stimulus consequence contingent on the infant reaching for the ambiguous object, and on when to initiate and terminate each trial. There was a 5-minute period of acclimatization to the laboratory at the beginning of each daily eight-trial session, and a 10-second intertrial interval.

Shaping and Prompting.   The looking-to-mother's-face referencing response was emitted at the start by all but two of the infant subjects. At the beginning of the training, when these two infants failed to exhibit a social referencing response within 55 seconds from the presentation of the ambiguous stimulus, the mother was asked to move an additional two feet away from her infant and/or to clap her hands, to prompt the infant's response of turning to, and looking at, her face. This prompting procedure succeeded rapidly in generating the referencing of mother's face in these two infants, and the prompts were rapidly terminated by a fading process.

Further, in case an infant did not exhibit a full reaching response to the object following the positive maternal cue, starting with the first treatment session (Session 2), the reaching response was modeled by the infant's mother and shaped by use of a *successive-approximations* technique, making the positive musical sound—the reinforcing stimulus—contingent on component arm movements toward the object that approximated successively the responses of reaching and touching the object. In addition, during the first three treatment (i.e., training) sessions, when an infant turned to reference its mother's face, the mother responded with a hand-to-face cue that was accompanied by a brief prompt (either a ⅓-second pleasant musical sound on a positive-consequence trial or a ⅓-second harsh sound on an aversive-consequence trial) that was a sample of the positive or aversive consequences being employed in the study. To preclude the possibility of elicitation or Pavlovian conditioning effects, these very brief prompts were implemented as a transitory discriminative stimulus (S^D) to facilitate the initiation of the training procedure and were faded out rapidly. All contingency prompts were faded out by the end of the third treatment session.

Immediately after the infant turned back from referencing the mother's face to look again at the ambiguous object, Experimenter A behind the theater removed the white cloth, leaving the object uncovered, and quietly propelled it forward to be within the infant's reach. If the infant responded by reaching for the object, Experimenter A immediately presented either the positive or the aversive stimulus. If the infant did *not* reach for the object within 10 seconds, that object was moved back out of the infant's reach but still in view, until the infant looked again toward the mother's face. That procedure was repeated for each of the eight trials of a session. Each trial lasted between 45 and 55 seconds.

Pretreatment Assessment.   A baseline was taken in the first eight-trial session for every infant subject. On four interspersed trials, a positive maternal facial cue was contingent upon the referencing response, but if there was subsequent reaching, that reaching was followed by no consequence at all. On the remaining four trials, a negative maternal facial cue was contingent upon the referencing response, but the ensuing reaching (if it occurred) was followed by no consequence at all. These two sets of four interspersed trials each generated two baseline scores for statistical comparison with last-treatment session scores. There were two subgroups due to the counterbalancing of the maternal cues.

Reliability of Observation.   To determine behavior-unit reliability, three pairs of observers independently scored the reaching responses of eight infants (40% of the subject sample) from videotape records, for all trials during those infants' entire experience as subjects. In all, 477 trials in 79 sessions were involved. Overall agreement on the number of reaching responses was 89%. The outcome measures in a trial was whether or not the infant reached for the ambiguous object after turning back from referencing the mother's facial expression in the ambiguous object's presence. The two outcome measures, for the baseline and the last treatment session, were the percentage of trials on which the infant reached for an ambiguous object following the positive maternal cue and the negative maternal cue.

Results and Implications

For within-subjects analyses of the data, Wilcoxon signed-rank non-parametric tests were used with the scores on the percentage of trials on which the infant reached for an ambiguous object following a positive maternal cue and separately following a negative maternal cue. Contrasts within infants were made for percentage reaching scores, separately for the positive and for the negative cues, between the pretreatment (baseline) session and the last treatment session (defined as the session during which there was attained the joint reaching-response criterion for the positive and for the negative cues). In addition, for the final treatment session an evaluation was made of the difference in median percentage reaching scores to positive compared to negative maternal cues. The scores of the total sample (N = 20) were used for the analysis of the data under the counterbalanced design, as between-group Mann-Whitney U tests yielded no reliable differences in reaching between the two different hand-to-face cue subgroups (fist-to-nose vs. palms-to-cheeks) that predicted the same consequences, either for the positive or the aversive consequence, or between the two gender groups under either positive or aversive consequences.

The Wilcoxon signed-rank tests comparing matched-distribution medians within subjects show that:

1. During the pretreatment baseline session, no reliable difference (p = .824, 2 tails) within infants was found on the median of reaching scores between the condition where infants' referencing looks were followed by positive cues with subsequent reaching followed

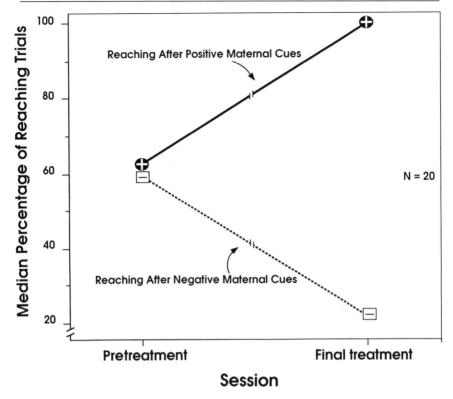

Figure 6. Median percentage reaching for ambiguous objects by 20 infants, after maternal expressive-response cues to infant referencing (of mother's face), under the two cue-and-consequence treatments: after the positive maternal cue (upper line), when reaching for the ambiguous object led to positive consequences, and after the negative maternal cue (lower line), when reaching for the ambiguous object led to aversive consequences.

by no consequence, and the condition where referencing looks were followed by the to-be-negative cues with subsequent reaching followed by no consequence. Figure 6 shows that the medians of infant reaching appeared essentially identical in the baseline session.

2. Within infants, the median percentage reaching scores after positive maternal cues were contingent upon the referencing looks with positive consequences contingent upon the subsequent reaching was reliably higher ($p = .0039$, 1 tail) during the final treatment session compared to the pretreatment baseline session.

3. Within infants, the median percentage reaching scores was reliably lower ($p = .0154$, 1 tail) for referencing looks upon which the negative maternal facial cues were contingent with *aversive* consequenc-

es contingent upon the subsequent reaching during the *final* treatment session, compared to the pretreatment/baseline session.
4. As would be expected from the preceding within-infants result patterns, a within-groups comparison showed that in the final treatment session the median of percentage reaching scores was reliably higher (p = .0001, 1 tail) in the condition where positive maternal facial cues were contingent upon infant referencing looks with positive consequences contingent upon subsequent reaching, compared to the condition where negative maternal facial cues were contingent upon social referencing looks with negative/aversive consequences contingent upon infant reaching.
5. The pattern of change in scores between pretreatment baseline and final session reflects discrimination learning by the infants. In the final session, differential rates of reaching by the infants were obtained after positive and negative maternal cues earlier had been differentially contingent upon the infant referencing response. Thus, every one of the 20 infant subjects reached for the ambiguous object after positive maternal cues were displayed contingent upon the infants' referencing the mother's face, and they did not reach for that object after negative maternal cues were provided contingent upon the infants' referencing responses.

DISCUSSION

Our basic assumption is that, very early in ontological development, experiential learning processes effected by systematic environmental cue and contingency stimulation can influence cued-response patterns of infants, patterns that might appear unconditioned to those unfamiliar with the behavior or its experiential history. In keeping with this assumption, it has been demonstrated in our paradigmatic experiment that infant reaching responses to ambiguous objects in contexts of uncertainty can be conditioned readily to originally meaningless facial cues presented by the mother following infant reference looking, on the basis of the stimulus contingencies that followed those cued infant reaching responses. In this way, this pattern of communicative interaction between the mother or caregiver and the child was shaped and maintained. Further, the results support our assumption that the maternal expressions that can operate in this manner to cue infant responses in uncertain contexts need not be limited to affective emotional information (such as fearful or joyful facial expressions of the mother) or to verbal information (that tells the infant how to behave or cope with the situation) or gestural information, to influence the infant's behavior in those uncertain contexts.

Until now, the literature has provided *no* process theory explanation of the mechanism underlying the infant social referencing phenomenon. Even so, we have noted nativist assertions in the literature to the effect that the human infant is prewired to reference and understand the message conveyed in its mother's facial emotional expressions on an unlearned basis, in order to disambiguate a context and regulate its behavior there. The results from our research support the notion that, rather than being an unlearned pattern, social referencing can emerge from a pattern of every-day learning experiences generated by contingencies in the interactions of the infant with its caregiver in ambiguous contexts. We have demonstrated that, in contexts of ambiguity or uncertainty, through a process of operant learning, two originally meaningless (neutral) maternal facial expressions can come to denote opposite consequences for infant reaching responses: one maternal hand-to-face "expression" came to predict for the infants *positive* auditory-kinetic consequences of their reaching for each of a series of ambiguous stimulus objects placed in front of them, and a second hand-to-face "expression" came to predict *aversive* consequences of their reaching for each of the remaining half of the series of ambiguous objects.

The differential conditioning procedure resulted in every one of the twenty 9- to 12-month-old infant subjects showing that they were, in the same way, influenced to responded differentially by the two distinct maternal facial-expressive cues. Infants in this experiment thus demonstrated having learned which maternal hand-to-face cue denoted which conse-quence, since they came reliably to reach for ambiguous objects after the maternal cue denoting positive consequences, and reliably to avoid objects after the maternal cue denoting negative consequences, before those con-tingent consequences were implemented on each new trial. The infant responses were based on the information communicated solely by their mothers' "facial expressions," without vocal or other affective cues being involved.

The results presented cannot rule out definitively the possibility that the infant is "prewired" to understand, in uncertain contexts, uncondi-tioned cues for its behavior from maternal facial expressions. To rule in or out the possibility that infants would respond on an unlearned basis to the maternal affective cues in emotional communication, research would be required at earlier points in the infant's life on the origins of the social referencing process and of the consequences of the action cued by the maternal emotional expressions (Peláez-Nogueras & Gewirtz, in prepara-tion). Even so, the results reported herein lend support to the notion that emotional or affective communication involving facial expressions in the visual modality does not differ from communication involving stimulation in any other modality–auditory, kinesthetic, etc. In the main, the phenom-enon of social referencing has been identified in studies with infants around one year of age. In other research, typically in seminatural settings, maternal facial and vocal emotional stimuli were often confounded, to obscure the role of each modality of maternal affective stimulation in the social referencing communication process (see, e.g., Bradshaw, Goldsmith, & Campos, 1987).

Our experimental tactic was to employ as stimulus cues that were originally meaningless maternal expressions. Even so, the infant subjects learned very efficiently the predictive value of these cues structured for them in the laboratory setting. This may suggest that the biologically meaningful maternal facial emotional cues are not acquired in a different manner by the infant. What has been shown in the research reported is that the valences of the cues maintaining social referencing responses can be trained in infants starting at 9 months of age, around the age when the social referencing process ordinarily appears "naturally." This work lends support to the notion that some portion of the social referencing process, if not all of it, is an outcome of the learning resulting from the commerce between mother and infant in the routine circumstances of everyday interactions.

Social Referencing and Infant Attachment

A corollary of our findings is that if, following the social referencing response, cued infant responses can be conditioned by their consequences on an operant basis, they can constitute one index among numerous potential ones of *attachment* under the social conditioning approach (Gewirtz, 1972a, 1972b, 1976, 1991; Gewirtz & Peláez-Nogueras, 1991). In this respect, the social referencing conception can be related to the conception of attachment. Under the social conditioning approach to attachment, instances of control of infant responses by stimulus cues provided by a caregiver's appearance or behavior have been conceived to be indices of infant-to-caregiver attachment.

It has been noted in the social conditioning approach that infant attachment could be seen as a *metaphor* for diverse infant discriminated operants being under maternal-stimulus control (Gewirtz & Peláez-Nogueras, 1991). In this context, the three conditioned events—infant social referencing, the maternal expressive-behavior cue, and the infant's ensuing approach or avoidance response in ambiguous contexts (like those trained in the experiment reported in this chapter)—may be prototypical behaviors learned during socialization that represent that pattern of infant responses cued by the mother or another attached figure and reinforced by contingent stimuli provided in those contexts. On this basis, in the first 9 to 12 months of life, infant referencing of the mother's facial expressions in ambiguous contexts can serve as one representative index of mother–

infant attachment. This is because the referencing process reflects control of the infant's referencing glances and ensuing responses by maternal response-produced stimuli.

CONCLUSION

The extent to which an infant turns to search its mother's face for expressive cues in contexts of uncertainty very likely depends on past success in obtaining such information, its validity, and its utility. That is, to become functional, maternal cues must be consistently contingent on infant referencing behavior and predict reliably the environmental consequences of the ensuing infant's approach or avoidance in the ambiguous contexts. This pattern will result in strengthening, or at least in maintenance, of the infant referencing pattern and the maternally cued responses, as well as in a reduction in referencing-response latencies. In contrast, it is expected that mothers who are unresponsive, or respond with delays, noncontingently, or inaccurately to their infants' soliciting information via referencing, would rear babies who reference their mother's facial expressions infrequently, if at all. These babies would not rely at all on their mothers for critical information about the world.

In a laboratory setting, it has been demonstrated that the operant-conditioning paradigm can account readily for the acquisition of cue value by maternal facial expressions that are provided (displayed) contingent upon the infant looking to the mother's face for information in an ambiguous context—the social referencing response. It is our assumption that a paradigm like the one employed in the design of this experiment is the basis for infant social referencing in the range of life settings. Even so, that assumption poses a question that awaits empirical validation.

REFERENCES

Bradshaw, D. L., Goldsmith, H. H., & Campos, J. J. (1987). Attachment, temperament, and social referencing: Interrelationships among three domains of infant affective behavior. *Infant Behavior and Development, 10,* 223–231.

Campos, J. J. (1983). The importance of affective communication in social referencing: A commentary on Feinman. *Merrill-Palmer Quarterly, 29,* 83–87.

Campos, J. J., Barrett, K. C., Lamb, M. E., Goldsmith, H. H., & Stenberg, C. (1983). Socioemotional development. In M. M. Haith & J. J. Campos (Eds.), *Handbook of child psychology: Vol. 2. Infancy and developmental psychobiology* (pp. 783–916). New York: Wiley.

Campos, J. J., & Stenberg, C. (1981). Perception, appraisal, and emotion: The onset of social referencing. In M. E. Lamb & L. R. Sherrod (Eds.), *Infant social cognition* (pp. 273–314). Hillsdale, NJ: Erlbaum.

DeCasper, A. J., & Spence, M. J. (1986). Prenatal maternal speech influences newborns' perception of speech sounds. *Infant Behavior and Development, 9,* 133–150.

Fantino, E., & Logan, C. A. (1979). *The experimental analysis of behavior: A biological perspective.* San Francisco: W. H. Freeman.

Feinman, S. (1982). Social referencing in infancy. *Merrill-Palmer Quarterly, 28,* 445–470.

Feinman, S. (1983). How does baby socially refer? Two views of social referencing: A reply to Campos. *Merrill-Palmer Quarterly, 29,* 467–471.

Feinman, S. (1985). Emotional expressions, social referencing and preparedness for learning in infancy: Mother knows best–but sometimes I know better. In G. Zivin (Ed.), *The development of expressive behavior: Biology–environment interactions* (pp. 291–318). New York: Academic Press.

Feinman, S., & Lewis, M. (1983). Social referencing at ten months: A second-order effect on infants' responses to strangers. *Child Development, 54,* 878–887.

Gewirtz, J. L. (1972a). Attachment, dependence, and a distinction in terms of stimulus control. In J. L. Gewirtz (Ed.), *Attachment and dependency* (pp. 179–215). Washington, DC: Winston.

Gewirtz, J. L. (1972b). On the selection and use of attachment and dependence indices. In J. L. Gewirtz (Ed.), *Attachment and dependency* (pp. 179–215). Washington, DC: Winston.

Gewirtz, J. L. (1976). The attachment acquisition process as evidenced in the maternal conditioning of cued infant responding (particularly crying). *Human Development, 19,* 143–155.

Gewirtz, J. L. (1991). Social influence on child and parent behavior via stimulation and operant-learning mechanisms. In M. Lewis & S. Feinman (Eds.), *Social influences and socialization in infancy* (pp. 137–163). New York: Plenum.

Gewirtz, J. L., & Peláez-Nogueras, M. (1991). The attachment metaphor and the conditioning of infant separation protests. In J. L. Gewirtz & W. M. Kurtines (Eds.), *Intersections with attachment* (pp. 123–144). Hillsdale, NJ: Erlbaum.

Gewirtz, J. L., Peláez-Nogueras, M., Díaz, L., & Villate, M. (1990, August). Infant social referencing as an instrumental conditioned process. Paper presented at the annual meeting of the American Psychological Association, Boston, MA.

Gottlieb, G. (1971). *Development of species identification in birds: An inquiry into the prenatal determinants of perception.* Chicago: The University of Chicago Press.

Gottlieb, G. (1973). Neglected developmental variables in the study of species identification in birds. *Psychological Bulletin, 79,* 362–372.

Gunnar, M. R., & Stone, C. (1984). The effects of positive maternal affect on infant responses to pleasant, ambiguous and fear-provoking toys. *Child Development, 55,* 1231–1236.

Hess, E. H. (1973). *Imprinting: Early experience and the developmental psychobiology of attachment.* New York: Van Nostrand.

Hess, E. H., & Petrovich, S. B. (1973). In J. R. Nesselroade & H. W. Reese (Eds.), *Life-span developmental psychology: Methodological issues* (pp. 25–42). New York: Academic Press.

Hornik, R., & Gunnar, M. (1988). A descriptive analysis of infant social referencing. *Child Development, 59,* 626–634.

Kenney, M. D., Mason, W. A., & Hill, S. D. (1979). Effects of age, objects, and visual experience on affective responses of Rhesus monkeys to strangers. *Developmental Psychology, 15,* 176–184.

Klinnert, M. D., Campos, J. J., Sorce, J. F., Emde, R. N., & Svejda, M. (1983). Emotions as behavior regulators: social referencing in infancy. In R. Plutchik & H. Kellerman (Eds.), *The emotions* (Vol. 2, pp. 57–86). New York: Academic Press.

Klinnert, M. D., Emde, R. N., Butterfield, P., & Campos, J. J. (1986). Social referencing: The infant's use of emotional signals from a friendly adult with mother present. *Developmental Psychology, 22,* 427–432.

Ling, B-C. (1941). Form discrimination as a learning cue in infants. *Comparative Psychology Monograph, 17*, No. 2.

Mendelson, M. J., Haith, M. M., Goldman-Rakic, P. S. (1982). Face scanning and responsiveness to social cues in infant Rhesus monkeys. *Developmental Psychology, 18*, 222–228.

Munn, N. L. (1965). *The evolution and growth of human behavior* (2nd Ed.). New York: Houghton Mifflin.

Peláez-Nogueras, M., & Gewirtz, J. L. (1990, May). *Discrimination training of infant protests.* Paper presented at the Annual Convention of The Association for Behavior Analysis: International (ABA), Nashville, TN.

Peláez-Nogueras, M. (1992). Infants learning to reference maternal emotional cues. Unpublished doctoral dissertation, Florida International University, Miami, Florida.

Petrovich, S. B., & Gewirtz, J. L. (1984). Learning in the context of evolutionary biology: In search of synthesis. *The Behavioral and Brain Sciences, 7*, 160–161.

Petrovich, S. B., & Gewirtz, J. L. (1985). The attachment learning process and its relation to cultural and biological evolution: Proximate and ultimate considerations. In M. Reite & T. Field (Eds.), *The psychobiology of attachment and separation* (pp. 257–289). New York: Academic Press.

Petrovich, S. B., & Gewirtz, J. L. (1991). Imprinting and attachment: Proximate and ultimate considerations. In J. L. Gewirtz & W. M. Kurtines (Eds.), *Intersections with attachment* (pp. 69–93). Hillsdale, NJ: Erlbaum.

Sackett, G. P. (1966). Monkeys reared in isolation with pictures as visual input: Evidence for an innate releasing mechanism. *Science, 154*, 1468–1473.

Simmons, M. W., & Lipsitt, L. P. (1961). An operant discrimination apparatus for infants. *Journal of Experimental Analysis of Behavior, 4*, 233–235.

Siqueland, E. R., & Lipsitt, L. P. (1966). Conditioned head-turning in human newborns. *Journal of Experimental Child Psychology, 3*, 356–376.

Staples, R. (1932). The responses of infants to color. *Journal of Experimental Psychology, 15*, 119–141.

Walden, T. A., & Ogan, T. A. (1988). The development of social referencing. *Child Development, 59*, 1230–1240.

Zarbatany, L., & Lamb, M. E. (1985). Social referencing as a function of information source: Mothers versus strangers. *Infant Behavior and Development, 8*, 25–33.

8

Social Cognitive Theory of Social Referencing

Albert Bandura

Effective functioning rests, in part, on the ability to predict the likely effects of different events and actions and to regulate one's behavior accordingly. Without such anticipatory capabilities, people would be forced to act blindly in ways that often are fruitless, if not injurious. Information about the outcomes likely to flow from different events and actions is conveyed by environmental predictors. One can be informed about what to expect by the distinctive features of places, persons, and things, by social signals in the words, affective expressions, and actions of others, and by functional rules that codify observed regularities.

In the earliest period of child development, environmental events, except those that are inherently aversive or attractive, exert no influence on affect or action. However, predictive signals are not treated indifferently for long. Through direct and vicarious experiences, children quickly gain increasing knowledge about which events have predictive value for guiding their actions in the transactions of everyday life. Most of the research conducted within the framework of social referencing concerns the predictive and regulatory function of the affective expressions of others.

In social referencing, one uses the manifest appraisal of another in-

ALBERT BANDURA • Department of Psychology, Stanford University, Stanford, CA 94305.

Social Referencing and the Social Construction of Reality in Infancy, edited by Saul Feinman. Plenum Press, New York, 1992.

dividual to comprehend ambiguous situations and to guide one's own actions. Although writers agree that social referencing involves social mediation of appraisal, they differ in how they view the scope of the phenomenon. Campos (1983) restricts social referencing mainly to situations where people use the affective expressions of others to know what to feel and how to behave. Feinman (1982, 1985) regards social referencing as a broader social influence process where human thought, affect, and action are modified by the actions and judgments of others as well as by their affective displays. An expanded scope increases the social import of the phenomenon. But a multifaceted conception of social referencing also poses some difficulties of analysis if it encompasses virtually every mode of social influence and type of psychosocial effect. In a wide-reaching conception, social referencing either means different things to different people, depending on which facets they emphasize, or it becomes indistinct in its meaning if multifold facets are embraced. However, the research on this topic has been more demarcated than the conceptions, in that almost all the studies are confined to the effects of affective social signaling. The present chapter, therefore, addresses the mechanisms governing the different functions of affective modeling.

Research on affective social referencing documents that infants use adult facial signals of emotion as a source of information in appraising unfamiliar people and things in ambiguous situations (Feinman, 1982; Klinnert, Campos, Sorce, Emde, & Svejda, 1983; Klinnert, Emde, Butterfield, & Campos, 1986). They then guide their actions on the basis of such information. For example, infants will cross the visual illusion of a table edge that does not look too scary when the mother mimics smiles, but halt their crawl if she mimics fear or anger. Infants similarly look to their mothers' emotional expressions when deciding whether to approach unfamiliar toys and strangers or to stay clear of them. Smiles encourage contact, fearful displays are read as warning for avoidance. However, when situations are clearly designated as safe or as dangerous by nonsocial cues (Sorce, Emde, Campos, & Klinnert, 1985), or by the nature of the objects themselves (Gunnar & Stone, 1984), affective signals are largely disregarded as guides for action. Such findings reveal that it is the predictive value of affective signals under conditions of uncertainty, rather than innate signal value, that seems important.

Although social referencing has been amply documented, the findings are by no means unequivocal. The results of studies are not always consistent on the signaling efficacy of different types of affective expressions, their directional effects on action, and whether they exert any influence on action in the presence of conflicting nonsocial cues of safety or danger (Gunnar & Stone, 1984; Hornik, Risenhoover, & Gunnar, 1987; Walden & Ogan, 1988). Social referencing is a multifaceted influence that can produce effects through a variety of mechanisms depending on the particular aspects of affective modeling that happen to be highlighted in any given instance. Specification of alternative mechanisms can help to explain some of the variability of effects.

Interactional Conception of Signaling Power

Signaling power does not reside as a fixed property in situational events. It is a relational property that depends on personal capabilities as well as on external factors. For example, judging the likelihood of painful happenings does not rely solely on reading external signs of danger or safety. Rather, it involves an interactional relation between personal coping capabilities and potentially hurtful aspects of the environment. A potentially aversive event will be judged as relatively safe by people with high perceived controlling efficacy but as hazardous by those who believe they cannot exercise control. Those who judge themselves as lacking controlling efficacy, whether the self-appraisal is objectively warranted or not, will perceive all kinds of dangers in situations and invest external events with high signaling value. If perceived controlling efficacy is enhanced, external signs of potential danger lose their signaling power (Bandura, 1986). To understand fully people's judgment of external events, it is, therefore, necessary to analyze their perceptions of their own controlling efficacy, which affect how realities are personally constructed. Research to be reviewed later on perceived self-efficacy underscores the need for an interactional model of social referencing.

Developmental analyses of social referencing tend to emphasize growth of perceptual skills in discriminating emotional expressions. Such research advances understanding of one aspect of the process. Unless children can recognize and differentiate positive and negative affective signals they cannot be affected by them. Perceptual development occurs rapidly so it does not take infants long to acquire the capability to distinguish the affective features of different emotional expressions (Klinnert *et al.*, 1983). However, perceptual differentiation is necessary but insufficient for affective social guidance. Unless emotional expressions have become invested with meaning and predictive value, simply noticing them is unlikely to have much impact on behavior. Children require correlated experiences that endow affective signals with predictive value. Through relational social learning, the smiles of people who have proven dependable can signify safety, while their fears forebode danger. Infants are therefore more inclined to use their mothers' happy or fearful expressions in interpreting unusual events than the same facial signals by strangers (Zarbatany & Lamb, 1985). The important issues center on how experiences must be socially structured to impart predictive information, and how that information is cognitively processed to confer predictive value on affective signals. Social and cognitive factors are accorded a central role in the social cognitive theory of social referencing (Bandura, 1986).

Multiple Functions of Affective Modeling

Affective modeling is the major vehicle for conveying information in the process of social referencing. Significant progress has been made in our understanding of how modeled affectivity influences the psychosocial functioning of others. Modeling of affective reactions can serve four separable functions that should be distinguished in efforts to clarify the determinants and mechanisms of social referencing. First, a model's affective expressions can activate emotional arousal in observers. This is designated as the *vicarious arousal function.*

If the affective reactions of models only aroused observers fleetingly, it would be of some interest as far as momentary communication is concerned, but of limited psychological import. Thus, if modeled affectivity got children to avoid a threat, but they learned nothing from that referencing experience, they would require the presence of an emoting model to tell them how to behave in every future encounter with the same threat. What gives significance to vicarious influence is that observers can acquire lasting ideational, affective, and behavioral proclivities toward persons, places, or things that have been associated with the model's emotional experiences. Thus, observers learn to fear the things that frightened models, to dislike what repulsed them, and to like what gratified them. This is the *vicarious acquisition function* of affective modeling. Acquisition is reflected in altered appraisals of, and reactions toward, previously referenced events in the absence of signaling models. Research conducted within the social cognitive framework has begun to delineate the conditions under which affective modeling fosters enduring appraisals of events.

The emotional reactions of models convey predictive information for regulating action as well as arouse emotions and create emotional proclivities in observers. If happy modeled expressions foretell positive response outcomes for observers, whereas angry or frightened ones forebode aversive outcomes, then the affective displays of models can be used by observers as highly informative guides for action. The *predictive regulatory function* of affective modeling operates principally through the cognitive mechanism of forethought. That is, actions are regulated anticipatorily by beliefs about the effects they are likely to have under given circumstances.

In the social referencing situations of everyday life, models do not merely emit facial expressions but otherwise remain impassive. Rather, they usually display their emotional reactions in transactions with the environment. They express the joys of success, the despondency of failure, the anger of thwarting, and the fear of inefficacy to exercise control over potential threats. The conjoint modeling of affective reactions and coping capabilities conveys information that can alter observers' judgments of their own personal efficacy and the formidableness of environmental demands (Bandura, 1982, 1986). Self-percepts of efficacy play a central role in the exercise of human agency. People's judgments of their personal efficacy influence what course of action they choose to pursue, how much effort they will mobilize in an endeavor, how long they will persevere in the face of difficulties, whether their thought patterns are self-hindering or self-aiding, and their emotional reactions in taxing or threatening situations (Bandura, 1986). The *self-efficacy and controllability function* can therefore have widespread impact on psychosocial functioning.

Theorizing and research on social referencing has focused extensively on how adults' emotive signals affect infants. However, neither the phenomenon nor the governing mechanisms are confined to early childhood years. People of all ages are stirred and guided by the emotional experiences of others. Affective modeling creates and alters emotional and evaluative proclivities in adults and children alike. Outcomes are usually determined by a multiplicity of interacting influences so that a given factor is associated with outcomes probabilistically rather than inevitably. Environments present causal uncertainties to people at all ages. In guiding their actions in uncertain situations, adults regularly draw on modeled predictive information as do children. Because each period of development brings with it new challenges, the self-efficacy and controllability function of coping modeling similarly impinges on most domains of functioning throughout the lifespan.

VICARIOUS ACTIVATION

Vicarious Activation and Expressive Cues

Observers are easily aroused by the emotional expressions of others. Vicarious activation is reflected in heightened autonomic reactivity and release of brain chemicals that serve as neurotransmitters (Berger, 1962; Welch & Welch, 1968). This capacity for vicarious arousal is of interest in its own right. However, it also plays a vital role in the development and modification of emotional proclivities.

Models communicate affective information partly through facial, vocal, and gestural cues. It is these observable expressions that serve as indicators and vicarious arousers of emotion (Izard, 1971). However, older children and adults use a broader range of emotive indicators. Indeed, when observers are exposed to verbal, vocal, and body expressions during social transactions, they read emotions more accurately from what the performers say and how they say it than from their facial expressions and gestures (Krauss, Apple, Morency, Wenzel, & Winton, 1981). However, the relative informativeness of verbal, vocal, and motoric indicants of affect can change substantially depending on social customs and sanctions which designate the appropriate mode of expression under particular circumstances.

Synchronous arousal in observers and models does not necessarily reflect vicarious activation. A nonsocial cue that has general signal value can directly activate emotional reactions in different individuals. When people become fearful upon hearing a fire alarm, they may be reacting similarly, but independently, to the same nonsocial alarm cue. However, assessing causal contributors to arousal is no easy task, because the activating power of even nonsocial instigators can be greatly augmented or diminished by how others react. The same fire alarm is substantially more emotionally arousing if others react with panic than if they respond calmly or ignore it altogether. Vicarious activation is most convincingly demonstrated when the model's affective expressions are the sole instigators of the observers' emotional reactions. This condition obtains when the situational events that arouse the model are either unobservable by, or neutral for, observers.

In social referencing situations observers' emotional arousal is determined by situational instigators as well as by modeled affective reactions. Observers must therefore integrate information from several sources. Even the meaning of modeled affective expressions can be significantly altered by what observers see as the situational instigators and how they interpret them. The relative weight given to expressive and contextual information in regulating affective arousal and actions depends on the clarity and predictive significance of the information. We return later to this issue of multiple predictors.

Cognitive Mediation of Vicarious Arousal

Vicarious arousal in infants depends mainly on the salient information conveyed by modeled affective expressions. Growth of knowledge and cognitive-processing capabilities confer increasing significance on contextual sources of information. As a result, modeled affectivity produces vicarious arousal largely through cognitive mediation. The same affective expression may thus take on different meanings in different social contexts and under different cognitive sets. Gestures of pain are vicariously arousing if observers know beforehand that models will undergo hurtful experiences, but the same gestures without the foreknowledge have little emotional impact (Craig & Lowery, 1969). The interpretations placed on environmental events similarly affect vicarious arousal. Seeing a filmed brutal fight elicits stronger autonomic reactions in observers if they look upon it as a vengeful or intentional beating than as a fictional enactment (Geen & Rakosky, 1973). In a series of experiments, Lazarus and his associates (Lazarus, Speisman, Mordkoff, & Davison, 1962) found that a filmed portrayal of a child undergoing a painful physical procedure generated less vicarious arousal when accompanied by commentaries minimizing the aversiveness of the procedure than when the commentary mentioned the suffering and hazards of the procedure.

One of the earliest developmental studies of vicarious arousal provides information on how experience and cognitive capabilities that come with age affect the social activation of emotion (Dysinger & Ruckmick, 1933). Movie scenes of danger and tragedy elicited the greatest physiological reactions in young children, but emotional reactions decreased progressively with increasing age. The authors explain the inverse relationship in terms of the greater ability of older children to distinguish fantasy from reality and to attenuate distress by forecasting eventual favorable outcomes. This interpretation receives support in a developmental analysis of children's cognitive strategies for coping with televised threats (Wilson, Hoffner, & Cantor, 1987). Compared to younger children, older children were more disposed to reduce their fear reactions by telling themselves the modeled threats were not real.

Vicarious Arousal and Predictive Relations

Learning experiences largely determine whether observers will be roused or unmoved by the emotional expressions of others. Expressive displays most likely acquire arousing capacity through correlated social experiences. That is, when individuals are in good spirits they treat others amiably, which produces positive affect. As a result of such occurrences, smiles and other expressions of happiness come to signify a positive state of affairs. Conversely, when individuals are dejected, ailing, distressed, or angry, the people around them are likely to suffer in one way or another. Expressive signs of anger or despondency forebode aversive experiences.

Research varying the degree of social conjointedness underscores the importance of correlated experience in development of the capability for vicarious arousal. Church (1959) found that cries of pain by an animal evoked strong emotional arousal in animals who had suffered pain together; the cries had less impact on animals who had undergone equally painful experiences always separately; but cries of pain left unmoved, animals who had never been subjected to painful treatment. That sensitivity to expressive displays grows out of social learning experiences receives further support from Miller, Caul, and Mirsky (1967). They found that monkeys reared in total social isolation during their infancy were unresponsive, either behaviorally or physiologically, to the facial expressions of emotion by other monkeys. Thus, even primates require correlative experiences to develop vicarious affective responsivity. Sackett (1966) similarly found no innate fear response to fear displays in monkeys reared under conditions where they had no visual access to, but could hear, other monkeys. They remained just as unresponsive to pictures of monkeys expressing fear as to pictures of monkeys in a neutral state. Threat displays left them unmoved for the first 2 months but later had a nonspecific effect, increasing all kinds of behavior including play and exploration as well as disturbance. There is little in the above research to support the strong inborn programming view that affective expressions are innate vicarious instigators of emotion.

People are innately equipped with the expressive and receptive structures for social activation of emotion and with sensitivities to affective information. Although people are endowed with the capacity for vicarious arousal, social experience largely determines the level and pattern of activation. To have the functional use of this capacity determined by experience provides substantial benefits. If people's affective reactions were automatically triggered by innate signals, they would be emotionally burdened much of the time by the expressions of pain, joy, grief, fear, anger, sadness, frustration, and disgust emitted by anyone and everyone in sight. No person could withstand such an emotional onslaught for long without a serious toll on physical and psychosocial well-being. Endowed capacities better serve adaptive purposes through experientially acquired selectivity in vicarious activation.

Past correlated experiences heighten vicarious arousal because they make what happens to others predictive of what might happen to oneself. This is why the injuries and delights of strangers are less vicariously arousing than the suffering and joy of close associates. The more one's well-being depends on others, the stronger the signaling power of their affective condition. Similarity to the model, either in performance roles or attributes, also enhances the power of vicarious instigators. In role similarity, seeing models undergo emotional experiences in performance situations that observers are, themselves, likely to face in the future has much greater emotional impact than if the observed activities have no personal relevance (Craig & Lowery, 1969). In attribute similarity, it is the possession of similar characteristics that enhances vicarious arousal (Krebs, 1975). These may involve sex, age, race, or socioeconomic status. However, not all shared characteristics heighten vicarious arousal (Brown, 1974). It is the attributes that observers, rightfully or wrongfully, assume to be predictive of similar outcomes for themselves that serve as the influential vicarious instigators.

Lanzetta and his associates document the central role correlative experience plays in creating proclivities for vicarious arousal. Past congruent experiences, in which modeled pleasure has signaled reward for observers and modeled distress has signaled pain, heighten an observer's emotional reactions to the model's emotional expression alone. Observers who have undergone discordant experiences, (e.g., model's joy brings suffering to oneself) respond indifferently or with discordant arousal to the model's joy and suffering (Englis, Vaughan, & Lanzetta, 1982). Different vicarious reactions to the emotional experiences of others are also activated when observers expect cooperative or competitive interactions, which from past experience foretells concordant or discordant outcomes, respectively. The joy and distress of a cooperative model elicit corresponding affective reactions from observers, whereas displays of joy by a competitive model distress observers, and displays of distress calm them (Lanzetta & Englis, 1989). The differential reactions to modeled affect generalize to situations in which the model and the observers no longer experience any outcomes together. Similarly, observers respond with concordant affective arousal to the emotional experiences of models depicted as in-group members, but discordantly to those portrayed as out-group members, in the absence of having shared any experiences with them (McHugo, Smith, & Lanzetta, 1982). If a sense of mutuality has been created, so that the joys and distresses of an out-group member foretell similar experiences for the observers, similarity of outcomes transforms discordant affective reactions to concordant ones. However, the concordant vicarious responsiveness does not necessarily generalize to other out-group members.

It is not unusual for people who have shared severe adversity and misery to become indifferent or callous to the suffering of others. There are several possible explanations for this apparently paradoxical effect. Repeated painful experiences may eventually blunt one's reactions to pain through habituation. Such experiences also create tougher standards for evaluating the hardships of others through contrast effects. To someone who has undergone intense suffering, the lesser adversity of others pales by comparison and thus reduces vicarious responsiveness. Another possible explanation is that self-protective reactions have been developed as a result of hypersensitivity to human distress. If, through past suffering, persons experience acute distress upon seeing others hurt, they can perfect attentional and cognitive ways to tune out vicarious arousers and this detachment leaves them seemingly unfeeling and uncaring (Bandura & Rosenthal, 1966).

Vicarious Activation through Cognitive Self-Arousal

In the social cognitive analysis, vicarious arousal operates mainly through an intervening self-arousal process. That is, seeing others react emotionally to evident instigators, or having foreknowledge of them, activates emotion-arousing thoughts and imagery in observers. Because of their capacity for cognitive self-arousal, people can generate physiological reactions to cues that are only suggestive of a model's emotional arousal. People's physiological reactions to these same expressive cues can vary markedly depending on what they know about the situational causes of the model's reactions (Craig & Lowrey, 1969). They can neutralize the impact of human distress by mobilizing tranquilizing trains of thought (Bandura & Rosenthal, 1966). The influential role of cognitive self-arousal in vicarious activation is further corroborated in studies where children are instructed to engage in different thought processes while observing a person undergoing a frightening experience (Cantor & Wilson, 1984). Children heighten their fear by visualizing themselves subjected to the modeled threat, but diminish their fear by thinking about the unreality of the threat. Young children, whose ability to generate and sustain a preselected line of thinking while watching absorbing events is limited, are less effective in altering their affective arousal in accordance with instructional sets. The development of cognitive skills also increases the capability for self-arousal through vivification of unrevealed or only intimated causes of observed distress. Thus children are less aroused subjectively and autonomically by modeled fearful expressions than by situational threats, whereas older children are aroused equally by affective expressions and situational threats (Wilson & Cantor, 1985).

Cognitive self-arousal obviously depends on level of cognitive development. Cognitive functioning involves knowledge and cognitive skills for operating on it. The issue of theoretical interest is whether the cognitive prerequisites for vicarious arousal are best analyzed as global cognitive stages or as specialized cognitive competencies. Social cognitive theory explains the mechanisms of vicarious arousal in terms of specialized ideational, attentional, self-referential, and self-regulatory subskills. As already noted, the degree of social correlation of personal outcomes also figures prominently in the social cognitive theory of vicarious arousal.

Cognitive self-arousal can take two forms—by personalizing the experiences of another, or by taking the perspective of another. In the personalizing form, observers get themselves emotionally aroused by imagining things happening to themselves that are either similar to the model's or have been generalized from previous positive and aversive experiences. Correlated prior experiences facilitate vicarious arousal not only because they bestow predictive significance on the model's plight. They also provide concrete and cognitively accessible reminders of past joys, pains, and sorrows for cognitively enhancing the activating power of vicarious influences.

In the perspective-taking form observers come to experience the emotional states of others by adopting their perspective. Research conducted within this framework has been concerned primarily with how role-taking skills develop and affect social behavior (Flavell, 1968; Iannotti, 1978). In developmental studies of other forms of social communication, greater explanatory power is achieved by considering cognitive subskills relevant to certain types of performances than by appeal to an omnibus cognitive structure or general cognitive role-taking ability (Dickson, 1982). However, experimental evidence is lacking on how vicarious arousal can be affected by putting oneself in a model's place. What little evidence does exist suggests that personalizing modeled experiences is more vicariously arousing than is role taking. Stotland (1969) found that observers react more emotionally to the sight of a person in pain if, at the time, they imagine how they themselves would feel than if they imagine how the other person feels. Studies of the development of empathetic understanding corroborate the importance of personalization (Hughes, Tingle, & Swain, 1981). Young children who focus on their own emotional reactions to the experiences of others gain better understanding of others' emotions than if they focus on how others might feel. Stotland regards the ability to visualize oneself undergoing the experiences to which others are being subjected as a fundamental aspect of vicarious activation. This imaginative self-involvement is facilitated by recall of similar past experiences to draw upon.

VICARIOUS ACQUISITION

Psychological theories have traditionally emphasized learning through the direct experience of action. Fortunately, virtually all learning phenomena, resulting from direct experience, can occur vicariously by observing other people's behavior and the effects it produces (Bandura, 1986). The mechanisms by which modeling influences instill competencies and alter motivation, which have been analyzed elsewhere (Bandura, 1986), fall beyond the scope of this chapter. It should be noted in passing, however, that modeling is not merely a process of behavioral mimicry. Models exemplify rules for generative behavior as well as particular behavioral patterns. Through the process of abstract modeling, observers extract rules underlying modeled activities for generating thought and behavior that go beyond what they have seen or heard.

Humans have evolved an advanced capacity for observational learning that is vital for both development and survival. Because mistakes can produce costly or even fatal outcomes, the prospects of survival would be slim indeed if one could learn only from the consequences of trial and error. The more costly and hazardous the possible missteps, the heavier must be the reliance on observational learning from proficient models. Much social learning occurs through modeling influences operating with in one's immediate environment. However, extraordinary advances in the technology of communications have greatly increased the scope and power of vicarious learning from the symbolic environment. Because of its prevalence and wide reach, symbolic modeling is playing an increasingly influential role in shaping human thought, affect, and action.

Affective modeling functions as an acquisition vehicle as well as a momentary arouser. In a commonly used paradigm to study vicarious affective learning (Berger, 1962), observers hear a neutral tone and then see a model react with pain ostensibly to a shock—which is actually feigned. Observers repeatedly witness the pairing of the tone and modeled distress. They begin to react physiologically to the tone alone, even though they themselves have never experienced any pain in conjunction with it. The more salient the model's pain reactions are, and the more consistent they are with the situational instigators, the more strongly observers come to fear the formerly neutral event (Berger, 1962; Kravetz, 1970, 1974).

Under natural conditions, arousal has many sources, so a variety of vicarious instigators, such as seeing persons distressed over failure or subjective threats, can promote vicarious affective learning (Bandura, Blanchard, & Ritter, 1969; Craig & Weinstein, 1965). Just as vicarious arousal is subject to cognitive modulation, so is vicarious affective learning. To achieve vicarious learning, observers have to recognize the events that foretell painful experiences for the model (Vaughan & Lanzetta, 1980). Unaware observers do not profit from the modeled affective co-occurrences even though they are repeatedly exposed to them. Observers thus learn from the emotional experiences of others by extracting predictive information rather than by being mechanically conditioned.

Level of Emotionality.   Exposure to the emotional experiences of others does not invariably leave lasting effects. We noted earlier that vicarious affective learning cannot occur unless observers are aroused by what they see and hear. Research, in which varying levels of arousal have been induced in the observers before they are exposed to affective modeling, shows that vicarious acquisition and elimination of emotional reactions are related to level of emotionality, but not in a simple linear fashion (Bandura & Rosenthal, 1966). Observers who have been moderately aroused acquire autonomic responses vicariously the most rapidly and enduringly, whereas those who have been either minimally or markedly aroused achieve the weakest vicarious acquisition of emotional proclivities. The curvilinear relationship obtained with induced arousal is further confirmed by correlations between observers' proneness to anxiety arousal, and their vicarious learning. Proneness to emotionality is positively related to vicarious learning under elevated arousal but negatively related under marked arousal.

Assessment of accompanying cognitions suggests that the facilitative and disruptive effects of arousal level on vicarious affective learning are mediated through attentional and cognitive mechanisms. Modeled anguish proved so upsetting to observers who were already beset by high personal arousal that they diverted their attention from the sufferer to distractions in the environment, and they conjured up distracting thoughts to escape the discomfort produced by the painful expressions being modeled. In the natural environment, physical detachment affords more efficient self-protection from the suffering of others than cognitive distraction does. The plight of sufferers cannot have much social impact if they are out of sight and out of mind.

Past Aversive Experiences.   People who have suffered pain are more likely to personalize the suffering of others and thus be more strongly affected by it. In studies examining this issue, observers who have undergone prior painful experiences learn more through socially mediated suffering than do observers who have experienced only mild unpleasantness, or none at all (Greco, 1973; Ogston & Davidson, 1972). However, if models show no signs of pain in hurtful situations, the effects of prior experience will not be activated (Hygge, 1978). Social cognitive theory posits that it is socially correlated, rather than simply prior, experience that wields the greatest influence on vicarious affective acquisition. The findings of Lanzetta and his coworkers cited earlier also speak to this issue—the degree of correlation between the prior experiences of models and observers is the critical determinant of vicarious affective acquisition.

Vicarious Acquisition of Intractable Fears.   When fear and distress are modeled in response to real dangers, vicarious acquisition serves useful social purposes. People can spare themselves a great deal of pain and misery by observing and acting with foresight on the information provided by the distress of others. However, if modeled fears are ill founded, as is sometimes the case, vicarious arousal creates much needless distress and wasted effort in self-protection against nonexistent objective threats.

Intractable fears often arise not from personally injurious experiences, but from seeing others respond fearfully toward, or be hurt by, threatening events. Thus, modeling of phobic reactions, usually by parents, is a prevalent factor in the development of phobic disorders. Children who fear dogs differ little from their nonfearful peers in injurious experiences with such animals, but their parents tend to display a phobic dread of dogs (Bandura & Menlove, 1968). Similarly, Windheuser (1977) found a close match between mothers' phobic reactions and the phobias that plague their children.

That intense and persistent fears can be acquired by observational experiences alone receives strong support from experimental studies by Mineka and her associates (Cook, Mineka, Wolkenstein, & Laitsch, 1985; Mineka, Davidson, Cook, & Keir, 1984). Most wild-reared monkeys display a fear of snakes, whereas lab-reared monkeys do not. In Mineka's studies, lab-reared monkeys who were fearless of snakes became highly fearful of them after having observed adult monkeys behave fearfully in the presence of a snake. The observers generalized the marked fear and avoidance to new settings and showed no diminution of fear when tested months later. The more intense the fear reactions of the model, the stronger was the observers' vicariously acquired fear. Whereas fearful modeling creates enduring fears in rhesus monkeys, nonfearful modeling which represents snakes as nondangerous immunizes observers against later, fearful modeling (Mineka & Cook, 1986). The information conveyed vicariously is a more powerful immunizer than is prior direct experience with the object.

This is not to say that phobias spring solely from vicarious experience or that direct experience plays only a secondary role in the process. Intractable fears usually have multiple origins, including direct aversive experiences, modeled fright or injury, and frightening portrayals of potential threats as highly dangerous and largely uncontrollable (Bandura *et al.*, 1969).

Experiential and Biological Preparedness

Some explanations of the origin of human fears assign considerable importance to innate preparedness. According to Seligman (1971), people are biologically predisposed to fear things that have threatened human survival through the ages. The predictive utility of the preparedness tenet has been tested with human fears acquired under both natural and controlled conditions. The naturalistic studies have compared the acquisition and modifiability of phobias judged to be either evolutionarily prepared or unprepared (DeSilva, Rachman, & Seligman, 1977: Zafiropoulou & McPherson, 1986). Judged preparedness failed to predict either suddenness, age of onset, or duration of the phobia, severity of impairment, or amenability to change.

In the social cognitive view (Bandura, 1986), all events are not equally susceptible to becoming objects of fear or phobic dread. There are certain properties of events—agential hurtfulness, unpredictability, and uncontrollability—that make them especially phobeogenic. Among the things that are correlated with aversive experiences, animate ones are more apt to produce phobias than are inanimate things. This is because animate threats, by virtue of their ability to act and roam around, can appear at unpredictable times and places and inflict injury despite self-protective efforts.

In addition to injurious agency, unpredictability and uncontrollability are other important properties of phobeogenic events. Predictable aversive events are less frightening than those one cannot foretell when or where they might happen, thus making it difficult to distinguish safe from unsafe circumstances. Similarly, ability to exercise control, or even the perception that one can do so, greatly reduces the threat of potentially painful events (Averill, 1973; Bandura, 1982; Miller, 1979, 1980). Active, unpredictable threats, over which one has only partial control, give more cause for generalized anxiety than equally aversive threats that are predictable, immobile, and safe, as long as one chooses to stay away from them. It is in the properties of events, then, rather than in the experiences of one's ancestors that answers to the selectivity of human phobias are most likely to be found. However, properties of events do not reflexively activate associative mechanisms. The impact of events on fear reactions is, in large part, dependent on cognitive processing, which defines the threatening-ness of particular objects under different circumstances.

A number of laboratory tests have been conducted on whether presumed innate preparedness affects the speed with which anticipatory autonomic reactions to threats are learned and eliminated. In these studies shock is associated either directly, vicariously, or by verbal threat with pictures of evolutionarily significant objects, such as snakes and spiders, or with biologically indifferent ones, such as houses, flowers, and geometrical forms. The basic assumption of the preparedness principle is that innately primed linkage ensures rapid learning of threats; otherwise preparedness would lack survival value because perilous threats usually permit few errors. An evolutionary legacy that did not facilitate acquisition of fears, but only slowed their extinction, would place the bias at the wrong end because slow learning of dangers is likely to extinguish the organism. The assumption of rapid acquisition of human fears judged to be biologically prepared receives little empirical support in laboratory studies. On the contrary, neither repeated shock, nor observing others suffering direct painful experiences, makes people fear prepared objects any faster than arbitrary ones (Dawson, Schell, & Banis, 1986; Hygge & Ohman, 1978; McNally, 1987; Ohman, Erixon, & Lofberg, 1975; Ohman & Hugdahl, 1979).

Knowledge that shocks have been discontinued is generally less effective in eliminating momentary orienting reactions to prepared rather than to arbitrary objects, but such assurance produces similar reductions in anticipatory reactions, whether triggered by prepared or by arbitrary objects. In some experiments, instated fear is eliminated by disconfirming experiences just as readily toward geometrical forms or fruit as toward snakes or spiders on every type of reaction measured, whether orienting, anticipatory, or hindmost (McNally & Foa, 1986; Merckelbach, van den Hout, & van der Molen, 1989; Ohman, Fredrikson, Hugdahl, & Rimmo, 1976). In a study testing for cognitive mediation of fear acquisition, Dawson et al. (1986) found that repeated aversive experiences failed to create fear of either biologically prepared or neutral objects without awareness that the object signified shock. When shock expectancies are controlled, acquired fear reactions toward biologically prepared objects are no more resistant to elimination than acquired fear of neutral objects. If correlated experiences are provided so that pictures of snakes and flowers come to signal safety from painful events, both of these objects are equally effective in diminishing fear toward other threats (McNally & Reiss, 1982, 1984). In the preparedness view, one would not expect that an object biologically predisposed for fear could be so readily transformed into a fear reducer and be just as tranquilizing as a dainty flower. Despite repeated disconfirmation of the effects of presumed preparedness on rate of fear acquisition and conflicting results on rate of fear extinction, these findings continue to be cited as evidence of biologically prepared learning.

A preparedness mechanism that does not help humans learn from the pain or calamities of others to fear dangers any faster and that has variable effects on the persistence of anticipatory arousal is not exactly the most reliable basis on which to rest survival chances. Forethought and advanced vicarious capacity to profit from the injuries of others, both of which are hallmarks of human adaptiveness, are more likely to ensure progeny than is reliance on blind associations. It is much wiser to trust one's survival to forethought concerning the properties of human creations because cultural evolution introduces new objects—guns, bombs, automobiles—that are considerably more prevalent and perilous in contemporary life than are tigers.

Even if it had been found that innate preparedness carried the burden of autonomic learning delegated to it, the evolutionary implications would be of lesser magnitude than is commonly assumed. This is because autonomic arousal does not control defensive behavior. Fear arousal and defensive behavior are largely coeffects of other determinants, rather than being causally linked (Bandura, 1986, 1988b; Bolles, 1975; Schwartz, 1978). From the standpoint of survival, the important factor is not that organisms become easily upset but that they make hasty retreats from perilous situations, which can cost them life or limb. It is smart protective action rather than internal upsetness that is of central concern to healthy longevity. Moreover, organisms that can guide their behavior on the knowledge of what is safe and what is dangerous are better equipped to survive and flourish than those that continued to cringe needlessly, knowing full well that what they have come to fear is now perfectly safe.

The innate preprogramming that enables animals to deal in a stereo-typed fashion with the recurring demands of a limited habitat would not be evolutionarily advantageous for humans, who must often cope with exceedingly complex and rapidly changing circumstances. Under such diverse and highly variable conditions of living, it is forethought rather than fixed, inborn linkage that is most adaptive. The evolved, advanced capability for thought, which sets humans apart from other species, rep-resents a more fundamental biological contribution to social referencing than does preset linkage or rudimentary social signals. Hence, thought that combines information from several predictors can readily override the influence of a particular social signal.

Innumerable studies have shown that painful experiences readily create experiential preparedness to fear selected types of objects and events. By varying the pattern of positive and negative experiences, one can carve out particular domains of sensitivities (Hoffman, 1969). Even after acquired fears are completely eliminated, the experientially created sensitivities remain. Years later, stressful experiences arising from unre-lated sources can reinstate fearful reactions toward former threats in the experientially sensitized domains.

Vicarious Induction of Social Anxiety

The vicarious induction of anxiety has more profound societal con-sequences than does direct experience because the vicarious mode, espe-cially televised modeling, can simultaneously affect the lives of vast num-bers of people in widely dispersed locales. There is another aspect of symbolic modeling that magnifies its psychological and social effects. During the course of their daily lives, people have direct contact with only a small sector of the physical and social environment. Consequently, their conceptions of social reality are greatly influenced by vicarious ex-periences—what they see, hear, and read in the mass media—without direct experiential correctives. The more people's images of reality de-pend upon the media's symbolic environment, the greater is its social impact.

Televised representations of social realities are heavily populated with villainous and assaultive characters (Gerbner, Gross, Signorielli, & Morgan, 1980). That heavy viewing of violence can frighten viewers has been shown in a comparison of how light and heavy viewers of television perceive their social reality (Bryant, Carveth, & Brown, 1981; Pingree & Hawkins, 1981). Heavy viewers are more distrustful of others and over-estimate their chances of being criminally assaulted than light viewers do. Exposure to the criminal assaults of others is most likely to instill strong fear of personal victimization when the assaults are portrayed as unpredictable and uncontrollable by randomness of victimization in the locale in which one resides (Heath, 1984).

Shaping Valuational Proclivities through Modeled Preferences

Values and tastes can be developed and altered vicariously by exposure to modeled preferences. Such valuational effects are strongly influenced by observed outcomes and the evaluative reactions of models. In an early experiment, Duncker (1938) demonstrated the long-term effects of modeled pleasure on food preferences. Young children consistently selected chocolate with a pleasant lemon flavor over a sugar with a disagreeable medicinal taste. They later heard a story in which a stalwart hero abhorred a tart substance, which tasted like the children's favored food, but enthusiastically relished a sweet tasting substance. The modeled reactions altered the children's preferences for foodstuffs and reversed their habitual liking for chocolate in favor of the medicated sugar in tests conducted over a period of several days. Brief recall of the story reinstated the vicariously created preferences after they had declined.

Modeling is an effective way of introducing young children to unfamiliar tastes and developing preferences for foods they have previously held in disfavor (Birch, 1980; Harper & Sanders, 1975). The food preferences of animals can be influenced in much the same way. Kittens seeing their mothers eating atypical food—forsaking meat for mashed potatoes—acquire a lasting preference for mashed potatoes that is most unusual for their species (Wyrwicka, 1978).

That evaluations created vicariously can affect action is shown most directly in therapeutic applications of modeling. Loathsome evaluations of long standing are changed to neutral or even favorable ones through modeling of positive reactions toward disliked phobic objects. The degree of change in evaluative reactions predicts the amount of behavioral change (Bandura *et al.,* 1969; Blanchard, 1970).

PREDICTIVE REGULATORY FUNCTION

In the occurrences of everyday life, vicarious instigators usually include both modeling of affective reactions and the situational events that arouse the models. For example, a snarling dog is the situational arouser, the frightened expression of a parent is the affective modeling. Both events convey predictive information about potential dangerousness. When situations contain multiple predictors, the extent to which they are attended to and used as guides for action depends on their relative informativeness about probable outcomes. Thus, in the research previously cited, infants pay little attention to parental affective signals when situational factors clearly convey danger or safety, but they draw heavily on affective signals when the situation is ambiguous (Gunnar & Stone, 1984; Sorce *et al.*, 1985). Infants are also selective in who they choose to reference if more than one adult is present. They ignore their mothers if a friendly adult is the better affective conveyer of predictive information (Klinnert *et al.*, 1986).

Once people discover that a particular cue is relatively effective in predicting what is likely to happen, they do not learn the predictive value of accompanying cues, even though these others may be equally informative. As a rule, anything that reduces the predictive value of signals by lowering or obscuring their correlation with outcomes diminishes their regulatory potential. It is only after people recognize the fallibility of their predictive system that they pay attention to the disregarded predictors.

Past experience influences how attention is deployed and what is learned in situations containing multiple predictors that are equally informative. Prior experience that a cue lacks predictive value leads people to pay little attention to it so they are slow in learning to use it when it later becomes a reliable predictor of outcomes. Conversely, a cue that has been predictive in the past will override other redundant predictors. Both of these effects have been demonstrated by Lanzetta and Orr (1980, 1981) in studies in which a neutral cue accompanied slides of either fearful facial expressions, happy expressions, or passive expressions, as joint predictors of painful events. Although objectively the neutral cue was equally predictive in all three expressive contexts, it was largely ignored when it competed with fearful expressions, which usually forebode painfulness and hence were selected as the predictor of painful occurrences. The neutral cue became the dominant predictor in the context of joyful expressions, which ordinarily contraindicate aversive outcomes, and it shared predictive functions with passive expressions, which do not bias attention one way or another.

A series of studies by Miller and his colleagues of cooperative avoidance reveal both the communicative and the regulative function of expressive signals (Miller, Banks, & Ogawa, 1962, 1963; Miller, Murphy, & Mirsky, 1959). Monkeys first learned to avoid shock, signaled by a light, by pressing a bar. The animals were then placed in different rooms so that the model could see the forewarning light come on, while the observer had the bar to forestall the shock. The model therefore had to communicate distress by facial and other expressions via video to the observing partner, who could take the protective action necessary to avoid shock for both of them. Modeled expressions of distress in anticipation of the shock elicited fear in the observing companion, as reflected in elevated heart rate and performance of protective acts. Even color slides of an animal showing fear of pain elicited protective action in observers. Protective behavior could be vicariously activated not only by the sight of their partner but also, through generalization, by an unfamiliar fearful monkey. Moreover, seeing another monkey express fear reinstated protective behavior in observers even after their fear had been thoroughly eliminated.

Research that systematically varies the accuracy with which social expressions and nonsocial events predict outcomes is essential for a full understanding of social referencing. Such studies would go a long way toward clarifying how people use social and nonsocial predictors to guide their actions when these factors convey unique, redundant, or conflicting predictive information. Some of the research in social referencing has begun to vary the signaling properties of the nonsocial factors but the informativeness of social expressions has not been varied in a systematic way.

SELF-EFFICACY AND CONTROLLABILITY FUNCTION

In dealing with their environment, models usually exhibit coping strategies both by their actions and by voicing their self-guiding thoughts. Observers can thus acquire, from informative modeling, strategies for managing challenging or threatening situations. This contribution is especially important when personal inefficacy reflects skill deficits rather than misappraisals of the skills one already possesses. In addition, modeling displays convey information about the nature of environmental tasks and the difficulties they present. Modeled transactions may reveal the tasks to be more or less difficult, and potential threats more or less manageable than observers originally believed. Adoption of serviceable strategies and altered perceptions of task difficulty will change observers' judgments of their personal efficacy.

Competent functioning involves a generative capability in which multiple subskills must be improvised to manage ever-changing circumstances, most of which contain ambiguous, unpredictable, and often stressful, elements. Therefore, in any activity, skills and self-beliefs of efficacy that insure their effective use are needed for successful functioning. Initiation and regulation of transactions with the environment are partly governed by judgments of operative capabilities—what people believe they can do under given circumstances.

Converging evidence from diverse lines of research indicates that perceived self-efficacy operates as a common cognitive mechanism governing different aspects of psychosocial functioning (Bandura, 1986). People who perceive themselves as inefficacious shy away from difficult tasks; they have low aspirations and weak commitment to the goals they choose to pursue. They slacken their efforts and give up quickly in the face of difficulties. They are slow to recover their sense of efficacy following adversity and harbor serious misgivings about their capabilities. In taxing situations they dwell on their personal deficiencies, the formidableness of the task, and adverse consequents, which only detract attention from the execution of the activity. They fall easy victim to stress and depression.

A high sense of perceived self-efficacy sponsors markedly different psychosocial functioning. People who judge themselves as highly efficacious approach difficult tasks as challenges to be mastered rather than as threats to be avoided. Such an orientation cultivates interest and deep involvement in activities. They set themselves challenging goals and maintain strong commitment to them. They heighten their efforts when their accomplishments fall short of their standards. They quickly recover their sense of efficacy after failures or setbacks. They ascribe failure to insufficient effort, which supports a success orientation. And they approach taxing situations with assurance that they can exercise control over them. As a result, they are less vulnerable to failure, stress, and depression.

Cognitive Processing of Vicarious Efficacy Information

Self-knowledge about one's efficacy is based on four principal sources of information. These include *enactive mastery experiences; vicarious experiences* for judging personal capabilities from the successes and failures of similar others; *verbal persuasion* and allied types of social influences that one possesses certain capabilities; and reading of *physiological states* which people partly use to judge their capableness, strength, and vulnerability to dysfunction. The present discussion centers on vicariously conveyed efficacy information because it is a prominent feature of many social referencing situations.

People do not rely on enactive experience as the sole source of information about their capabilities. Self-efficacy appraisals are partly based on social comparative evaluation of modeling experiences. Seeing other people perform successfully can raise self-percepts of efficacy in observers that they too possess the capabilities to master comparable activities (Bandura, Reese, & Adams, 1982). By the same token, observing others perceived to be similarly competent fail despite high effort lowers observers' judgments of their own capabilities and undermines their motivation (Brown & Inouye, 1978).

There are several conditions under which self-efficacy appraisals are especially sensitive to vicarious information. The amount of uncertainty about one's capabilities is one such factor. Perceived self-efficacy can be readily changed by relevant modeling influences when people have had little prior experience on which to base evaluations of their personal capabilities. Lacking direct knowledge of their own capabilities, they rely extensively on modeled indicators (Takata & Takata, 1976). This is not to say that a great deal of prior experience necessarily nullifies the potential influence of social modeling. Informative modeling that conveys effective coping strategies supplants well-entrenched beliefs of self-inefficacy with an enhanced sense of personal efficacy (Bandura, 1977; Bandura *et al.*, 1982).

Information that is relevant for judging personal capabilities is not inherently enlightening. Rather, it becomes instructive only through cognitive appraisal. A distinction must, therefore, be drawn between information conveyed by modeling events and information as selected, weighted, and integrated into self-efficacy judgments. The impact of modeling on observers' perceived efficacy relies heavily on social comparison processes. Similarity to a model is one factor that increases the personal relevance of modeled performance information for observers' appraisal of their own efficacy. Persons who are similar or slightly higher in ability provide the most informative comparative information for gauging one's own capabilities (Festinger, 1954; Suls & Miller, 1977). Neither outperforming those of much lesser ability nor being surpassed by the greatly superior convey much information about one's own level of competence. In general, modeled successes by similar others raise, and modeled failures lower, self-appraisals of efficacy.

In judging personal efficacy through social comparisons, observers may rely on similarity either in the model's past performances or in the model's attributes that are presumably predictive of the ability in question. The influential role of prior performance similarity on vicarious efficacy appraisal is revealed in a study by Brown and Inouye (1978). Observers who believed themselves to be superior to a model whom they later saw perform poorly maintained a high sense of personal efficacy and did not slacken their effort at all, despite repeated failure. In contrast, modeled failure had a devastating effect on observers' self-judged efficacy when they perceived themselves of comparable ability to the model. They expressed a very low sense of personal efficacy and gave up quickly when they encountered difficulties. The lower their perceived self-efficacy the quicker they gave up.

Efficacy appraisals are often based, not on comparative performance experiences, but on similarity to models on personal characteristics that are assumed to be predictive of performance capabilities (Suls & Miller, 1977). People develop preconceptions of capabilities according to age, sex, educational and socioeconomic level, race, and ethnic designation, even though the performances of individuals within these groups are extremely varied. Such preconceptions usually arise from a combination of cultural stereotyping and overgeneralization from salient personal experiences. Attributes invested with predictive significance operate as influential factors in comparative self-appraisals. Thus, the same physical stamina modeled by a female raises women's perceived physical efficacy and actual muscular endurance, whereas that of a male model does not (Gould & Weiss, 1981).

Attribute similarity generally increases the force of modeling influences even though the personal characteristics may be spurious indicants of performance capabilities (Rosenthal & Bandura, 1978). For example, similarity in age and sex to coping models emboldens phobic observers, although these characteristics do not really affect how well one can perform the feared activities. Such misjudgments reflect overgeneralization from activities in which these attributes would predict performance, at least to some extent. Indeed, when model attributes irrelevant to the new task are salient and overweighted in their predictive value, these irrelevant model characteristics sway observers more than do relevant ability indicants (Kazdin, 1978). When the successes of models who possess similar attributes lead others to try things they would otherwise shun, spurious indicants can have beneficial social effects. But comparative self-efficacy appraisals through faulty preconceptions often lead those who are uncertain about their abilities to judge valuable pursuits to be beyond their reach. In such instances, judging efficacy by social comparison is self-limiting, especially if models verbalize self-doubts about their own capabilities (Gould & Weiss, 1981).

Diversified modeling, in which different people master difficult tasks, is superior to exposure to the same performances by a single model (Bandura & Menlove, 1968; Kazdin, 1978). If people of widely differing characteristics can succeed, then observers have a reasonable basis for increasing their own sense of efficacy. Observers also generally benefit more from seeing models overcome their difficulties by determined effort than from observing facile performances by adept models (Kazdin, 1973; Meichenbaum, 1971; Schunk, Hanson, & Cox, 1987). Showing the gains achieved by intensified effort not only reduces negative effects of temporary setbacks, but demonstrates that perseverance eventually brings success. Modeled perseverant success alters the diagnosticity of failure experiences as reflecting difficult situational predicaments rather than personal inefficacy. However, variations on the coping–mastery dimension have produced somewhat mixed results (Kato & Fukushima, 1977; Klorman, Hilpert, Michael, LaGana, & Sveen, 1980). Coping modeling contains two separable factors—models display decreasing fear as they struggle with the task, and they demonstrate techniques for managing difficult situations. Instruction in coping techniques is more helpful than is emotive modeling. Therefore, whether coping modeling is weaker, equipotent, or stronger than mastery modeling may largely depend on the number of serviceable coping strategies these two forms of modeling convey.

Models can exhibit coping strategies both by their actions and by voicing their thoughts about how to analyze task demands, find alternative solutions, assess the effects of their actions, correct errors, and deal effectively with stress. In complex activities, the thinking skills guiding actions are, in many respects, more informative than are the modeled actions themselves. People who lack coping skills benefit more from observing people model self-guiding thoughts in conjunction with actions, than from seeing the actions alone (Sarason, 1975).

Vicariously Instated Self-Efficacy and Coping Behavior

Social referencing has focused extensively on modeled affectivity. Therefore, the research on the effects of vicariously instated self-efficacy on fear arousal and coping behavior is especially pertinent. Modeling influences designed to alter coping behavior emphasize two aspects—predictability and controllability—that are conducive to the enhancement of self-percepts of efficacy (Bandura et al., 1982). In demonstrating predictability, models repeatedly engage in threatening activities in ways that exemplify how feared persons or objects are most likely to behave in each of many different situations. Predictability reduces stress and increases preparedness for coping with threats (Averill, 1973; Miller, 1981). When modeling controllability, the model demonstrates effective strategies for managing threats in whatever situations might arise. In studies in which perceived coping efficacy is vicariously raised to differential levels, the higher the perceived self-efficacy the greater are observers' subsequent performance accomplishments (Bandura et al., 1982). Microanalyses of efficacy–action congruences reveal a close fit between self-percepts of efficacy and successful coping behavior.

Affective Signaling versus Mastery Modeling. The discussion thus far has centered on enhancement of coping efficacy by vicarious means. Mastery modeling is the most powerful means of instilling a strong sense of coping efficacy (Bandura, 1988a). Guided mastery modeling relies on mastery experiences as the principal vehicle of psychological change. Mastery experiences are structured so as to develop coping skills and to provide persuasive confirmatory tests that one can exercise control over threats. This is achieved by enlisting a variety of performance mastery aids, including modeling of coping strategies, graduated subtasks, enactment of threatening activities for progressively longer periods, joint performance, use of protective aids that reduce the likelihood of feared consequences, and modulation of the severity of threats (Bandura et al., 1969; Bandura, Jeffery, & Wright, 1974). As skillfulness is developed, self-directed mastery experiences, designed to provide varied confirmatory tests of coping capabilities, are arranged to strengthen and generalize the sense of coping self-efficacy.

Within a relatively short time, mastery modeling achieves widespread psychological changes that typically generalize across different modalities of functioning. In addition to cultivating capabilities, personal mastery eliminates anxiety arousal, instills positive attitudes, and eradicates perturbing ruminations and nightmares (Bandura, Jeffery, & Gajdos, 1975). That mastery of threats profoundly affects dream activity is a particularly striking effect. The favorable changes remain very much in evidence months and years later. The nature and scope of the changes people achieve is predictable from the generality of their self-percepts of coping efficacy. There is a good deal of evidence to suggest that mastery modeling would be more powerful in altering appraisal of threats and coping behavior than modeling alone or merely affective signaling. An enhanced sense of coping efficacy reduces perceived personal vulnerability and perceived risk (Ozer & Bandura, 1990). A strong sense of coping efficacy also reduces aversive thoughts and anxiety arousal by strengthening perceived self-efficacy to exercise control over one's own thought processes.

Perceived Self-Efficacy and Stress Reactions

Self-percepts of efficacy affect emotional reactions as well as motivation and action. This is especially true of anxiety and stress reactions to unfamiliar or potentially aversive events. Recent years have witnessed the convergence of theory and research on the influential role of perceived control in stress reactions (Averill, 1973; Lazarus & Folkman, 1984; Miller, 1980). A sense of controllability can be achieved either behaviorally or cognitively. In behavioral control, individuals take action that forestalls or attenuates aversive events. In cognitive control, people believe they can manage environmental threats should they arise. These two forms of controllability are distinguished because the relationship between actual and perceived control is far from perfect.

Being able to exercise control over potential threats can diminish arousal because the capability can be used to reduce or to prevent painful experiences. But there is much more to the process of stress reduction by behavioral control than simply curtailing painful events. In some studies of controllability, ordinarily stressful events occur undiminished, but they are promptly transformed to pleasant ones when their occurrence is personally controlled (Gunnar-vonGnechten, 1978). Here it is exercise of personal control, not the curtailment of the events, themselves, that reduces stress. That a sense of controllability diminishes stress is strikingly demonstrated by Mineka, Gunnar, and Champoux (1986) in a developmental study with primates. Early experience in the exercise of control over appetitive events reduces subsequent fear arousal to novel threats. In situations in which the opportunity to wield control exists but is unexercised, it is the self-knowledge that one can exercise control should one choose to do so rather than its application that reduces stress reactions (Glass, Reim, & Singer, 1971). These lines of evidence suggest that much of the stress reductive effects of behavioral control stem anticipatorily from perceived capability to wield control over troublesome events rather than simply from attenuating aversive events.

As the above studies indicate, the phenomenon of particular interest is the impact of perceived control on stress reactions. Perceived control without the actuality has been shown to reduce stress reactions. People who are led to believe they can exercise some control over painful events display lower autonomic arousal and less impairment in performance than do those who believe they lack personal control, even though they are subjected equally to the painful events (Geer, Davison, & Gatchel, 1970; Glass, Singer, Leonard, Krantz, & Cummings, 1973). Repeated failures create stress reactions when ascribed to personal incapability, but the same painful experiences leave people unperturbed if ascribed to situational factors (Wortman, Panciera, Shusterman, & Hibscher, 1976).

In the social cognitive analysis, perceived self-efficacy operates as a cognitive mechanism by which controllability reduces stress reactions. It is mainly perceived inefficacy to cope with potentially aversive events that makes them stressful (Bandura, 1986). To the extent that people believe they can prevent, terminate, or lessen the severity of aversive events, they have little reason to be perturbed by them. People who judge themselves inefficacious in coping with environmental threats dwell on their vulner-abilities and perceive many situations as fraught with danger (Beck, Laude, & Bohnert, 1974). As a result, they experience a high level of cognitively generated stress.

Several lines of research provide corroborative evidence that per-ceived self-efficacy operates as a cognitive mediator of stress reactions during coping with phobic threats. In some studies phobics' perceptions of their coping efficacy are raised vicariously to differential levels, where-upon their subjective stress is measured (Bandura et al., 1982). The more efficacious they perceived themselves to be in coping with various threat-ening tasks, the weaker the stress reactions they experience while antici-pating or performing the activities.

The generality of the relationship between perceived coping inefficacy and stress reactions has been further corroborated using autonomic indices of stress reactions (Bandura et al., 1982). Phobics display little autonomic reactivity while coping with tasks they regard with utmost self-efficacy. But as they cope with tasks for which they distrust their coping efficacy their heart rate accelerates and their blood pressure rises. After their self-efficacy beliefs are strengthened to maximal level, they perform the previously threatening tasks without experiencing any stress or autonomic arousal.

To further clarify psychobiological mechanisms of operation, this line of research was extended by linking strength of perceived self-efficacy to catecholamine secretion at a microlevel (Bandura, Taylor, Williams, Mefford, & Barchas, 1985). After phobics' range of perceived self-efficacy was expanded through modeling, their plasma catecholamines were measured as they were administered tasks corresponding to their strong, medium, and weak strengths of perceived self-efficacy. High perceived self-efficacy was accompanied by low levels of plasma epinephrine and norepinephrine, whereas moderate perceived self-inefficacy gave rise to substantial increases in these plasma catecholamines. Both catecholamines dropped sharply when phobics declined tasks for which they judged themselves completely inefficacious. After perceived self-efficacy was strengthened to the maximal level by mastery modeling, all of the previously intimidating tasks were performed without any differential catecholamine secretion. Microanalyses, whether conducted at the level of phenomenal experience, autonomic reactivity, or catecholamine release, provide converging evidence for close linkage between self-percepts of efficacy and level of psychophysiological stress.

Interactive but Asymmetric Relation

Social cognitive theory posits an interactive, though asymmetric, relation between perceived self-efficacy and fear arousal, with coping efficacy exercising the much greater sway. That is, perceived self-inefficacy in coping with potential threats leads people to approach such situations anxiously, and experience of disruptive arousal may further lower their sense of efficacy that they will perform skillfully. People are much more likely to act on their self-percepts of efficacy inferred from many sources of information rather than rely primarily on visceral cues. This is not surprising because self-knowledge based on information about one's coping skills, past accomplishments, and social comparison is considerably more indicative of capability than are the indefinite stirrings of the viscera.

Given a sufficient level of perceived self-efficacy to take on threatening tasks, people perform them with varying amounts of fear arousal depending on the strength of their perceived self-efficacy. Because people can perform activities at weaker strengths of perceived self-efficacy, despite high anxiety, they are able to overcome inappropriate fears and function effectively even in the face of anticipated aversive consequences. Thus, perceived coping efficacy predicts phobic behavior much better than do fearful anticipations (Lee, 1984a, 1984b; Williams & Watson, 1985).

Perceived self-efficacy retains its predictiveness of phobic behavior when variations in anticipatory and performance anxiety are partialed out, whereas the relationship between anxiety and phobic behavior essentially disappears when the influence of perceived self-efficacy is controlled (Williams, Dooseman, & Kleifield, 1984; Williams, Turner, & Peer, 1985; Williams & Watson, 1985). Studies of academic activities corroborate the generality of this finding (Hackett & Betz, 1982). Perceived self-inefficacy predicts avoidance of academic activities whereas anxiety does not.

CONCLUDING REMARKS

Social referencing is rooted in the information conveyed by the affective expressions, verbalized thoughts, and actions of others. The research reviewed in the present chapter clarifies the different mechanisms by which such modeling, especially the affective forms, can alter psychosocial functioning. Social cognitive theory accords a central role to the interplay of social and cognitive factors in the determination of social referencing effects. Social mutualities and conditional relations between events make affective signals predictors of outcomes. Knowledge structures and cognitive skills determine how the available predictive information is extracted, weighted, and integrated in the guidance of action. Vicarious transmission of coping skills and social comparative information alter self-appraisal of coping self-efficacy, which also operates as an important mechanism through which social influences affect emotional arousal and action. Enhanced perceived self-efficacy to exercise control over unfamiliar and potentially aversive events reduces stress reactions and fosters contact with them.

Search for the biological contributions to social referencing has centered mainly on the innate signal value of affective expressions and the types of emotional reactions they trigger. Analyses of psychobiological mechanisms of social referencing must consider not only rudimentary expressive signals but also the evolution of an advanced cognitive capability. Thought functions as a powerful tool for comprehending and dealing effectively with the environment. A comprehensive theory must, therefore, encompass the influential role played by cognition in the regulation of affect and action through social referencing.

REFERENCES

Averill, J. R. (1973). Personal control over aversive stimuli and its relationship to stress. *Psychological Bulletin, 80,* 286–303.

Bandura, A. (1977). Self-efficacy: Toward a unifying theory of behavioral change. *Psychological Review, 84,* 191–215.

Bandura, A. (1982). Self-efficacy mechanism in human agency. *American Psychologist, 37,* 122–147.

Bandura, A. (1986). *Social foundations of thought and action: A social cognitive theory.* Englewood Cliffs, NJ: Prentice-Hall.

Bandura, A. (1988a). Perceived self-efficacy: Exercise of control through self-belief. In J. P. Dauwalder, M. Perrez, & V. Hobi (Eds.), *Annual series of European research in behavior therapy* (Vol. 2, pp. 27–59). Lisse (NL): Swets & Zeitlinger.

Bandura, A. (1988b). Self-efficacy conception of anxiety. *Anxiety Research, 1,* 77–98.

Bandura, A., Blanchard, E. B., & Ritter, B. (1969). Relative efficacy of desensitization and modeling approaches for inducing behavioral, affective, and attitudinal changes. *Journal of Personality and Social Psychology, 13,* 173–199.

Bandura, A., Jeffery, R. W., & Gajdos, E. (1975). Generalizing change through participant modeling with self-directed mastery. *Behaviour Research and Therapy, 13,* 141–152.

Bandura, A., Jeffery, R. W., & Wright, C. L. (1974). Efficacy of participant modeling as a function of response induction aids. *Journal of Abnormal Psychology, 83,* 56–64.

Bandura, A., & Menlove, F. L. (1968). Factors determining vicarious extinction of avoidance behavior through symbolic modeling. *Journal of Personality and Social Psychology, 8,* 99–108.

Bandura, A., Reese, L., & Adams, N. E. (1982). Microanalysis of action and fear arousal as a function of differential levels of perceived self-efficacy. *Journal of Personality and Social Psychology, 43,* 5–21.

Bandura, A., & Rosenthal, T. L. (1966). Vicarious classical conditioning as a function of arousal level. *Journal of Personality and Social Psychology, 3,* 54–62.

Bandura, A., Taylor, C. B., Williams, S. L., Mefford, I. N., & Barchas, J. D. (1985). Catecholamine secretion as a function of perceived coping self-efficacy. *Journal of Consulting and Clinical Psychology, 53,* 406–414.

Beck, A. T., Laude, R., & Bohnert, M. (1974). Ideational components of anxiety neurosis. *Archives of General Psychiatry, 31,* 319–325.

Berger, S. M. (1962). Conditioning through vicarious instigation. *Psychological Review, 69,* 450–466.

Birch, L. L. (1980). Effects of peer models' food choices and eating behaviors on preschoolers' food preferences. *Child Development, 51,* 489–496.

Blanchard, E. B. (1970). Relative contributions of modeling, informational influences, and physical contact in extinction of phobic behavior. *Journal of Abnormal Psychology, 76,* 55–61.

Bolles, R. C. (1975). *Learning theory.* New York: Holt, Rinehart & Winston.

Brown, I., Jr. (1974). Effects of perceived similarity on vicarious emotional conditioning. *Behavior Research and Therapy, 12,* 165–174.

Brown, I., Jr., & Inouye, D. K. (1978). Learned helplessness through modeling: The role of perceived similarity in competence. *Journal of Personality and Social Psychology, 36,* 900–908.

Bryant, J., Carveth, R. A., & Brown, D. (1981). Television viewing and anxiety: An experimental examination. *The Journal of Communication, 31,* 106–119.

Campos, J. J. (1983). The importance of affective communication in social referencing: A commentary on Feinman. *Merrill-Palmer Quarterly, 29,* 83–87.

Cantor, J., & Wilson, B. J. (1984). Modifying fear responses to mass media in preschool and elementary school children. *Journal of Broadcasting, 28,* 431–443.

Church, R. M. (1959). Emotional reactions of rats to the pain of others. *Journal of Comparative and Physiological Psychology, 52,* 132–134.

Cook, M., Mineka, S., Wolkenstein, B., & Laitsch, K. (1985). Observational conditioning of snake fear in unrelated rhesus monkeys. *Journal of Abnormal Psychology, 94,* 591–610.

Craig, K. D., & Lowery, H. J. (1969). Heart-rate components of conditioned vicarious autonomic responses. *Journal of Personality and Social Psychology, 11,* 381–387.

Craig, K. D., & Weinstein, M. S. (1965). Conditioning vicarious affective arousal. *Psychological Reports, 17,* 955–963.

Dawson, M. E., Schell, A. M., Banis, H. T. (1986). Greater resistance to extinction of electrodermal responses conditioned to potentially phobic CSs: A noncognitive process? *Psychophysiology, 23,* 552–561.

DeSilva, P., Rachman, S., & Seligman, M. E. P. (1977). Prepared phobias and obsessions: Therapeutic outcome. *Behaviour Research and Therapy, 15,* 65–77.

Dickson, W. P. (1982). Two decades of referential communication research: A review and meta-analysis. In C. J. Brainerd & M. Pressley (Eds.), *Verbal processes in children* (pp. 1–33). New York: Springer-Verlag.

Duncker, K. (1938). Experimental modification of children's food preferences through social suggestion. *Journal of Abnormal Social Psychology, 33,* 489–507.

Dysinger, W. S., & Ruckmick, C. A. (1933). *The emotional responses of children to the motion-picture situation.* New York: Macmillan.

Englis, B. G., Vaughan, K. B., & Lanzetta, J. T. (1982). Conditioning of counter-empathetic emotional responses. *Journal of Experimental Social Psychology, 18,* 375–391.

Feinman, S. (1982). Social referencing in infancy. *Merrill-Palmer Quarterly, 28,* 445–470.

Feinman, S. (1985). Mother knows best—but sometimes I know better: Emotional expression, social referencing and preparedness for learning in infancy. In G. Zivin (Ed.), *The development of expressive behavior: Biology–environment interactions* (pp. 291–318). Orlando, FL: Academic Press.

Festinger, L., (1954). A theory of social comparison processes. *Human Relations, 7,* 117–140.

Flavell, J. H. (1968). *The development of role-taking and communication skills in children.* New York: Wiley.

Geen, R. G., & Rakosky, J. J. (1973). Interpretations of observed aggression and their effect on GSR. *Journal of Experimental Research in Personality, 6,* 289–292.

Geer, J. H., Davidson, G. C., & Gatchel, R. I. (1970). Reduction of stress in humans through nonveridical perceived control of aversive stimulation. *Journal of Personality and Social Psychology, 16,* 731–738.

Gerbner, G., Gross, L., Signorielli, N., & Morgan, M. (1980). Aging with television: Images on television drama and conceptions of social reality. *Journal of Communication, 30,* 37–47.

Glass, D. C., Reim, B., & Singer, J. (1971). Behavioral consequences of adaptation to controllable and uncontrollable noise. *Journal of Experimental Social Psychology, 7,* 244–257.

Glass, D. C., Singer, J. E., Leonard, H. S., Krantz, D., & Cummings, H. (1973). Perceived control of aversive stimulation and the reduction of stress responses. *Journal of Personality, 41,* 577–595.

Gould, D., & Weiss, M. (1981). Effect of model similarity and model self-talk on self-efficacy in muscular endurance. *Journal of Sport Psychology, 3,* 17–29.

Greco, T. S. (1973). The effects of prior situational and aversive experience on vicarious emotional arousal (Doctoral dissertation, University of Georgia). *Dissertation Abstracts International, 33,* 4506-B. (University Microfilms No. 73–670a, 98)

Gunnar, M. R., & Stone, C. (1984). The effects of positive maternal affect on infant responses to pleasant, ambiguous and fear-provoking toys. *Child Development, 55,* 1231–1236.

Gunnar-vonGnechten, M. R. (1978). Changing a frightening toy into a pleasant toy by allowing the infant to control its actions. *Development Psychology, 14,* 147–152.

Hackett, G., & Betz, N. E. (1982, April). *Mathematics performance, mathematics self-efficacy, and the prediction of science-based college majors*. Paper presented at the Annual Meeting of the Educational Research Association, New York.

Harper, L. V., & Sanders, K. M. (1975). The effect of adults' eating on young children's acceptance of unfamiliar foods. *Journal of Experimental Child Psychology, 20,* 206–214.

Heath, L. (1984). Impact of newspaper crime reports on fear of crime: Multimethodological investigation. *Journal of Personality and Social Psychology, 47,* 263–276.

Hoffman, H. S. (1969). Stimulus factors in conditioned suppression. In B. A. Campbell & R. M. Church (Eds.) *Punishment and aversive behavior* (pp. 185–234). New York: Appleton-Century-Crofts.

Hornik, R., Risenhoover, N., & Gunnar, M. (1987). The effects of maternal positive, neutral, and negative affective communications on infant responses to new toys. *Child Development, 58,* 937–944.

Hughes, R., Jr., Tingle, B. A., & Swain, D. B. (1981). Development of empathic understanding in children. *Child Development, 52,* 122–128.

Hygge, S. (1978). The observer's acquaintance with the models' stimulus in vicarious classical conditioning. *Scandinavian Journal of Psychology, 19,* 231–239.

Hygge, S., & Ohman, A. (1978). Modeling processes in the acquisition of fears: Vicarious electrodermal conditioning to fear-relevant stimuli. *Journal of Personality and Social Psychology, 36,* 271–279.

Iannotti, R. J. (1978). Effect of role-taking experiences on role taking, empathy, altruism, and aggression. *Developmental Psychology, 14,* 119–124.

Izard, C. E. (1971). *The face of emotion.* New York: Appleton-Century-Crofts.

Kato, M., & Fukushima, O. (1977). The effects of covert modeling in reducing avoidance behavior. *Japanese Psychological Research, 19,* 199–203.

Kazdin, A. E. (1973). Covert modeling and the reduction of avoidance behavior. *Journal of Abnormal Psychology, 81,* 87–95.

Kazdin, A. E. (1978). Covert modeling—Therapeutic application of imagined rehearsal. In J. L. Singer & K. S. Pope (Eds.), *The power of human imagination: New methods in psychotherapy. Emotions, personality, and psychotherapy* (pp. 255–278). New York: Plenum.

Klinnert, M. D., Campos, J. J., Sorce, J. F., Emde, R. N., & Svejda, M. (1983). Emotions as behavior regulators: Social referencing in infancy. In R. Plutchik & H. Kellerman (Eds.), *Emotion: Theory, research, and experience* (Vol. 2, pp. 57–86). New York: Academic Press.

Klinnert, M. D., Emde, R. N., Butterfield, P., & Campos, J. J. (1986). Social referencing: The infant's use of emotional signals from a friendly adult with mother present. *Developmental Psychology, 22,* 427–432.

Klorman, R., Hilpert, P. L., Michael, R., LaGana, C., & Sveen, O. B. (1980). Effects of coping and mastery modeling on experienced and inexperienced pedodontic patients' disruptiveness. *Behavior Therapy, 11,* 156–168.

Krauss, R. M., Apple, W., Morency, N., Wenzel, C., & Winton, W. (1981). Verbal, vocal, and visible factors in judgments of another's affect. *Journal of Personality and Social Psychology, 40,* 312–320.

Kravetz, D. F. (1970). Heart rate as a minimal cue for the occurrence of conditioned vicarious autonomic responses. *Psychonomic Science, 19,* 90–91.

Kravetz, D. F. (1974). Heart rate as a minimal cue for the occurrence of vicarious classical conditioning. *Journal of Personality and Social Psychology, 29,* 125–131.

Krebs, D. (1975). Empathy and altruism. *Journal of Personality and Social Psychology, 32,* 1134–1146.

Lanzetta, J. T., & Englis, B. G. (1989). Expectations of cooperation and competition and their effects on observers' vicarious emotional responses. *Journal of Personality and Social Psychology, 56,* 543–554.

Lanzetta, J. T., & Orr, S. P. (1980). Influence of facial expressions on the classical conditioning of fear. *Journal of Personality and Social Psychology, 39*, 1081–1087.

Lanzetta, J. T., & Orr, S. P. (1981). Stimulus properties of facial expressions and their influence on the classical conditioning of fear. *Motivation and Emotion, 5*, 225–234.

Lazarus, R. S., & Folkman, S. (1984). *Stress, appraisal, and coping.* New York: Springer.

Lazarus, R. S., Speisman, J. C., Mordkoff, A. M., & Davison, L. A. (1962). A laboratory study of psychological stress produced by a motion picture film. *Psychological Monographs, 76* (No. 34, Whole No. 554).

Lee, C. (1984a). Accuracy of efficacy and outcome expectations in predicting performance in a simulated assertiveness task. *Cognitive Therapy and Research, 8*, 37–48.

Lee, C. (1984b). Efficacy expectations and outcome expectations as predictors of performance in a snake-handling task. *Cognitive Therapy and Research, 8*, 509–516.

McHugo, G. J., Smith, C. A., & Lanzetta, J. T. (1982). The structure of self-reports of emotional responses to film segments. *Motivation and Emotion, 6*, 365–385.

McNally, R. J. (1987). Preparedness and phobias: A review. *Psychology Bulletin, 101*, 283–303.

McNally, R. J., & Foa, E. B. (1986). Preparedness and resistance to extinction to fear-relevant stimuli: A failure to replicate. *Behaviour Research and Therapy, 24*, 529–535.

McNally, R. J., & Reiss, S. (1982). The preparedness theory of phobia and human safety-signal conditioning. *Behaviour Research and Therapy, 20*, 153–159.

McNally, R. J., & Reiss, S. (1984). The preparedness theory of phobias: The effects of initial fear level on safety-signal conditioning to fear-relevant stimuli. *Psychophysiology, 21*, 647–652.

Meichenbaum, D. H. (1971). Examination of model characteristics in reducing avoidance behavior. *Journal of Personality and Social Psychology, 17*, 298–307.

Merckelbach, H., van den Hout, M. A., & van der Molen, G. M. (1989). The phylogenetic origin of phobias: A review of the evidence. In P. Emmelkamp *et al.* (Ed.), *Fresh perspectives on anxiety disorders; biological, behavioral, and cognitive models.* Amsterdam: Swets.

Miller, R. E., Banks, J. H., Jr., & Ogawa, N. (1962). Communication of affect in "cooperative conditioning" of rhesus monkeys. *Journal of Abnormal and Social Psychology, 64*, 343–348.

Miller, R. E., Banks, J. H., Jr., & Ogawa, N. (1963). Role of facial expression in "cooperative-avoidance conditioning" in monkeys. *Journal of Abnormal and Social Psychology, 67*, 24–30.

Miller, R. E., Caul, W. F., & Mirsky, I. A. (1967). Communication of affect between feral and socially isolated monkeys. *Journal of Personality and Social Psychology, 7*, 231–239.

Miller, R. E., Murphy, J. V., & Mirsky, I. A. (1959). Nonverbal communication of affect. *Journal of Clinical Psychology, 15*, 155–158.

Miller, S. M. (1979). Controllability and human stress: Method, evidence and theory. *Behaviour Research and Therapy, 17*, 287–304.

Miller, S. M. (1980). Why having control reduces stress: If I can stop the rollercoaster I don't want to get off. In J. Garber & M. E. P. Seligman (Eds.), *Human helplessness: Theory and applications* (pp. 71–95). New York: Academic Press.

Miller, S. M. (1981). Predictability and human stress: Towards a clarification of evidence and theory. In. L. Berkowitz (Ed.), *Advances in experimental social psychology* (Vol. 14, pp. 204–256). New York: Academic Press.

Mineka, S., & Cook, M. (1986). Immunization against the observational conditioning of snake fear in rhesus monkeys. *Journal of Abnormal Psychology, 95*, 307–318.

Mineka, S., Davidson, M., Cook, M., & Keir, R. (1984). Observational conditioning of snake fear in rhesus monkeys. *Journal of Abnormal Psychology, 93*, 355–372.

Mineka, S., Gunnar, M., & Champoux, M. (1986). Control and early socioemotional development: Infant rhesus monkeys reared in controllable versus uncontrollable environments. *Child Development, 57*, 1241–1256.

Ogston, K. M., & Davidson, P. O. (1972). The effects of cognitive expectancies on vicarious conditioning. *The British Journal of Social and Clinical Psychology, 11*, 126–134.

Ohman, A., Erixon, G., & Lofberg, I. (1975). Phobias and preparedness: Phobic versus neutral pictures as conditioned stimuli for human autonomic responses. *Journal of Abnormal Psychology, 84*, 41–45.

Ohman, A., Fredrikson, M., Hugdahl, K., & Rimmo, P. (1976). The premise of equipotentiality in human classical conditioning: Conditioned electrodermal responses to potentially phobic stimuli. *Journal of Experimental Psychology, 105*, 313–337.

Ohman, A., & Hugdahl, K. (1979). Instructional control of autonomic respondents: Fear relevance as a critical factor. In N. Birbaumer and H. D. Kimmerl (Eds.), *Biofeedback and self-regulation* (pp. 149–165). Hillsdale, NJ: Erlbaum.

Ozer, E., & Bandura, A. (1990). Mechanisms governing empowerment effects: A self-efficacy analysis. *Journal of Personality and Social Psychology, 58*, 472–486.

Pingree, S., & Hawkins, R. (1981). U.S. programs on Australian television: The cultivation effect. *The Journal of Communication, 31*, 97–105.

Rosenthal, T. L., & Bandura, A. (1978). Psychological modeling: Theory and practice. In S. L. Garfield & A. E. Bergin (Eds.), *Handbook of psychotherapy and behavior change: An empirical analysis* (2nd ed., pp. 621–658). New York: Wiley.

Sackett, G. P. (1966). Monkeys reared in isolation with pictures as visual input: Evidence for an innate releasing mechanism. *Science, 154*, 1468–1473.

Sarason, I. G. (1975). Test anxiety and the self-disclosing coping model. *Journal of Consulting and Clinical Psychology, 43*, 148–153.

Schunk, D. H., Hanson, A. R., & Cox, P. D. (1987). Peer-model attributes and children's achievement behaviors. *Journal of Educational Psychology, 79*, 54–61.

Schwartz, B. (1978). *Psychology of learning and behavior.* New York: Norton.

Seligman, M. E. P. (1971). Phobias and preparedness. *Behavior Therapy, 2*, 307–320.

Sorce, J. F., Emde, R. N., Campos, J. J., & Klinnert, M. D. (1985). Maternal emotional signaling: Its effect on the visual cliff behavior of 1-year-olds. *Developmental Psychology, 21*, 195–200.

Stotland, E. (1969). Exploratory investigations of empathy. In L. Berkowitz (Ed.), *Advances in experimental social psychology* (Vol. 4, pp. 271–314). New York: Academic Press.

Suls, J. M., & Miller, R. L. (Eds.). (1977). *Social comparison processes: Theoretical and empirical perspectives.* Washington, DC: Hemisphere.

Takata, C., & Takata, T. (1976). The influence of models in the evaluation of ability: Two functions of social comparison processes. *The Japanese Journal of Psychology, 47*, 74–84.

Vaughan, K. B., & Lanzetta, J. T. (1980). Vicarious instigation and conditioning of facial expressive and autonomic responses to a model's expressive display of pain. *Journal of Personality and Social Psychology, 38*, 909–923.

Walden, T. A., & Ogan, T. A. (1988). The development of social referencing. *Child Development, 59*, 1230–1240.

Welch, A. S., & Welch, B. L. (1968). Reduction of norepinephrine in the lower brainstem by psychological stimulus. *Proceedings of the National Academy of Sciences, 60*, 478–481.

Williams, S. L., Dooseman, G., & Kleifield, E. (1984). Comparative power of guided mastery and exposure treatments for intractable phobias. *Journal of Consulting and Clinical Psychology, 52*, 505–518.

Williams, S. L., Turner, S. M., & Peer, D. F. (1985). Guided mastery and performance desensitization treatments for severe acrophobia. *Journal of Consulting and Clinical Psychology, 53*, 237–247.

Williams, S. L., & Watson, N. (1985). Perceived danger and perceived self-efficacy as cognitive mediators of acrophobic behavior. *Behavior Therapy, 16*, 136–146.

Wilson, B. J., & Cantor, J. (1985). Developmental differences in empathy with a television protagonist's fear. *Journal of Experimental Child Psychology, 39*, 284–299.

Wilson, B. J., Hoffner, C., & Cantor, J. (1987). Children's perception of the effectiveness of techniques to reduce fear from mass media. *Journal of Applied Developmental Psychology, 8,* 39–52.

Windheuser, H. J. (1977). Anxious mothers as models for coping with anxiety. *Behavioral Analysis and Modification, 2,* 39–58.

Wortman, C. B., Panciera, L., Shusterman, L., & Hibscher, J. (1976). Attributions of causality and reactions to uncontrollable outcomes. *Journal of Experimental Social Psychology, 12,* 301–316.

Wyrwicka, W. (1978). Imitation of mother's inappropriate food preference in weaning kittens. *The Pavlovian Journal of Biological Science, 13,* 55–72.

Zafiropoulou, M., & McPerson, F. M. (1986). Preparedness and the severity and outcome of clinical phobias. *Behaviour Research Therapy, 24,* 221–222.

Zarbatany, L., & Lamb, M. E. (1985). Social referencing as a function of information source: Mothers versus strangers. *Infant Behavior and Development, 8,* 25–33.

9

Control, Social Referencing, and the Infant's Appraisal of Threat

Robin Hornik Parritz, Sarah Mangelsdorf, and Megan R. Gunnar

Current theories of infant fear emphasize the importance of the infant's cognitive appraisal of threat (e.g., Campos & Stenberg, 1981; Sroufe, Waters, & Matas, 1974). Rather than arguing that the infant responds primarily to the arousing properties of a stimulus, these theories propose that the infant, by the end of the first year, actively evaluates and assigns meaning to events. Some form of active appraisal seems necessary to explain why the same event can sometimes elicit fear and sometimes laughter (Sroufe *et al.*, 1974). However, without an understanding of the factors that enter into the infant's appraisal of threat, appraisal theory does not provide a satisfying explanation for why the infant finds some events scary and others pleasurable.

Most social referencing research has focused on one explanation of how infants appraise threat: they reference another person's emotional

ROBIN HORNIK PARRITZ • Department of Psychology, Hamline University, St. Paul, Minnesota 55104.   SARAH MANGELSDORF • Department of Psychology, University of Illinois, Champaign–Urbana, Illinois 61820.   MEGAN R. GUN-NAR • Institute of Child Development, University of Minnesota, Minneapolis, Minnesota 55455.

Social Referencing and the Social Construction of Reality in Infancy, edited by Saul Feinman. Plenum Press, New York, 1992.

response (Campos & Stenberg, 1981). If the person acts frightened, the infant decides the event is scary; if the person acts happy, the infant decides that the event is pleasant. Along with this type of affective referencing, Feinman (1983) has argued that babies also engage in instrumental referencing: they also look to others to find out what to do to influence new events. In this chapter, we argue that social referencing is indeed a part of infant threat appraisal. However, we suggest that referencing of both the affective and instrumental varieties enters into threat appraisal primarily because it provides information that increases predictability and control. We believe that control and predictability are two of the three major factors in threat appraisal during infancy, the third factor being the availability of primary attachment figures (Sroufe et al., 1974).

PREDICTABILITY, CONTROL, AND FEAR

There are now numerous studies which indicate that both the controllability and predictability of events play an important role in regulating fear in human adults and animals (see reviews by Averill, 1973; Seligman, 1975). Control over an event, even a painful one, reduces emotional distress and buffers physiological stress reactions (see Weiss, 1971). Objective control is not necessary. In the absence of "true" control, false perceptions of control suffice to reduce fear and stress among adults (Glass & Singer, 1972). Conversely, objective control may not be enough. Without feedback that threat has been avoided, objective control does not reduce fear, and may in fact increase it (Weiss, 1971).

Results such as these have led Bandura (1977) to argue that control moderates threat appraisal to the extent that it affects the person's sense of self-efficacy. But why should a sense of control or efficacy reduce perceived threat? Opinions differ, but most center around some aspect of predictability. When people believe that they are competent to control an event, then they can predict with confidence the nature, intensity, and severity of the experience (Miller, 1981).

Control and prediction are intimately linked. Having control means knowing what will happen (Seligman, 1975). Of course, predictability can exist in the absence of control, although predictability alone probably never provides as certain a sense of safety as does control. Both animals and human adults will choose signaled noxious events over unsignaled ones (Badia, Culbertson, & Harsh, 1973; Badia, Harsh, & Coker, 1975; Pervin, 1968). Surprisingly, the need to predict noxious stimulation is so strong that animals will choose signaled shock that is several times more intense than unsignaled shock, even though there is nothing that the increased predictability allows them to do to avoid or modify the stimulation. Seligman (Seligman & Binik, 1977) has argued that choice of predictable over unpredictable shock reflects the animal's need to predict safety. Without knowing when noxious events will happen, one has no way to predict when they will not occur. Without knowing when one is safe, one can never relax.

Miller (1981) has examined another type of predictability in research with human adults. As with predicting the "when" of noxious events, people often choose to know *what* will happen, even when the "what" is bad news. Miller argues that choosing to know, rather than ignore, bad news is also regulated by the need to predict safety. Knowing what is *really* going to happen saves one from imagining consequences that are worse than the real thing. Not all human adults, however, choose predictability over unpredictability. Miller believes that this is because human beings use distraction and denial as major coping strategies. Denying that anything bad will happen sometimes can be more effective in reducing perceived threat than knowing the worst. Similarly, tuning out sometimes can be more effective at reducing threat perceptions than monitoring when a noxious event will and will not occur. Some bad things are harder to deny than others, and some situations facilitate distraction better than others. Thus, there should be situational differences in both the preference for and effectiveness of predictability in reducing fear. Individuals also differ in their reliance on denial and their ability to distract, thus, there also should be individual differences in the effects of predictability on fear. Some people, as Miller (1981) notes, tend to be Monitors, who seek increased predictability, and others Blunters, who use denial and distraction. Predictability tends to reduce fear for Monitors, and increase it for Blunters.

Thus, both control and predictability play central roles in threat appraisal, and both appear to reduce distress to the extent that they permit individuals to increase their perceptions of safety. People, however, are not always in a position to control or predict when and what will happen. Among adults, there is evidence that seeking assistance from a trusted other who is more competent or capable also reduces threat appraisal (Glass & Singer, 1972). Using more competent others to control events can be termed *mediated control*. This is the type of control characteristic of early childhood. The concept of mediated control is similar to Rothbaum, Weisz, and Snyder's (1982) concept of vicarious primary control.

Children must often appeal to more powerful and competent adults for help. While the presence of a familiar adult may have a direct impact on the child's affect (Panksepp, Herman, Vilberg, Bishop, & DeEskinazi, 1978), the adult's history of sensitivity and responsiveness should also matter (Gunnar, 1982; Lewis & Goldberg, 1969; Watson, 1977). The more sensitive and responsive the child knows the adult to be, the greater the child's sense of mediated control. Thus, the presence of a responsive adult should be especially fear reducing, while the presence of an unresponsive or preoccupied adult should have less of a fear-reducing effect (Main, 1973; Sorce & Emde, 1981).

CONTROL, PREDICTABILITY, AND INFANT FEAR

Control

Although much of the infant's control over events must be mediated through the responsiveness of adults, with development the infant increasingly acquires skills that permit direct control. The idea that direct control might mediate fear in infancy is not new. Bronson (1972) suggested that control over proximity to a stationary object explained why infants were less distressed by it than by a mobile object. Similarly, Rheingold and Eckerman (1969) argued that infants are only distressed by separation when they are not the ones to control the initiation and termination of the separation interval. Jersild and Holmes (1935), in their classic studies of children's fears, noted that fear of the dark could be modified by teaching preschoolers how to turn on the lights in a darkened room. Finally, Horner (1980) argued that stranger fear was a function of lack of control over the stranger's behavior.

Unfortunately, in none of the above studies were yoked comparison groups employed; thus none of these studies provide an adequate test of the controllability hypothesis. To directly test the hypothesis that control mediates fear in infancy, one of us (Gunnar-vonGnechten, 1978) permitted one group of 12-month-olds to control the actions of a noisy, mechanical monkey and compared the reactions of the Controlling infants to those of yoked, Noncontrolling infants who received the same stimulation uncontrollably. Reactions to two nonaversive training toys did not differ by condition. In contrast, reactions to the noisy monkey differed sharply by whether the infant did or did not have control. Not only were the Controlling infants quite willing to self-activate the noisy monkey toy, but they also cried less (boys), and smiled and laughed more (both sexes) than did the yoked infants (see Figures 1 & 2). Furthermore, when given the opportunity, the Controlling infants were more likely than their yoked partners to approach and handle the toy. Thus, by 12 months, direct control over the activation of a noisy toy changed it from a threatening stimulus into a pleasant one. How early does this kind of direct control reduce distress? In a subsequent study (Gunnar, 1980), when the same paradigm was used to test 6-, 9-, and 12-month-olds, only the 12-month-olds showed the fear-reducing effects of control.

We have recently replicated this pattern of developmental change in the effects of control on threat appraisal in several studies of stranger fear

(Mangelsdorf, 1988; Mangelsdorf, Lehr, & Friedman, 1986). In these studies we were interested in understanding why babies are more fearful and wary of some strangers than others (Rheingold & Eckerman, 1973; Scarr & Salapatek, 1970). We expected that a significant portion of the difference could be attributed to the ways strangers interact with babies. We expected that babies would respond more positively to strangers who acted more predictably and who allowed the baby more control. To test this hypothesis we had three strangers interact with each baby. Coders blind to the

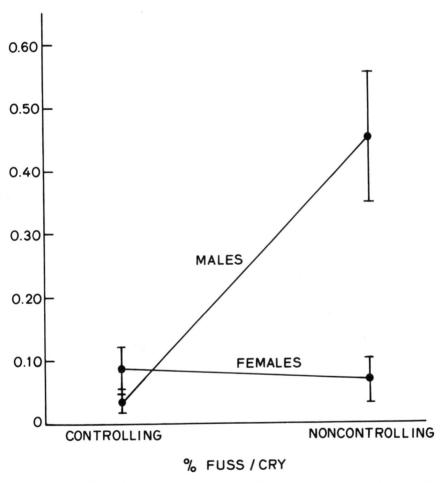

Figure 1. The effects of control on percentage of coding intervals spent crying in response to the fear-eliciting toy. Bars reflect standard error of the mean. Gunnar-vonGnechten, 1978. Copyright (1978) by the American Psychological Association. Reprinted with permission of the publisher.

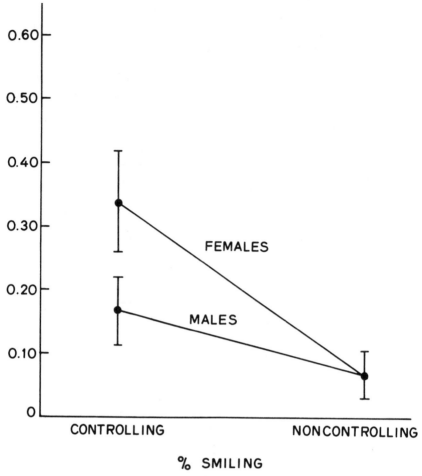

Figure 2. The effects of control on the percentage of coding intervals spent smiling at the potentially fear-eliciting toy. Bars reflect standard error of the mean. Gunnar-vonGnechten, 1978. Copyright (1978) by the American Psychological Association. Reprinted with permission of the publisher.

hypotheses separately scored stranger behavior in the first minutes and infant affect in the last minutes of each interaction.

In an initial pilot study (Mangelsdorf *et al.*, 1986), the reactions of 10-month-olds were examined. The 10-month-olds responded more positively to the more controllable and predictable strangers. In a subsequent study (Mangelsdorf, 1988), the reactions of 6-, 12- and 18-month-olds were examined. As shown in Table 1, control and predictability did not enter into the 6-month-olds' appraisal of the strangers. Instead, at 6 months, it was the stranger's friendliness or smiling that mattered. Conversely, at 12 and 18 months, friendliness was not enough. The 12- and 18-month-olds were also sensitive to whether the stranger was controllable and predictable. Twelve and 18-month-olds who were initially wary of a stranger would warm up if the stranger was controllable and predictable; conversely, initially friendly babies would become wary and fearful of unpredictable and uncontrollable strangers.

The importance of control in regulating stranger fear by the end of the first year has been confirmed in an experimental study (Mangelsdorf, Watkins, & Lehn, in preparation). Adult females were trained either to allow 12-month-olds to control the play sessions or to be controlling of the babies' actions. All babies interacted with both a Controllable and a Controlling stranger, and both of the strangers in this study served in each of the two stranger roles. As predicted, the 12-month-olds were more positive and more relaxed with the Controllable as compared to the Controlling stranger, even though both types of strangers displayed equivalent amounts of positive affect. These data complement earlier work by Levitt (1980) showing that 10-month-olds smiled more during peek-a-boo if they could touch a cylinder to make the adult "peek-a-boo," than if the adult "peek-a-booed" on her own schedule.

To summarize, perceived control is a pivotal determinant of infant distress to arousing events. Furthermore, its importance as a modulator of distress appears to emerge during the last quarter of the first year. This is when others have targeted the transition from affect based primarily on the intensity of arousing qualities of stimulation, to affect based on appraisal of the meaning of stimulation (Sroufe, 1979). Control does not alter the intensity or quality of stimulation: for control to have an impact it must alter the meaning of the event. Thus, our data are highly consistent with

Table 1.   Infant Positive Reactivity Correlates with Stranger Behavior[a]

	Infant age (months)		
Stranger behaviors	6	12	18
Friendliness	.33**[b]	.26**	.25**
Control and predictability	.10	.36**	.27**

[a]Correlation coefficients reflect the average of three correlations at each age.
[b]Significance based on meta-analysis of the three coefficients computed for each stranger variable at each age.
*$p < .05$.
**$p < .10$.

the idea that affect becomes the product of cognitive appraisal by the end of the first year, and they implicate "control" as a central factor in that appraisal.

Predictability

In studies described above, control and predictability were confounded. Infants who turned on the noisy monkey themselves knew when it would come on and when it would not. And controllable strangers were also highly predictable in their actions. To examine the effects of predictability alone, we conducted a number of studies in which potentially threatening toys were made to act predictably without the infant being able to control them. All of the studies were conducted with 12-month-olds, and the bottom line appears to be that infants of this age do *not* find warning signals reassuring. In fact, warning signals increase distress reactions. Infants of this age, however, quickly pick up on predictable patterns of stimulation (autocontingencies) and appear to use these to moderate threat appraisal. The studies leading to these conclusions are now briefly outlined.

We (Gunnar, 1980) first examined warning signals in conjunction with studies of control. Twelve-month-olds either were allowed to turn on the noisy monkey toy, heard a tone for 1.5 seconds prior to each uncontrollable toy activation, or were given neither the opportunity to control nor predict the toy's actions. Although the infants looked at the toy when the tone came on and before the toy began to operate, as shown in Figure 3, the warning signal did not reduce distress for boys and it increased distress for girls. Because the toy only came on a few times in that study, we conducted a second study (Gunnar, Leighton, & Peleaux, 1984) in which 12-month-olds experienced a total of 36 activations of the toy monkey over 6 minutes. These activations were either preceded by a 2-second tone or were accompanied by a randomly occurring tone. In addition, the interactivation interval was either fixed (predictable) or variable (unpredictable). As shown in Figure 4, again the warning signal increased negative reactions to the toy.

In a final attempt to find that warning signals could reduce distress reactions by 12 months, we (Gunnar & Nanez, 1985) conducted a study in which the safe, or no-signal no-toy, time was much longer than the threat, or signal plus toy, time. We thought that perhaps the warning signal was not working because in our previous studies the periods of safety were too short to override the fact that having a warning signal increased the amount of unsafe time during testing. We observed 12-month-olds for 30 minutes with our noisy monkey. On average, every minute, the infants in the warning-signal condition experienced 20 seconds of "unsafe" (signal

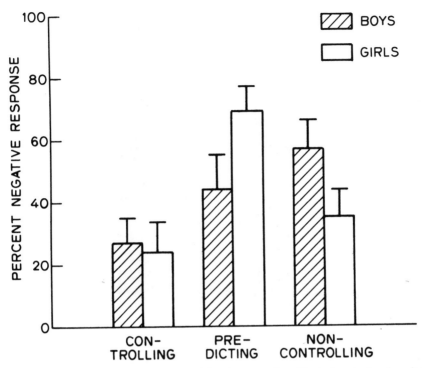

Figure 3. The effects of control, predictability (no control) and lack of control and predict-ability on infants' reactions to a potentially frightening toy. Bars reflect standard error of the mean. Gunnar, 1980. Copyright (1980) by the American Psychological Association. Reprinted with permission of the publisher.

plus toy) time and 40 seconds of "safety." In contrast, infants in the random signal and no-signal conditions experienced 60 seconds of unsafe time every minute because without a contingent signal, they could never pre-dict safety. Again the warning or contingent signal was not effective in reducing threat. Instead, it prolonged vigilant, wary, and negative reac-tions to the toy (Figure 5).

Since these studies were completed, we have examined the kinds of behavioral strategies infants use to cope with potentially threatening events. Similar to the results reported by others (e.g., Gianino & Tronik, 1987), we (Hornik & Gunnar, 1987; Parritz, 1989) have found that 12- and 18-month-olds rely heavily on distraction to cope with potentially threat-ening, arousing events. In research on adults, Miller (1981) has found that warning signals disrupt the use of distraction as a strategy. Furthermore, individuals who rely on distraction to cope (i.e., Blunters) are more dis-tressed by being warned than by not being warned about impending,

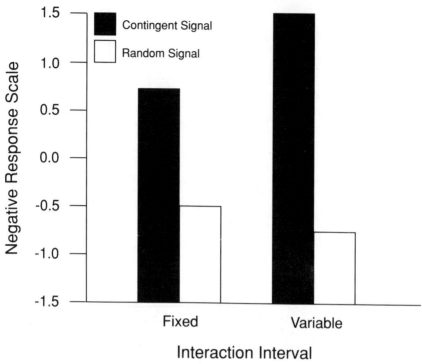

Figure 4. The effects of contingent (warning) signals on distress reactions to an aversive toy using fixed versus variable interaction intervals. Adapted from Gunnar, Leighton, & Peleaux, 1984. Copyright (1984) by the American Psychological Association. Adapted with permission of the publisher.

noxious stimulation. We began to suspect that the warning signals increased distress in our studies because they disrupted a primary coping strategy of infancy.

This type of reasoning led us to examine the effects of autocontingencies on infant distress. That is, we examined whether noisy toys elicited less distress if they operated on fixed as compared to variable on–off schedules. We expected that it would be especially easy to use distraction (i.e., free play with toys) and ignore the noisy toy if the toy came on and went off repeatedly on a fixed, unvarying schedule (4-sec on/4-sec off). Conversely, if it operated on a random, variable schedule, it should be quite intrusive and hard to ignore. These expectations were bolstered by evidence that autocontingencies reduce stress reactions in animals (Davis, Memmott, & Hurwitz, 1975), and that even very young infants are sensitive to such contingencies (Rovee-Collier & Lipsitt, 1982).

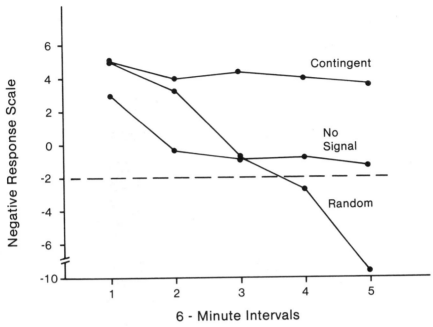

Figure 5. Reactions to an aversive toy over a 30-minute period as a function of a random versus contingent versus no signal. (Dotted line represents reactions to the signal when the toy is never activated. Gunnar & Nanez, 1985).

To our surprise, not only did we find that autocontingencies reduced negative reactions to the toy monkey among 12-month-olds, but we found that the babies were very particular about the aspect of stimulation that needed to occur on a fixed schedule. Only the interactivation intervals mattered (see Figure 6). As long as the toy always stayed off for the same period of time (4 sec), then the baby was able to get off the mother's lap, play with the age appropriate toys in the room, and ignore the noisy monkey.

CONTROL, PREDICTABILITY, AND SOCIAL REFERENCING

Thus far we have argued that control and predictability are two major factors in the infant's appraisal of threat. The focus of this volume, however, is on social referencing: the infant's use of another person's behavior in threat appraisal. Can social referencing be understood from a control and predictability framework? We believe it can. Information gleaned

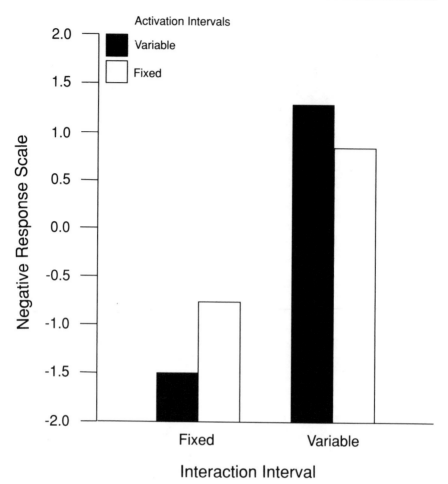

Figure 6. Infant reactions to fixed versus variable activation and interactivation intervals. Adapted from Gunnar *et al.*, 1984. Copyright (1984) by the American Psychological Association. Adapted with permission of the publisher.

through observing another's affective response to a new event should affect the infant's ability to predict whether the event will be pleasant or not. And, information obtained through watching how another acts on the event should increase the infant's understanding of how to control it.

Social Referencing and Predictability

If referencing increases predictability, it follows that referencing should occur most frequently under conditions of low predictability or high uncertainty (see also Campos & Stenberg, 1981). There are now several studies which support this argument. Sorce, Emde, Campos, and Klinnert (1985) showed that infants were more responsive to maternal facial expressions of emotion when confronted with a visual cliff drop-off of intermediate depth, as opposed to a large drop-off or no drop-off. We (Gunnar & Stone, 1984) also found that 12-month-old infants shown toys that were pleasant, fear-eliciting, or ambiguous were only responsive to maternal expressions of positive affect when confronted with the ambiguous toy. In a subsequent study (Hornik, Risenhoover, & Gunnar, 1987), infants were responsive to maternal affect regardless of whether the stimulus toy was designated as ambiguous or not. However, in that study mothers expressed disgust and the stimulus toys had plastic bugs attached to them. We reasoned that the plastic bugs may have made all of the stimulus toys seem ambiguous.

In the Gunnar and Stone (1984) study we presented each toy twice, once with the mother expressing neutral affect and once with her expressing positive affect. The order of maternal expression was, of course, counterbalanced. Interestingly, we found the effect of positive affect only on the second trial with the ambiguous stimulus (see Table 2). Campos and Stenberg (1981) originally suggested that social referencing was part of a secondary appraisal process. Accordingly, infants should first attempt to appraise the event on their own, and then when they are unable to do so, they should seek help from the actions and reactions of others. The results of the Gunnar and Stone (1984) study support this hypothesis. The infants were responsive to their mother's affective reactions to the ambiguous toy, but only on the second trial with the toy. On the first trial, which lasted 1.5 minutes, they appeared to ignore their mother's reactions and attempted to appraise the stimulus on their own.

Table 2. Means and Standard Errors of the Negative Response Scale Scores in Reaction to the Stimulus Toys

Order of maternal simulated affect from Trial 1 to 2	Ferris wheel		Robot		Monkey	
	Trial 1	Trial 2	Trial 1	Trial 2	Trial 1	Trial 2
Positive to neutral	4.7	5.6	6.9	7.4	7.7	7.3
	(.5)[a]	(.6)	(.5)	(.6)	(.6)	(.7)
Neutral to positive	5.3	4.5	6.9	5.8	6.7	6.7
	(.6)	(.6)	(.5)	(.6)	(.6)	(.5)

[a]Standard error of the mean.
Note. Higher values represent more negative reactions. From Gunnar and Stone, 1984. Copyright 1984 by the Society for Research in Child Development. Reprinted with permission of the publishers.

Evidence that referencing occurs in response to uncertainty and is part of a secondary appraisal process, paradoxically, creates a problem. As with Kagan's (1974) discrepancy theory of fear, it is difficult, *a priori*, to determine whether an infant will find an event ambiguous and whether, following initial appraisal, the infant will be unable to make an independent judgment about it. The danger of circular argument, however, can be avoided by independently assessing the infant's affective expression. We (Hornik & Gunnar, 1988; Hornik & Larson, 1988) have attempted to do this by assessing infant affect in the first minute with a stimulus, and then scoring social referencing in the later minutes of the trial. When this is done, we have repeatedly noted that referencing is associated with wary affect. Compared to infants expressing positive affect, wary infants reference their mothers more. This relationship is stronger when stimulus-specific wariness is used to predict social referencing, than when maternal reports of generalized wariness (approach–withdrawal on the Toddler Temperament Scale) are used (Hornik & Larson, 1988).

Referencing versus Affective Sharing

Another way to show that referencing can be understood from a predictability framework is to compare referencing looks to affective-sharing looks. In affective sharing the infant smiles and then turns and shares the positive experience with another person, often an attachment figure. In referencing, the infant expresses neutral or wary affect when turning to look at the other person. Affective sharing should occur more frequently when the infant is certain about an event, and it should decrease in frequency when events become uncertain. The reverse should be the case for social referencing. We (Hornik & Larson, 1988) have recently examined both types of looks in response to four situations. One, a free-play condition, was designed to be unambiguously pleasant. The other three situations were designed to elicit wariness and approach–avoidance conflicts. The three challenging situations were: a live, caged rabbit; a spinning, mechanical toy; and a male stranger who sat in a chair with attractive toys arranged about his feet. As shown in Table 3, affective sharing occurred more often than referencing during free play, and less often than referencing during the challenge situations.

Active Participation, Instrumental Referencing, and Control

Much of the work on infant referencing has dealt with the infant's use of another person's affective reactions. Termed affective social referencing, this can be contrasted with instrumental social referencing, in which the infant observes others to learn the actions to perform in new situations (see

Table 3. Frequency of Referencing and Sharing in
Free-Play and Challenge Situations

	Situations	
Type of look	Free-play situation	Average of 3 challenge situations[a]
Affect sharing	6.3	1.6
Social referencing	1.0	2.9

[a]Average of rabbit, toy, and stranger situations.

Feinman, 1983, and Chapter 2, this volume). In new situations, infants are highly motivated to get their parents to actively participate in exploration (see Ainsworth, Blehar, Waters, & Wall, 1978); and anecdotally, parents often respond to the infant's social referencing by helping the infant explore, providing information about the object or event ("It's a rabbit. It's a nice Bun Bun. He won't bite you. Look, he has big, long ears. Oh, he's so soft.") and by showing the infant what to do ("See, I can pet him. Oh, he likes that.").

Most of the studies of infant social referencing have prevented parents from engaging in such active participation. By doing so, the opportunity to examine the impact of instrumental social referencing has been missed. Instrumental social referencing, or modeling (see Bandura, 1977), is a potent method of increasing self-efficacy (control) perceptions as shown in studies of older children and adults. In one of our referencing studies (Hornik & Gunnar, 1988), during one segment of the testing with the live, caged rabbit (Blacky), we asked the mother to go over to the cage and do whatever she wanted to help her baby feel relaxed and happy about the rabbit. Not surprisingly, nearly all of the infants approached Blacky's cage during this segment. Positive affect also increased sharply. Both of these changes could be attributed to increased maternal proximity. One change, however, seemed to point specifically to the power of instrumental social referencing.

When the mothers came over to the cage, all but three reached in and petted Blacky. During the first segments of the testing, nearly all of the infants seemed to want to pet him, but only one or two actually found the courage to do so. With mother close to the cage, half of the babies reached in and touched Blacky. But, none of the infants touched Blacky until they watched their mothers touch him first. Indeed, the infants whose mothers did not touch the rabbit also did not touch him.

As noted, the importance of instrumental social referencing has been largely overlooked in the infant social referencing literature (see Feinman,

1983, for a similar argument). Studies of infant imitation have revealed that infants are capable of modeling by the end of the first year (see Užgiris & Kruper, Chapter 6, this volume). Given the dramatic changes in infant behavior that we observed once the infants could engage in instrumental referencing, it would seem especially important to begin to explore the role of this process in infant threat appraisal. Knowing what to do with an ambiguous new object or event should increase the infant's sense of control. By increasing the baby's sense of control or efficacy, instrumental referencing should be even more potent than affective referencing in regulating fear and wariness.

Individual Differences

The history of research on control and predictability is replete with evidence of individual differences (e.g., Rotter, 1966; Seligman, 1975). There is good reason to expect that individual differences will also characterize the infant's use of social referencing in appraising threat. The need to consider differences among individuals is underscored by the results of studies in which the referrer has displayed only facial expressions of affect. In these studies, typically 20–25% of infants fail to reference. Were 25% of the infants in these studies not wary, or were they not likely ever to reference? We (Parritz, 1989) examined whether some babies simply do not reference by showing 12- and 18-month olds a variety of different events that could elicit wary reactions. Examined event by event, about a quarter of the infants failed to reference. However, summing across events, only 1–2% of the infants failed to do so. The use of social referencing, therefore, does appear to characterize the threat appraisal repertoire of most infants during the second year. At the same time, individual differences were still apparent. At both 12 and 18 months, the amount of social referencing was positively correlated across events. Infants who referenced more to one event referenced more to the other events.

What accounts for these differences in referencing? Several researchers have suggested that temperament may play a role. Bradshaw, Goldsmith, and Campos (1987) found that infants with more negative temperaments were slightly, but not significantly, less likely to seek information and significantly less likely to use information from mother to guide their behavior. Similarly, Feinman and Lewis (1983; Feinman, 1985) found that difficult infants did not seem to be influenced as much as easier infants by the mother's message during stranger approach. These data are in conflict with our own. Fear or wariness to the unfamiliar is a component of both difficult and negative temperament. Rather than referencing less, we (Hornik & Larson, 1988) noted a slight tendency among temperamentally wary babies to reference more. The apparent conflict among results may have to do with the threat potential of the stimulus materials. Referencing should occur most when the baby is wary, and the intensity of events eliciting wariness should differ for bold, easy babies versus fearful, difficult ones. If the stimuli used in a study elicit wariness in bold babies, then the bold babies will appear to reference more. The converse should be found in studies in which wariness is produced primarily in the difficult, fearful babies.

In addition to wary temperament, the quality of the infant's relationship to the referrer should also affect the likelihood of referencing. This possibility has been examined in several studies without much success. Dickstein, Thompson, Estes, Malkin, and Lamb (1984) found that insecure–resistant infants referenced more, and insecure–avoidant infants referenced less than secure infants. Because resistant and avoidant infants differ in parental reports of wariness (Gunnar, Mangelsdorf, Larson, & Hertsgaard, 1989), the Dickstein *et al.* (1984) result may merely reflect the wariness–referencing link discussed above. Furthermore, Bradshaw and colleagues (1987) were unable to find any relation between referencing and either the avoidance or resistance scale used to assign infants to attachment classification. Neither of these studies involved enough babies to examine relations between attachment quality and referencing while controlling for infant wariness. This needs to be done before any firm conclusions can be drawn about the relations between attachment quality and referencing.

SUMMARY

Predictability and control serve as major factors in the infant's appraisal of threat by the last part of the first year. Controllable events elicit more approach and more positive affect than uncontrollable events. This is true whether the event is a noise-making toy or an adult stranger. Likewise, events that start and stop predictably and strangers who act predictably are less fear provoking for the baby. We have argued in this chapter that both control and predictability decrease fear when they increase perceptions of safety. Furthermore, we have argued that perceived safety is more certain when events are controllable than when they are merely predictable. Finally, we have argued that social referencing is involved in infant threat appraisal because it serves as one of the infant's strategies for increasing predictability and determining the controllability of new events. Social referencing subserves the baby's need to predict and control.

We have noted that the relation between referencing and predictability is amply supported by evidence that referencing is more likely in the presence of ambiguous than unambiguous stimuli, that wariness is positively associated with referencing, and that positive affect sharing decreases under conditions that elicit increased referencing. The importance of referencing to control is less well documented. However, we have argued in this chapter that this may be because work on infant social referencing has largely neglected the study of instrumental referencing. This type of referencing, we suggest, may have even more potent effects on infant threat appraisal than referencing that only allows the infant to learn what another person feels about a new event. Finally, we have noted that there are individual differences in referencing, and have pointed out that to some extent these differences may be attributed to temperamental differences in wariness. However, we have argued that other factors associated with referencing, such as the quality of the relationship, need to be more adequately explored.

Acknowledgments: Work on this chapter was supported by Dissertation Fellowships to the first two authors and a Research Career Development Award from NIH to the third author. We would like to thank Saul Feinman for his comments on this chapter, and Lonnie Behrendt and LuJean Huffman-Nordberg for their secretarial help.

REFERENCES

Ainsworth, M. D. S., Blehar, M., Waters, E., & Wall, S. (1978). *Patterns of attachment: A psychological study of the strange situation.* Hillsdale, NJ: Erlbaum.

Averill, J. R. (1973). Personal control over aversive stimuli and its relationship to stress. *Psychological Bulletin, 80,* 286–303.

Badia, P., Culbertson, S., & Harsh, J. (1973). Choice of longer or stronger signalled shock over shorter or weaker unsignalled shock. *Journal of the Experimental Analysis of Behavior, 19,* 25–32.

Badia, P., Harsh, J., & Coker, C. (1975). Choosing between fixed time and variable time shock. *Learning and Motivation, 6,* 264–278.

Bandura, A. (1977). Self-efficacy: Toward a unifying theory of behavioral change. *Psychological Review, 84,* 191–215.

Bradshaw, D. L., Goldsmith, H. H., & Campos, J. J. (1987). Attachment, temperament, and social referencing: Interrelationships among three domains of infant affective behavior. *Infant Behavior and Development, 10,* 223–232.

Bronson, G. W. (1972). Infant's reactions to unfamiliar persons and novel objects. *Monographs of the Society for Research in Child Development, 37*(3 Serial No. 148).

Campos, J., & Stenberg, C. (1981). Perception, appraisal and emotion: The onset of social referencing. In M. Lamb & L. Sherrod (Eds.), *Infant social cognition: Empirical and theoretical considerations* (pp. 273–314). Hillsdale, NJ: Erlbaum.

Davis, H., Memmott, J., & Hurwitz, H. (1975). Autocontingencies: A model for subtle behavioral control. *Journal of Experimental Psychology: General, 104,* 169–188.

Dickstein, S., Thompson, R. A., Estes, D., Malkin, C., & Lamb, M. E. (1984). Social referencing and the security of attachment. *Infant Behavior and Development, 7,* 507–516.

Feinman, S. (1983). How does baby socially refer? Two views of social referencing: A reply to Campos. *Merrill-Palmer Quarterly, 29,* 467–471.

Feinman, S. (1985). Emotional expression, social referencing, and preparedness for learning in infancy—Mother knows best, but sometimes I know better. In G. Zivin (Ed.), *The development of expressive behavior: Biology–environment interactions* (pp. 291–318). Orlando: Academic Press.

Feinman, S., & Lewis, M. (1983). Social referencing at 10 months: A second-order effect on infants' responses to strangers. *Child Development, 54,* 878–887.

Gianino, A., & Tronick, E. (1987). The mutual regulation model: The infant's self and inter-active regulation, coping and defensive capacities. In T. Field, P. McCabe, & N. Schneiderman (Eds.), *Stress and coping, Vol. 2* (pp. 47–68). Hillsdale, NJ: Erlbaum.

Glass, D. C., & Singer, J. W. (1972). *Urban stress: Experiments on noise and social stressors.* New York: Academic Press.

Gunnar, M. (1980). Control, warning signals and distress in infancy. *Developmental Psychology, 16(4),* 281–289.

Gunnar, M. (1982). The development of control in infancy: Effects of poverty and malnutrition. *Baroda Journal of Nutrition, 9,* 110–115.

Gunnar, M. R., Leighton, K., & Peleaux, R. (1984). Effects of temporal predictability on the reactions of one-year-olds to potentially frightening toys. *Developmental Psychology, 20,* 449–458.

Gunnar, M., Mangelsdorf, S., Larson, M., & Hertsgaard, L. (1989). Attachment, temperament and adrenocortical activity in infancy: A study of psychoendocrine regulation. *Developmental Psychology, 25,* 355–363.

Gunnar, M. R., & Nanez, J. (1985). *Warning signals are not safety signals for one-year-olds.* Unpublished manuscript.

Gunnar, M. R., & Stone, C. (1984). The effects of positive maternal affect on infant responses to pleasant, ambiguous, and fear-provoking toys. *Child Development, 55,* 1231–1236.

Gunnar-vonGnechten, M. R. (1978). Changing a frightening toy into a pleasant toy by allowing the infant to control its actions. *Developmental Psychology, 14(2),* 157–162.

Horner, T. M. (1980). Two methods of studying stranger reactivity in infants: A review. *Journal of Child Psychology and Psychiatry, 21,* 203–219.

Hornik, R., & Gunnar, M. (1987, April). Towards a taxonomy of infant coping strategies. Paper presented at the biennial meeting of the Society for Research in Child Development, Baltimore.

Hornik, R., & Gunnar, M. R. (1988). A descriptive analysis of infant social referencing. *Child Development, 59,* 626–634.

Hornik, R., & Larson, M. (1988). *Social referencing: Relations between temperament and patterns of looking.* Paper presented at the International Conference on Infant Studies, Washington, DC.

Hornik, R., Risenhoover, N., & Gunnar, M. R. (1987). The effects of maternal positive, neutral, and negative affective communications on infant responses to new toys. *Child Development, 58,* 937–944.

Jersild, A. T., & Holmes, F. B. (1935). Children's fears. *Child Developmental Monograph, 20.*

Kagan, J. (1974). Discrepancy, temperament and infant distress. In M. Lewis & L. Rosenblum (Eds.), *The origins of fear* (pp. 229–248). New York: Wiley.

Levitt, M. J. (1980). Contingent feedback, familiarization, and infant affect: How a stranger becomes a friend. *Developmental Psychology, 16,* 425–432.

Lewis, M., & Goldberg, S. (1969). Perceptual-cognitive development in infancy: A generalized expectancy model as a function of the mother–infant interaction. *Merrill-Palmer Quarterly, 15,* 81–100.

Main, M. (1973). *Play, exploration and competence as related to child–adult attachment.* Unpublished doctoral dissertation, The Johns Hopkins University, Baltimore.

Mangelsdorf, S. (1988). *The development of social appraisal processes in infancy.* Unpublished doctoral dissertation, University of Minnesota, Minneapolis.

Mangelsdorf, S., Lehr, C., & Friedman, J. (1986). *Control, predictability and the infant's appraisal of strangers.* Paper presented at the International Conference on Infant Studies, Los Angeles.

Mangelsdorf, S., Watkins, S., & Lehn, L. (in preparation). *The role of control in infants' appraisal of strangers.*

Miller, S. (1981). Predictability and human stress: Towards a clarification of evidence and theory. In L. Berkowitz (Ed.), *Advances in experimental social psychology* (Vol 14., pp. 203–256). New York: Academic Press.

Panksepp, J., Herman, B., Vilberg, T., Bishop, P., & DeEskinazi, F. G. (1978). Endogenous opioids and social behavior. *Neuroscience Behavioral Reviews, 4,* 473–487.

Parritz, R. H. (1989). *An examination of toddler coping in three challenging situations.* Unpublished doctoral dissertation, University of Minnesota, Minneapolis.

Pervin, L. (1968). The need to predict and control under conditions of threat. *Journal of Personality, 31,* 570.

Rheingold, H., & Eckerman, C. (1969). The infant's free entry into a new environment. *Journal of Experimental Child Psychology, 8,* 271–283.

Rheingold, H., & Eckerman, C. (1973). Fear of the stranger: A critical examination. In H. Reese (Ed.), *Advances in child development and behavior, Vol. 8* (pp. 185–222). New York: Academic Press.

Rothbaum, F., Weisz, J. R., & Snyder, S. S. (1982). Changing the world and changing the self: A two-process model of perceived control. *Journal of Personality and Social Psychology, 42,* 5–37.

Rotter, J. B. (1966). Generalized expectancies for internal versus external control of reinforcement. *Psychological Monographs, 80* (Whole No. 609).

Rovee-Collier, C., & Lipsitt, L. (1982). Learning, adaptation and memory in the newborn. In P. Stratton (Ed.), *Psychology of the human newborn* (pp. 147–190). New York: Wiley.

Scarr, S., & Salapatek, P. (1970). Patterns of fear development during infancy. *Merrill-Palmer Quarterly, 16,* 53–90.

Seligman, M. (1975). *Learned helplessness: On development, depression, and death.* San Francisco: Freeman.

Seligman, M., & Binik, Y. (1977). The safety-signal hypothesis. In H. Davis & H. Hurwitz (Eds.), *Pavlovian-operant interactions* (pp. 165–180). Hillsdale, NJ: Erlbaum.

Sorce, J. F., & Emde, R. N. (1981). Mother's presence is not enough: The effect of emotional availability on infant exploration. *Developmental Psychology, 17,* 737–745.

Sorce, J. F., Emde, R. N., Campos, J. J., & Klinnert, M. D. (1985). Maternal emotional signaling: Its effects on the visual cliff behavior of one-year-olds. *Developmental Psychology, 20,* 195–200.

Sroufe, L. A. (1979). Socioemotional development. In J. Osofsky (Ed.), *Handbook of infant development* (pp. 462–515). New York: John Wiley.

Sroufe, L. A., Waters, E., & Matas, L. (1974). Contextual determinants of infant affective response. In M. Lewis & L. Rosenblum (Eds.), *The origins of fear* (pp. 49–72). New York: Wiley.

Watson, J. S. (1977). Depression and the perception of control in early childhood. In J. G. Schulterbrandt & A. Raskin (Eds.), *Depression in childhood: Diagnosis, treatment and conceptual models* (pp. 123–133). New York: Raven Press.

Weiss, J. M. (1971). Effects of coping behavior with and without a feedback signal on stress pathology in rats. *Journal of Comparative and Physiological Psychology, 77,* 22–30.

10

Social Referencing and Conformity

Saul Feinman

About 30 years ago, university students in Oslo and Paris participated in a study of conformity (Milgram, 1961), in which they were asked to determine which of two acoustic tones was the longer one. To answer this relatively simple question—the two tones were of obviously different lengths—the student sat in a booth and responded only after hearing what appeared to be the judgments of five other students who communicated via intercom from adjacent booths. In truth, the "voices" actually were tape recordings of answers to the tone length judgment question. In the critical trials when the "other students" gave the obviously wrong answer, the French students went along with the others' judgment 50% of the time, and the Norwegian students 62% of the time.

About 10 years ago, 10-month-old infants and their mothers participated in a study of social referencing in Princeton, New Jersey (Feinman & Lewis, 1983). Mother and baby sat in a laboratory room, and when an adult female stranger approached, some mothers were asked to talk in a positive tone of voice to the infant about the stranger, and others talked in a neutral tone. Infants whose mothers provided a positive interpretation were subsequently friendlier to the stranger than were those whose

SAUL FEINMAN • Child and Family Studies, Department of Home Economics, University of Wyoming, Laramie, Wyoming 82071.

Social Referencing and the Social Construction of Reality in Infancy, edited by Saul Feinman. Plenum Press, New York, 1992.

mothers provided a neutral interpretation. This pattern was especially prominent for infants of easier temperament, and it was not found for all infants.

Although these two studies differ in terms of experimental paradigm, nature of subjects, and ambiguity of the situation, there is a common thread that runs through them—as it does through many studies of conformity in adults and verbal children, and of social referencing in infants and toddlers. In either case, the participant is being provided with someone else's definition of the situation, and is being asked, encouraged, or pressured to go along with this interpretation. In both phenomena, there is considerable individual variation. Just as infants did not always adopt their mothers' definition of the stranger, some of the students' responses did not conform to their peers' assessments of the tone lengths. The fact that the university students were confronted with an unambiguous stimulus while the infants were in a more uncertain situation (it is easier to determine which of two obviously different tone lengths is longer than to decide how to behave to a stranger) is not germane to the distinction between studies of conformity and social referencing. Many conformity studies present confusing and unstructured situations to the participants (e.g., Sherif, 1958), while studies of social referencing have investigated infants' responses to clear-cut stimuli as well (e.g., Hornik, Risenhoover, & Gunnar, 1987).

The connection between social referencing and conformity is also revealed by an examination of statements made about each of these processes. Consider, for example, the following three quotations:

> From birth on, we learn that the perceptions and judgments of others are frequently reliable sources of evidence about reality.

> . . . individual perception is influenced by others' interpretations of the situation . . . reality is socially constructed so that action is founded upon interpretation which has been socially influenced by others' opinions.

> Human beings face uncertainty constantly. . . . The role of the social context for the resolution of uncertainty was neglected.

Clearly, there is a fair share of commonality among these three statements, so much so that each could easily be applied to social referencing or conformity. Actually, the first citation comes from the conformity literature (Deutsch & Gerard, 1955, p. 635), and the other two derive from social referencing (Feinman, 1982, p. 446; Campos, 1983, p. 83). The location of one of the major origins of social referencing theory in the study of conformity, social influence, and reference groups certainly implies that a conceptual link between referencing and conformity is to be expected.

The central question posed in this chapter takes the form, metaphorically, of a two-sided coin. To what extent is it possible to understand social referencing as conformity? And, in a corollary fashion, to what extent is it possible to understand conformity as social referencing? To what degree do the nature and dynamics of these phenomena overlap? To examine these issues, a comparative analysis of referencing and conformity is performed, and considers the following major topics: (1) definitions; (2) measurement and methods of investigation; (3) classifications and dimensions; and (4) forces that drive and mediate these processes. Most basically, this chapter focuses on the question of what each phenomenon has to "say" to and about the other. What insights can we gain about social referencing by examining it as conformity, and what can we learn about conformity by examining it in the context of referencing?

DEFINITIONS AND NATURE OF SOCIAL REFERENCING AND CONFORMITY

The Definition of Social Referencing

Let us look first at the definition and key characteristics of social referencing. Although there has been some disagreement as to a number of points of definition (see exchange between Feinman, 1982, 1983, and Campos, 1983), there appears to be consensus that social referencing should be viewed as an evaluative or appraisal process influenced by others' interpretations. Two essential features of this process are that sensations must be constructed into meaning, and that this construction is influenced by other persons' expressed appraisal of the situation. Indeed, if the link between sensation and behavior turned out to be a mechanistic one, then social referencing would be unlikely to play much of a role.

Three entities can be identified in social referencing: (1) the referer—the person who seeks and/or accepts interpretations of the situations from others; (2) the referee—the person who provides that interpretation; and (3) the referent—the topic of the interpretative communication (Feinman, 1985). When, for example, a 12-month-old encounters a modified visual cliff (i.e., a 30-cm visual "step"), as in the investigation done by Sorce, Emde, Campos, and Klinnert (1985), the referer is the infant, the referee is the mother, and the referent is the visual cliff apparatus and the illusion which it generates.

There appears to be considerable agreement as to the cognitive underpinnings of social referencing (Feinman, 1982; Klinnert, Campos, Sorce, Emde, & Svejda, 1983). The referer must be capable of appraising rather than merely reacting to stimuli, be open to interpretations from referees, be able to comprehend interpretive cues, and be able to identify the referent of the referee's message. Misunderstanding by the infant of the referee's cues, or miscommunication of these signals by the referee could easily lead to an unanticipated outcome in the referencing process.

The Definition of Conformity

Although the concept of conformity is constructed somewhat differently by various theorists and researchers, there is a reasonably solid common definitional core. Consider the following three conceptualizations of conformity:

> ... behavior which is influenced by a group, the result being to create increased congruence between the individual and the group. (Allen 1965, p. 134)

> ... display of attitudes and behavior in accord with the social norms. (Webster 1975, p. 51)

> ... a change in a person's behavior or opinions as a result of real or imagined pressure from a person or a group of people. (Aronson, 1984, p. 17)

In all three of these definitions—as well as in most others—several common elements can be found. First, a change in behavior, and possibly in attitude as well, occurs. Second, this change is the result of explicit or implicit pressure to do so. Even the definition which places the least emphasis upon the role of pressure (Webster's) uses the phrase "in accord with the social norms," which implies that there is some normative force which acts upon the individual. Third, the source of the pressure can be either a group or a single individual. While many of the classic experiments were done within group settings (Asch, 1951/1963; Sherif, 1958), conformity can occur with respect to the expectations expressed by a single individual, especially one of higher status and greater expertise. Indeed, some of the most interesting and insightful theoretical work about typologies of conformity and nonconformity has focused upon social influence within the dyad *per se* (Willis, 1965a). Although Milgram (1974) argues that obedience is not the same as conformity—he sees conformity as due to peer pressure, and obedience as due to pressure from an authority— typically, obedience is viewed simply as conformity to a source of authority (Kiesler, 1969).

A Comparison of Definitions

There is obviously much in the way of common conceptual ground shared by these two concepts. First, the three entities of referer, referee, and referent that have been identified in social referencing are present in conformity as well. Second, the cognitive underpinnings proposed for social referencing would also need to be in place for conformity to occur. In the context of research on conformity, which has focused exclusively upon adults or children who are mature enough to fulfill these cognitive prerequisites effortlessly, these developmental issues are very much a moot point. In contrast, the focus of social referencing research on infants and toddlers leads to much interest in whether the cognitive prerequisites indeed are possessed by the child. Third, both social referencing and conformity are ineffective if sensation leads to behavior in a mechanistic, prewired way. And fourth, both processes depend upon influence from others to generate changes in behavior and cognition.

In addition to these crucial similarities, there are several important differences. The most important divergence is that while conformity's hallmark is a change in behavior, possibly accompanied by a change in attitude, the key feature of social referencing is that it involves a change in interpretation. Indeed, social referencing has been conceptualized as being a type of conformity in which a change in attitude as well as behavior takes place (Feinman, 1982; Feinman & Lewis, 1984). In this sense, referencing can be considered to be a subset of conformity.

Two other differences are matters more of emphasis than definition. Although both conformity and social referencing allow for input from one person or several persons, referencing research has focused mostly upon influence of the former type, while conformity research has been more mixed. In addition, while the definition of referencing tends to view the referer in a more active light, as someone who *uses* others' interpretations, the definition of conformity seems to envision an individual who is on the receiving end of social *pressure*. Nevertheless, in many social referencing studies, input from others is provided regardless of whether the infant asks for it or not (e.g., Feinman & Lewis, 1983; Svejda and Campos, 1982). And, such input may be provided in a relatively gentle manner in some conformity studies, so that other people merely state their views rather than directly pressure the individual to accept these opinions (e.g., Alexander, Zucker, & Brody, 1970; Insko, Drenan, Solomon, Smith, & Wade, 1983). Except for the issue of whether attitudes as well as behavior must change, all of the differences between the definitions of referencing and conformity are matters of degree rather than of kind.

MEASUREMENT OF SOCIAL REFERENCING AND CONFORMITY

The definition of social referencing implies that an individual might change her understanding of the situation as a result of utilizing another person's interpretation of that situation. Or, if change *per se* is not measured, then it would be expected that there will be a difference in interpretation between people who have versus those who have not engaged in social referencing. Furthermore, it would be expected that, among individuals who have engaged in referencing, different messages would produce dissimilar understandings of the situation. Thus, in social referencing studies, measures of change or difference in infant behavior are utilized to reflect shifts or variations in situational understanding.

A rather similar line of reasoning links definition with measurement for conformity. Definitions which emphasize change translate into measuring the modification of attitudes and/or behavior as a consequence of social pressure. If change *per se* is not measured, as when the definition highlights the accordance of behavior and attitudes with normative expectations, then measurement focuses on the extent to which individuals exposed to normative pressure think and act differently than those not exposed. Furthermore, consideration is given to the examination of how much the specific attitudes and behaviors which result from exposure to social or normative pressure vary as a function of the content of this pressure.

Basically, studies of referencing and conformity measure the effect of social input upon individual interpretation and action in fundamentally the same manner. Nonetheless, one significant difference must be noted. Since conformity studies typically are performed with adults or verbal children, it is possible to measure changes or differences in attitude by asking subjects about their definitions of the situation, without having to infer opinion from behavior. Thus, it is possible to obtain independent assessments of behavior and interpretation. However, due to developmental restrictions, infants' interpretations can be measured only by inference from behavior, thus making it considerably more difficult to discriminate operationally between meaning and action.

Experimental Design: Independent Variable Conditions

Typically, conformity studies are designed to compare the effects of social input versus no social input. For example, Asch (1951/1963) contrasted the line length judgments made by solitary subjects (i.e., no social input) to those who had seen several other people make inaccurate judgments. A minority of conformity studies do, however, investigate the impact of one norm versus another. For example, Hood and Sherif (1962) exposed some subjects to a confederate who expressed the judgment that a point of light moved between 1 inch and 5 inches, while other subjects were exposed to a confederate whose judgments ranged from 6 to 10 inches. Similarly, in a more recent study, Campbell, Tesser, and Fairey (1986) varied the extremity of norms to which subjects were exposed.

Referencing studies, on the other hand, usually are designed to examine the difference between two or more conditions of social input. For example, in the Sorce *et al.* (1985) study, infants' behavior on the visual "step" was measured after they had received a happy, fearful, sad, interested, or angry emotional message from their mothers. There are some exceptions to this general inclination; thus, the comparison of social input versus no social input can be seen in the Feinman and Lewis (1983) investigation, which incorporated a control condition in which mothers did nothing during the stranger approach. It is important to note, however, that the no-input condition in conformity studies typically is one in which the individual subject is alone, while in social referencing studies an adult is present but noncommunicative.

Change versus Difference Measures

For both phenomena, the method of study typically employed is one of cross-sectional differences in which individuals are assigned to different conditions, and then compared after exposure to these treatments. An alternative paradigm involves gauging an individual's initial response to a stimulus, then exposing her to another person's or a group's judgment, and finally noting whether the initial judgment has changed after this exposure. This longitudinal change method must, in the interest of internal validity, also incorporate an examination of the comparative effects of different message conditions. Just such a technique has been used in conformity research, for example, in Willis's (1963) study of a typology of conformity and nonconformity. First, Willis asked each subject to express an initial individual opinion about the stimulus. The subject was then exposed to the opinion of a model, and was given another opportunity to respond. With such a method, change scores can be calculated. But, because Willis also varied the model's opinion, comparison among as well as within subjects can be examined.

Before versus after comparison has not been used in the analysis of social referencing. Nonetheless, the data collected in some studies could lend themselves to such analytical considerations. In particular, when the referee does not provide input immediately, it should be possible to compare behavior prior to versus after the referencing message. In the Klinnert (1984) study, because the mother did not provide a message about the stimulus toy until after the infant had looked to her, it is possible to distinguish between behavior before versus after the message. It is important, however, to realize that the practice, in some of the investigations designed in this manner, of eliminating from the data base those infants who did not solicit input from the referee would probably skew any pretest versus posttest analysis. Probably the most interesting data set which could be subjected to such an analysis is the Zarbatany and Lamb

(1985) investigation, which distinguished between infants who were initially fearful of the toy and those who were not. There are a good number of studies, however, in which the social referencing message was proffered almost immediately by the referee, thus preventing any over-time analysis within the experiment (e.g., Feinman, Roberts, & Hsieh, 1988; Gunnar & Stone, 1984).

Is It Conformity or Coincidence?

One issue of theoretical as well as methodological importance that has been raised in the conformity literature, and which is germane to referencing as well, is the question of how we can be reassured that observed conformity is not just coincidental. Could the accordance of the referer's behavior with that of the referee occur because she was going to engage in that behavior anyway? One alternative explanation of what appears to be conformity is that it is merely coentropic behavior, that is, responses which are in agreement due to independent learning of isomorphic actions (Hollander & Willis, 1967; Kiesler & Kiesler, 1969; Willis, 1963).

In studying group differences, this issue is resolved by random assignment to different experimental or control groups. It is highly unlikely that differences in later behavior between infants randomly assigned to positive versus negative message is coincidental (indeed, that is the rationale for utilizing random assignment). But on the more finely grained level of individual differences, this issue has not been addressed in either the referencing or conformity literatures. Individuals who behave in accordance with normative expectations may do so because they have been persuaded by the referee's message. But, on the other hand, some conformity may indeed be coincidental. The random assignment technique solves the coincidental conformity problem in terms of group differences, but not with regard to individual differences.

A possible solution for the coincidental conformity quandary lies in the distinction between measuring conformity in a congruence paradigm versus a movement paradigm (Hollander & Willis, 1967). In a congruence paradigm, the similarity of the referer's and the referee's behavior is the key measure of conformity. On the other hand, movement conformity is measured by obtaining a reading of the individual's interpretation of the stimulus prior to exposure to the referee, and then examining the extent to which change in this interpretation occurs after the referee's message. Hollander and Willis (1967) argue that the coincidental conformity issue is solved on the individual level of analysis through the utilization of a movement conformity paradigm, but not with a congruence approach. However, I would suggest that neither paradigm alone provides a solution to understanding individual differences in coincidental versus true conformity. Perhaps an infant who is initially afraid of a new toy, and then becomes more accepting of it after the mother provides a positive message, would have exhibited this change anyway. In other words, variability may occur independently of interpretative information from others. Indeed, Willis (1965a) describes, as one type of conformity-related behavior, a pattern which he terms "variability," in which the individual changes behavior regardless of what is done by the model. The movement paradigm alone does not discriminate between those individuals who change due to the influence of the referee versus those who change independently.

One reason that solving the coincidence predicament in conformity and referencing research is so enigmatic is that the data collection and analysis which result from the predominant bias for utilizing averaging methods rather than variational methods (Valsiner, 1984) is not well suited for teasing apart individual differences. Indeed, in general, we know considerably less about variation than about central tendencies in both of these phenomena. The placement of greater emphasis upon individual differences would be of overall benefit in the study of both referencing and conformity, and would assist considerably in resolving the coincidence dilemma, in particular.

CLASSIFICATIONS, MODELS, AND DIMENSIONS

The simplest way to classify individual response in conformity or social referencing is the elementary dichotomy of whether the behavior is conforming or nonconforming, of whether or not it is in accordance with the referencing message. Thus, in the Asch (1951/1963) study, we can discriminate between responses which conform with the group's incorrect answer and those which do not. Similarly, in the Sorce *et al.* (1985) investigation, we can ask whether or not the infant acts in accordance with the mother's communication. Beyond this most fundamental categorization, more finely grained distinctions can be drawn. First of all, we can ask the question of *how* influence is exerted. Second, other classification schemes focus upon the behavioral outcomes of influence, indicating *what* responses occur. Third, we can inquire into the individual's motivations, that is, *why* does the individual conform or deviate. For the most part, typologies of social referencing have sorted out variation in how the referee provides influence. In contrast, conformity research has emphasized descriptive classifications of what subjects do in responding to such influence and motivational classifications of why they do it.

Types of Social Referencing

Emotional versus Instrumental Referencing. Social referencing can be either emotional or instrumental, in that messages may convey information about how to feel or about what to do (Feinman, 1982). Although others have suggested that the important thing about referencing is its contribution to emotional communication and experience (Campos, 1983), referees can and do provide instrumental interpretations. For example, an older sister could try to persuade her toddler brother that a set of blocks should be built up into a tower, rather than scattered on the floor. Furthermore, representational and symbolic play can be viewed as examples of instrumental referencing, in which an adult attempts to convince a young child to define a situation as something it is not (e.g., to behave to a shoe as if it were a baby doll, or to make believe that an empty cup actually has juice in it; Bretherton, O'Connell, Shore, & Bates, 1984).

Almost all investigations of social referencing have focused primarily upon emotional referencing, indicating quite clearly that infants' responses to referent objects and events are shaped by the emotional messages which they receive from other people (e.g., Boccia & Campos, 1983; Walden & Ogan, 1988). Hornik and Gunnar's investigation (1988), however, considered instrumental as well as emotional referencing and found that infants' use of their mothers' messages about a large black rabbit had an impact not only upon their emotional reactions but also upon the specifics of how they contacted the rabbit. Furthermore, there is some indication that instrumental referencing may be the more potent force for increasing the referer's self-efficacy and confidence in coping with events and stimuli (Bandura, Chapter 8, this volume; Hornik-Parritz, Mangelsdorf, & Gunnar, Chapter 9, this volume).

How can the emotional versus instrumental distinction be applied to conformity? In most conformity studies, it is an instrumental message which is conveyed. The common use of judgment tasks results in the subject receiving influence as to how she should perceive the stimulus, for example, tone length (Milgram, 1961), light movement (Polis, Montgomery, & Smith, 1975; Sorrels & Kelly, 1984), line length (Amir, 1984), and fashionability of clothing (Davis, 1984). On the other hand, a few studies of conformity and attitude change can be thought of as efforts to modify not only instrumental behavior but affect as well. For example, research on the effects of adults' prohibitions upon children's play with and feelings about prohibited toys (Aronson & Carlsmith, 1963; Freedman, 1965) seem to involve an affective as well as an instrumental component. Generally, however, social referencing research has concentrated predominantly upon emotional influence, while conformity research has emphasized instrumental effects.

Direct versus Indirect Referencing.   Another distinction in social referencing is that between direct and indirect attempts to influence the infant. In direct communication, a mother might, in talking to her baby, convey through voice tone and other nonverbal cues her emotional definition of a toy, or a stranger. For example, Gunnar and Stone (1984) asked the mother to talk to her infant about stimulus toys. On the other hand, in the indirect approach, the mother enables the infant to observe her interact with the toy or stranger, so that the baby may infer from this behavior the mother's emotional and/or instrumental definition of that referent. In this way, two of the conditions in Feinman and Lewis's (1983) study called for the mother to greet the stranger either positively or neutrally while the infant watched. Sometimes, a mixture of these two methods is utilized, as when the mother smiles to both the infant and the stranger in the Boccia and Campos (1983) study. In other studies, it is a bit difficult to precisely classify the directness of the referencing message. For example, in the Sorce et al. (1985) study, the mother's facial display reflects her reaction to the visual cliff (an indirect communication), but that expression is directed to the infant. The directness of vocally expressed emotion is somewhat easier to determine. There is some evidence that directly conveyed messages are understood earlier in development than indirect ones (Feinman & Lewis, 1983; Lewis & Feiring, Chapter 12, this volume).

Social referencing studies tend to be quite mixed with regard to the use of direct versus indirect messages. In contrast, studies of conformity most often employ an indirect method in which group members or a single model simply express their judgments or preferences (Asch, 1951/1963; Deutsch & Gerard, 1955; Willis & Hollander, 1964). In some investigations, such input is transmitted through audiotaped recordings of fictive group members (Milgram, 1961), or through a machine panel in which patterns of lights indicate one's own and others' judgments of a perceptual task— the so-called Crutchfield apparatus (Crutchfield, 1955). There have been a few conformity studies, however, in which a direct procedure is utilized. In Milgram's (1974) investigation of obedience to authority, an authority figure tells the reluctant subject, "the experiment requires that you continue" with a procedure in which the subject administers what she thinks are powerful electric shocks to another person. One variation of this procedure includes both direct and indirect forces. In the "two peers rebel" variation, confederates refuse to go along with the experimenter's demand. Thus, the subject is caught between direct pressure from the experimenter and indirect, vicarious modeling by the confederates.

Solicited versus Offered Referencing.   Social referencing investigations can also be classified as to whether the referee waits for the referer to request input (solicited referencing) or provides that input without being asked (offered referencing). It has been suggested that social referencing be definitionally restricted to those incidents in which information is solicited (Klinnert et al., 1983). In accordance with this point of view, some investigations have excluded from their samples any infants who did not seem to solicit information from the referee (Klinnert, 1984; Klinnert, Emde, Butterfield, & Campos, 1986; Sorce et al., 1985; Zarbatany & Lamb, 1985).

In contrast, a more inclusive view (Feinman, 1982) acknowledges the possibility that referencing messages could influence the infant, even if this information is not solicited. Indeed, it seems likely, in everyday life, that caregivers often offer referencing messages before these messages are requested, frequently acting so as to "catch the gaze" of the infant (Langhorst, 1983). From this perspective, it can be noted that the Svejda and Campos (1982) study calls for the mother to provide the message after the infant reacts initially to the stimulus but without requiring that the infant solicit the message. In several other studies (Boccia & Campos, 1983; Feinman & Lewis, 1983; Feinman, Roberts, & Morissette, 1986; Feinman et al., 1988; Gunnar & Stone, 1984; Hornik et al., 1987), the message is offered early on in the procedure, possibly before the infant can formulate an initial reaction. Clearly, there is a good deal of variation among referencing studies as to how they handle the solicited versus offered dimension. Conformity studies, in contrast, have leaned toward the offered side of this continuum. Subjects do not need to request information from others; rather, it is provided routinely.

Referencing as Initial Appraisal versus Referencing as Reappraisal.   Building on the work of Lazarus (1968), Klinnert et al. (1983) suggested a conceptualization of referencing as reappraisal, in which the infant makes an initial evaluation of the situation, then seeks out social referencing information and, as a consequence, reappraises the situation. The visual cliff study (Sorce et al., 1985) is typical of studies in this reappraisal mold. It is presumed that the infant, by looking first at the cliff and then to the mother, has made an initial appraisal of the situation and is requesting further input. Although referencing as reappraisal is often solicited, this linkage is not absolute. Thus, Svejda and Campos (1982) wait until the infant has indicated an initial reaction to the toy before providing a vocally expressed message, but the infant does not have to request such information.

If the referencing message is offered before the infant can form an initial appraisal of the stimulus, then the information could contribute to that evaluation. Studies in which the message is offered very soon after or just as the infant first encounters the stimulus are most likely to reflect this referencing-as-initial-appraisal quality. It is possible that the infant will formulate the initial appraisal so rapidly on her own that it precedes even the most hastily offered messages; that is, offered referencing would then influence the reappraisal. Or, a stimulus which is highly complex could leave the infant without an initial appraisal for a long enough time that the message provided in response to the infant's solicitation could still contribute to the formulation of the initial appraisal. Furthermore, as Klinnert *et al.* (1986) have noted, reappraisal referencing can occur even when the primary individual appraisal has been entirely successful. The infant who has formulated an initial appraisal of the referent may still remain interested in others' opinions about it.

A reappraisal process clearly is at the heart of conformity investigations in which the subject provides an initial response, is next exposed to a model, and then responds a second time to the stimulus (Willis, 1963). But if the subject is provided with a group's response prior to making her own judgment of the situation (Sherif, 1958), then an initial appraisal process may be occurring. Provision of the group's input prior to the individual's expression of her judgment does not necessarily mean that the group influences initial appraisal, since the individual may have privately made a preliminary assessment of the situation. In the Asch (1951/1963) experiment, which employs as easy perceptual task, the procedure is temporally structured so that the other group members offer their responses before the subject expresses her answer but probably after she has formed an initial impression of the stimulus.

Typologies in Conformity

Classifications of "What" Subjects Do in Response to Influence

Willis (1965b). The most elaborate explication of conformity is that provided by Willis (1965b), who begins by delineating four unidimensional models (see Figure 1). The first model simply distinguishes between conformity and nonconformity. The second is a bit more complex; it places nonconformity on either side of conformity, thus suggesting that nonconformity can be expressed as deviation either above or below the norm. Both of these rudimentary models derive from Allport's (1934) work on norms of automobile driving behavior. Similar models can be found in more strictly sociological approaches, but the term *nonconformity* is likely to be replaced by that of *deviance* (Lofland, 1969; Merton, 1968).

Model 3 places conformity at one pole, and independence at the other; it was very often used in earlier work on conformity (Asch, 1951/1963, 1956). The fourth model places independence in the middle, with conformity and boomerang on either side. The individual may either (1) not take into account the group's opinion (remain independent), (2) go along

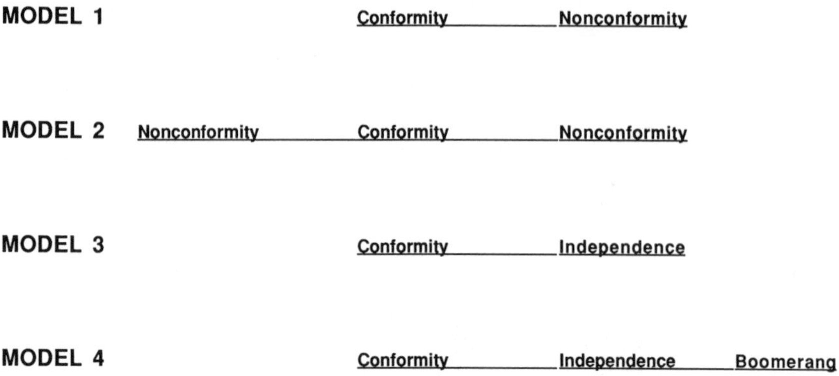

MODEL 1   Conformity_____Nonconformity

MODEL 2   Nonconformity_____Conformity_____Nonconformity

MODEL 3   Conformity_____Independence

MODEL 4   Conformity_____Independence_____Boomerang

Figure 1.   Simple models of conformity (adapted from Willis, 1965b, and Kiesler, 1969).

with the group (conform), or (3) react against the group and adopt an even more extreme and opposite position that she would have done independently (boomerang). It is noteworthy that both of the unidimensional models which include more than two categories (the second and fourth models) divide up the nonconformity side of the distinction, thus indicating only one way to conform, but two ways not to conform.

Figure 2 depicts three models of greater complexity. Model 5 is a two dimensional combination of Models 1 and 3, which splits nonconformity into independence and "counterformity" (Krech, Crutchfield, & Ballachey, 1962). The counterformity strategy is not an independent response, because the individual's nonconformity represents a reaction against the group (negative reference group). The sixth and seventh models represent the earlier and later stages, respectively, of Willis's own theoretical work on conformity (Willis, 1963, 1965a). Model 6 specifies two dimensions— independence–dependence and conformity–anticonformity. All points along the conformity–anticonformity axis represent dependent responses, in that they are based upon reaction to the group's standard: positively in the case of conformity, and negatively in the case of anticonformity. Willis's "anticonformity" has much the same meaning as Crutchfield's "counterformity."

Model 7 extends the independence–dependence dimension of Model 6. In this more complex scheme, two types of independence are distinguished, and each is located at one end of the continuum, with dependence in the middle. At the "independence" end of the spectrum, the individual maintains a consistent response, regardless of what input she receives from others. At the other end, "variability" indicates an inconsistent pattern of behavior in which the individual modifies her response indecisively, but does so independently of the group.

Although Willis's diagram of this seventh model (Willis, 1965b) is two

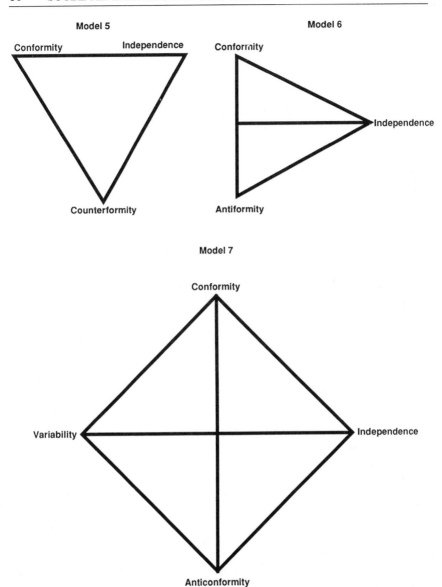

Figure 2. Complex models of conformity (adapted from Willis, 1965b, and Kiesler, 1969).

dimensional, actually there is a third dimension: relevance–irrelevance. Willis argues that the first issue for the individual is whether or not the normative expectations are perceived as relevant to the behavioral choice she faces. If she determines these expectations to be irrelevant to the situation, then conformity becomes a moot issue. I would suggest that an additional dimension be introduced into the model prior to the consideration of relevance. Willis assumes that the individual is cognizant of the model's normative expectations. But what if these expectations, although expressed, are not noticed by the individual? In this case, even the relevance versus irrelevance question would not be germane. If awareness occurs, then relevance would become an issue. If not, then the flowchart would terminate at that beginning question. This prior dimension could be labeled awareness–unawareness.

   Cooley (1922/1964).   A more modest but rather provocative classification of nonconformity was formulated many years ago by Charles Horton Cooley—provocative because it does not recognize the possibility of truly independent response. Rather, Cooley suggests that nonconformity either reflects a rebellious impulse ("contrary suggestion") or is the product of conformity to a distant reference group (Cooley, 1922/1964, pp. 297–298). The former type is quite similar to Crutchfield's counterformity and Willis's anticonformity, and implies that nonconformity occurs for the sake of being contrary or rebellious. The latter type is nonconformity in appearance only; in actuality, it does conform, but to a remote reference group. Indeed, Cooley states that "independence is only relative to the more immediate and obvious environment, and never constitutes a real revolt from the social order" (Cooley, 1922/1964, p. 303). This view suggests that behavior cannot ever be truly independent of social context, and that reality *always* is socially constructed. The claim that nonconformity is more apparent than real, and that it is due to conformity to remote reference groups, has been supported by research on deviant behavior (Becker, 1953; Cohen, 1964).

   Relevance of Willis's and Cooley's Models to Social Referencing.   These classifications of nonconformity may indeed be of considerable value in guiding the consideration of individual differences in referencing. Consider, for example, the finding that infants of easier temperament are influenced to a greater extent than their more difficult counterparts by the mother's referencing communication (Feinman & Lewis, 1983). Difficult infants may either be more independent or be acting in a contrary manner. Or, it may be that some infants did not behave in accordance with the social referencing message because they had not perceived it as relevant to the stranger, or had simply been unaware of it. As has been noted (Boccia & Campos, 1983; Feinman, 1985), referencing stays on track only if the infant accurately identifies the referent of the referee's message. If she perceives the referent as being the mother's mood, then the message may be seen as irrelevant to the issue of how to respond to the stranger.

Zarbatany and Lamb's (1985) finding that the referencing message made a more powerful impression upon infants who were initially uncertain about the stimulus (a large toy spider) than upon those who were initially fearful also may be interpreted within the context of conformity classifications. The fearful infants, because they had formulated an initial assessment of the spider, may have been less dependent upon the referee for definitional messages and, thus, fell along the axis of independence (Model 7, Figure 2). In contrast, the initially uncertain infants are located on the axis of dependency in that model, leaning strongly toward the conformity end of that dimension. Generally, analysis of the role of awareness, relevance, independence, and dependence may be particularly useful in sorting out the various reasons why infants do not appear to be going along with the referencing message.

Classifications of "Why" Subjects Conform

Being Right versus Being Liked. A critical motivational distinction can be made between the desire to be correct in responding to the task at hand versus the desire to please other people. For example, did the subjects in Milgram's (1974) obedience study administer the shocks because they wished to satisfy the experimenter, or because they believed that he was correct in his interpretation of the situation? This dichotomy has been described as the need to be right versus the need to be liked (Insko *et al.*, 1983; Kiesler, 1969), informational versus normative social influence (Deutsch & Gerard, 1955), social reality versus group locomotion forces (Jackson & Saltzstein, 1958), and task set versus group set (Thibaut & Strickland, 1956). The fundamental theme in the midst of all this semantic diversity is the common focus on the difference between being correct versus being liked and accepted by others.

One characteristic of the being-liked motivation is that conforming behavior will probably not be accompanied by a change of attitude. Thus, behavior and thought may not correspond, in that the individual can conform behaviorally to satisfy the group but not believe in the correctness of these actions. This dichotomy has been recognized by a number of theorists, who have referred to it by a variety of names: private acceptance versus public conformity (Festinger, 1953), the true believer versus the compliant skeptic (Kiesler & Kiesler, 1969), own versus induced forces (Lewin, 1951), and independent consent versus compliance (Jahoda, 1959). Each of these pairs represents the distinction of action versus thought and/or feeling, and reflects the age-old dualism between mind and body.

Kelman (1961). More complex classifications have been formulated around this central theme of correctness versus social acceptance. Perhaps the most widely known system is that proposed by Kelman (1961), which includes the categories of compliance, identification, and internalization. In compliance, the individual is motivated by the desire to obtain rewards and escape punishment; consequently, public behavior conforms to the normative expectations but private thoughts do not. Since this behavior is performed only to please others, it will not occur when the individual is not being watched. Thus, studies have found higher rates of conformity, in some groups, under conditions of surveillance (Eagly & Chrvala, 1986).

In identification, conforming behavior is performed to satisfy the desire to be similar to an attractive model or to meet the requirements of a desirable role. Unlike compliance, however, this type of conformity reflects a corresponding shift in beliefs, and does not cease when the individual is out of the public eye. But, since it is based upon the attractiveness of the source of interpretation, identification-based conformity is weakened if the relationship with the source of information weakens, or if the attractiveness of the role wanes.

In internalization, the individual conforms because she finds the behavior to be satisfying and valid in itself. Conforming behavior is accompanied, in internalization, by a corresponding belief. The intrinsic satisfaction provided by such conformity may occur because the behavior fits with the individual's own value system or because she "finds it useful for the solution of a problem" (Kelman, 1961, p. 65).

In discussing Kelman's scheme, Aronson (1984) argues that internalization is motivated by the desire to be right. Therefore, behavior does not cease to conform to the norm when the individual is alone, or if the source becomes less attractive. Due to the differences in motivation among these three forms of conformity, it has been suggested that compliance is the least and internalization the most enduring and deeply rooted. Furthermore, it is possible, as Aronson (1984) notes, for compliance to become transfigured into internalization through self-justification of counterattitudinal behavior, or the discovery of positive consequences other than rewards. It is reasonable to suggest that, in much the same way, identification could be translated into internalization, and become less dependent upon the individual's relationship with the source of information.

Clearly, there is a certain element of deceit in compliance. Because public behavior is not congruent with private thought, the individual is presenting herself in a manner that misleads the observer (intentionally perhaps) as to her actual feelings. Perhaps the tension from this deception generates the dissonance which leads to the transformation of compliance into internalization.

Hooper (1983); French and Raven (1959). Although an individual can, according to Kelman (1961), comply either to gain rewards and/or to avoid punishments, other classification schemes distinguish between these two sources of influence. In an effort to delineate the motivational foundations of compliant political behavior, Hooper (1983) distinguished between a penalty avoidance orientation (i.e., escaping punishments) and an instrumental orientation (i.e., obtaining rewards). A similar distinction has also been formulated by French and Raven (1959), who refer to reward power versus coercive power.

The identification form of conformity has been noted in other classification efforts. Hooper (1983) talks about a duty orientation in which the individual conforms in order to satisfy a role requirement or out of a sense of identification with an authority or with an attractive other. French and Raven (1959) further dissect this category by differentiating between legitimate power and referent power. Legitimate power operates when the person believes that a social agent possesses a justifiable right to define behavior—suggesting that a role relationship is operating between the person and the agent. In referent power, however, the personal attraction to the source motivates conformity.

The internalization mode has also been identified in Hooper's (1983) and in French and Raven's (1959) schemes of conformity. Hooper refers to a *values orientation*, while French and Raven use the term *expert power*. In the values orientation, the individual truly is persuaded that the model is correct and finds the proposed solution to be intrinsically satisfying. In expert power, the person perceives the social agent as someone who possesses special understanding or expertise. Furthermore, it may be worth distinguishing between two forms of internalization. In what we might call "values-internalization," the individual is motivated to accept, both publicly and privately, the message of the model because it is congruent with her own value system. As Kelman notes, however, such internalization is not necessarily "rational," because the individual's values may be dysfunctional, inappropriate, or self-destructive. On the other hand, what we might call "correctness-internalization" is motivated purely by a desire to formulate an accurate and adaptive definition of the situation.

Making Empirical Distinctions. How can we distinguish in practice among these motivations for conformity? The most commonly suggested method for differentiating compliance from the other two types of conformity is to observe the individual first with the group, and then in private. If her behavior conforms while under surveillance but not when alone, then compliance is most likely to be occurring. But if public and private behavior correspond, then either identification or internalization is indicated (Allen, 1965; Aronson, 1984; Kelman, 1961).

Because compliance is theorized to occur in response to rewards and punishments, it also might be useful to determine the extent to which these sources of power actually are evident and exercised by the social agent. If rewards and punishments cannot be found in the relationship or, more likely, if they are not used by the social agent, then compliance becomes less likely as an explanation of observed conformity.

Furthermore, since compliance involves deception, which is likely to produce anxiety, it would be instructive to observe the level of stress exhibited by the person. For example, the subjects in Sherif's (1958) auto-kinetic studies (in which internalization occurred) rarely displayed tension. In contrast, the behavior of those in the Asch (1956) and Milgram (1974) paradigms (in which compliance was much more common) often seemed strained. Indeed, Asch (1951/1963, 1956) suggested that it is possible to differentiate between subjects who comply versus those who have become convinced that the group is correct; one of the indicators used in making that discrimination is the level of exhibited tension. Along this line, it is interesting that Ekman (1985), in discussing facial cues of deceit, noted the existence of a "compliance smile" which "acknowledges that a bitter pill will be swallowed without protest. No one thinks the person showing it is happy, but this smile shows that the person is accepting an unwanted fate" (p. 156).

Finally, it has been suggested that compliance is more short lived and ephemeral than either identification or internalization (Aronson, 1984; Kelman, 1961). Consequently, the relative endurance of conforming behavior over time might be a useful differentiating marker of the particular motivational type of conformity which is operating.

If the actions turn out not to reflect compliance, how might we then determine whether it is identification or internalization which is occurring? Because, as Kelman suggests, beliefs acquired through internalization generally are more firmly held, strength of conviction and temporal durability may be points of discrimination. One other source of differentiation resides in identification's foundation upon the wish to be like an attractive model, or to partake in a valued role. Conformity which is based upon such attraction will decay if the relationship or the role goes sour. Since internalization is less socially dependent, it will not dissipate if the social agent or role becomes less salient. Furthermore, if identification is based upon the desire to fulfill role requirements, then behavior outside of that role would be unlikely to conform to the same norms. In contrast, internalization will result in a less contained effect, in which the behavior acquired through conformity will be displayed in various contexts and roles.

Both Kelman and Hooper have attempted either to induce the various types of conformity which they delineate or to classify actual behavior with their categorization systems. Indeed, most investigators who have discussed motivational differences have also used such distinctions as the basis of empirical considerations (e.g., Deutsch & Gerard's 1955 study of informational versus normative conformity). Along a similar line, Insko *et al.* (1983) used the private versus public distinction to investigate the motivations for being right versus being liked. The categorization of power bases formulated by French and Raven (1959) has also been subjected to empirical consideration, and has formed the foundation for research on the operation of power within families (Cromwell & Olson, 1975).

Applicability of Conformity Classifications to Social Referencing. Because social referencing is a process in which others' opinions modify the infant's interpretation of the situation, it falls, conceptually at least, under the rubric of internalization (Feinman, 1982; Feinman & Lewis, 1984). Compliance prototypically is characterized by a false presentation of self, by a deceptive display of behavior which is incongruent with internal beliefs. In this light, infant social referencing could reflect a compliance process only if the very young child is capable of such deceit and incongruence. It seems extremely unlikely, however, that going along with the referee's message could reflect, during infancy, an attempt to misrepresent or deceive. As Bretherton (1984) notes, infants do not appear to have a well-developed capacity to understand or practice deceit.

Another way to approach this question is to ask whether rewards and/or punishments were utilized in conveying the social referencing message. For the most part, the answer clearly denies this possibility—unless one wants to argue that any positive cue from the referee is potentially rewarding and any negative cue is potentially punishing. Concern that referencing communications which contain prohibitions might produce compliance has led some investigators to avoid using directives or "No" statements (Feinman *et al.*, 1988; Walden & Baxter, 1989). Furthermore, there is evidence that infants and toddlers can interpret prohibitive statements, especially when expressed by sensitive and nurturant caregivers, as informative messages about environmental events; indeed, such guidance is often internalized (Stayton, Hogan, & Ainsworth, 1971; Ainsworth, Chapter 14, this volume; Emde, Chapter 4, this volume).

Similarly, three of the negative emotional messages which typically are conveyed in social referencing investigations, namely, fear, sadness, and disgust, are probably most sensibly interpreted as expressions of how the referee feels about the situation rather than as indications of punishment or disapproval. Anger, however, would seem to have greater potential to be interpreted as punishing and, therefore, to elicit compliance rather than internalization. Nonetheless, the finding that the impact of anger upon infant behavior usually is not significantly different than that of fear (Sorce *et al.*, 1985; Svejda & Campos, 1982) or disgust (Bradshaw, Campos, & Klinnert, 1986) suggests that infants are interpreting it as a message about the referent stimulus rather than about the adult's intention to punish. Generally, it would appear that the emotional communications utilized in infant social referencing studies convey, from the child's perspective, neither promises of desired rewards nor threats of feared punishments. Indeed, very young children seem to differentiate between signals that serve an anticipation-of-action mechanism, which enables them to predict conspecifics' behavior (such as intended rewards and punishments), and those which provide situational reference, in which a conspecific's communication refers to an environmental event (Frijda, 1969; Leung & Rheingold, 1981; Murphy & Messer, 1977).

The hypothesis that duration of the conformity effect may discriminate among motivational types suggests that it would be worth examining the longevity of referencing's impact in regulating behavior. When studies have confined message provision to a delimited period of time (a signal phase) after which it does not continue (e.g., Walden & Ogan, 1988), there have been no reports indicating that the social referencing effect decays over time. Furthermore, Bradshaw et al. (1986) found that an effect could still be detected 30 minutes after the message was provided. The short time frame of all other social referencing studies (usually a few minutes) does, however, limit the degree to which the matter of duration can be assessed with the extant evidence. Perhaps future studies will more consistently investigate the longer-term impact of social referencing messages and generate a substantial data base for considering the endurance issue.

French and Raven's classification scheme may also be able to shed some light upon the type of conformity which transpires in social referencing. Perhaps Klinnert et al.'s (1986) finding that 12-month-olds are influenced by a stranger's emotional message about a robot, when the mother pretends to be puzzled, is a case of putting referent power up against expert power. Since 12-month-olds typically are attached to their mothers, the mother may have referent power, in which influence is based upon her attractiveness to the infant. In contrast, the mother's puzzled expression in reaction to the robot suggests that she has little, if any, expertise in this situation. The stranger, on the other hand, although not perceived as being exceptionally attractive, may be viewed as possessing expertise about the room and the toy, because these may be seen as falling specifically within her domain of knowledge, and because her clear reaction to the robot suggests that she is confident in this knowledge. The finding that infants behave in accordance with the stranger's message, rather than adopting their mothers' puzzlement, suggests that they may have opted for expertise over attractiveness, that is, to have been more swayed by expert power than by referent power. Thus, the infant's desire to be correct would appear to be more compelling than the desire to follow her mother's lead, particularly when mother appears to be confused and the stranger is confident.

There is other evidence which is consistent with this interpretation. When two infants and their mothers are together, the infant who sees that a peer is crying can either turn to her own mother, who would be a source of referent power, or to the peer's mother, as a source of expert power. After all, who would be a more expert interpreter of a baby's crying than that child's own mother? And, indeed, it is to this more knowledgeable source that infants more often turn upon observing a peer in distress (Hay, Nash, & Pedersen, 1981).

The application of motivational models of conformity behavior to the study of infant social referencing is somewhat of a speculative enterprise at this time, and clearly there is a need for further consideration of this issue, utilizing data collected intentionally for this specific purpose. Nonetheless, the extant evidence does suggest that social referencing operates through an internalization process, in which the infant's desire to formulate accurate and adaptive interpretations is the prevailing motivational force.

PATTERNS OF BEHAVIOR IN SOCIAL REFERENCING AND CONFORMITY

The final method to be utilized in this comparative analysis of social referencing and conformity is the examination of forces which have been hypothesized and/or found to influence these processes. Three particular types of variables are considered: (1) the nature of the situation; (2) the relationship that the individual possesses with the referee; and (3) the techniques that are used to induce conformity or social referencing.

The Nature of the Situation

Ambiguity.   Although referencing is not assumed to occur *exclusively* in uncertain situations (Campos & Stenberg, 1981; Feinman, 1982; Klinnert *et al.*, 1986), the ambiguity postulate (Feinman, 1982) hypothesizes that ambiguity increases the potency of referencing, making infants more receptive to others' interpretative messages. Situational clarity, in contrast, typically is expected to enhance the infant's self-reliance, encouraging her to process and interpret stimuli more independently (Feinman, 1991).

Theory about conformity has made essentially the same prediction: that receptivity to others' influence will increase as the situation becomes more ambiguous and the task, therefore, more difficult (Allen, 1965; Deutsch & Gerard, 1955; Festinger, 1954; Kiesler, 1969); much evidence can be mustered in support of this proposition (Alexander *et al.*, 1970; Deutsch & Gerard, 1955; Luchins, 1945; Pollis *et al.*, 1975; see the reviews in Allen, 1965, and in Kiesler, 1969). Experiments using the Sherif paradigm, in which subjects are confronted with the highly ambiguous autokinetic effect—a stationary point of light that appears to move randomly—elicit a much higher level of conforming behavior than do experiments using the unambiguous Asch paradigm, in which subjects are asked to match a test line with one of several other lines, only one of which is the obviously correct answer (Asch, 1956; Sherif, 1958). It is instructive to note that when Asch (1952) made his line-matching task more ambiguous, conformity to the group increased.

Graham (1962) has noted a theoretically salient distinction between the objective ambiguity of the stimulus and the individual's subjective certainty. Usually, these two variables are highly correlated; that is, individuals feel certain of their judgments in clear-cut situations, but the association is not a perfect one. Thus, a person may feel subjectively certain under the most enigmatic of circumstances. There is a fair amount of evidence indicating that, as confidence in one's own judgment increases, conformity decreases (see Allen, 1965, Aronson, 1984, and Stang, 1981, for reviews of this literature).

The evidence concerning the impact of ambiguity upon referencing is mixed. Sorce and his colleagues (Sorce et al., 1985) found that although no infant would cross an ambiguous 30-cm visual "step" when the mother displayed fear, most crossed when she smiled. When confronted with a flat surface devoid of depth cues (a clear-cut situation), most infants showed little interest in using their mothers' messages (Sorce et al., 1985). For those who did look toward their mothers, the negative message which they received elicited an affective reaction, motor hesitation, and further attending to mother. They seemed to be acting as if they were experiencing the sort of strain that adults feel when confronted in clear-cut situations with the group's conspicuously incorrect interpretation (Asch, 1956). Despite this tension, the infants did cross the obviously safe surface, as if saying that in this clear-cut situation "Mother knows best, but sometimes I know better" (Feinman, 1985). Furthermore, pretesting indicated little interest in referencing information when infants were confronted with the clear-cut danger of the full visual cliff (Campos, personal communication, 1981). All of this evidence is consistent with the expectation that referencing would be more powerful in ambiguous than clear-cut situations. However, when Bradshaw, Goldsmith, and Campos (1987) replicated the smiling condition with the visual "step," the majority of infants would not cross.

Similarly, support for the ambiguity postulate has been equivocal with regard to toys as well. Gunnar and Stone (1984) reported a stronger influence of mother's message when the infant encountered an ambiguous toy rather than clearly pleasurable or aversive toys. Similarly, although infants who initially were afraid of a new toy were not influenced by the referee's affective message, this message did have an impact upon the behavior of those who initially seemed less certain (Zarbatany & Lamb,

1985). In contrast, although they used the same stimuli as Gunnar and Stone (1984), Hornik *et al.* (1987) found that ambiguity did not mediate the impact of referencing messages. In addition, Hornik and Gunnar (1988) noted that there were no significant referencing differences between initially wary versus bold infants in response to a large black rabbit, other than the much stronger inclination of the wary group than the bold group to cast a referencing look toward the mother after first encountering the rabbit.

Overall, conformity studies with adults provide support for the postulate that receptivity to others' cues is heightened by ambiguity. In contrast, the evidence from referencing research is somewhat equivocal. Perhaps other factors overshadowed the ambiguity effect in these infant studies. On the other hand, it may be that uncertainty is less salient for infants and toddlers than for adults.

The Relevance of the Situation.   Willingness to accept influence from others may depend upon how important or relevant the situation is perceived to be. Cooley (1922/1964) proposed the following relevance-oriented strategy: "Assert your individuality in matters which you deem important; conform in those you deem unimportant" (p. 304). Similarly, Jahoda (1959) suggested that influence is less readily accepted with regard to issues and objects in which the person is ego invested. More recently, research on persuasion and attitude change has indicated that while individuals *can* be influenced with regard to high-relevance issues, the form that this influence takes is very different from that which modifies low-relevance attitudes (Petty & Cacioppo, 1981, 1984; Petty, Cacioppo, & Goldman, 1981).

Petty and his colleagues have suggested that there are two major routes of influence. In the "central route," it is the quality of the arguments that persuades the individual. In the "peripheral route," factors associated with the communication, such as the expertise of the source, and pleasurable or noxious events paired with the message transmission result in opinion change. It is suggested that the central route is most effective for high-relevance issues, while the peripheral route is most effective for low-relevance issues. Petty and Cacioppo (1984) also suggest that the desire to be correct is diminished in low-relevance situations. Furthermore, individuals are likely to be more motivated to think clearly about high-relevance matters and, in all likelihood, probably have engaged in such thought prior to receiving any persuasive communication. High-relevance topics—as the result of having been the focus of previous contemplation—may be perceived as more clear-cut matters and, as a consequence, be less subject to influence from others.

How does the distinction between central and peripheral routes of influence apply to very young children? Clearly, infants could be influenced by factors which are associated with the peripheral route (e.g., pleasant or unpleasant stimuli associated with the message). But the possibility that they could be influenced through the central route, by the strength and logic of the arguments *per se*, seems rather remote. Infants' closure to the central route would make it particularly difficult to modify their interpretations concerning high-relevance matters. While it is possible to influence adults with respect to strong fears, such influence may be diminished in infancy because the cognitive skills needed to gain access to the central route of persuasion are not yet in place.

The referents in social referencing studies usually are high- rather than low-relevance issues. Matters such as depth cues, strangers, and new toys are likely to be especially salient in infancy. In contrast, much of the research on conformity in adults focuses upon what are best interpreted as low-relevance items (Jahoda, 1959). After all, how many of the subjects (typically college students) in studies about the duration of sounds (Milgram, 1961), the length of lines (Asch, 1956), or the movement of a point of light (Sherif, 1958) would perceive these issues as central to their lives? It is not difficult to imagine that there are particular individuals and occupational groups for whom these referents would be of high salience (e.g., musicians may be interested in sound duration, just as airplane pilots would find the apparent movement of a stationary point of light to be a relevant topic), but these special populations are not the focus of conformity research. Jahoda argues that the focus upon such low-relevance issues has resulted in an artificially high estimate of the degree to which people will conform. In this perspective, perhaps the consideration of only high-relevance referents in infant social referencing research has led us to underestimate the extent to which referencing messages can influence infant behavior.

The Relationship with the Referee

How does the individual's relationship with the referee mediate receptivity to social influence? The selectivity postulate hypothesizes that social referencing is characterized by the inclination to be more receptive to communication about the situation from some people than from others: "individuals tend to refer socially to people whose thought and behavior seem to improve the probability of receiving rewarding consequences" (Feinman, 1982, p. 460). Nurturance, power, expertise, and status are some of the dimensions that may be relevant to the selective referencing of others.

It has been suggested that conformity is more likely to occur when the individual is attracted to the source of influence (Allen, 1965; Kiesler,

1969), and there is a substantial literature which supports this claim for the most part (Jackson & Saltzstein, 1958; Thibaut & Strickland, 1956; see review in Kiesler, 1969). Furthermore, it has been claimed that the more cohesive the group, the greater the conformity (Festinger, 1950; Lott & Lott, 1961). Related to this hypothesis is the finding (Pollis & Montgomery, 1966) that natural groups are more effective at inducing conformity—and not just of the compliance type—than are experimental groups of strangers. Since it is reasonable to assume that natural groups possess a higher level of cohesiveness and "groupness," this finding lends further support to the cohesiveness hypothesis. When based upon interpersonal attraction, cohesiveness induces conformity even when it is detrimental to the individual and/or the group (Sakurai, 1975). But cohesiveness that is based upon a more task-related interdependence is capable of leading to conformity only in directions which are beneficial. And, it should be noted that McKelvey and Kerr (1988) reported higher levels of conformity to strangers than to friends—suggesting that the impact of attractiveness and cohesiveness of the group upon conformity is a complex multivariate affair.

Jackson and Saltzstein (1958) have further suggested that the relationship with the group can be classified not only in terms of the individual's attraction to it, but also along the dimension of whether the group accepts the individual. They postulated that when the group applied normative pressure, individuals who were not accepted by the group would simply seek to behave in accordance with a standard of correctness; in contrast, those who were accepted by the group would be more motivated by group locomotion forces. While the latter prediction was supported, the former was not. Instead, it was found that nonaccepted individuals conformed more than expected, perhaps because their status of nonacceptance implied either rejection or low task ability, or because they were still attempting to gain the group's acceptance.

The issue of expertise has been considered already in discussing French and Raven's (1959) classification of power bases. There is a fair amount of evidence that conformity is greater when the referee is perceived as possessing expertise about the situation (Deutsch & Gerard, 1955; Hollander & Willis, 1967; Mausner, 1954). But expertise alone is not enough; the referee also must be seen as trustworthy (Kiesler & Kiesler, 1969). Expertise without trustworthiness, or trustworthiness without expertise, produces zero credibility and, therefore, no social influence. It is credibility, as the multiplicative product of expertise and trustworthiness, which mediates the impact of others' opinions upon the individual (Liska, 1978; Petty & Cacioppo, 1981).

How do these predictions—and the issue of selectivity more generally—fare within infant social referencing research? Intimate caregivers seem to be equally accepted. Thus, Hirshberg and Svejda (1990) found that infants were just as likely to accept referencing influence from their fathers as from their mothers. But strangers may be less well received, as reflected in Zarbatany and Lamb's (1985) report that infants engaged in referencing with their mothers but not with a familiarized stranger. Yet this preference does have its limits. In the Klinnert et al. (1986) investigation, when the mother acted puzzled, the stranger's affective message served as a source of referencing information for the infant.

Although selectivity seems to mediate the degree to which the referee's message regulates the infant's response to the referent, there is little evidence for selectivity in social referencing looking. Thus, although the infant's behavior to the toy spider was more influenced by the mother's than the stranger's affective message, no selectivity differences were found for latency of initial looking or overall looking to the referee's affective display (Zarbatany & Lamb, 1985). Similarly, Dickstein and Parke (1988) found that the frequency of social referencing looks to mother versus father did not differ. And, Bradshaw et al. (1987) noted that infants looked just as often to an experimenter as to the mother when confronted with a reduced visual cliff. In contrast, when the mother appears puzzled and the stranger appears knowledgeable, infants look more to the latter than the former source (Klinnert et al., 1986). The general rule seems to be that when referees are equally communicative and knowledgeable, selective information seeking is not found in infant social referencing.

Research on conformity suggests that social referencing will be more potent when the infant is attracted to and accepted by the individual providing the referencing message. Terms such as *attraction, acceptance,* and *trustworthiness* bring to mind the concept of attachment. The infant's attachment classification has been found to be associated with the frequency of social referencing looking to mother during a modified strange situation, especially when the stranger talked to the mother, with the most looking from resistant–insecure babies and the least from avoidant–insecure babies (Dickstein, Thompson, Estes, Malkin, & Lamb, 1984). In contrast, no attachment differences in looking were found by Bradshaw et al. (1987). This inconsistency is further confounded by the lack of affective specificity in the definition of referencing looking in these studies. A smiling or fearful look at the mother right after looking at the referent might be more reflective of affect sharing or comfort seeking than solicitation of information. Furthermore, the relative paucity of information which emanated from the mother in these procedures may have rendered her a less than maximally useful source of referencing.

Feinman and Lewis (1983) suggested that the failure of indirectly conveyed messages to influence infant behavior to the stranger, and the presence of an effect upon behavior to the mother, might be interpreted within the context of the attachment relationship. Since infants were friendlier to mothers who spoke neutrally rather than positively to the stranger, we speculated that the infants may have seen the mother's friendly communication to the stranger primarily as a threat to attachment, and had expressed their concern with this maternal behavior. Similarly, in the Dickstein et al. (1984) study, if infant looking served a comfort-seeking function, then the finding that attachment classification differences in looking to the mother were most evident when the stranger and mother talked might also be better interpreted as reflecting attachment behavior, rather than as differences in information seeking.

That infants are attached to their mothers but not to a stranger may have been a key factor in leading infants to selectively accept influence from the mother in Zarbatany and Lamb's (1985) study. Alternatively, the mother's absence when the infant was with the stranger may have distracted the baby from the stranger's message. There were, indeed, several infants paired with the stranger–referee who were so upset about their mother's absence that they could not participate. The contrast between this finding and Klinnert et al.'s (1986) report that the infant accepted influence from the stranger when the mother was present, although apparently puzzled, suggests that attachment relationships can play an unexpected role in referencing—namely, that the infant's concern with attachment may take precedence over her interest in referencing.

Of related interest is Dickstein and Parke's (1988) finding that infants engaged in more looking to mothers and fathers when fathers were experiencing high marital satisfaction. Mothers' marital satisfaction had a weaker impact in the opposite direction upon looking to the mother— infants looked more often to mothers who were experiencing low marital satisfaction, particularly if the marital satisfaction of the father was high. The complexity of these marital satisfaction differences, combined with the use of a measure of social referencing looking which could also reflect affect sharing or requests for proximity and comfort, makes the interpretation of these findings rather difficult. Nonetheless, the weaker effect of mothers' than fathers' marital satisfaction upon infant looking could mean that mothers are more uniformly trusted sources of information, while fathers may be perceived as being somewhat variable. Indeed, Dickstein and Parke (1988) suggest that infants may perceive maritally dissatisfied fathers as being less available and/or less reliable sources of information. Mothers, regardless of interpersonal differences, are perhaps more uniformly viewed as physically, emotionally, and informationally available.

Selectivity findings in the extant social referencing literature cannot be interpreted precisely, because the factors of attachment, expertise, and trustworthiness are fairly well confounded in these investigations. And interpretation of selectivity in information gathering is further complicated by the way in which social referencing looking has been operationalized in some studies. Nevertheless, these results do suggest that selectivity, especially in acceptance of influence, is apparent in infant social referencing. Further delineation of just how selectivity operates in infant referencing will call for the sorting out of expertise, trustworthiness, attraction, acceptance, and attachment as they coexist within the context of infants' relationships with potential referees—a formidable task, to say the least.

Methods of Influence

Consistency.   There has been considerable interest in the effect of message consistency upon conformity. Within the group setting, consistency is operationalized by whether the group is unanimous in the message that it conveys. There is considerable evidence that unanimity is much more effective in inducing conformity than even a nearly unanimous majority norm. Even if only one confederate gave an answer which was at variance with that of the others, the rate of conformity plummeted (Asch, 1956; Graham, 1962). Similarly, independence of response is considerably more likely to occur when subjects are exposed to dissent; indeed, consistent dissent leads to total independence (Nemeth & Chiles, 1988).

When one individual is the sole source of influence, an internally consistent message is considerably more effective than an inconsistent one in inducing conforming behavior (Crano, 1970). The infamous Miss X incident in Sherif's classic study provides a colorful and dramatic demonstration of the importance of message consistency. In this episode, a confederate influenced the subject—the unfortunate "Miss X"—to change her judgment in the autokinetic effect paradigm. Once she had done so, the confederate then changed his norm and influenced her to modify her judgments to fit the revised norm. This went on several times; each time Miss X conformed to the newly changed norm, the confederate modified it again. After being a good sport for a while, Miss X apparently had enough; she said, "Get me out of here," and left (Sherif, 1958; Webster, 1975, Ch. 1).

Although social referencing theory has not offered any specific predictions about the effects of consistency, an implicit understanding of its importance is indicated by the way in which methods of influence have been utilized in referencing studies. For example, Boccia and Campos (1983) specifically note that the mother's facial and vocal cues about the stranger were presented in an emotionally congruent manner, thus intimating that incongruence would probably have reduced the power of the message. That this would be the case is indicated in Barrett's (1985) finding that inconsistent signals trigger more looking to the referee, very possibly in order to elicit further clarification. Furthermore, the uncertainty and inhibition induced by such cues result in ambivalence of behavior to the referent toys. Similarly, Hirshberg (1990) found that when infants received opposing referencing messages from mother versus father, their contact with the referent toy was reduced and uneasy. Generally, it appears that message inconsistency has the same effect upon infants as it does upon adults, namely, that of decreasing the acceptance of influence.

Pressure to Conform: The Use of Rewards and Punishments. Although almost all conformity studies use indirect methods to induce conformity, it is well recognized that, in everyday life, methods which are either more enticing or more threatening are utilized (Milgram, 1974). While confederates in the Asch paradigm are instructed not to pressure the subject to go along with the group, stronger efforts are likely to be used in naturally occurring situations. In light of the more enticing or threatening uses of rewards and punishments that occur in daily life situations, there has been some interest in the effects of such methods upon conformity and attitude change.

Given that the application of rewards and punishments is associated with the compliance form of conformity (French & Raven, 1959; Kiesler, 1969), it might be expected that efforts to induce conformity through the application of these reinforcers would not be especially effective at generating enduring changes in how the individual defines the situation. Since dissonance is a common motivator of attitude change, and changing one's behavior because of either temptation or threat is not likely to generate much dissonance, the use of rewards and punishments to induce conforming behavior would seem unlikely to lay the psychological groundwork for internalization.

Two studies of the effect of adults' prohibitions upon children's play with toys (Aronson & Carlsmith, 1963; Freedman, 1965) have examined the impact of threat. Regardless of whether the children were instructed not to play with a particular desirable toy (mild threat) or were told that the experimenter would be angry and/or disappointed if they played with the toy (severe threat), the children did not play with the prohibited toy when the experimenter left the room. But future behavior and attitudes toward the toys were more affected by the mild-threat than the high-threat condition.

Analogously, parents and other caregivers often try to increase children's consumption of nonpreferred foods (e.g., vegetables) by offering rewards for "instrumental eating" of such foods (e.g., "if you eat your vegetables, you can have a cookie"). Although such efforts may increase food consumption at the moment, foods which are instrumentally eaten to obtain a treat actually become devalued and less preferred (Birch, Birch, Marlin, & Kramer, 1982; Birch, Marlin, & Rotter, 1984). Thus, treats are not any more effective than threats in producing internalized modifications of thought and situational definition.

Although theory about social referencing has not grappled with the issue of threatening or enticing messages, there are some data which are relevant to this question. As noted earlier, the referee's emotional message does not seem to be mistaken for a rewarding or punishing communication; rather, it appears to be taken as information about the referent. Furthermore, imagining that infants could be engaging in compliance sorely tries our understanding of their limited capacity for deceit—for doing one thing while feeling another. It is also important to note that the major explanation for why mild threat produces deeper and more enduring changes in older children is that of dissonance reduction (Aronson & Carlsmith, 1963; Freedman, 1965)—a capacity that seems to be way beyond what infants are able to do.

Emotional versus Instrumental Messages.   Referencing theory's distinction between instrumental and emotional communication (Feinman, 1982, 1985; Hornik & Gunnar, 1988) poses the question of whether one is more effective than the other in producing the desired social referencing result. The paucity of instrumental social referencing studies denies us a sufficient data base for considering this question empirically. Furthermore, the fact that almost all conformity studies are of the instrumental type restricts our ability to consider this matter in that literature as well. There is, however, some reason for suspecting that instrumental referencing is easier to produce than affective referencing. Issues for which emotional messages would be salient to the infant are probably high-relevance matters on which they are not going to be easily influenced. In contrast, many instrumental issues may be of lesser importance, so that receptivity to modification would be greater. To the extent that these assumptions are valid, one would predict more success at instrumental than emotional referencing—a suggestion also made by Hornik and Gunnar (1988; see also Hornik-Parritz et al., Chapter 9, this volume).

Direct versus Indirect Messages.   The one study which has systematically varied whether the message is conveyed directly or indirectly (Feinman & Lewis, 1983) found that the former method of delivery was quite effective, while the latter seemed to lead to an error in which, in interpreting the message, infants focused on the mother–infant attachment relationship rather than the stranger. Since comprehension of the indirect message would seem to require more sophisticated cognitive skill, it is not unreasonable to expect that the direct message will be more effective during infancy. On the other hand, because adults and older children clearly possess the requisite cognitive skills to comprehend indirectly transmitted communications, there is no reason to suspect that direct messages would be more effective in inducing conformity beyond infancy and toddlerhood. Indeed, there may be an advantage, then, to the indirect approach, given that it is less likely to produce reactance formation in adults. The fact that most of the studies of conformity utilize indirect approaches indicates clearly that such methods are quite effective, although it does not answer the question of whether they would be more successful than direct methods in producing conforming behavior in adulthood.

Solicited versus Offered Referencing and Initial Appraisal versus Reappraisal. Some infants who receive social referencing messages which they did not request may not be especially interested in that information. In contrast, request of information portends receptivity to the message. By this criterion, one would predict that solicited social referencing is going to be more effective in modifying interpretation than is offered referencing. Nevertheless, no apparent differences in the effects of offered versus solicited messages can be detected in social referencing research.

Related to this issue is the question of whether social referencing is more effective as initial appraisal or as reappraisal. On the one hand, initial appraisal would seem to be more potent since an initial judgment has not yet been formed; that is, there is no prior interpretation to be challenged by the referencing message. On the other hand, when reappraisal is associated with solicited referencing, then perhaps the effectiveness of reappraisal would be greater.

Since these two factors tend to be confounded in the empirical investigation of referencing (although they are not necessarily confounded conceptually, as noted above) and are sometimes even further confounded with other factors as well, it is difficult to rigorously examine these predictions in the extant literature. Because conformity studies are rarely, if ever, designed to utilize a solicited form of message conveyance, they do not lend themselves to the investigation of the relative power of solicited versus offered messages. The consideration of the initial appraisal versus reappraisal dimension in conformity research would be easier since both forms seem to be included in the investigation of conformity. However, because this dimension has not been manipulated systematically in conformity research, and because it is confounded with other design and methodological factors, it would be difficult to compare these two formats. Nonetheless, upon initial empirical inspection, there do not seem to be any obvious differences between initial appraisal and reappraisal processes in producing conformity.

EPILOGUE

There is a great deal of similarity between social referencing in infancy and conformity in adulthood. They seem to be powered by some the same major motivations, and to run according to rather comparable operating mechanisms. Consideration of points of differences between them is quite helpful in determining how each process fits within the broader social construction of reality framework. Furthermore, the examination of each process often suggests new directions for research on the other.

In ending, let us bring our comparative analysis of social referencing and conformity back to the most basic question, that of the overall extent to which infants and adults go along with others' interpretations. In conformity research, it is very rare indeed to find a situation in which all individuals conform or all deviate. How much conformity or deviance we require in order to be "impressed" depends largely upon the parameters of the situation (e.g., the difficulty of the task). Thus, even though it can be noted that subjects more often remain independent than yield to the majority in the Asch paradigm (Harris, 1985), the finding that one-third of the responses conform to the group (Asch, 1951/1963, 1956) can only be meaningfully interpreted when we keep in mind the remarkably clear-cut nature of the stimulus, and the fact that, in the absence of group input, subjects almost never make a mistake.

A similar approach must be taken in interpreting the magnitude of the social referencing effects found in the extant literature. That some infants seem to go along with the referencing message, while others do not, is a pattern which is consistent with the finding of individual differences in conformity research. Furthermore, the strong probability that referencing research has focused upon highly cathected topics in the lives of infants and toddlers makes the degree to which social referencing effects are found even more impressive. In contrast, many if not most of the conformity studies seem to focus on low-relevance situations (for a major exception, see Milgram, 1974).

Interest in the central tendencies of infants' behavior in social referencing and of adults' behavior in conformity must not lead to the neglect of the variation which occurs in such investigations. In most studies, some subjects conform to the expectations and others deviate. The logical question is: what accounts for such differences? One potentially useful strategy may be to distinguish among deviant responses which are due to resistance to the referee's influence versus those which are due not to resistance but, rather, to errors in comprehending the intent of that influence. Indeed, such interest in sources of resistance and/or errors in social referencing can be found in the extant literature (Feinman, 1985; Feinman & Lewis, 1984; Klinnert, 1984; Walden & Ogan, 1988). When social referencing is examined within the context of conformity, an additional feature is added to this consideration—namely, the conceptualization of resistance and errors within the framework of nonconforming or deviant behavior. In this light, the investigation of individual differences in infants' responses to social referencing boils down to the basic social psychological question of understanding why, in a given situation, some people conform more than others.

REFERENCES

Alexander, C. N., Zucker, L. G., & Brody, C. L. (1970). Experimental expectations and autokinetic experiences: Consistency theories and judgmental convergence. *Sociometry, 33,* 108–122.

Allen, V. L. (1965). Situational factors in conformity. In L. Berkowitz (Ed.), *Advances in experimental social psychology* (Vol. 2, pp. 133–175). New York: Academic Press.

Allport, F. H. (1934). The J-curve hypothesis of conforming behavior. *Journal of Social Psychology, 5,* 141–183.

Amir, T. (1984). The Asch conformity effect: A study in Kuwait. *Social Behavior and Personality, 12,* 187–190.

Aronson, E. (1984). *The social animal* (4th ed.). New York: W. H. Freeman.

Aronson, E., & Carlsmith, J. M. (1963). Effect of the severity of threat on the devaluation of forbidden behavior. *Journal of Abnormal and Social Psychology, 66,* 584–588.

Asch, S. E. (1952). *Social psychology.* Englewood Cliffs, NJ: Prentice-Hall.

Asch, S. E. (1956). Studies of independence and conformity: A minority of one against a unanimous majority. *Psychological Monographs, 70* (9, 177–190).

Asch, S. E. (1963). Effects of group pressure upon the modification and distortion of judgments. In H. Guetzkow (Ed.), *Groups, leadership and men* (pp. 177–190). New York: Russell & Russell. (Original work published 1951)

Barrett, K. C. (1985). Infants' use of conflicting emotion signals. (Doctoral dissertation, University of Denver, 1984). *Dissertation Abstracts international, 46,* 321B–322B.

Becker, H. S. (1953). Becoming a marijuana user. *American Journal of Sociology, 59,* 235–242.

Birch, L. L., Birch, D., Marlin, D., & Kramer, L. (1982). Effects of instrumental eating on children's food preferences. *Appetite, 3,* 125–134.

Birch, L. L., Marlin, D., & Rotter, J. (1984). Eating as the "means" activity in a contingency: Effects on young children's food preference. *Child Development, 55,* 431–439.

Boccia, M. L., & Campos, J. J. (1983, April). *Maternal emotional signals and infants' reactions to strangers.* Paper presented at the biennial meeting of the Society for Research in Child Development, Detroit.

Bradshaw, D. L., Campos, J. J., & Klinnert, M. D. (1986, April). *Emotional expressions as determinants of infants' immediate and delayed responses to prohibitions.* Paper presented at the Fifth International Conference on Infant Studies, Los Angeles.

Bradshaw, D. L., Goldsmith, H. H., & Campos, J. J. (1987). Attachment, temperament, and social referencing: Interrelationships among three domains of infant affective behavior. *Infant Behavior and Development, 10,* 223–231.

Bretherton, I. (1984). Social referencing and the interfacing of minds: A commentary on the views of Feinman and Campos. *Merrill-Palmer Quarterly, 30,* 419–427.

Bretherton, I., O'Connell, B., Shore, C., & Bates, E. (1984). The effect of contextual variation on symbolic play: Development from 20 to 28 months. In I. Bretherton (Ed.), *Symbolic play: The development of social understanding* (pp. 271–298). New York: Academic Press.

Campbell, J. D., Tesser, A., & Fairey, P. J. (1986). Conformity and attention to the stimulus: Some temporal and contextual dynamics. *Journal of Personality and Social Psychology, 51,* 315–324.

Campos, J. J. (1983). The importance of affective communication in social referencing: A commentary on Feinman. *Merrill-Palmer Quarterly, 29,* 83–87.

Campos, J. J., & Stenberg, C. (1981). Perception, appraisal, and emotion: The onset of social referencing. In M. Lamb & L. Sherrod (Eds.), *Infant social cognition* (pp. 273–314). Hillsdale, NJ: Erlbaum.

Cohen, A. K. (1964). *Deviance and control.* Englewood Cliffs, NJ: Prentice-Hall.

Cooley, C. H. (1964). *Human nature and the social order* (rev. ed.). New York: Schocken. (Original work published 1922)

Crano, W. D. (1970). Effects of sex, response order, and expertise in conformity: A dispositional approach. *Sociometry, 33,* 239–252.

Cromwell, R. E., & Olson, D. H. (Eds.). (1975). *Power in families.* New York: Wiley.

Crutchfield, R. S. (1955). Conformity and character. *American Psychologist, 10,* 191–198.

Davis, L. L. (1984). Judgement ambiguity, self-consciousness, and conformity in judgements of fashionability. *Psychological Reports, 54,* 671–675.

Deutsch, M., & Gerard, H. (1955). A study of normative and informational social influences upon individual judgement. *Journal of Abnormal and Social Psychology, 51,* 629–636.

Dickstein, S., & Parke, R. D. (1988). Social referencing in infancy: A glance at fathers and marriage. *Child Development, 59,* 506–511.

Dickstein, S., Thompson, R. A., Estes, D., Malkin, C., & Lamb, M. E. (1984). Social referencing and the security of attachment. *Infant Behavior and Development, 7,* 507–516.

Eagly, A. H., & Chrvala, C. (1986). Sex differences in conformity: Status and gender role interpretations. *Psychology of Women Quarterly, 10,* 203–220.

Ekman, P. (1985). *Telling lies: Clues to deceit in the marketplace, politics and marriage.* New York: W. W. Norton.

Feinman, S. (1982). Social referencing in infancy. *Merrill-Palmer Quarterly, 28,* 445–470.

Feinman, S. (1983). How does baby socially refer? Two views of social referencing: A reply to Campos. *Merrill-Palmer Quarterly, 29,* 467–471.

Feinman, S. (1985). Emotional expression, social referencing, and preparedness for learning in infancy—Mother knows best, but sometimes I know better. In G. Zivin (Ed.), *The development of expressive behavior: Biology–environment interactions* (pp. 291–318). New York: Academic Press.

Feinman, S. (1991). Bringing babies back into the social world. In M. Lewis & S. Feinman (Eds.), *Social influences and socialization in infancy* (pp. 281–325). New York: Plenum.

Feinman, S., & Lewis, M. (1983). Social referencing at ten months: A second-order effect on infants' responses to strangers. *Child Development, 54,* 878–887.

Feinman, S., & Lewis, M. (1984). Is there social life beyond the dyad? A social-psychological view of social connections in infancy. In M. Lewis (Ed.), *Beyond the dyad* (pp. 13–41). New York: Plenum.

Feinman, S., Roberts, D., & Hsieh, K. (1988, April). *Social referencing within the context of the infant–sibling–mother triad.* Paper presented at the Sixth International Conference on Infant Studies, Washington, D.C..

Feinman, S., Roberts, D., & Morissette, P. L. (1986, April). *The effect of social referencing on 12-month-olds' responses to a stranger's attempts to "make friends."* Paper presented at the Fifth International Conference on Infant Studies, Los Angeles.

Festinger, L. (1950). Informal social communication. *Psychological Review, 57,* 271–292.

Festinger, L. (1953). An analysis of compliant behavior. In M. Sherif & O. Wilson (Eds.), *Group relations as the crossroads* (pp. 232–256). New York: Harper.

Festinger, L. (1954). A theory of social comparison processes. *Human Relations, 7,* 117–140.

Freedman, J. L. (1965). Long-term behavioral effects of cognitive dissonance. *Journal of Experimental Social Psychology, 1,* 145–155.

French, J. R. P., Jr., & Raven, B. (1959). The bases of social power. In D. Cartwright (Ed.), *Studies in social power* (pp. 150–167). Ann Arbor, MI: University of Michigan Institute for Social Research.

Frijda, N. H. (1969). Recognition of emotion. In L. Berkowitz (Ed.), *Advances in experimental social psychology* (Vol. 4, pp. 167–223). New York: Academic Press.

Graham, D. (1962). Experimental studies of social influence in simple judgement situations. *Journal of Social Psychology, 56,* 245–269.

Gunnar, M. R., & Stone, C. (1984). The effects of positive maternal affect on infant responses to pleasant, ambiguous, and fear-provoking toys. *Child Development, 55,* 1231–1236.

Harris, P. R. (1985). Asch's data and the "Asch effect": A critical note. *British Journal of Social Psychology, 24,* 229–230.

Hay, D. F., Nash, A., & Pedersen, J. (1981). Responses of six-month-olds to the distress of their peers. *Child Development, 52,* 1071–1075.

Hirshberg, L. (1990). When infants look to their parents: II. Twelve-month-olds' response to conflicting parental emotional signals. *Child Development, 61,* 1187–1191.

Hirshberg, L. M., & Svejda, M. (1990). When infants look to their parents: I. Infants' social referencing of mothers compared to fathers. *Child Development, 61,* 1175–1186.

Hollander, E. P., & Willis, R. H. (1967). Some current issues in the psychology of conformity and nonconformity. *Psychological Bulletin, 68,* 62–76.

Hood, W. R., & Sherif, M. (1962). Verbal report and judgement of an unstructured stimulus. *Journal of Psychology, 54,* 121–130.

Hooper, M. (1983). The motivational basis of political behavior: A new concept and measurement procedure. *Public Opinion Quarterly, 47,* 497–515.

Hornik, R., & Gunnar, M. (1988). A descriptive analysis of infant social referencing. *Child Development, 59,* 626–634.

Hornik, R., Risenhoover, N., & Gunnar, M. (1987). The effects of maternal positive, neutral, and negative affective communications on infant responses to new toys. *Child Development, 58,* 937–944.

Insko, C. A., Drenan, S., Solomon, M. R., Smith, R., & Wade, T. J. (1983). Conformity as a function of the consistency of positive self-evaluation with being liked and being right. *Journal of Experimental Social Psychology, 19,* 341–358.

Jackson, J. M., & Saltzstein, H. D. (1958). The effect of person–group relationships on conformity processes. *Journal of Abnormal and Social Psychology, 57,* 17–24.

Jahoda, M. (1959). Conformity and independence. *Human Relations, 12,* 99–120.

Kelman, H. C. (1961). Processes of opinion change. *Public Opinion Quarterly, 25,* 57–78.

Kiesler, C. A. (1969). Group pressure and conformity. In J. Mills (Ed.), *Experimental social psychology* (pp. 235–306). New York: Macmillan.

Kiesler, C. A., & Kiesler, S. B. (1969). *Conformity.* Reading, MA: Addison-Wesley.

Klinnert, M. D. (1984). The regulation of infant behavior by maternal facial expression. *Infant Behavior and Development, 7,* 447–465.

Klinnert, M. D., Campos, J. J., Sorce, J. F., Emde, R. N., & Svejda, M. (1983). Emotions as behavior regulators: Social referencing in infancy. In R. Plutchik & H. Kellerman (Eds.), *The emotions* (Vol. 2, pp. 57–86). New York: Academic Press.

Klinnert, M. D., Emde, R. N., Butterfield, P., & Campos, J. J. (1986). Social referencing: The infant's use of emotional signals from a friendly adult with mother present. *Developmental Psychology, 22,* 427–432.

Krech, D., Crutchfield, R. S., & Ballachey, E. L. (1962). *Individual in society.* New York: McGraw-Hill.

Langhorst, B. H. (1983, April). *Early antecedents of affect referencing.* Paper presented at the biennial meeting of the Society for Research in Child Development, Detroit.

Lazarus, R. S. (1968). Emotions and adaptation: Conceptual and empirical relations. In W. J. Arnold (Ed.), *Nebraska symposium on motivation* (Vol. 16, pp. 175–270). Lincoln, NE: University of Nebraska Press.

Leung, E. H. L., & Rheingold, H. L. (1981). Development of pointing as a social gesture. *Developmental Psychology, 17,* 215–220.

Lewin, K. (1951). *Field theory in social science.* New York: Harper & Row.

Liska, J. (1978). Situational and topical variations in credibility criteria. *Communication Monographs, 45,* 85–92.

Lofland, J. (1969). *Deviance and identity.* Englewood Cliffs, NJ: Prentice-Hall.

Lott, A. J., & Lott, B. E. (1961). Group cohesiveness, communication level, and conformity. *Journal of Abnormal and Social Psychology, 62,* 408–412.

Luchins, A. S. (1945). Social influences on perceptions of complex drawings. *Journal of Social Psychology, 21,* 257–273.

Mausner, B. (1954). The effect of one partner's success in a relevant task on the interaction of observer pairs. *Journal of Abnormal and Social Psychology, 49,* 557–560.

McKelvey, W., & Kerr, N. H. (1988). Differences in conformity among friends and strangers. *Psychological Reports, 62,* 759–762.

Merton, R. K. (1968). *Social theory and social structure.* New York: Free Press.

Milgram, S. (1961). Nationality and conformity. *Scientific American, 205* (6), 45–51.

Milgram, S. (1974). *Obedience to authority.* New York: Harper & Row.

Murphy, C. M., & Messer, D. J. (1977). Mothers, infants and pointing: A study of a gesture. In H. R. Schaffer (Ed.), *Studies in mother–infant interaction* (pp. 325–354). London: Academic Press.

Nemeth, C., & Chiles, C. (1988). Modelling courage: The role of dissent in fostering independence. *European Journal of Social Psychology, 18,* 275–280.

Petty, R. E., & Cacioppo, J. T. (1981). *Attitudes and persuasion: Classic and contemporary approaches.* Dubuque, IA: Wm. C. Brown.

Petty, R. E., & Cacioppo, J. T. (1984). The effects of involvement on responses to argument quantity and quality: Central and peripheral routes to persuasion. *Journal of Personality and Social Psychology, 46,* 69–81.

Petty, E. E., Cacioppo, J. T., & Goldman, R. (1981). Personal involvement as a determinant of argument-based persuasion. *Journal of Personality and Social Psychology, 41,* 847–855.

Pollis, N. P., & Montgomery, R. L. (1966). Conformity and resistance to compliance. *Journal of Psychology, 63,* 35–41.

Pollis, N. P., Montgomery, R. L., & Smith, T. G. (1975). Autokinetic paradigms: A reply to Alexander, Zucker and Brody. *Sociometry, 38,* 358–373.

Sakurai, M. M. (1975). Small group cohesiveness and detrimental conformity. *Sociometry, 38,* 340–357.

Sherif, M. (1958). Group influences upon the formation of norms and attitudes. In E. Maccoby, T. Newcomb, & E. Hartley (Eds.), *Readings in social psychology* (pp. 219–232). New York: Holt, Rinehart & Winston.

Sorce, J. F., Emde, R. N., Campos, J. J., & Klinnert, M. D. (1985). Maternal emotional signaling: Its effect on the visual cliff behavior of 1-year-olds. *Developmental Psychology, 21,* 195–200.

Sorrels, J. P., & Kelly, J. (1984). Conformity by omission. *Personality and Social Psychology Bulletin, 10,* 302–305.

Stang, D. J. (1981). *Introduction to social psychology.* Monterey, CA: Brooks/Cole.

Stayton, D. J., Hogan, R., & Ainsworth, M. D. S. (1971). Infant obedience and maternal behavior: The origins of socialization reconsidered. *Child Development, 42,* 1057–1069.

Svejda, M. J., & Campos, J. J. (1982, March). *Mother's vocal expression of emotion as a behavior regulator.* Paper presented at the Third International Conference on Infant Studies, Austin, TX.

Thibaut, J. W., & Strickland, L. H. (1956). Psychological set and social conformity. *Journal of Personality, 25,* 115–129.

Valsiner, J. (1984). Two alternative epistemological frameworks in psychology: The typological and variational modes of thinking. *The Journal of Mind and Behavior, 5,* 449–470.

Walden, T. A., & Baxter, A. (1989). The effect of context and age on social referencing. *Child Development, 60,* 1511–1518.

Walden, T. A., & Ogan, T. A. (1988). The development of social referencing. *Child Development, 59,* 1230–1240.

Webster, M. (1975). *Actions and actors: Principles of social psychology.* Cambridge, MA: Winthrop.

Willis, R. H. (1963). Two dimensions of conformity–nonconformity, *Sociometry, 26,* 499–513.

Willis, R. H. (1965a). Conformity, independence, and anticonformity. *Human Relations, 18,* 373–388.

Willis, R. H. (1965b, September). *Descriptive models of social response.* Paper presented at the meeting of the American Psychological Association, Chicago.

Willis, R. H., & Hollander, E. P. (1964). An experimental study of three response modes in social influence situations. *Journal of Abnormal and Social Psychology, 69,* 150–156.

Zarbatany, L., & Lamb, M. E. (1985). Social referencing as a function of information source: Mothers versus strangers. *Infant Behavior and Development, 8,* 25–33.

11

Social Referencing and Theories of Status and Social Interaction

Murray Webster, Jr., and Martha Foschi

INTRODUCTION

Social referencing is a phenomenon of clear significance. Many studies, including those in this volume, document the importance of referencing in the lives of young children and their guardians. Even before the end of their first year, children use adults to define what is dangerous and what is delightful or, in a process similar to modeling, to develop competencies.

As modeling theorists have pointed out (e.g., Bandura, 1965), vicarious learning is the one way to learn complex social behaviors (not to mention the complexities of attitudes and manners). Even something as taken for granted as learning to drive a car would be impossible through either classical or operant conditioning. The learner could too readily suffer "one-trial extinction," due to task complexity.

There is more to referencing than behavioral learning. As most investigators use the term, referencing involves cognition, understanding,

MURRAY WEBSTER, JR. • Department of Sociology, San Jose State University, San Jose, California 95192. MARTHA FOSCHI • Associate Professor of Sociology, University of British Columbia, Vancouver, British Columbia V6T 2B2, Canada.

Social Referencing and the Social Construction of Reality in Infancy, edited by Saul Feinman. Plenum Press, New York, 1992.

and awareness. It is how we learn attitudes and manners. Thus referencing is symbolic learning. It involves interpreting situations and attributing significance. Referencing tells what is going on in a situation, or what the evidence means to the referer.[1]

Social psychologists trained in sociology know W. I. Thomas's (1928) dictum that definition of a situation is crucial: "If [people] believe situations are real, they are real in their consequences." For most referencing in the life of a child, that is certainly true. If the mother looks alarmed, it is probably because the child is approaching some real danger. Even if the mother is wrong and the danger is not real, the child will become frightened. Referencing must be a basic way in which life or death information comes to us.

Another giant in sociologists' intellectual history is George Herbert Mead (1934), probably best remembered for his analysis of "taking the role of the other." Mead's conception of role taking is somewhat more subtle than the term might suggest. It involves, first, understanding what the other person is about to do. This step is comparable to the child feeling fear when the mother feels fear.[2] Second, often the referer must prepare to take not the same, but complementary actions. For instance, if the referer sees that the referee is about to toss something his way, the referer must prepare to catch it or move out of the way.

This second step is complex. It requires understanding and acting on symbolic meanings. Sometimes the symbolic meanings entail deliberate communication. For instance, a father may make several gestures to focus his daughter's attention before actually throwing her a toy. Sometimes the referee intentionally conceals attitudes such as anger. Sometimes the referee doesn't know what will happen, as with a wild pitch of a baseball. In all cases, however, the referer must prepare actions based upon an interpretation of the situation and a guess about what the referee is about to do.

Taking the role of the other is a difficult process, fraught with chances for mistakes. Mead believed role-taking ability to be the most important element of intelligence, and recent studies show that the two at least correlate strongly. Whatever its relation to intelligence, role taking is a crucial process in everyone's life. Studying referencing may specify some mechanisms in this process.

[1]We use the terms *referer* and *referee* consistently with other chapters in this volume.

[2]Mead taught at a time when sociologists and psychologists were trying to free themselves from the relatively unempirical speculation practiced by psychoanalysts of that day. Like many others, Mead felt attracted to behaviorism as the solution. Some students of Mead today object to speaking of thoughts and feelings; they might prefer the phrase ". . . looking fearful when the mother looks fearful." Our view is that Mead's greatest contribution to theory comes precisely from his ideas on manipulating symbols and the self-concept, and we do not see how those ideas can be preserved in a strictly behavioral interpretation.

Referencing studies connect to many theoretical perspectives in contemporary social psychology: symbolic interaction (the study of communicating meanings and how they affect people's behavior), information processing (how people combine disparate bits of information to form aggregate impressions), self-concept (how we know what kind of people we are), social control (how to get people to act, or not to act, in particular ways), and social learning.

As a new field with findings collecting rapidly, social referencing has not to date developed a coherent, explicit theoretical framework for research. There is no doubt about the value of a theoretical framework. It identifies new areas to study, increases understanding of important phenomena such as referencing, tells where and when to expect referencing phenomena to appear and when other processes are more likely.

Here, we plan to discuss the theoretical context of social referencing. Rather than drawing links to all the theoretical perspectives mentioned above, we wish to focus upon three "theoretical research programs."[3] The three describe work we know well, which looks closely related to some phenomena studied as referencing. Each is part of a continuing program of studies on how status characteristics influence and organize face-to-face interaction (for description of several other branches of the larger program, see Berger, Wagner, & Zelditch, 1985, 1989).

In the next sections, we describe briefly each theoretical research program, and relate it to interests and findings in the study of social referencing. After we describe each program, we try to identify two types of links between the program and studies of social referencing—ways in which studies of social referencing may advance through ideas or evidence from the program, and ways in which the program might advance by using ideas or evidence from studies of social referencing. The first program is on sources of self-evaluation. The second incorporates standards for evaluation. The third tells how referent actors help overcome status generalization. All three of these programs are within the sociological tradition described above. All appear to us to be fully compatible with the orientation and findings of research into social referencing.

SOURCES OF SELF-EVALUATION

Investigators began this research program in the late 1960s. Their goal was to specify in greater detail the processes by which individuals form their self-evaluations, or ideas of how well they can do something. Self-

---

[3]The term is Lakatos's (1970). We use it here to mean a series of empirical studies related by common approaches, empirical methods, and explicit theories using many overlapping core concepts.

evaluation is one part of the self-concept, not the only one. It may not hold strong interest for some. However, self-evaluation remains the part of the self most widely studied. The most likely reason for this is measurement. It is relatively straightforward to design instruments asking respondents how well they think they can do something, be it succeed in school, win friends, or play basketball. By contrast, scales to measure unevaluated aspects of the self have proved difficult to devise, and are fewer in number.[4]

Sociological traditions for study of the self usually trace to Cooley's (1902) idea of the looking-glass self, Mead's (1934) idea of taking the role of the other and the generalized other, and Sullivan's (1947) idea of significant others. The sources of self-evaluation program builds upon their ideas.

Cooley probably intended to oppose nineteenth-century individualism, for he emphasized the importance of the social in forming an individual's idea of who he or she is.[5] The looking-glass self is the reflection we see of our actions, personal traits, and abilities from others' eyes. Those reflections determine who, and what sort of person, we think we are. This view, that the self is essentially social in origin, is now universal in sociological social psychology.

Implicit in Cooley's conception of the self is the idea that individuals make mistakes. We perceive others' opinions more or less accurately. Our translation of others' opinions into the self-concept is neither automatic nor perfect. Mead extended Cooley's idea with his notion of the generalized other. These are opinions of the entire community in which the individual lives. An early study based upon Mead's ideas (Miyamoto & Dornbusch, 1956) found individuals' self-evaluations were (1) fairly close to what others in their groups actually thought of them; (2) closer still to what individuals *thought* others thought of them; and (3) virtually the same as the perceived opinions of "most people." These results show the importance of others in forming the self [finding (1)]; the effect of some misperception of others' opinions [comparison of findings (1) and (2)]; and powerful effects of the generalized other [finding (3)].

Harry Stack Sullivan (1947) developed the term *significant other*. Significant others are those whose opinions especially matter in forming a

---

[4]Some interesting measures of unevaluated aspects of the self have been constructed by Ralph H. Turner and his colleagues and students (see, e.g., Turner, 1976). For discussion of mechanisms by which individuals change roles, see Turner, 1990.

[5]Ironically, Cooley's famous quote, "Each to each a looking glass / Reflects the other that doth pass," comes from the poem "Astrae" by the champion of individualism, Ralph Waldo Emerson. Emerson celebrated an internal sense of self. The lines Cooley quotes describe the sort of person Emerson opposed to the more heroic, self-reliant individual he favored. Cooley's point was that nobody has an internal sense of self. We all are products of the looking glass.

person's self-concept. As a psychoanalyst speaking to clinical audiences, Sullivan did not form a precise or explicit definition of the term. Significant others to Sullivan were those who nurtured the child: parents, nursemaids, and housekeepers. The sources program began by trying to explicate the abstract characteristics which a potential source must possess to be effective.[6]

Let us restrict attention to evaluative aspects of the self. From the social-self perspective, the self forms socially; that is, it is heavily influenced by others' opinions. A sufficient condition for an evaluator to become a significant other is to have greater ability than the evaluated person. More precisely, the person being evaluated *believes* the evaluator has the greater ability. If I want to know how good a paper I have written, I seek the opinions of someone I consider an expert in that field.[7] The first laboratory test of the theory (Webster, 1969) confirmed that idea. Evaluations from someone described as having low ability to perform a task produced much less effect upon subjects' self-evaluations than did evaluations from someone described as having high ability.

Next, investigators extended the original theory to answer "What happens when the individual does not know the ability of those evaluating him?" From the larger theoretical research program, Webster and Sobieszek (1974a,b) adopted an idea developed in another context. It came to be called (Webster & Driskell, 1978, 1985; Webster & Foschi, 1988) *status generalization*. Under certain conditions, if individuals do not know the ability of interactants, they will act as if status external to the interaction revealed the specific abilities immediately required. That is, people with the high state of some culturally defined status characteristic (such as race,

---

[6]This research program uses somewhat different terminology from what is standard in other literature on self-evaluation. This is to avoid confusion of similar terms, as concepts in the source theory tradition sometimes have more restricted meanings than the same words when used informally. For example, we use the terms *self-expectation states* instead of *self-evaluations*. We intend to emphasize that what is significant about holding, say, high expectations for oneself is the idea that "I expect my future performances to be correct." As we use terms in this program, *self-expectation* differs from *self-evaluation* in being specific to: (1) a particular group of individuals, (2) a particular task, and (3) a particular situation. With those restrictions, most statements which could be made about self-evaluation could be made about self-expectations. Please see Webster and Sobieszek (1974b) for discussion of the exact terminology of this program. For most of this chapter, we adopt the more usual terms of the self-evaluation literature.

[7]The phenomenon appears early. Most schoolchildren learn that reliable evaluations of performance come from teachers but not from other children. By preadolescence, children often dismiss their parents' judgments because of presumed differences in values or parents' supposed use of irrelevant standards. By college age, most children believe their parents' evaluations are not useful because they always are positive. For a discussion of early development of several aspects of self-evaluation in children, see Pallas, Entwisle, Alexander, and Weinstein, 1990.

sex, age, or ethnicity) were treated as if they had high task ability, and vice versa for those with the low state of the status characteristic.

For self-evaluation, this implies that individuals may treat status as a surrogate for ability information. Then they accept evaluations from a high-status evaluator and ignore them from a low-status evaluator. An experiment employing the same design as the first one confirmed that prediction.[8]

An issue which arose from these experiments is the "negative source": someone whose evaluative opinions are so bad as to indicate that the correct answer is the opposite of this person's choice. If it existed, a negative source would raise a host of additional questions for the theory. Intuitively, the idea has appeal. So Webster and Sobieszek (1974b) designed an experiment to investigate the negative source phenomenon. They defined it as an evaluator scoring 4 correct answers out of 20, with 12–15 being average. If negative ability existed, this evaluator certainly had it. Perhaps surprisingly, results showed that nearly all subjects simply ignored the evaluator's opinions. If a negative source exists, the phenomenon does not appear in the simplified social setting of these experiments.[9]

What about two evaluators? Sobieszek and Webster (1973) investigated first the situation in which the two evaluators differed in ability (one high and one low), and where they agreed or disagreed in their evaluations of the focal subject. Both ability of the evaluators and the nature of their evaluations showed measurable effects. Subjects formed the highest self-evaluations when given positive evaluations by both evaluators; next highest when the high-ability evaluator gave positive evaluations and the low-ability evaluator gave negative evaluations; next highest where the high-ability evaluator gave negative evaluations and the low-ability evaluator gave positive evaluations; and lowest where both gave negative evaluations.

The situation could be even more difficult. Sobieszek and Webster (1973) designed an experiment in which people received evaluations from two highly competent evaluators, and they almost always disagreed.[10] We might imagine any of three outcomes.

[8]Interestingly, experiments by Feinman and Lewis (1983) show what may be status generalization or a similar process in referencing. Children generally treat unfamiliar adults in a more friendly manner after receiving positive messages about the stranger.

[9]Perhaps a series of demonstrated failures by an evaluator could lead to his becoming a negative source. A negative source might come into existence, but only after long experience with a particular evaluator's opinions.

[10]Hirshberg (1988, 1990) has studied the effects of conflicting information in infant referencing. Hirshberg's studies use a single referee giving inconsistent signals to the infant. The phenomenon appears to have similarities with the more highly controlled conflicting sources experiment described here.

1. With such confusion, the person might withhold evaluation. If two experts disagree, a person might not form any ideas at all.
2. People might reduce ambiguity by picking only one evaluator and sticking with that person's judgments, forming whatever self-evaluation that evaluator intended to create.
3. People might distribute agreements among the evaluators, now accepting an evaluation from one, then from the other.

Experimental results showed that people actually followed the third option. Most formed intermediate-level self-evaluations based upon the combination of positive and negative evaluations they had received.

Results of these experiments, as well as some additional analyses, are in Webster and Sobieszek (1974a). Entwisle and Webster (1972; Webster & Entwisle, 1976) and Entwisle and Hayduk (1978) brought this program out of the experimental laboratory into the school classroom.

The first classroom experiments explicate a phenomenon which attracted much attention in the late 1960s and early 1970s—teacher expectancy (see, e.g., Rosenthal & Jacobson, 1968; Brophy & Good, 1970). In a typical teacher expectancy study, the investigator would enter a classroom and give a test purported to identify "potential academic bloomers." About 20% of the class, actually picked at random, got that name attached to them. In some studies, selected students actually did show the improvement expected on the basis of the counterfeit test scores. The first experiment by Entwisle and Webster (1972) illuminates the mechanism producing the teacher expectancy phenomenon, and also shows why it did not work reliably.

In theoretical terms, a teacher in a classroom is like a source in the laboratory experiments described earlier. That is, a teacher has the right to evaluate, high ability at the task, and high status. Therefore, if a teacher gives a child positive evaluations, that should raise the child's self-evaluation. Why should a teacher give positive evaluations to a child called a potential academic bloomer? Because, according to the theoretical context of this work, expectations affect the distribution of evaluations. What the child says in class begins to sound better, more nearly correct. In a teacher expectancy experiment, *if the teacher believes the investigator*, selected children will receive more chances to perform in class (the teacher will call on them more often), and they will get positive evaluations more frequently.[11]

A child who receives positive evaluations will surely increase his or her self-evaluation about schoolwork. That leads to greater interaction (raising hands, talking about schoolwork), which leads to greater actual

[11]Early teacher expectancy experiments later proved difficult to replicate. We believe this is because teachers did not always believe the experimental manipulation attempted by identifying "potential academic bloomers."

achievement. So the teacher expectancy phenomenon results partly from teachers marking selected children higher, and partly from the children actually performing better at standardized tests.

The first experiments show that having an adult give positive evaluations to children (third and fourth graders) increases their likelihood of hand raising, a sign of propensity to interact and a measure of self-evaluation. In a three-phase experiment, Entwisle and Webster (1972) first measured each child's baseline frequency of hand raising in response to group-directed questions. Then they selected one child responding near the mean for his or her group and gave a heavy dose of positive evaluations. Following that, they reconstituted the group and again measured hand raising without evaluations. As predicted, self-evaluation increased considerably from this treatment.

The second experiments (Entwisle & Webster, 1973) extended the age range (grades 1–4) and demographic range (black or white inner city, suburban, rural) of children. Comparable results show the effect to be quite general.

At first the experimenters were unsuccessful at raising self-evaluations of black, inner-city youngsters. The positive evaluations in the experimental groups did not produce the expected effect. We can imagine at least two possible reasons for this.

1. The "debilitating effect of school" hypothesis, popular at the time, held that going through the school system lowered self-evaluations for black children. Perhaps the brief experimental treatment could not overcome years of failure in schools.
2. The "mistrust of whites" hypothesis noted that the research team members all were white. Perhaps black children did not trust evaluations from whites.

To assess these hypotheses, black researchers repeated the experiments. This time, children did raise self-evaluations, supporting the second hypothesis. (Related studies by Dornbusch and colleagues [Natriello & Dornbusch, 1984] show similar cross-race mistrust among high school students.)

A behaviorist interpretation of these experiments would be inadequate. The children were not, we believe, simply increasing the rate of a behavior (hand raising) that had been rewarded. Rather, the treatment affected their relative confidence to perform this task. The raised self-evaluation led to the increase in hand raising. Supporting this conclusion, some "special control" experiments were run in which two children received the experimental treatment (Webster & Entwisle, 1976). In these, one child received the positive evaluations which we claim are crucial. The second child received all the same attention and warmth, but without evaluations. Only the first child showed the increase in hand raising.

The last Entwisle and Webster experiments (1978) involve transfer of evaluation effects across tasks. These experiments were designed with applications in mind. For raising children's self-evaluations, the procedure developed was effective. However, it depended upon giving clear positive evaluations of a child's performances. In a classroom where a teacher might wish to raise a given child's self-evaluation, sometimes the teacher cannot give positive evaluations honestly. Fortunately, according to the theory guiding this work, evaluations in one area will, under certain circumstances, transfer to a second area. That means a teacher need not wait, perhaps in vain, for a praiseworthy performance in, say, arithmetic to raise a child's self-evaluation at that task. A heavy dose of positive evaluations at spelling or reading will, with some attenuation, transfer to the new area. To test this idea, Entwisle and Webster gave experimental group children positive evaluations for one task (meal planning), and then measured their self-evaluations at the criterion task (storytelling). As predicted, the treatment raised self-evaluation at storytelling, though not so much as in other groups where children received positive evaluations for performing the criterion task (Entwisle & Webster, 1978). (For a fuller discussion of transfer phenomena, please see Berger, Wagner, & Zelditch, 1989.)

Entwisle and Hayduk (1978, 1982) extended this line of research by moving into early elementary classrooms to study determinants of the *formation* of children's ideas of their abilities. They were able to separate effects of parents' expectations, children's preschool expectations, and teachers' evaluations (school marks) upon children's self-evaluations. As we might expect, parents' and children's own expectations were the main determinants of children's self-evaluations as they entered school.

These are longitudinal studies. The investigators tracked children through school years, watching changes in their evaluations, as well as other effects. One important finding from this program is that most children, and especially working-class black children in the inner city, enter school with expectations so high as to be unrealistic. They expect to receive much higher marks than they eventually do. Black, inner-city children are the most overly optimistic; white suburban children, least so. This shows an error in one of the assumptions behind many social programs of the 1960s, such as Head Start, that disadvantaged children do poorly because they expect to fail. Disadvantaged children do not, in most cases, expect to fail. In fact, their expectations for success are more optimistic than those of middle-class children.

Other results of Entwisle and Hayduk's (1982) findings illuminate effects of a discrepancy between expected and actual marks. When the discrepancy is small, it motivates. Children bring up their marks at the next grading period to approximate their earlier expectations. When the discrepancy is large, as it most often is for black inner-city children, it may discourage children. The larger the initial discrepancy, the lower the marks at the second grading period. Thus, social programs, when they were effective at their stated goal of raising children's expectations, actually may have discouraged some and lowered their marks.

All the above work uses the initial ideas about what characteristics enable an individual to become an effective significant other: either high ability or high status. Work by Crundall and Foddy (Crundall & Foddy, 1981; Crundall, 1985; Foddy, 1988) extends the theory to "the coach phenomenon." Many times, individuals are willing to accept an evaluator's opinions even when the evaluator does not have higher ability. For instance, a swim team member is willing to believe his coach's evaluations, even knowing the coach could not swim well enough to make the team. This theoretical extension posits that experience, through a high level of exposure to similar performances, is another sufficient condition for acceptance as a significant other (or "source").

Themes and Issues in Referencing Studies and Source Studies

It is obvious that referencing and source processes have much overlap. In some referencing studies (e.g., Sorce, Emde, Campos, & Klinnert, 1985; Walden & Baxter, 1989), the parallels with source experiments are especially apparent. Both research traditions deal with efforts to define certain aspects of a situation by relying upon others, both regard certain others as particularly significant, and both investigate what happens when a source (or a referee) communicates certain information to the individual (referer). Briefly, we now point out some specific areas in which the theory or the research in one program either answers questions in the other, suggests modifications of theoretical ideas in the other, or points to further research topics.

Some Ideas for Studies of Referencing. 1. The source theories and research program concern *who* will be a source (or referee). Referencing theory and research have not, as yet, directly addressed this question, perhaps for the same reason that Sullivan did not ask who might be a significant other. That is, the referee is so close at hand (often, indeed, holding the referer in her arms) that the answer would be obvious.

Still, it would be profitable to inquire into abstract properties which make this or that person more or less likely to become a referee. The source theory identifies ability, status, and experience as each being sufficient. We do not think that nurturing or affection is necessary or sufficient. As we read the literature on infant referencing, researchers assume those two qualities to be effective in referencing phenomena. It would be interesting to investigate whether they actually *are* sufficient.

2. Researchers in the source program have tried to specify just which elements of the situation get defined during referencing. This program identifies three general classes of such elements. First, source processes determine elements of self-evaluations. This suggests that referencing theorists, when they ask what happens during the process, might look for changes in, or formation of, some areas of self-evaluation. Perhaps, in the situation commonly employed in referencing studies, the infant's ideas of his or her own competence to scale a visual cliff are affected. Some research on referencing could be so interpreted.

Second, the source program has shown that these processes affect *relative* conceptions of competence for two or more actors. Referencing studies concentrate upon early infancy, but perhaps referencing phenomena in childhood similarly affect siblings' ideas about their relative skills at, for example, playing ball or doing schoolwork.

Third, source theories apply to interactive behavioral effects of performance evaluations, an area approached only indirectly in referencing studies. In the source research program, we see behavioral effects especially in two areas: propensity to interact in the future, and likelihood of accepting influence attempts from others. There are other effects, such as likelihood of receiving positive evaluations, but the first two have been especially good behavioral indicators of the effects of evaluations. It might be worthwhile in studies of referencing phenomena to look for additional interactive behaviors which are affected by a referee.

3. The source program, like the older self-evaluation literature from which it derives, explicitly recognizes the chance of mistakes and misperceptions in reading others' signals. For unintentional referees, such as a parent who does not know the child is watching, or who is momentarily unable to control a sudden reaction, it might be worthwhile to ask when, and under what circumstances, referers are most likely correctly to understand a communication from a referee.

Some Ideas for Source Studies.   1. The most exciting implication of referencing studies for source studies is that the former show influence processes occurring well within the first year of life.[12]Source theories have treated much more advanced stages, children entering first grade, and college students. The age range at which source phenomena occur may be greater than we realized before referencing studies appeared. This raises the question of just how many source phenomena occur during infancy.

[12]We are indebted to Saul Feinman for first suggesting this idea.

For instance, do status effects of sources, well documented among college student adults, appear also among infants?

2. The natural course of self-evaluation in elementary school and the significance of schoolteachers are well documented. Since infant referencing studies make use of what is usually the only available adult—the parent—this raises the question of when others, such as teachers, get the ability to be effective sources. Transfer of the source (or referee) role probably occurs during elementary school for most children. However, we do not know the abstract conditions which make the transfer possible, or the time of their appearance.

3. As noted, the source program includes attempts to specify additional bases of "sourcehood" beyond the three already documented. Referencing studies suggest that certain characteristics of evaluators (or referees) may make them effective in certain types of circumstances, while other characteristics affect behavior in other types of circumstances. Perhaps specific status characteristics of evaluators have limited effects, while diffuse status characteristics are effective over a wider range.[13]

EVALUATIVE STANDARDS

This program focuses on the role of standards for performance in the assignment of ability levels. The program is newer than the one on sources of self-evaluation, going back only to the late 1970s, and hence it is less fully developed. It does, however, include some new theoretical directions. In particular it includes a Bayesian approach to the study of how individuals process evaluations about self and others. Foschi and her colleagues and students developed both theoretical and empirical work on evaluative standards in a series of papers and articles.

In general terms, *standards* in this research refers to how well a person must perform to receive an ability attribution, and conversely, how poorly a person has to perform before receiving an attribution of lack of ability. The assignment of ability or lack of ability is seen from the point of view of the "self" who interacts with a partner, or "other." The focus is on situations in which performance evaluations lead to ability inferences. In this context, standards are a key variable affecting how individuals process

[13]The term *diffuse status characteristic,* as used here, refers to such facts about a person as race, sex, age, wealth, or fame. More generally, diffuse status characteristics have the following three properties: (1) there are at least two differentially evaluated states, such that it is culturally considered better or preferable to possess one of the states; (2) associated with each state are certain cultural beliefs about specific performance abilities, such as the idea that men are more mathematical than women; and (3) also associated with each state are general beliefs about performance at "most tasks," or at "things in general." For a formal definition of diffuse status characteristic, see Berger *et al.,* 1977.

evaluations and what performance expectations result. For example, depending on the standards used, people may interpret the same level of success as a major accomplishment or dismiss it as unimportant. The same is true for interpretation of failure.

Although defined in somewhat different terms, the notion of standards appears under several labels and in a variety of research contexts in the social psychological literature. For example, "level of aspiration" and "goal setting" have some similarities with "standards" as used here. However, although there is an extensive literature on the relationship between level of aspiration, inferred competence, and self esteem, this work deals mostly with the level of performance that a person who values success would strive for or would like to achieve, or with the effects of goal setting on the performance and the performer. That is, the work has not focused on requirements for inferences of ability or lack of ability. (For reviews on goal setting and task performances, see Latham & Yukl, 1975; and Locke, Shaw, Saari, & Latham, 1981. For emotional reactions to performances that either meet or do not meet a given standard, see Higgins, Strautman, & Klein, 1986.)

The literature on social comparison, stemming from Festinger's (1954) formulation, also relates to work on standards in that it investigates how people use the ability level of comparison others as a yardstick. However, again the focus is different here. Work on standards concerns requirements for performance defined in objective terms relative to the task. Festinger's theory, on the other hand, focuses on situations lacking such standards. He argues that in those cases one judges one's performance against the performances of other people. Thus the comparison is social, and research in this tradition has centered around the issue of who is chosen as the comparison other. Findings show that individuals tend to shift comparison others depending upon how important the performance is, the ability level of others compared to self, or how immediately previous performances rate (see, e.g., Allen & Wilder, 1977; and Suls, 1977).

Standards as defined above are a key parameter in a Bayesian model on the formation of performance expectations constructed by Foschi and Foschi (1976, 1979). Given a situation where two people, A and B, perform a task consisting of a series of performances, and where person C knows the evaluations A and B received at each step of this series, the model accounts for C's expectations about A and B as a function of the evaluations. The theory assumes that each person's expectations include his or her own standard, or definition of what it means to be better or worse than, or equal to, another person at the task. The approach involves looking at the problem of formation of expectations as a special case of information processing. Thus, instead of asking about the effect of a given evaluation on C's expectations, the question becomes how a piece of evidence affects the subjective probability or confidence that C attaches to a given hypothesis. In this way, we can use the logic of inductive inference as expressed in Bayes's theorem for constructing the model.

Bayes's theorem specifies the way in which an ideal person C would process information. That is, Bayesian models provide normative quantities and cannot themselves be tested. However, the models can be used as a framework against which the behavior of real people in different conditions may be studied. Foschi (1986) put the model to such a use in an experiment having three conditions: actors evaluated as performing better than their partners, actors evaluated as performing worse, and observers of the two actors. Foschi measured each subject's standards for ability and for lack of ability at the task and relative to a partner, and then used these standards to calculate how each subject would process the evaluations if Bayes's theorem were followed. For each person, normative and actual probability revisions were then compared. This comparison investigates two variables: conservatism and deviation. Results showed that, of the three conditions, subjects performing worse than their partners were most conservative in processing the received evaluations—that is, they did not go as far in their revisions as Bayes's theorem would prescribe—but also that they deviated the least from the direction of change specified by the model. These results suggest that people interpret negative evaluations of self more cautiously than positive ones, but also that they attend to the former more carefully than the latter.

Foschi, Warriner, and Hart (1985) report results from a study in which subject in same-sex dyads received either higher or lower scores at a task than the partner. At each level of relative success and failure, subjects received one of two levels of experimentally created standards. The dependent measure was level of acceptance of influence from the partner. Standards had the predicted effects on influence in the success conditions: subjects who performed better than their partners and whose performances met the standard for ability accepted less influence than subjects whose performances did not meet the standard. The experimental manipulations, however, were not successful at creating two levels of standards for male subjects who performed worse than their partners. A study by Foschi and Freeman (1991) replicated this finding, which the authors explain as an effect of status of subject relative to status of source of expectations. Research on this topic continues, with a special interest in identifying factors affecting the differential acceptance of standards in success and failure conditions.

Currently, the research program focuses on different origins of standards, that is, whether a third party such as the experimenter sets them, or whether the interactants themselves do. One promising theoretical lead is the idea that different states of a diffuse status characteristic can set in motion the use of double or multiple standards by individuals who have no access to others (Foddy & Smithson, 1989; Foschi, 1989). For example, it has often been observed that stricter performance standards are applied to women than to men. Foschi (1990) recently completed an experiment in which male and female subjects in opposite-sex dyads performed a task defined as masculine. Results give clear evidence of a stricter standard for the performances of females.[14] Note, however, that on other occasions women are patronized and judged by lenient standards. Another example of shifting standards in the judgment of performances is the following. Performers known to be successful at a task often enjoy a more lenient standard than previously unsuccessful performers, although it is not unusual to observe circumstances in which the opposite shift occurs. Current work studies conditions under which both types of double standards (i.e., either stricter or more lenient for the lower-status person) get activated, and their effects upon expectations and group interaction.

Finally, a paper by Foschi and Foddy (1988) presents an expanded conceptualization of standards. All of the experimental work described above involves defining standards by the number of correct responses in a single task consisting of a series of trials. Thus, for example, one may set 70% (or more) correct responses as the standard for ability, and 30% (or fewer) correct responses as the standard for lack of ability. In addition to this variable, the latest conceptualization includes the degree of difficulty of the task, the number of times a performer must repeat the series, and the number of additional tasks requiring the same or related abilities. Current work aims to incorporate this more complex definition of standards in propositions for empirical testing.

Themes and Issues in Referencing Studies and Evaluative Standards Studies

Some Ideas for Referencing.   1. Referencing and source studies assume a referer does not use all potential referees in a situation. Although this idea has not received full development in social referencing, obviously no individual, infant or adult, can use every other individual indiscriminately in making sense of the world. The question here is not how to select

---

[14]The substantial number of studies exploring sex differences in attribution also are relevant here. These studies test the hypothesis that success by a man will tend to be attributed to ability, whereas success by a woman will tend to be seen as due to other factors such as good luck and, perhaps, to effort. The opposite pattern of attributions has been hypothesized for failure. Support for these ideas, however, has been only moderate and inconsistent. Foschi and Plecash (1983) and Foschi (1989) discuss reasons for such findings, and propose a reformulation and explanation of the attribution hypotheses in terms of expectation states and standards for performance. They argue that in mixed-sex groups, success by women often is seen as due to factors other than ability because their performances tend to be evaluated with stricter standards than men's performances.

a potential referee (as it was when we discussed the source theories), but rather what makes a referee, once selected, lose that position. Research on effects of standards suggests that a referee who sets too high standards for the referer—such that he or she cannot ever achieve the referee's definition of success—may also cease to be effective.

2. Setting standards by referees may involve early, though slow, processes of individuating the self from others. If so, they are important in early socialization. Children certainly learn that referees (e.g., parents) set different standards for themselves and for children, and even differentiate among siblings. Learning to identify oneself as a child, that is, as someone who can "succeed" with less than an adult level of performance, may take place this way. Similarly, such statements from a referee as "that's a pretty good pitch for a girl" may facilitate learning to identify oneself in terms of gender role.

3. The Bayesian approach in work on evaluative standards involves a process of continual redefinition of performance capacities from repeated trials. Ideas of self-worth, self-evaluation, and other similar notions probably get refined this way through the opinions of others. As self-evaluations change in this theory, the effects of a given new unit of information also change. A single positive evaluation has one effect coming after a lifetime of negative evaluations, and quite a different effect in a field of positive evaluations. Referencing theories probably should incorporate this idea. The child referer is not simply a passive recipient of the referee's opinions, but an active processor, who assimilates and modifies them.

Some Ideas for Evaluative Standards. 1. Referencing research emphasizes social sources of evaluations and standards, consistent with Festinger's (1954) theory of social comparison processes. Research into evaluative standards also focuses upon standards which come socially, from others. The referee may accept such others because of their roles (e.g., experimenter) or may choose them because of their status characteristics. Although social factors play a major role in determining what standards are used, the nature of the task, such as its complexity or difficulty, also places limits on what may be required (Foschi & Foddy, 1988).

2. Referencing research reminds us that an effect of standards from certain referees may be to limit the level of aspiration of actors. Robert Rosenthal (1966) noted that when companies introduced Hollerith machines, office managers set what they considered a reasonable day's output on them. Operators who exceeded that limit often suffered significant symptoms of fatigue and stress. But operators not told the "normal" production levels happily exceeded them several times over. How referees not only communicate immediate interpretations of a situation but also affect performances through setting evaluative standards deserves more investigation.

REFERENT ACTORS

Studies of referent actors make up a branch of a large research program investigating ways to ameliorate undesirable effects of status characteristic differences among schoolchildren (for summaries of the main findings of this program, see Cohen, 1982, 1988). Investigators in this program wish to modify certain interaction patterns between children from different ethnic groups, such as typically occur in black–white or Chicano–Anglo classrooms.

Together these undesirable behaviors form a pattern investigators call "interracial interaction disability" (Cohen & Roper, 1972, 1985). As used, interracial interaction disability results from a self-fulfilling prophecy of stereotypes children (as well as adults) activate in racially mixed groups. In outline, a high-status member such as a white child expects to be more competent at new tasks and so initiates more interaction, and is more influential during the group's life. The lower-status child, such as a black or Chicano child, initiates less interaction, overvalues contributions of the more talkative high-status child and undervalues his or her own, and exerts less influence over group discussion and outcome.

These phenomena have attracted considerable attention and a search for ways to alter interaction patterns. What makes the work of Cohen and her colleagues distinctive is its basis in established theories of status generalization.[15] It is a theoretically based application of techniques to solve a problem of obvious practical significance.

According to Cohen's analysis, interracial interaction disability results from status generalization. Children of "minority" status do not interact so much, and are not so influential, as children having culturally favored states of the status characteristic. This occurs because both groups activate stereotypes of supposed abilities having the same relative evaluations as their statuses: high ability for high-status children, low ability for low-status children.

In some of the first studies, Cohen successfully reduced interracial interaction disability by giving black children special training and information and then letting them teach white children how to perform a simple task (making a two-transistor radio). Investigators dramatically pointed out instances of the blacks' superior knowledge and skills to all children, both black and white. Then biracial groups of the children played

[15]As mentioned earlier in this chapter, status generalization describes the process of using initially irrelevant status characteristics as the basis for inferences regarding ability. For example, if children, both black and white, assume without evidence that white children can learn to write cursively faster and better, status generalization has taken place from the status characteristic race to the skill writing ability. See Webster and Driskell, 1985, and Webster and Foschi, 1988, for a formal theoretical description of status generalization, along with some relevant experimental data.

a board game and investigators recorded interaction rates and influence. Compared to control groups which had not received the "expectation training" on radio assembly, experimental groups showed much greater equality of participation and influence.

Cohen's research differs from other approaches to this problem in that it does not locate the source of difficulty in some peculiar attributes of black or Chicano children. Treatments are not designed to help minority children overcome a supposed inferiority such as poor preparation, inadequate study habits, lack of assertiveness, or low IQ. Rather, the interaction effects of status differences in society are identified as the source of the problem. Therefore, intervention takes the form of modifying some well-understood properties of unequal status interaction. Success is measured as much in the lowered interaction rates of whites as in the increased rates achieved by blacks or Chicanos in biracial groups.

A student of Cohen's, Mark Lohman (1970), devised the first successful treatment in this program which involved referent actors. Lohman's intervention showed children a videotape of a black teacher instructing white students. Later, a black adult instructed all students in the training task. At the time of Lohman's research, the theoretical basis for using blacks in the roles of teacher and experimenter was not fully developed. However, there has long been a concern for finding appropriate role models (such as black teachers, or women scientists) for students at all levels.

What Lohman's research did in theoretical terms can be shown better with graphs, such as the ones on the following pages.

Figure 1 shows the simplest possible case of mixed-status interaction (two actors differentiated by a single status characteristic). Actor p possesses the low state of a diffuse status characteristic $(D-)$ such as race; for example, p could be black. Actor o possesses the high state $(D+)$; o is white. We show the stereotypical belief cluster people associate with states of D by Γ, with $\Gamma-$ linked to or associated with p and $\Gamma+$ associated with o. States of Γ connect to ideas of the specific ability required to perform the group task, such as playing a board game (C^*). Ideas of task ability connect to outcome states "success" $(T+)$ and "failure" $(T-)$. In this example, p becomes connected to "failure" and o connected (in p's mind, as well as o's) to "success" through the links of γ and C^*.[16]

---

[16]We omit several technicalities of the graph version of the theory. However note that the "expectation advantage" of an actor depends upon three things: (1) The number of paths connecting each actor to outcome states, which is a function of the status characteristics salient in the situation. Thus, if in Figure 1, p were female (D_2-) and o were male (D_2+), p's expectation disadvantage would become greater. (2) The length of paths connecting actors to outcome states. Thus if actors knew for sure that o possessed the needed ability C^*+ and p did not, p would be directly connected to C^*- and o to C^*+. The inferential process through stereotypes would be unnecessary, and o's expectation advantage again would be greater. (3) The consistency of states of status. Figure 2 shows what happens when p and o both possess one positively and one negatively evaluated state of two status characteristics.

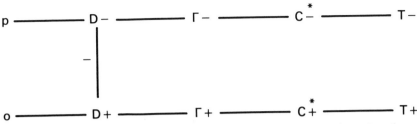

Figure 1. Status generalization from the characteristic race (see text for discussion of symbols).

Figure 2 shows what happened in Cohen's experimental condition. Here, p also has the high state (+) of a specific status characteristic C, which is building a radio. $C+$ is associated with the necessary skills (wiring, reading diagrams, etc), represented by $\tau+$. That connects with the idea of success at tasks in general, $\gamma+$. And $\gamma+$ connects to success at the specific group task $T+$. Now p is connected to both outcome states of T. The link through $D-$ leads to $T-$ and the link through $C+$ leads to $T+$. Thus, p's expectation disadvantage decreases, in this case to zero (since path lengths are equal and no other factors apply). We consequently expect interracial interaction equality, and that is what Cohen and Roper (1972, 1985) found.

Figure 3 diagrams Lohman's technique. Here, there is an additional actor, the black role model o_2, linked to p through their mutual possession of $D-$. However, o_2 has the high state of C, knowing how to assemble a radio. $C+$ connects to $T+$ through the inferential links described in the discussion of Figure 2.[17] Thus, o's expectation advantage decreases because of the existence of referent actor o_2.

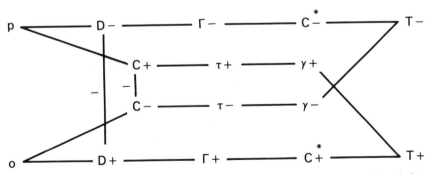

Figure 2. Status generalization from ability and race (see text for discussion of symbols).

[17]The path connecting p to $T+$ has length 6, making it a very weak path. Thus we predict only a small effect of the role model here at increasing equality between p and o. That is what Lohman found.

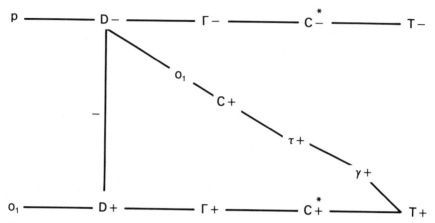

Figure 3. Status generalization from referent actor, ability, and race (see text for discussion of symbols).

Pugh and Wahrman (1983) devised another use of the referent actor phenomenon, this time with the applied concern of reducing one type of sexism, the belief that a typical man can do most tasks better than a typical woman. Pugh and Wahrman adopted a basic experimental setting commonly used in status characteristic studies (see Berger *et al.*, 1977, Ch. 5). The criterion task here is a series of group judgments about binary choice slides (i.e., which of two patterns contains more white area), and experimentally controlled disagreements are introduced. The disagreement resolution measure P(s), the proportion of disagreements resolved in favor of self, is a reliable measure of relative expectation advantage.

An interesting sidelight of Pugh and Wahrman's research is that they employed college student subjects, a group sometimes said to be beyond sexist beliefs. However, in the baseline condition, with no information other than the fact that one's partner was of the opposite sex, a clear, significant P(s) difference favors men.

The second condition in this study had the experimenter use his authority to tell subjects that previous research shows that women and men do equally well at the criterion task. Here again, Pugh and Wahrman found strong, significant P(s) differences favoring men.

In the third condition, the investigators showed both individuals in each group that women actually did perform as well as men. Subjects took a test of ability, and received feedback on each judgment and overall scores. In spite of this, substantial P(s) differences again appeared. Only in the fourth condition, in which women performed better than men, could Pugh and Wahrman produce equal status interaction at the criterion task.

To understand graphically what happened, imagine each person directly connected to a C^* having an opposite sign from the sign on his or her D characteristic. Compared with the first two conditions, we find the P(s) for men here lower, and the P(s) for women higher.[18]

The most interesting findings come from the fifth condition, "transfer." Here, subjects who had completed condition four returned to the laboratory and interacted with a new other-sex partner. Investigators predicted that each person's first partner would now become a referent actor. When the referent actor was a man, as it was for female subjects, he possessed $D+$ and also C^*-. When the referent actor was a woman, as it was for male subjects, she possessed $D-$ and also C^*+.

This referent actor connects to the new partner through their common possession of D. Both the referent actor and the new partner for a man were women; both the referent actor and the new partner for a woman were men. As anticipated, the increased equality found in condition four transferred to condition five. Not all subjects interacted as perfect equals with their new partners, but they definitely showed greater equality in condition five than in conditions one and two.

Theoretically based use of referent actors to increase equality among adults is only beginning. However, the phenomenon has clear parallels to social referencing phenomena. For instance, several referencing studies have shown that multiple cues produce stronger effects than single cues. Furthermore, when a referee communicates through multiple channels such as facial expression and voice, the message also has greater effect. (For examples, please see Boccia & Campos, 1983; Hornik & Gunner, 1988; Svejda & Campos, 1982; Walden & Baxter, 1989; Walden & Ogan, 1988). The theory Pugh and Wahrman used proposes a mechanism through which social referencing occurs.

Themes and Issues in Referencing Studies and Referent Actor Studies

Some Ideas for Referencing. 1. Referent actor research emphasizes that an effective referent must have links to the individual for these processes to appear. For example, they may both possess states of a particular status characteristic, such as being women. Implicitly, referencing studies also assume some link. Referent actor theories are more specific about what that link is. It goes through common possession of either specific or diffuse status characteristics. Research in referencing suggests

---

[18]Also of interest, Pugh and Wahrman (1983) reported that in their third and fourth conditions, male subjects were more easily convinced than female subjects of a female's equal or superior ability.

that familiarity or trust are sufficient conditions for the process to occur. Would those be sufficient without the link through status characteristics? In other words, would social referencing occur between actors who have nothing in common, but who trust each other, or who are closely familiar with each other? It seems unlikely.[19]

2. In referent actor theories, a "memory" gets created which transfers to similar situations and to actors having similar status characteristics. Referencing studies also may assume a memory, but without making its significance explicit. Referencing research would gain determinacy by specifying ways individuals incorporate referencing effects from previous encounters. For instance, referent actor theories predict that such transfer effects should be weaker than status effects produced in immediate interaction. Such an assumption, or one similar, might improve theoretical and applied work in social referencing.

3. Referent actor theories stress the need for interaction in changing beliefs. Usually it is not enough for an individual to gain information. He or she must *act* upon it before it becomes part of a knowledge store. So we ask whether learning by referencing is effective if the individual does not act upon it. Does a child who infers that cars are dangerous from a parent's frightened look effectively learn the lesson if the child then ignores the implied warning? Referent actor theories would predict that the child does not learn without acting. We know that children learn to fear cars without actually being struck by them, but most parents do not trust solely in worried looks to get the message across. As Feinman, Roberts, Hsieh, Sawyer, and Swanson note (Chapter 2, this volume), in cases of potential danger most parents combine oral warnings with warning glances.

Some Ideas for Referent Actor Studies.   1. Referencing processes usually are more subtle than processes studied to date with referent actors. In referencing studies, a look, even a smile, can have great significance. Experimental studies of referent actors have not used such subtle cues, though subtle cues probably would be effective here too. This points to the importance of communicative and evaluative cues between referents and actors, and suggests a search to identify what those cues might be.

2. When does experience override the information from a referent actor? Studies of social referencing have documented cases where a child will ignore a mother's smiles and refuse to cross a visual cliff (Feinman,

[19]More usefully, we might ask: What sorts of links between individuals must exist before social referencing phenomena can occur? Common possession of some status characteristic may not be essential even though sufficient. It would be useful to identify other effective links.

1985).[20] Similarly, certainly there must be cases where referent actors give one type of information and individuals reinterpret or ignore it. Determining the class of situations which give rise to such a phenomenon would improve referent actor theories.

CONCLUSION

Social referencing involves behavioral as well as symbolic learning, and occurs in a wide variety of interaction contexts. The phenomenon has clear importance, and connects to several of the major perspectives of contemporary social psychology. Those include the traditions of reference group, social comparison, and self-evaluation studies. Through these intellectual ties, social referencing also connects to more recent theoretical research programs. In this chapter we describe three: (1) selection and effects of sources of self-evaluation, (2) setting evaluative standards and resulting ability inferences, and (3) the role of referent actors in overcoming status generalization. We try to identify points of commonality between each program and social referencing studies, and suggest ways the comparisons may be mutually useful. Thus, we illustrate how the concepts and propositions from one area may be refined using those from another, and propose research extensions of each area from the ideas and findings of the other.

REFERENCES

Allen, V. L., & Wilder, D. A. (1977). Social comparison, self-evaluation, and conformity to the group. In J. M. Suls & R. L. Miller (Eds.), *Social comparison processes: Theoretical and empirical perspectives* (pp. 187–208). Washington, DC: Hemisphere.

Bandura, A. (1965). Vicarious processes: A case of no-trial learning. In L. Berkowitz (Ed.), *Advances in experimental social psychology* (Vol. 2, pp. 1–55). New York: Academic Press.

Berger, J., Fisek, M. H., Norman, R. Z., & Zelditch, M., Jr. (1977). *Status characteristics and social interaction: An expectation states approach.* New York: Elsevier.

Berger, J., Wagner, D. G., & Zelditch, M., Jr. (1985). Expectation states theory: Review and assessment. In J. Berger & M. Zelditch, Jr. (Eds.), *Status, rewards, and influence* (pp. 1–72). San Francisco: Jossey-Bass.

Berger, J., Wagner, D. G., & Zelditch, M., Jr. (1989). Theory growth, social processes, and metatheory. In J. H. Turner (Ed.), *Theory building in sociology: Assessing theoretical cumulation* (pp. 19–42). Newbury Park, CA: Sage.

---

[20]Feinman's paper implies that some unlearned survival response acts in this case. If so, we would not expect override in cases where the referee signals danger and the objective facts do not. That would be an interesting test.

Boccia, M. L., & Campos, J. J. (1983, April). *Maternal emotional signals and infants' reactions to strangers.* Paper presented at the biennial meeting of the Society for Research in Child Development, Detroit.

Brophy, J. E., & Good, T. L. (1970). Teachers' communication of differential expectations for children's classroom performance. *Journal of Educational Psychology, 61,* 367–374.

Cohen, E. G. (1982). Expectation states and interracial interaction in school settings. In A. Inkeles & R. H. Turner (Eds.), *Annual review of sociology, Vol. 8* (pp. 209–235). Palo Alto, CA: Annual Reviews.

Cohen, E. G. (1988). Can expectations for competence be altered in the classroom? In M. Webster, Jr., & M. Foschi (Eds.), *Status generalization: New theory and research* (pp. 27–54 & 478–480). Stanford, CA: Stanford University Press.

Cohen, E. G. & Roper, S. S. (1972). Modification of interracial interaction disability: An application of status characteristic theory. *American Sociological Review, 37,* 643–657.

Cohen, E. G., & Roper, S. S. (1985). Modification of interracial interaction disability. In J. Berger & M. Zelditch, Jr. (Eds.), *Status, rewards, and influence* (pp. 350–378). San Francisco: Jossey-Bass.

Cooley, C. H. (1902). *Human nature and the social order.* New York: Scribners.

Crundall, I. (1985). *Practice, exposure, and reputation as sources of influence in task oriented situations.* Unpublished doctoral dissertation, Australian National University, Canberra.

Crundall, I., & Foddy, M. (1981). Vicarious exposure to a task as a basis of evaluative competence. *Social Psychology Quarterly, 44,* 331–338.

Entwisle, D. R., & Hayduk, L. A. (1978). *Too great expectations: The academic outlook of young children.* Baltimore: Johns Hopkins University Press.

Entwisle, D. R., & Hayduk, L. A. (1982). *Early schooling: Cognitive and affective outcomes.* Baltimore: Johns Hopkins University Press.

Entwisle, D. R., & Webster, M., Jr. (1972). Raising children's performance expectations. *Social Science Research, 1,* 147–158.

Entwisle, D. R., & Webster, M., Jr. (1973). Research note: Status factors in expectation raising. *Sociology of Education, 46,* 115–126.

Entwisle, D. R., & Webster, M., Jr. (1978). Raising expectations indirectly. *Social Forces, 57,* 257–264.

Feinman, S. (1985). Emotional expression, social referencing, and preparedness for learning in infancy—Mother knows best, but sometimes I know better. In G. Zivin (Ed.), *The development of expressive behavior: Biology–environment interactions* (pp. 291–318). Orlando, FL: Academic Press.

Feinman, S., & Lewis, M. (1983). Social referencing at ten months: A second-order effect on infants' responses to strangers. *Child Development, 54,* 878–887.

Festinger, L. (1954). A theory of social comparison processes. *Human Relations, 7,* 117–140.

Foddy, M. (1988). Paths of relevance and evaluative competence. In M. Webster, Jr., & M. Foschi (Eds.), *Status generalization: New theory and research* (pp. 232–247 & 501). Stanford, CA: Stanford University Press.

Foddy, M., & Smithson, M. (1989). Fuzzy sets and double standards: Modeling the process of ability inference. In J. Berger, M. Zelditch, Jr., & B. Anderson (Eds.), *Sociological theories in progress: New formulations* (pp. 73–99). Newbury Park, CA: Sage.

Foschi, M. (1986). Actors, observers, and performance expectations: A Bayesian model and an experimental study. In E. J. Lawler (Ed.), *Advances in group processes, Vol. 3* (pp. 181–208). Greenwich, CT: JAI Press.

Foschi, M. (1989). Status characteristics, standards, and attributions. In J. Berger, M. Zelditch, Jr., & B. Anderson (Eds.), *Sociological theories in progress: New formulations* (pp. 58–72). Newbury Park, CA: Sage.

Foschi, M. (1990, May). *Double standards in the evaluation of men and women.* Paper presented at the annual meeting of the Canadian Sociology and Anthropology Association, Victoria, B.C.

Foschi, M., & Foddy, M. (1988). Standards, performances, and the formation of self–other expectations. In M. Webster, Jr., & M. Foschi (Eds.), *Status generalization: New theory and research* (pp. 248–260 & 501–503). Stanford, CA: Stanford University Press.

Foschi, M., & Foschi, R. (1976). Evaluations and expectations: A Bayesian model. *Journal of Mathematical Sociology, 4,* 279–293.

Foschi, M., & Foschi, R. (1979). A Bayesian model for performance expectations: Extension and simulation. *Social Psychology Quarterly, 42,* 232–241.

Foschi, M., & Freeman, S. (1991). Inferior performance, standards, and influence in same-sex dyads. *Canadian Journal of Behavioural Science 23,* 99–113.

Foschi, M., & Plecash, J. S. (1983, June). *Sex differences in the attribution of success and failure: An expectation-states explanation.* Paper presented at the annual meeting of the Canadian Sociology and Anthropology Association, Vancouver, B.C.

Foschi, M., Warriner, G. K., & Hart, S. D. (1985). Standards, expectations, and interpersonal influence. *Social Psychology Quarterly, 48,* 108–117.

Higgins, E. T., Strautman, T., & Klein, R. (1986). Standards and the process of self-evaluation: Multiple effects from multiple stages. In R. M. Sorrentino & E. T. Higgins (Eds.), *Handbook of motivation and cognition: Foundations of social behavior* (pp. 23–63). New York: The Guilford Press.

Hirshberg, L. M. (1988, April). *Patterns of coping with conflict in infancy: 12-month olds' response to conflicting parental emotional signals.* Paper presented at the Sixth International Conference on Infant Studies, Washington, DC

Hirshberg, L. M. (1990). When infants look to their parents: II. Twelve-month-olds' response to conflicting parental emotional signals. *Child Development 61,* 1187–1191.

Hornik, R., & Gunnar, M. (1988). A descriptive analysis of infant social referencing. *Child Development 59,* 626–634.

Lakatos, I. (1970). Falsification and the methodology of scientific research programmes. In I. Lakatos & A. Mosgrave (Eds.), *Criticism and the growth of knowledge* (pp. 91–195). Cambridge: Cambridge University Press.

Latham, G. P., & Yukl, G. A. (1975). A review of research on the application of goal setting in organizations. *Academy of Management Journal, 18,* 824–845.

Locke, E. A., Shaw, K. N., Saari, L. M., & Latham, G. P. (1981). Goal setting and task performance: 1969–1980. *Psychological Bulletin, 90,* 125–152.

Lohman, M. (1970). *Changing a racial status ordering by means of role modeling* (Technical Report #3). Stanford, CA: Stanford University, School of Education.

Mead, G. H. (1934). *Mind, self and society.* Chicago: University of Chicago Press.

Miyamoto, S. F., & Dornbusch, S. M. (1956). A test of interactionist hypotheses of self-conception. *American Journal of Sociology, 41,* 399–403.

Natriello, G., & Dornbusch, S. M. (1984). *Teacher evaluative standards and student effort.* New York: Longmans.

Pallas, A. M., Entwisle, D. R., Alexander, K. L., & Weinstein, P. (1990). Social structure and the development of self-evaluation in young children. *Social Psychology Quarterly, 53,* 302–315.

Pugh, M. D., & Wahrman, R. (1983). Neutralizing sexism: Do women have to be better than men? *American Journal of Sociology, 88,* 746–762.

Rosenthal, R. (1966). *Experimenter effects in behavioral research.* New York: Appleton-Century-Crofts.

Rosenthal, R., & Jacobson, L. (1968). *Pygmalion in the classroom.* New York: Holt, Rinehart & Winston.

Sobieszek, B. I., & Webster, M., Jr. (1973). Conflicting sources of evaluations. *Sociometry, 36,* 550–560.

Sorce, J. F., Emde, R. N., Campos, J. J., & Klinnert, M. D. (1985). Maternal emotional signaling: Its effect on the visual cliff behavior of 1-year-olds. *Developmental Psychology, 21,* 195–200.

Sullivan, H. S. (1947). *Conceptions of modern psychiatry.* Washington, DC: W. H. White Psychiatric Foundation.

Suls, J. M. (1977). Social comparison theory and research: An overview from 1954. In J. M. Suls & R. L. Miller (Eds.), *Social comparison processes: Theoretical and empirical perspectives* (pp. 1–19). Washington, DC: Hemisphere.

Svejda, M. J., & Campos, J. J. (1982, March). *Mother's vocal expression of emotion as a behavior regulator.* Paper presented at the Third International Conference on Infant Studies, Austin, TX.

Thomas, W. I. (1928). *The child in America.* New York: Knopf.

Turner, R. H. (1976). The real self: From institution to impulse. *American Journal of Sociology, 81,* 989–1016.

Turner, R. H. (1990). Role change. In *Annual Review of Sociology, Vol. 16* (pp. 87–110). Palo Alto, CA: Annual Reviews.

Walden, T. A., & Baxter, A. (1989). The effect of context and age on social referencing. *Child Development 60,* 1511–1518.

Walden, T. A., & Ogan, T. A. (1988). The development of social referencing. *Child Development 59,* 1230–1240.

Webster, M., Jr. (1969). Source of evaluations and expectations for performance. *Sociometry, 32,* 243–258.

Webster, M., Jr., & Driskell, J. E., Jr. (1978). Status generalization: A review and some new data. *American Sociological Review, 43,* 220–236.

Webster, M., Jr., & Driskell, J. E., Jr. (1985). Status generalization. In J. Berger & M. Zelditch, Jr. (Eds.), *Status, rewards, and influence* (pp. 108–141). San Francisco: Jossey-Bass.

Webster, M., Jr., & Entwisle, D. R. (1976). Expectations and evaluations. *Social Forces, 55,* 493–502.

Webster, M., Jr., & Foschi, M. (1988). Overview of status generalization. In M. Webster, Jr., & M. Foschi (Eds.), *Status generalization: New theory and research* (pp. 1–20 & 477–478). Stanford, CA: Stanford University Press.

Webster, M., Jr., & Sobieszek, B. I. (1974a). Sources of evaluations and expectation states. In J. Berger, T. L. Conner, & M. H. Fisek (Eds.), *Expectation states theory: A theoretical research program* (pp. 115–158). Boston: Winthrop Publishers.

Webster, M., Jr., & Sobieszek, B. I. (1974b). *Sources of self-evaluation: A formal theory of significant others and social influence.* New York: Wiley-Interscience.

IV
Relationships and Interaction

12

Indirect and Direct Effects and Family Interaction

Michael Lewis and Candice Feiring

In this chapter we consider the issue of social referencing from the broader perspective of social influences in general and direct and indirect effects in particular. First, we consider the question of why indirect effects should be studied, focusing on the inherent problems in the study of social influences. Direct and indirect effects are defined in the next section. Then, the relationship between indirect effects and social referencing is discussed. Following this, the model of direct and indirect effects and a review of the relevant literature is presented. Our work on the family at dinner is presented in order to demonstrate how indirect effects operate within the dinner context. Discussion of these data as they pertain to our focus ends the chapter.

WHY STUDY INDIRECT EFFECTS

The study of children's development is dominated by a model which argues for the impact of a single adult (usually mother) on the child's subsequent outcome. This direct effects model is based on the premise that

MICHAEL LEWIS and CANDICE FEIRING • Institute for the Study of Child Development, Robert Wood Johnson Medical School, University of Medicine and Dentistry of New Jersey, New Brunswick, New Jersey 08903.

Social Referencing and the Social Construction of Reality in Infancy, edited by Saul Feinman. Plenum Press, New York, 1992.

person A (e.g., mother) interacts with person B (e.g., child), and through A's behavior toward B, A influences B's behavior or personality. Thus, for example, the mother's speech patterns toward her young infant are used to predict the child's subsequent language behavior. This model suggests (1) a dyadic view of social behavior and (2) that children's language acquisition is the result of mother's behavior directed toward them. Such a model assumes that mother and child constitute the only people in the child's social world and that children's development will be a consequence of only those maternal behaviors directed toward them.

Such a limited view of the organism's development as a function of the dyad is predicted on biological and educational models as well as on methodological limitations. In the biological model, the emphasis on the mother–infant dyad is based on the belief that this dyad constitutes a biological unit endowed with characteristics that are essential for infant survival. Rosenblum and Moltz (1983) conceive of it as a symbiotic relationship having evolutionary significance. While recent studies have shown the impact of other members of the child's family, the data gathered still use the dyadic formulation (Lewis & Rosenblum, 1979). Few studies beyond the dyad, focusing on the family or other polyadic groups as the unit of inquiry, have been undertaken (Lewis, 1986; Lewis & Feiring, 1982; Vuchinich, Emery, & Cassidy, 1988).

The teacher–pupil relationship represents another powerful model of a dyad. Focusing on information exchange, this educational model argues for information dissemination in a single teacher–learner unit. As in the mother–child dyad, it is the adult teacher who informs and educates the pupil. This model assumes that the learning environment contains only teacher and pupil and does not consider the role of the others in the classroom, certainly not other students if not other teachers. While there are some studies which focus on the role of the pupil–pupil dyad in the learning process, there are few polyadic studies of classroom behavior itself.

Both the biological and educational models suffer from the bias of utilizing the dyad as the unit of measurement. This bias is perpetuated by the exclusive focus on one specific dyad (i.e., teacher–child, mother–child), for once we begin to even consider other dyads (e.g., father–child, pupil–pupil) the need for expanding our view to a larger social context becomes more obvious. Nevertheless, the focus on only two-person systems, regardless of the diversity in membership of the dyad, results in a restriction of interactions and effects considered to be direct ones. It neglects to consider the impact of each member's behavior on others not in the dyad under study. Indirect effects do not operate through the direct interaction of one person with another. Indirect effects usually involve influences that result from social situations or contexts that involve more than one person.

One such indirect effect, taken from our language example, would be a child's *observation* of parental conversation at dinner influencing the child's expressive language skills. These indirect effects (something we will return to in more detail shortly) are understudied.

One central problem that restricts studies of children's development to the dyad pertains to measurement difficulties when we study units larger than the dyad. Prior to the late 1960s, the measurement of interaction was dependent on scales and questionnaires. More recent direct observational methods have resulted in new measurement procedures (Cairns, 1979; Lamb, Suomi, & Stephenson, 1979; Sackett, 1978). However, except for a few studies, these methods have been restricted to dyads. More complex procedures such as sequential analysis techniques are difficult to use with units larger than dyads (see Gottman & Bakeman, 1979 for exceptions). This is especially true when a larger number of measures is employed. Thus, in most cases, measurement difficulty has restricted research to dyads. As such, the effects of indirect actions have received little study in relation to direct effects.

Except for those arguing for a strong biological model, it has become clear that we need to go beyond the dyad in studying social development (Lewis, 1985). This requires that we focus more attention on group processes, and to do so means that we must deal with indirect as well as direct effects.

DEFINITION OF DIRECT AND INDIRECT EFFECTS

Direct Effects

Direct effects have been defined as those interactions which represent the effect or influence of one person on the behaviors of another when both are engaged in mutual interaction (Lewis & Weinraub, 1976). In the study of social behavior, direct effects are usually observed in dyadic interactions but could occur in polyadic groups, as when a teacher instructs a class of students. Direct effects may involve information gathered from participation in an interaction with another person or object and always involve the target person as one of the focused participants in the interaction. For example, a child learns about how puzzles work by playing with puzzles, or develops an aggressive interaction style from being picked on by a sibling.

Indirect Effects

Indirect effects include two classes of events. The first class of indirect effects contains the sets of interactions which affect the target person but which occur in the absence of that person. These sets of interactions may best be described as influences which play their role in development as they affect direct effects (or interactions). For example, the husband–wife interaction that takes place in the bedroom outside of the child's experience can influence the parents' sense of well-being, and this sense of well-being can influence the parent–child interaction.

More important for the present discussion and for the consideration of social referencing is the second class of indirect effects. This refers to interactions among members of the system that occur in the presence of the target person even though the interaction is not directed toward and does not involve that person such as when toddlers observe parents and older siblings converse (Dunn, 1988; Dunn & Shatz, 1989). These kinds of indirect effects are based on information which is gathered from sources other than the direct interaction with another person or object. These effects may be the result of observation of another's interaction with persons or objects or may be the result of information gathered from another about the attitudes, behaviors, traits, or actions of a third person. Indirect effects refer to a varied range of phenomena. These include modeling and imitation, incidental and vicarious learning, and identification. Campos and Stenberg (1981), Feinman (1982), and Feinman and Lewis (1983) have discussed a phenomenon which also can be considered a subclass of the second general class of indirect effects; they have called this indirect effect social referencing.

THE RELATIONSHIP BETWEEN INDIRECT EFFECTS
AND SOCIAL REFERENCING

As noted above, indirect effects involve two different kinds of processes. In the first, the action of two people which occurs in the child's absence influences the child; for example, the support provided by the father to the mother may influence the mother's subsequent behavior to the child. The second type of indirect effect refers to consequences of action which occur in the child's presence. In the first case, there is little resemblance to the phenomenon of social referencing since the child cannot observe the action in question. It is only within the context of the second case, in which the child observes the actions of people to one another, that social referencing can be discussed. The second type of indirect effects involves influences that occur through means other than direct interaction of one person to another and which involve at least three people (or two people and an object) in the same space. The target person is not involved in the direct interaction but, rather, observes the interaction and thus has the opportunity to gather information on and/or act on knowledge of the other party's performance.

There has been a long history of research on this second class of indirect effects. The relevant question here is: How might these indirect effects be viewed in terms of social referencing? Indirect forms of information acquisition have been considered under a wide rubric which includes identification, modeling, imitation, and incidental-, vicarious-, and observational-learning. In considering each of these in relationship to social referencing, we need to ask whether social referencing specifies something different or more specific than what has already been considered by others, especially under the rubric of vicarious or observational learning (see Bandura, Chapter 8, this volume).

Social referencing can be characterized as using the perception of another's reaction or evaluation of a situation to form one's own understanding of that situation. Two features are of importance: (1) *mental activity*, an appraisal and evaluation process by which interpretation is formed, and (2) *sensation*. Thus, a child may or may not actively seek information but, in either case, once the information is received it is appraised, evaluated, and interpreted. In the first case, the child has a question which it seeks to initially consider from the sensation available; while in the second case, sensation which is offered is then evaluated and interpreted. Nevertheless, in both cases, the child uses the information to form an interpretation. Notice that in these cases the definition relies heavily on an *active cognitive* process on the part of the child. In other words, the child intends to process information—that is, to form an understanding. This understanding is a cognitive one (Feinman, 1982). The definition of social referencing is cognitive in approach and, as such, eliminates direct influences vis à vis affective exchanges. That is, the claim of this definition is that information (sensation) results in an evaluative/appraisal process, and it is this process which leads the child to action. Thus, for Feinman (1982), a child's response of wariness to a mother's wariness of a stranger is not caused by the transmission of wariness *per se*, but rather the mother's wariness provides information about the situation which is cognitively utilized to produce wariness in the child. This information can be obtained through question asking or through evaluation of others' actions without a prior question. Such a view of cognitive appraisal, especially as it results in affective behavior, is consistent with Lazarus, Kanner, and Folkman (1980) as well as Weiner and Graham (1984). In contrast, this definition of social referencing, especially as it refers to emotion, is inconsistent with the view of emotional exchange between people *independent* of cognitive processes (e.g. Zajonc, 1980). Empathetic distress, as discussed by Hoffman (1981) and Zahn-Waxler, Yarrow, and King (1979), allows for direct conveying of emotion as a kind of contiguous process. Thus, the child, seeing the distress of another, rather than evaluating the experience, is said to automatically have empathetic distress as a type of reflex response (Hoffman, 1981). In this case, there is little cognitive evaluative processing except for the perception of the situation itself.

If, then, social referencing is defined as a cognitive evaluative process, its relationship to other processes becomes clearer. Modeling and imitation (Bandura, 1973; Piaget, 1951; Poulson, Nunes, & Warren, 1989) assume an active process on the part of the child, whereby the child compares the behavior of the model to a goal or outcome and actively chooses to behave in a like manner to the model, presumably to obtain a similar goal. Modeling and imitation are instrumental means of obtaining for the self something another person has or does. There may be an emotional component in modeling and imitation such that the child feels good behaving like the other, both because of actually obtaining the goal *as well as* because acting like an important other may be a goal in itself. This is the difference between modeling and identification: For identification, unlike modeling, the instrumental act is not necessarily goal directed but is carried out in order to be like the important other (Freud, 1953). For example, we have found that a 2-year-old will often sit in the chair formerly occupied by her mother after she has left the room. Rather than simply going to the door and trying to get to her mother (modeling of the action of her mother's leaving the room), the child will choose to sit in the chair the mother formerly occupied. Thus, modeling and imitation can be considered to be a form of social referencing; similarly, the case for observational learning has been made by Bandura (1973; this volume).

Incidental learning (Hagen & Hale, 1973; Toyota, 1989) has not received the attention that it deserves. Recall the underlying model of this process. If you require a child to attend to particular features of a situation (a set of stimuli), the child will learn the focused information (information the experimenter requested) but also appears to learn other information as well—incidental information. For example, in the case of learning to sort squares and circles, a child may also learn something about the color or texture of the stimuli. Such learning may involve no interpretation or appraisal. In the case of a person, the child may learn that a particular stranger, who is female and approaches slowly with a smile and to whom mother reacts positively, is the type of person with whom interaction is safe—an interpretation. However, the child may also acquire information concerning the quality of voice, and the mode of dress of a particular stranger. The child's gathering of information, related to its set of expectations for evaluation of strangers, thus may include "relevant" and irrelevant pieces of information. Relevant information from the adult's point of view could include cues that identify a "safe person"; incidental cues which are also learned do not necessarily enter into judging a "safe stranger." In this case, the incidental learning may not constitute a type of social referencing.

Given the emphasis in social referencing on the cognitive appraisal function—rather than, for example, on emotional exchange—the question remains as to how social referencing might differ from previous concepts such as imitation or vicarious learning. Clearly, cognitive appraisal is not the only manner in which children obtain information from their social environments. Elsewhere, Lewis and Michalson (1983), in discussing information acquisition and emotional behavior, have suggested that more automatic (less cognitive) processes as well are involved in social behavior. Thus, the distress of another may produce a more automatic consequence. In like fashion, the organization of simultaneous menstruation in women living and working together can be thought of as a similar noncognitive process by which the behavior of one social member of a group affects another. Such examples are numerous, for example, group effects of audience behavior in coughing or laughing. It would be a mistake to assume that all social influences are cognitive in nature. One task for social referencing research is to specify how to determine whether such cognitive or appraisal processes are at work.

Indirect effects as used in this chapter make no stipulation of how children obtain information from their environment except to call attention to the fact that such a process is an important feature of how children learn about their social world. Children acquire information not only through appraisal and evaluation, but also through more direct transfer of emotional states from significant others.

SOCIAL REFERENCING AND THE APPRAISAL PROCESS

Although just how infants use the information from others to adjust their behaviors is not known, it is safe to say that there is evidence that they can use such information. There is some experimental evidence for the occurrence of social referencing early in the child's development. At around 6–7 months of age infants begin to appraise events in ways suggesting they evaluate their consequences and act consistently with such evaluations (Piaget, 1951; Schaffer, Greenwood, & Parry, 1972). When faced with an uncertain situation, an unfamiliar object, or an unfamiliar person, the infant may look back and forth from significant other (caregiver) to the unknown object in question (Carr, Dabbs, & Carr, 1975; Rheingold & Eckerman, 1973). This type of checking with caregiver for reaction may reflect the infant's use of the significant other as a source of information, or of another's reaction to directly produce an emotional state in the child. Further, infants around 6 months and older may imitate unfamiliar behaviors (Eckerman, Whatley, & McGhee, 1979), which may index their attempts at using other persons' behaviors to guide their own reaction or behavior. This would be social referencing only if it could be demonstrated that subsequent behavior was a consequence of the child's appraisal rather than simply an imitation of the mother's response. That is, is it the result of appraisal or a more immediate response such as contagion?

The effect of social referencing upon infants' visual cliff behavior has been used to demonstrate how infants use their mother's reaction to them to guide their behavior in an uncertain situation (Sorce, Emde, Campos, & Klinnert, 1985). Twelve-month-old infants were placed on the shallow side of a modified visual cliff with the appearance of a drop of 12 inches, while the mother stood at the deep side and smiled at the child as the child crossed the shallow side. Subsequently, mothers showed either smiles or a fear face to the child when the infant came to cross the deep side of the visual cliff. The majority of infants who had smiling mothers crossed the deep side, while none of the infants who saw their mothers make a fear face did so. These results, however, are ambiguous vis à vis the cognitive definition of social referencing. This may suggest that 1-year-olds utilize their mothers' affective expression as a source of information for guiding their behavior in an uncertain situation. Alternatively, their behavior may be the result of a more direct form of emotional exchange. Mother's fear face may inhibit child's actions through the child's fear. Thus, no cognitive appraisal is necessary.

In a study of 10-month-old infants, boys and girls received positive or neutral messages or no message about a stranger, either from the mother to the infant or when the mother spoke with the stranger (Feinman & Lewis, 1983). Infants behaved more positively toward the stranger when they received positive rather than neutral information about the stranger from the mother. However, infant behavior to the stranger was not influenced by the mother's affect when the infant saw her speak to the stranger. The results of this study suggest that, although 10-month-old infants may use their mothers as a source of information about the stranger when the information is conveyed to them—that is, mother tells infant about stranger—the ability of the infant to gather information from a mother who is not directing the information to the child may be limited.

In the middle of the second year, however, it appears that the child can gather information indirectly from the mother's interaction with a stranger. In a study of 15-month-old children, Feiring, Lewis, and Starr (1984) examined whether a child's reaction to a stranger would be influenced by the observation of a stranger's interactions with others. In some cases this other was the mother; in some cases the other was a second unfamiliar adult. The results of this study suggested that, by 15 months, children were able to gather information from observation of the stranger's interactions and that the stranger–mother versus the stranger–stranger interaction had more impact on subsequent child behavior. Children were more likely to watch a dyad that included their mother in interaction with a stranger than a dyad that included two strangers interacting. Moreover, if the child observed a positive mother–stranger interaction prior to her own interaction with the stranger, the child was less wary of the stranger and showed more prolonged positive affect than if the child observed the stranger–stranger interaction.

Children 12 and 18 months of age may use their mothers' reactions to novel toys as a way to evaluate these objects. Children may be more likely to approach a novel object if their mother is showing joy as compared to fear or neutral expression in the presence of the child and object (Klinnert, 1984). It may be that children's evaluation of a new toy can be influenced or modified by their mothers' messages concerning that toy. On the other hand, more direct exchange of emotional behavior may be the cause of the child's behavior.

It appears reasonable to suggest that children can utilize information which affects their behavior. Still to be determined is whether the child *evaluated* (i.e., used cognitive appraisal) the information or whether the process at work is one of *affective exchange*. Feinman and Lewis (1983) argued that this effect was not mood induction by showing that their subjects displayed no increase in positive affect to mother but they did to a stranger. Such a demonstration does not directly test the basic process of appraisal, it only shows that it is not mood induction. Nonetheless, this study is the only attempt to demonstrate social referencing as a cognitive appraisal process. The failure to find any effect when the mother talked directly to the stranger rather than directly to the child raises the question about the role of information exchange. Why was there no information exchange when the child observed the mother's behavior to the stranger directly?

This brief review also suggests that children within the first year of life can utilize information which is directed at them to affect their behavior. It is not until later, perhaps by the middle of the second year of life, that they can utilize information which is not directed at them to affect their behavior. The Feinman and Lewis (1983) study is an example. While children were able to utilize the information given to them directly by their mothers, they were not able to utilize the same information when it was directed toward the stranger rather than toward them. Thus, two types of information utilization need to be considered. In the first case is information which is directed at the child about another person or event. Children in the first year of life are able to utilize this information, and it affects their behavior. The second case is information which is not directed at the child but which is available for children to utilize if they can. This information is harder to utilize and probably takes longer for the child to learn how to do so. Feiring *et al.* (1984) have suggested that, by 15 months of age, infants are able to utilize this indirect information.

Lewis and Feiring (1981) have focused on these two types of information as they impact on children's social life. They have tried to capture the general operation of direct and indirect effects through the use of model building. We continue that effort in this chapter. Social referencing can take place with information that is both directed at the child or at others in the child's company. By 2 years of age, children appear to utilize both forms. The issue to which we now turn is the differentiated effect between these two forms of information utilization.

A HEURISTIC MODEL OF DIRECT AND INDIRECT EFFECTS

From a more general learning point of view, direct information effects are usually studied; however, we have little idea of how the impacts of direct and indirect sources of information on children's behavior differ. We can state that children acquire knowledge through both direct and indirect effects:

Child behavior (knowledge) = f(direct effect + indirect effect)

In this general case, the direct effect refers to those actions (or interactions) which are directed toward the child by others. In the case of families or groups this could involve the actions directed toward the child by any number of different people. When there is more than one person, the direct term becomes the sum of the actions of X_n people directed toward the child. In a family size of three, including mother, father, and child, the direct action would be that of the mother and father toward the child. In a family of four, it would be the direct action of mother, father, and sibling toward the child. Indirect effects always involve three or more people, including the child, and, therefore, contain two terms; the first term refers to the interaction between the two people in child's presence which the child observes, and the second term refers to the child's relationship to these people. In the family system, for example, the child has a history of interaction and has formed relationships with family members. Thus, any current interaction will be influenced by that interaction as well as by expectations for the interaction based on the relationship of the child to the persons being observed. In a contrasting example, the child may observe an interaction between two people, neither of whom is known to the child; here the relationship term will be zero. The relationship factor is important to consider in addition to the effects of the immediate interaction (Hinde, 1979). Research has shown the importance of the child's relationship to the persons involved in the indirect effects; that is, the child's knowledge of either/or both people in the interaction influences the child's subsequent knowledge or action (Feiring *et al.*, 1984). Consequently, in a family of mother, father, and child, indirect effects refer to both the interaction of mother and father and the child's relationship to each. In a family of mother, father, sibling, and child, indirect effects refer to the interactions of mother and father, as well as mother and sibling and father and sibling and the child's relationship to each member.

Our model allows us to consider not only the effects of action directed toward the child but the effects of actions directed toward others in the presence of the child (these we call indirect effects). It is our hypothesis that in order to understand the child's action or knowledge we need to consider both direct and indirect effects as well as the child's relationship to the people involved in the interaction. In order to study direct and indirect influences within a context in which the child has a significant relationship to the persons involved in the interaction, we have chosen to look at families, in particular, families at dinner.

FAMILIES AT DINNER

Examination of the child within the context of her family provides an opportunity to study multiple relationships among people who live together and the processes, both indirect and direct, which describe how these relationships operate and influence each other. By and large, studies of family interaction, like studies of child development, have focused on the direct influence and interaction of the child with a family member. Occasionally parent-to-parent interactions within a family setting are considered for their impact on parent–child interaction (e.g., Lewis & Feiring, 1982; Minuchin, Montalvo, Guerney, Rosman, & Schurer, 1967; Pedersen, Anderson, & Cain, 1980). In general, however, an examination of the exclusive and mutual influences of direct and indirect effects in a common context has been neglected. The need to include nonchild focused as well as child focused exchanges in the consideration of development has been noted (Lewis & Feiring, 1978; Lewis, Feiring, & Weinraub, 1981; Pedersen, Yarrow, Anderson, & Cain, 1979), although little empirical work on this problem has been done (Jones & Adamson, 1987; Oshima-Takane, 1988).

The situation of the family at dinner is a context which enables one to examine social referencing as a function of indirect and direct influences vis-à-vis the child and other family members, especially when we consider the direct and indirect effects of information seeking. One reason for choosing information seeking as a function upon which to focus is because it may be similar to the information-gathering aspects of social referencing.

Social referencing in regard to the infancy period usually involves non-verbal indices such as looking at the mother. In this report, we focus on 3-year-old children who are more capable of seeking and gathering information in a verbal as well as nonverbal way. However, the processes whereby children as well as adults monitor the reaction to behavior of others, whether they are in interaction with a person or not, are social referencing processes which have application to all age groups.

The family is a rich situation for examining how social referencing as defined by the indirect processes of observing another's actions may operate in a dyadic interaction in which the subject does not participate. Several characteristics of the family dinner make it of interest for this examination (Lewis & Feiring, 1982): (1) all family members are present, (2) interaction between family members is the common experience, (3) the situation elicits important family functions such as information exchange, and (4) a family meal occurs with high frequency. The family dinner situation is one in which dyadic interaction takes place within the context of a larger group. Because it is not likely that more than two people will talk at once (for any length of time), it is often possible that, in a 2 + n system, one person may observe the interaction between two others. Consequently, the potential for social referencing or other kinds of indirect effects is high because a sequence of family interaction involves a series of exchanges in which actor and observer roles are changing. For example, in act 1, the mother is the actor, the father, the direct recipient, and the child is the observer; while in act 2, the father is the actor, the child is the recipient, and the mother is the observer. The family context, especially at dinnertime, where (1) the express purpose is often for family members all to be together and exchange information, and where (2) people take turns being actor, receiver, and observer, is an excellent context for examining the kinds of indirect effects to which young children have exposure on a regular basis.

Family Characteristics and Observational Procedures

The dinnertime interaction of 31 families was examined for this report. All the families were nuclear in structure, consisting of mother, father, and child(ren). Each family contained a 3-year-old target child who was the focus of the study. All the families were participants in a longitudinal study in which the social and cognitive characteristics of children at 3, 12, 24, and 36 months of age were examined.

Nineteen families were from the upper-middle socioeconomic group and 12 were from the middle socioeconomic group (as determined by both parents' education and occupation, using a modified Hollingshead category system; Feiring & Lewis, 1982). The families were distributed by family size as follows: family size 3, $n=5$ (target children (TC) were the only born); family size 4, n=14 (TC=5 first borns, 9 second borns); family size 5, n=12 (TC=12 third borns). There were 16 female and 15 male target children.

Before the child's third birthday, the parents were contacted and asked to participate in a study of families at dinner. Parents were told that we wished to gather information about the behavior of the target child (whom we had observed previously at 3 months at home and at 12- and 24- months in the laboratory) in the family environment. Permission was given by the families contacted to videotape a mealtime interaction during which all nuclear family members were present. The majority of families indicated that all family members did not always eat dinner together but that a meal with all members present took place at least twice a week. Before the meal began, the camera crew set up the video equipment so that all family members were in the view of the camera, turned on the equipment, and then left the home. The videotape ran for an hour or until the family finished dinner and turned it off. Families were told that we were interested in recording the kinds of things they did at mealtime and were asked to try as much as possible to go about their "normal" business, as if the camera were not present. After the film crew returned, many families showed interest in watching themselves on the videotape.

In capturing a segment of family interaction, we chose to use videotape rather than trained observers for several reasons. First and perhaps most important, we wished to obtain the most complete sample of ongoing behavior of the family members. Videotaping is a technique that does not impose a predetermined observation system on the recording of the data (Willems, 1969). Another advantage is that videotape makes it easy to observe interaction among all family members. The number of observers necessary to code all dyadic interactions among three to five family members would have been more intrusive than the presence of a video camera. The disadvantages of videotape is that the family members knew they were being taped and thus may have altered their behavior. This problem also exists using live observers. Since the camera was not run by a person, its presence may have been more readily forgotten than an observer's would have been. Interviews with the families following the taping sessions indicated that they became less aware of the camera as the meal progressed; nevertheless, the adults and older siblings obviously were more aware that they were being filmed. For example, one father became quite angry when his son took a long time eating and was fooling around with his food. The father raised his voice and said "Stop messing with your food!" and then after a pause, during which it appeared he recalled the camera, he began speaking again, "And the reasons why you should not play with your food are because . . . " Younger children were somewhat less affected by the presence of the camera. For example, one 3-year-old target child announced in the middle of the meal, "Daddy, I have to go make." The mother said, "I knew this would happen," while the father was obliged to take his son to the bathroom.

In our examination of the data, we were also able to discover more systematic quantitative evidence that observation of families may have influenced interaction patterns. For all families, age of family member was related to the amount of interaction time the family member commanded, both as actor and recipient of verbal interaction. Specifically, the older the family member the more interaction time they commanded. Adults commanded more time than children, older siblings more than younger siblings. However, there was one exception to this general rule. The target child tended to receive more interaction time from parents, as compared to the older nontarget sibling, who by the age "rule" would have received more interaction from parents than the target child. This finding suggests that one way our observation changed the "typical" family interaction patterns was to elevate the amount of interaction the target child received from parents. This is not surprising given the fact that the parents knew we were interested in the behavior of the target child. Parents thus may have acted to elicit target child behavior to a greater extent than they normally would have if not being observed. This bias was consistent across families.

Once family interaction had been recorded, the tapes were scored for the duration of time each family member spent talking to every other family member for a period of 20 minutes during which all family members were present. Thus, we obtained the total amount of time each family member spoke to and received verbal input from every other family member. In addition to duration of vocalization, we also coded information exchange. Information exchange duration was defined as verbal interaction, in the form of a question or an answer to a question, which informed family members about past, present, and/or future events of family members, friends, relatives, or events and objects. Interrater reliability on nine families (three families each for family size three, four, and five) was calculated by correlating the observations for total verbal interaction and information exchange for each actor to recipient unit for the 20 minutes of interaction coded. Interrater reliabilities were adequate. For verbal interaction they ranged from .69 to .99, and for information exchange from .65 to .91.

Our coding was based on a dyadic analysis. Every possible dyadic exchange was noted; these dyadic exchanges constitute the basis of the analysis. From this coding scheme we were able to determine both direct and indirect dyadic interaction relative to the target child.

Table 1 lists, for the target child, the possible direct and indirect dyadic effects by family size. Thus, Table 1 presents the terms that make up the total of direct and indirect effects. The number of effects increases

Table 1. Direct and Indirect Dyad Identities for Target Child

Family size	Three	Four	Five
Direct dyads	$M \rightarrow TC$	$M \rightarrow TC$	$M \rightarrow TC$
	$F \rightarrow TC$	$F \rightarrow TC$	$F \rightarrow TC$
		$S_1 \rightarrow TC$	$S_1 \rightarrow TC$
			$S_2 \rightarrow TC$
Indirect dyads	$M \leftrightarrow F$	$M \leftrightarrow F$	$M \leftrightarrow F$
		$M \leftrightarrow S_1$	$M \leftrightarrow S_1$
		$F \leftrightarrow S_1$	$F \leftrightarrow S_1$
			$M \leftrightarrow S_2$
			$F \leftrightarrow S_2$
			$S_1 \leftrightarrow S_2$

Note. M, mother; F, father; TC, target child; S, sibling.

with family size. While the number of direct dyads increases simply by a factor of one, (i.e., the number of direct dyads is always n-1, where n=family size), the number of indirect dyads grows more rapidly with an increase in family size. In addition, Table 1 shows how in family size three the number of child-focused dyads (direct effects) is greater than nonchild-focusing dyads (indirect effects); in family size four the number of direct and indirect dyads is equal; in family size five the number of indirect dyads exceeds the number of direct dyads. This distribution of indirect and direct dyads by family size suggests that, in family size five, the role of indirect effects may become more important than in family size three or four.

Assessment of Target Child's Mental Status

At approximately 1 week following the home observation of the family dinner, the child was scheduled to come to the laboratory to take the Stanford Binet Mental Status IQ Test (FORM LM, 1969). All children came to the laboratory with their mothers and completed the Binet in a 1-hour testing session.

THE ROLE OF DIRECT AND INDIRECT EFFECTS ON THE CHILD OUTCOMES

The working hypothesis is that developmental outcomes are to be best understood by considering the role of *both* direct and indirect effects. As we (Lewis & Feiring, 1981) have argued previously, although direct effects should exert a more powerful influence than indirect effects, both need to be considered. In the analysis of family behavior at dinner, we are interested in two classes of outcomes: those related to interactive behavior at the table and those related to child performance in general. First we consider behaviors at the dinner table; these are the target child's vocalization and information-seeking behavior. Second, we examine the general developmental outcome of the target child's general IQ score.

The basic problem of interest is the relation between direct and indirect effects and child outcomes, since these correlations should inform us as to the form of information young children can best use in their social referencing. Two statistical methods can be used to investigate how much of the variance of the outcome measure can be accounted for using *both* direct and indirect effect measures as predictors at the same time. Since our formulation suggests that any outcome is a function of the combination of direct and indirect effects, multiple regression techniques would aid in determining how much of child outcome variance the direct and indirect factors can account for together. Multiple regression also allows us to examine, using the standardized beta weights, the relative importance of each factor as it relates to a change in the outcome score.

A second statistical procedure for examining the relation of direct and indirect effects to child outcomes is to consider contribution of the direct and indirect effects, one at a time, on the outcome variable using partial correlations. For example, in this approach, the correlation between the direct effect and child IQ can be examined with the indirect effect held constant. The portion of IQ variance (Y) associated with X_2 (indirect) is removed from the IQ variance and the remaining variance due to X_1 (direct) is estimated. It is important to keep in mind in the discussion to follow that squared partial correlations represent the portion of *remaining* variance explained by a given variable (e.g., direct effect, X_1) once the portion of the variance due to another variable (e.g., indirect effect, X_2) has been removed from the total variance (e.g., IQ, Y). Consequently, partial correlations give us some indication of how much a factor contributes to the variance in an outcome from which other possible explanatory variables have been removed. Although this second approach of using squared partial correlations does not allow us to consider the effect of both direct and indirect factors together, we have chosen to use it as our major exploratory tool in this chapter. The partial correlation analyses presented are used as a preliminary tool for exploring the possible impact of direct and indirect effects.

Table 2 gives the zero-order correlations and the partial correlations for the direct and indirect effects and the child outcomes of information seeking, vocalization, and IQ for the total sample and for family sizes three, four, and five separately. In the discussion to follow, we refer to variance estimates.[1] The reader should note that the variance estimates given are subject to a broad range of fluctuation due to the small sample sizes.

Family Information Seeking

Child's Information-Seeking Outcome.   In order to observe the relationship of family information seeking (IS) and the target child's IS, we correlated the target child's IS with the direct IS (directed toward the child) as well as the target child's IS with the indirect IS (those exchanges between family members not directed toward the child). Next, partial correlations were calculated in order to estimate the portion of variance in the child's IS (Y) due to the direct effect (X_1) with the indirect effect removed from Y and also the portion of variance in Y due to the indirect effect (X_2) with the direct effect (X_1) removed (see Table 2).

For the sample as a whole, the amount of variance accounted for by the direct effect is 18.5% (with the indirect effect partialed out of the Y variance), while, for the indirect, it is essentially zero (with the direct effect partialed out of the Y variance). Family size appears to influence the relative impact of direct versus indirect effects upon the outcome variables: there is a tendency for the indirect effect to become more influential as family size increases. Family size three has too few subjects to allow us to reliably estimate the effect. In family sizes four and five, indirect effects account for as much if not more of the variance between family behavior and the target child's outcome. Holding one factor constant in family size four, direct and indirect factors each account for 28% of the variance. In family size five, the indirect factor accounts for 50% of the variance, while, in contrast, the direct factor accounts for only 1% of the variance in the outcome.

Child's IQ Outcome.   Examination of the relationship between family IS and the outcome of the target child's overall IQ score also yields suggestive findings concerning the operation of direct and indirect effects. For the sample as a whole, direct effects account for 11.6% of the variance, while the indirect effects account for only 2.3% of the variance. For family size four, the direct factor accounts for 20.3%, while the indirect factor accounts for only 1.0%. However, for family size five, the direct and

---

[1]If the reader wishes to clarify the components of interaction used to calculate the direct and indirect effects, refer to Table 1. For example, for family size four, the direct effect is the sum total of all vocalization from parent and sibling to the child, while the indirect effect is the sum total of all vocalization of parent to parent, sibling to parents, and parent to siblings.

Table 2. Zero-order Correlations and Partial Correlations for Direct and Indirect Effects and Child Outcomes of Query, Vocalization and Stanford Binet IQ

	Total sample			Family size 3		
	Zero-order correlations	Direct with indirect partialed out	Indirect with direct partialed out	Zero-order correlations	Direct with indirect partialed out	Indirect with direct partialed out
Information seeking (IS)						
Child IS and direct IS	.43*	.44*		−.33	−.32	
Child IS and indirect IS	.01		−.10	−.09		.02
Direct IS and IQ	.36*	.34+		.08	−.02	
Indirect IS and IQ	.20		.15	.47		.47
Vocalization (Voc)						
Child voc & direct voc	.49**	.53**		.71	.78	
Child voc & indirect voc	.08		.25	−.83+		−.99**
Direct voc & IQ	.31+	.23		−.13	.02	
Indirect voc & IQ	−.44*		−.39*	.16		.16

+$p \le .10$. *$p \le .05$.
**$p \le .01$.

indirect factors each account for 84.6% of the proportion of variance due to each factor with the other removed.[2] While our analyses are based on a small sample, they suggest that both direct and indirect family IS affect various child outcomes.

First, family IS behavior at the dinner table is related to the target child's IS behavior and general IQ. Second, direct and indirect effects each seem to be related to both kinds of outcome variables. Of particular interest to us is the suggestion that indirect factors are related to a child outcome outside of the immediate interaction, that is, to the target child's IQ. A third notable trend is that the indirect factor seems to play a greater role in regard to child's information seeking as family size increases. Fourth, for the total sample, direct and indirect IS are positively related to the child's

[2]When estimating variance, it is possible to obtain values which, when added together, are greater than 1.0. Such problems in variance estimation can come about when two variables are highly correlated with one another. Such findings must be viewed, therefore, with some caution.

| | Family size 4 | | | Family size 5 | |
Zero-order correlations	Direct with indirect partialed out	Indirect with direct partialed out	Zero-order correlations	Direct with indirect partialed out	Indirect with direct partialed out
.36	.53⁺		.30	−.11	
−.37		−.54⁺	.74**		.71*
.48⁺	.45		−.47	−.92**	
.23		.10	.47		.91**
.56*	.56*		.52⁺	.33	
−.29		−.30	.57⁺		.42
.46⁺	.46		−.21	−.28	
−.13		−.10	.07		.20

IQ. Furthermore, strong relations appear to be more characteristic of the larger families.

Family Vocalization

Child's Vocalization Outcome.   The same analyses as for family information seeking were performed examining the family vocalization data. For the sample as a whole, direct vocalization to the child with the indirect factor removed (from the Y variance) accounts for 28.1% of the remaining variance, while indirect vocalization with the direct factor removed only accounts for 6.3% of the remaining variance. Again, as with information seeking, family size appears to be related to the direct and indirect factors' impact on child outcome. For family size four, the variances for children's vocalization are 31.4% for the direct factor and 9% for indirect factor. For family size five, the direct factor yields a variance estimate of 10.9%, while the indirect factor yields 17.6%. These findings

indicate that child vocalization is positively related to direct family vocalization to the child; this holds for all family sizes. For indirect family
vocalization, the pattern is more variable, with family size five showing a
positive relation between family indirect vocalization and child vocalization but showing a negative relation with family sizes three and four.

Child's IQ Outcome.   Examining family vocalization data and target child IQ data for the total sample, we find direct vocalization accounts
for 5.3% of the child's IQ variance, while the indirect vocalization accounts
for 15.2%. For family size four, the partial correlations yield variance
estimates of 21.2% and 1% for the direct and indirect factors, respectively.
In family size five, the target child's IQ and the direct factor shows that
7.8% of the variance is accounted for, while for the indirect factor the
variance is 4.0%. These vocalization findings, broken down by family
size, appear to indicate that both direct and indirect effects play a role
in children's behavior, with direct effects, in general, having a greater
impact.

Summary of Information-Seeking and Vocalization Results

These results support our belief that children's behavior, both specific
behavior in a given context (i.e., dinnertime interaction) and more general
outcome variables (i.e., child IQ), are influenced both by what family
members do directly to the child and by what they do to each other in the
child's company. Moreover, it appears reasonable to suggest that, over all
families, the direct factor is a more powerful determinant of outcome than
the indirect factor. The valence of the correlations between direct and
indirect effects and outcome fluctuate considerably and are related to
family size. However, due to the small sample sizes, the differences in
family size need further study.

Family size appears to influence the differential amounts of variance
accounted for by direct and indirect factors. As family size increases, the
indirect factor becomes increasingly important. We can only speculate as
to why this may be the case. Given the small sample sizes we have used,
this trend may be a sample size artifact; however, as we noted in Table 1,
the number of indirect sources increases rapidly from family size three to
five. Thus, it may be the case that the large number of possible indirect
effects makes them increasingly salient relative to direct effects.

Specific Types of Indirect Effects within Family Size Five

Within family size five, the overall indirect effect comprises three
types of indirect terms: parent–parent, parent–sibling, sibling–sibling. Be-

cause indirect effects appear to be more salient and because we have noted previously the importance of sibling effects for child outcomes, we decided to explore how the specific components of the indirect effects in family size five would operate on target child behavior (Lewis & Feiring, 1982). In this sample, the sibling–sibling effect comprised two older siblings because the target child was the third born.

The older sibling–middle sibling indirect effect can potentially serve as a model or reference for target child behavior, as can the parent–parent or parent–sibling subsystems. While the parent–parent subsystem would be a salient model due to its characteristic of expert status (i.e., adults converse and "know" more than children), the sibling–sibling subsystem would be salient to model because older sibling interaction is both more expert as well as more similar to target children capabilities. Bandura (1973) and Lewis, Young, Brooks, and Michalson (1975) have argued that expertise and similarity are two important factors that can influence a child's tendency to model another's behavior. Based on these ideas, one might expect that in a family size of five, in which the target child is the youngest family member, indirect sibling effects should be at least as central to child behavior as parent–parent effects; however, the parent–sibling effect, having both expertise and similarity, might be even more powerful.

In order to explore the operation of specific indirect effects, and, in particular, the importance of parent–parent, parent–sibling, and sibling–sibling subsystems on the child's behavior, we employed a multiple regression procedure. The multiple regression technique was used to get an idea of what components of indirect effects and direct effects would be entered into an equation to predict the child outcomes of information seeking, vocalization, and IQ. Since this analysis was used as an exploratory tool, we do not present the results formally but rather indicate what the analysis suggests about the operation of specific indirect effects in family size five. Our discussion is thus meant to be suggestive, especially for planning future research on larger samples of families.

In regard to predicting child vocalization from the indirect effects of parent–parent, sibling–sibling and sibling–parent interactions, we found that sibling–sibling interaction was the most important factor, followed by parent–parent interaction. The parent–sibling interaction did not influence child vocalization. Thus, as we expected, the sibling–sibling indirect effect appeared most salient for child vocalization. In regard to child IQ, the sibling–sibling component is the only factor to appear in the regression.

The analyses for child information seeking showed that only the parent–sibling indirect component was present in the regression equation predicting child information seeking. However, for IQ, parent–sibling information seeking followed by sibling–sibling information seeking predicted child outcome.

CONCLUSIONS

In general, our exploration of the operation of direct and indirect factors suggests that both can play a role in regard to child outcomes. When each of these effects is examined for its relation to child outcomes, we find that direct effects may account for more variance than indirect effects. More specifically, when we examine the direct effects of information seeking and vocalization on child information seeking, vocalization, and IQ with indirect effects held constant, we note that these relations tend to be of greater magnitude than those for the indirect effects with the direct effects held constant. It is interesting to note that, for the total sample, indirect vocalization more than direct vocalization relates to IQ, and this indirect relation is a negative one. For information seeking, however, the direct compared to indirect is more related to IQ, and both relations are positive. While it does appear that the valences of the direct (positive) and indirect (negative) effects for vocalization are different, the results are too preliminary to draw any conclusions about the positive versus negative impact of each type of effect on IQ. Our analyses give us some idea as to the relative impact of direct and indirect factors on certain child outcomes, although they do not speak to how direct and indirect effects operate in combination to influence child outcomes. Such analyses would be important for understanding how the direct and indirect effects influence the developmental processes.

Although the direct effect does appear to account for more variance than the indirect effect, this statement is qualified by the consideration of family size. The preliminary analyses presented here suggest that as we move from smaller to larger family sizes, the relative influence of the indirect factor increases. Especially in family size five, where the number of indirect effects is greater than the number of direct effects, we note that indirect factors are as related to child outcomes as the direct effects.

The sibling–sibling indirect effect in which older siblings interact in the presence of the younger target child may be particularly important to explore in regard to child outcomes. While the Zajonc and Markus model (1975) predicts that this sibling interaction is negatively related to child cognitive development, our data do not consistently support this view. While the indirect effect of sibling–sibling vocalization is negatively related to child IQ, sibling–sibling information seeking, as well as parent–sibling information seeking, is positively related to the child's intellectual performance. Exploration of particular family subsystems that involve specific types of indirect effects (e.g., sibling–sibling vs. parent–parent) will be important to examine in future studies of indirect effects as they operate in larger families. Also, the importance of the particular child outcome is highlighted by the data on family size five and the components of indirect effects. The indirect effects of vocalization and information seeking do not always yield similar outcomes. For example, sibling–sibling indirect effects for vocalization are salient for child vocalization, whereas parent–sibling indirect effects appear more salient for information seeking.

Finally, what does our analysis tell us about indirect effects and social referencing? Social referencing, as discussed previously, implies that the child monitors the mother's or a significant other's interaction with a third party or object. Our data suggest that during a family dinner a child has the opportunity to observe family members interacting and references these behaviors. Our outcome measures do not speak specifically to behavior as a consequence of referencing by the child. However, the data do reflect a situation wherein a child can learn about interaction patterns by observing interactions of others in which she does not directly participate. As such, these data lend support to the belief that young children do reference the behavior of others and that such referencing impacts on both concurrent and subsequent behavior.

Acknowledgment: Support for this chapter came from the W. T. Grant Foundation.

REFERENCES

Bandura, A. (1973). *Aggression: A social learning analysis.* Englewood Cliffs, NJ: Prentice-Hall.

Cairns, R. B. (Ed.). (1979). *The analysis of social interactions: Methods, issues and illustrations.* Hillsdale, NJ: Erlbaum.

Campos, J. J., & Stenberg, C. R. (1981). Perception, appraisal and emotion: The onset of social referencing. In M. Lamb & L. Sherrod (Eds.), *Infant social cognition: Empirical and theoretical considerations* (pp. 273–314). Hillsdale, NJ: Erlbaum.

Carr, S., Dabbs, J., & Carr, T. (1975). Mother–infant attachment: The importance of the mother's visual field. *Child Development, 46,* 331–338.

Dunn, J. (1988). *The beginnings of social understanding.* Cambridge, MA: Harvard University Press.

Dunn, J., & Shatz, M. (1989). Becoming a conversationalist despite (or because of) having an older sibling. *Child Development, 60,* 399–410.

Eckerman, C. O., Whatley, J. L., & McGhee, L. J. (1979). Approaching and contacting the object another manipulates: A social skill of the 1-year-old. *Development Psychology, 15,* 585–593.

Feinman, S. (1982). Social referencing in infancy. *Merril-Palmer Quarterly, 28,* 445–470.

Feinman, S., & Lewis, M. (1983). Social referencing at ten months: A second-order effect on infants' responses to stranger. *Child Development, 54,* 878–887.

Feiring, C., & Lewis, M. (1982). Middle class differences in the mother–child interaction and the child's cognitive development. In T. M. Field, A. M. Sostek, P. Vietze, & P. H. Leiderman (Eds.), *Culture and early interactions* (pp. 63–91). Hillsdale, NJ: Erlbaum.

Feiring, C., Lewis, M., & Starr, M. D. (1984). Indirect effects and infants' reaction to strangers. *Developmental Psychology, 20,* 485–491.

Freud, S. (1953). Three essays on the theory of sexuality. In J. Strachey (Ed. & trans.) in collaboration with A. Freud, *The standard edition of the complete psychological works of Sigmund Freud* (Vol. 7). London: The Hogarth Press and the Institute of Psycho-Analysis. (original work published 1905)

Gottman, J. M., & Bakeman, R. (1979). The sequential analysis of observation data. In M. E. Lamb, S. J. Suomi, & G. R. Stephenson (Eds.), *Social interaction analysis* (pp. 185–206). Madison: The University of Wisconsin Press.

Hagen, J., & Hale, G. (1973). The development of attention in children. In A. Pick (Ed.), *Minnesota symposia on child psychology* (Vol. 7, pp. 117–140). Minneapolis: University of Minnesota Press.

Hinde, R. (1979). *Towards understanding relationships.* New York: Academic Press.

Hoffman, M. L. (1981). The development of empathy. In J. P. Rushton & R. M. Sorrentino (Eds.), *Altruism and helping behavior: Social personality and developmental perspective* (pp. 41–63). Hillsdale, NJ: Erlbaum.

Jones, C., & Adamson, L. B. (1987). Language use in mother–child and mother–child–sibling interactions. *Child Development, 58,* 356–366.

Klinnert, M. D. (1984). The regulation of infant behavior by maternal facial expression. *Infant Behavior and Development, 7,* 447–465.

Lamb, M. E., Suomi, S. J., & Stephenson, G. R. (Eds.). (1979). *Social interaction analysis: Methodological issues.* Madison: University of Wisconsin Press.

Lazarus, R. S., Kanner, A. D., & Folkman, S. (1980). Emotions: A cognitive phenomenological analysis. In R. Plutchik & H. Kellerman (Eds.), *Emotion: Theory, research, and experience* (Vol. 1, pp. 189–217). New York: Academic Press.

Lewis, M. (1986). Origins of self-knowledge and individual differences in early self-recognition. In A. Greenwald & J. Suls (Eds.), *Psychological perspective on the self* (Vol. 3, pp. 55–78). Hillsdale, NJ: Erlbaum.

Lewis, M., & Feiring, C. (1978). The child's social world. In R. M. Lerner & G. D. Spanier (Eds.), *Child influences on marital and family interaction: A life-span perspective* (pp. 47–69). New York: Academic Press.

Lewis, M., & Feiring, C. (1981). Direct and indirect interactions in social relationships. In L. Lipsitt (Ed.), *Advances in infancy research* (pp. 129–146). New York: Ablex.

Lewis, M., & Feiring, C. (1982). Some American families at dinner. In L. M. Laosa & I. E. Sigel (Eds.), *Families as learning environments for children* (pp. 115–146). New York: Plenum.

Lewis, M., Feiring, C., & Weinraub, M. (1981). The father as a member of the child's social network. In M. Lamb (Ed.), *The role of the father in child development* (2nd ed., pp. 259–294). New York: Wiley.

Lewis, M., & Michalson, L. (1983). *Children's emotions and moods.* New York: Plenum.

Lewis, M., & Rosenblum, L. A. (Eds.). (1979). *The child and its family.* New York: Plenum.

Lewis, M., & Weinraub, M. (1976). The father's role in the infant's social network. In M. Lamb (Ed.), *The role of the father in child development,* Vol. 1 (pp. 157–184). New York: Wiley.

Lewis, M., Young, G., Brooks, J., & Michalson, L. (1975). The beginning of friendship. In M. Lewis & L. Rosenblum (Eds.), *Friendship and peer relations: The origins of behavior* (Vol. 4, pp. 27–66). New York: Wiley.

Minuchin, S., Montalvo, B., Guerney, B. G., Jr., Rosman, B. L., & Schurer, F. (1967). *Families of the slums: An explanation of their structure and treatment.* New York: Basic Books.

Oshima-Takane, Y. (1988). Children learn from speech not addressed to them: The case of personal pronouns. *Journal of Child Language, 15,* 95–108.

Pederson, F. A., Anderson, B. J., & Cain, R. L., Jr. (1980). Parent–infant and husband–wife interactions observed at age five months. In F. A. Pederson (Ed.), *The father–infant relationship* (pp. 71–86). New York: Praeger.

Pederson, F. A., Yarrow, L., Anderson, B., & Cain, R. (1979). Conceptualization of father influences in the infancy period. In M. Lewis & L. Rosenblum (Eds.), *The child and its family* (pp. 45–66). New York: Plenum.

Piaget, J. (1951). *Play, dreams, and imitation in childhood.* (C. Gattegno & F. M. Hodgson, trans.). New York: W. W. Norton & Co., Inc. (Original French edition, 1945).

Poulson, C. L., Nunes, L. R. P., & Warren, S. F. (1989). Imitation in infancy: A critical review. In H. W. Reese (Ed.), *Advances in child development and behavior, Vol. 22* (pp. 271–298). San Diego, CA: Academic Press.

Rheingold, H. L., & Eckerman, C. O. (1973). Fear of the stranger: A critical examination. In H. W. Reese (Ed.), *Advances in child development and behavior* (Vol. 8, pp. 185–222). New York: Academic Press.

Rosenblum, L. A., & Moltz, H. (1983). *Symbiosis in parent–offspring interaction.* New York: Plenum.

Sackett, G. P. (1978). The lag sequential analysis of contingency and cyclicity in behavioral interaction research. In J. Osofsky (Ed.), *Handbook of infant development* (pp. 623–649). New York: Wiley.

Schaffer, H. R., Greenwood, A., & Parry, M. H. (1972). The onset of wariness. *Child Development, 43*, 165–175.

Sorce, J. F., Emde, R. N., Campos, J. J., & Klinnert, M. D. (1985). Maternal emotional signalling: Its effect on the visual cliff behavior of one-year-olds. *Developmental Psychology, 21*, 195–200.

Toyota, H. (1989). Effects of autobiographical elaboration on incidental learning. *Japanese Journal of Educational Psychology, 37*, 234–242.

Vuchinich, S., Emery, R. E., & Cassidy, J. (1988). Family members as third parties in dyadic family conflict: Strategies, alliances, and outcomes. *Child Development, 59*, 1293–1302.

Weiner, B., & Graham, S. (1984). An attributional approach to emotional development. In C. Izard, J. Kagan, & R. Zajonc (Eds.), *Emotions, cognition and behavior* (pp. 167–191). Cambridge: Harvard University Press.

Willems, E. P. (1969). Planning a rationale for naturalistic research. In E. P. Willems & H. L. Rausch (Eds.), *Naturalistic viewpoints in psychological research* (pp. 44–71). New York: Holt, Rinehart & Winston.

Zahn-Waxler, C., Radke-Yarrow, M., & King, R. (1979). Child rearing and children's prosocial initiations towards victims of distress. *Child Development, 50*, 319–330.

Zajonc, R. B. (1980). Feeling and thinking: Preferences need no inferences. *American Psychologist, 35*, 151–175.

Zajonc, R. B., & Markus, G. B. (1975). Birth order and intellectual development. *Psychological Review, 82*, 74–88.

13

Infants' Instrumental Social Interaction with Adults

Barbara Rogoff, Jayanthi Mistry, Barbara Radziszewska, and Jamie Germond

The role of social interaction in guiding children's development is receiving increasing attention as an explanation for children's rapid learning (Azmitia, 1988; Newman, Griffin, & Cole, 1989; Rogoff, 1986, 1990; Valsiner, 1987; Vygotsky, 1978; Wertsch, 1979). This increasing emphasis on the facilitating role of adults and peers helps to place child development in context, rather than focusing on individual children as if they develop in a vacuum, uninfluenced by the people around them and by the social and technological inventions they learn to employ.

However, a balance is needed in which the child's own efforts to learn and to employ social tools is recognized, along with the socialization attempts of those around the child (Rogoff, 1990, 1991). Child development is a collaborative process, with active involvement of children as well as of

BARBARA ROGOFF • Department of Psychology, University of Utah, Salt Lake City, Utah 84112.   JAYANTHI MISTRY • Department of Child Study, Tufts University, Medford, Massachusetts 02155.   BARBARA RADZISZEWSKA • Institute for Prevention Research, University of Southern California, Alhambra, California 91803. JAMIE GERMOND • Department of Psychology, University of Maine at Orono, Maine 04473.

Social Referencing and the Social Construction of Reality in Infancy, edited by Saul Feinman. Plenum Press, New York, 1992.

caregivers. This chapter examines the play interaction of infants and adults, focusing on the attempts of infants to direct the actions of adults, as they deliberately attempt to use others to accomplish actions of which they are not independently capable or which require mutual involvement.

Our focus on adult–child communication as a forum for children's development can be related to research on social referencing that points out that infants attend to the intents and emotions of adults as a means of guiding their understanding of new situations (Feinman, 1982; Gunnar & Stone, 1984; Sorce, Emde, Campos, & Klinnert, 1985). Adults provide infants with cues regarding the nature of situations, models of how to behave, and interpretations of behavior and events (Rogoff, 1990).

Like the literature on social influences on children's learning, the literature on social referencing has thus far limited the child's role to being a recipient of adult messages. However, we propose that social referencing is a mutual activity, embedded in a stream of two-way social interaction, where both participants are motivated by their own goals and engage in social referencing as a way to negotiate their goals. Social referencing often has been examined as one-way communication, in which an adult displays some type of emotional reaction to an unusual stimulus (such as a large toy spider), and a child's use of these cues to interpret the situation is studied. The interpretation of their communication does not take into account the information and influence provided by the child.

While it has been very fruitful to examine children's social referencing of adults, it is also important to recognize that children may be sources of information, as adults attempt to understand their intentions in ongoing social interaction, and infants may actively attempt to influence adults' understanding of situations to promote the infants' own goals. In this chapter, we focus on infants' contributions to mutual social referencing as adults and infants attempt to understand and influence each other. Since infants' skill in and methods for providing communication to influence adults' actions presumably change with age, we examine developmental changes, focusing on infants' strategies for using adults instrumentally to achieve goals which infants are unable to reach alone.

We examine the development of infants' instrumental use of adults using longitudinal observations of one or the other of two middle-class U.S. infants interacting with 21 middle-class adults at 2- or 3-week intervals from the age of 4 to 15 months. We explore developmental changes in the extent to which the babies initiated an episode that appeared designed to use an adult instrumentally, the degree of agreement of independent observers that this had occurred, and developmental changes in the nature of the babies' goals and the means they used to reach them.

Our perspective is built on Bruner's work on intentional communication in infancy and Vygotsky's theory which emphasizes the role of children's social interactions in their developing abilities to use the material and conceptual tools of society. Among the most important tools for infants are their caregivers, who provide the means for infants to satisfy their needs, as well as guiding the meaning of infants' encounters with the social and physical world. While caregivers interpret infants' actions and focus the meaning in them (e.g., interpreting an arched back as an attempt to communicate), infants develop skills in using the available means to communicate and to use adults as tools to achieve goals.

Our working definition of instrumental interaction (presented in detail in the next section) differs from several related efforts to study the development of children's influence on adults and children's intentional communication. Some scholars argue that younger babies than those we studied also use adults instrumentally (see Dunn's [1982] thoughtful discussion of alternate definitions of intentionality). Rheingold (1969) argued persuasively that infants socialize their caregivers, teaching them what the infants need to have them do through the power of the cry and the rewards of smiles and vocalization. "From his behavior they learn what he wants and what he will accept, what produces in him a state of well-being and good nature, and what will keep him from whining" (p. 786). While we are open to the possibility that very early parent–child interaction may involve intentionality of some sort on the part of the infant, our study focuses on more deliberate efforts of infants to use adults instrumentally. Our definition of instrumental use of an adult involves deliberate goal-directed behavior by the infant.

On the other hand, we do not assume that instrumental use of an adult necessarily involves awareness of the adult as a "person." The infant can be deliberately attempting to use the adult as a tool without intending to modify the adult's understanding of the situation. At early ages, modifications in the adult's understanding may be an inadvertent product of the infant's attempts to use the adult to reach the infant's own goals. Our definition of instrumental use of adults is deliberately broad, so as to include what we expect to be early deliberate, instrumental acts that do not involve trying to communicate a new understanding to the adult, as well as person-oriented communication that truly attempts to modify the other person's understanding in order to use them instrumentally.

Since our goal is to study the rudiments of early efforts to use others instrumentally, our definition is relaxed compared to those employed by Feinman for "true" social referencing, and by researchers studying intentional communication (e.g., Bretherton, McNew, & Beeghly-Smith, 1981; Sugarman-Bell, 1978). While we share an interest in infants' expression of intent, we focus on infants' intent to get the adult to do something rather than infants' intent to communicate. Intent to communicate requires evidence that the baby recognizes that the adult is another person and that a message is transmitted. This may be shown through eye contact as a baby requests an object, for example. Intent to use an adult as a tool is simpler, in that it could involve moves that treat the adult, or part of the adult (e.g., the hand) as an instrument, without signs of recognition that there is person "running" the hand (see Harding & Golinkoff, 1979; Piaget, 1952). The baby could attempt to get the hand to assist in reaching an object without making eye contact with the adult (Bates, 1979; Harding, 1982b). Instrumental use of an adult could also include communicative moves. We attempt to distinguish these levels of instrumental use of adults—tool-oriented versus interpersonal—by documenting the subtleties of changes in the infants' means of communication, especially their use of mutual gaze.

One could hypothesize a developmental sequence in infancy to begin with infants expressing contentment or distress, with adults learning to use these cues to satisfy wants. Later, infants become more goal directed (learning the effects of their cues) and begin to use cues such as crying and smiling deliberately, not simply reflecting the infants' current emotional state. But their actions are not yet interpersonally directed to adults as other thinking persons, but to adults as tools instrumental in reaching goals. The repertoire of actions is also becoming more extensive, and more flexible and persistent in application. Although at this point, infants may not be trying to modify adults' understanding, middle-class adults' efforts to understand situations from an infant's point of view may bring about changes in adults' understanding of infants' intentions. Eventually, adults' efforts to assist infants in clarifying intentions, along with mysterious processes leading infants to become more aware of others as persons, lead to the development of instrumental actions that involve attempts to communicate intentionally and interpersonally, using increasingly sophisticated and indirect means.

The following sections of the chapter specify the operational definition we used in detecting and coding infants' instrumental interactions with adults, and describe the data base of our observations. We present our findings regarding developmental changes in frequency of instrumental episodes as well as changes in the infants' purposes, means used to influence adults, and persistence in trying to reach their goals. In our discussion of developmental changes in the means used by infants, we focus on the infants' use of gaze (both avoidant and self-initiated eye contact), stylized gestures, and conventional gestures or vocalizations, in order to follow the course of instrumental interaction from hints of rudimentary efforts to use adults instrumentally, to clear intentional communication. We illustrate the texture of these developments with examples from our transcripts of the play interactions.

DETECTING INFANTS' ATTEMPTS TO
USE ADULTS INSTRUMENTALLY

To study infants' attempts to use adults instrumentally, it is necessary to apply some criteria to their ongoing behavior that are precise enough to apply only to episodes that would qualify as attempts to use adults instrumentally, yet adaptable enough to apply to infants of quite different ages. The analysis requires attention to the structure of action, that is, how the episode unfolds and how each person's actions build on those of the other. It also requires inference regarding the participants' purposes, based on the interactive evidence they provide in the interaction (see McDermott, Gospodinoff, & Aron, 1978). They are, we assume, actively trying to tailor their behavior to fit with each other's intentions and, thus, frequently test hypotheses regarding the direction in which the other means to take the interaction.

Our definition of an instrumental episode required observers to be certain that the baby had a definite goal, that the baby used multiple actions (simultaneously or in succession) to indicate to the adult what they wanted done, and that the baby evidenced satisfaction upon achieving the goal or dissatisfaction if thwarted. Our definition did not require the participants to be "conscious" of their purposes or actions, in the sense of being able to introspect or to describe them (see Lunzer's [1979] definitions of consciousness, and Piaget's [1952] discussion of intentionality). Our definition resembles Miller, Galanter, and Pribram's (1960) Test-Operate-Test-Exit cycle of planning, and is elaborated directly from Bruner's (1981) definition of intentional actions:

> An intention is present when an individual operates persistently toward achieving an end state, chooses among alternative means and/or routes to achieve that end state, persists in deploying means and corrects the deployment of means to get closer to the end state, and finally ceases the line of activity when specifiable features of the state are achieved. The elements of the cycle, then, comprise aim, option of means, persistence and correction, and a terminal stop order. (p. 41)

Specifically, the following criteria were applied to the videotaped play interactions of adults and babies to define an episode as instrumental:

1. The baby had to signal clearly that he or she wanted something, and must have either indicated clearly what was wanted or persistently attempted to clarify what was wanted over the course of the episode. The observer had to be certain that the baby's actions were goal-directed, though the goal may not have been clearly specifiable. The observer must have stated a goal (specific or diffuse) or alternative goals that would fit the event.

2. The baby's signaling must have been more than fleeting. It must have been quite clear initially what the baby wanted, or else the baby must have shown clear and/or persistent attempts to get the adult to do something on her or his behalf. If the baby's expression of intent was brief and effective, it must nevertheless have involved several kinds of evidence indicating goal-directed behavior (e.g., simultaneous gazing and vocalizing toward an object). For clear requests to which adults responded rapidly, it was not necessary that the baby show persistence or adjustment of strategies. For less clear, more extended episodes, the baby must have been persistent or have adjusted strategies to get closer to achieving the goal or to clarify what the goal was.

3. The baby must have ceased efforts when the goal was reached or became unreachable. The baby may have shown either satisfaction or acknowledgment when the goal was achieved or distress or avoidance if the adult did not understand or responded in a manner inconsistent with the baby's goal. If the goal was not met because of an interruption or if the outcome was ambiguous, the episode may still have been considered instrumental if there was other good evidence that the baby was attempting to use the adult to reach a goal.

4. In order to exclude reflexive activities by the baby, or cyclical variations in the baby's state, or indications simply of interest in an object (rather than attempts to use the adult to get access to an object), the evidence for instrumental intent must have been stronger than any of these other explanations. If the baby's behavior was as easily explained in terms of intent to do something with an object as intent to use the adult to do something with an object, the event was not considered instrumental use of an adult.

5. Adults' comments on the baby's intentions (e.g., "You want the jack-in-the-box, don't you?") were *not* taken by themselves as evidence of an instrumental episode; middle-class adults frequently make such comments (Harding, 1982a; Kruper & Uzgiris, 1985). Often the adults in this study appeared to be thinking aloud as they tried to figure out what to do next with the baby. At times their comments appeared to be a way of communicating their own intentions to the experimenter (e.g., "You're ready to quit now, aren't you, baby?").

However, if the observers felt that the baby's actions provided evidence of an attempt to use the adult instrumentally, the adult's interpretation was sometimes useful in untangling the interaction, especially as the consequences of the adult's interpretation could be observed as the adult tested a hypothesis regarding the baby's intent.

Scoville (1984) argued that intentionality is in the eye of the beholder. In the present study, the beholders of interest were the trained observers, who used the evidence provided by the infants and the attempts of the adults to understand the infants' actions.

To increase the stringency of the criteria, observers were instructed to propose as instrumental episodes only those episodes that they felt personally willing to argue for, rather than to include episodes about which they felt any doubt.

To increase the appropriateness of developmental comparisons, the observers attempted to apply the criteria similarly across all ages. For example, they tried not to leave out episodes at older ages in which babies used rudimentary strategies even though at these ages babies are capable of more sophisticated strategies.

There are undoubtedly instances in which the babies used an adult instrumentally but the evidence for inferring this was not clear enough for the observers. For example, if the communication between infant and adult is very smooth, the adult may anticipate the infant's desires before the infant needs to make them clear, and the observer does not have the chance to see if the infant can use alternative means to make the intention clear. This possibility is supported by evidence that babies aged 9 to 18 months are more likely to attempt to regulate games with adults during an interruption than when the game is proceeding smoothly (Ross & Lollis, 1987). Since much of infant–adult interaction does function smoothly, with adults supporting infants' actions in what appears to be a fine-tuned fashion (Bruner, 1983; Rogoff, Malkin, & Gilbride, 1984), this definition of infants' instrumental use of adults is rather conservative, and would miss many incidents that transpire smoothly between babies and those who are familiar with them.

The data that we analyze in this chapter involve adults who were somewhat or entirely unfamiliar with these babies, and some of the adults were not familiar with any babies at all. Such relative unfamiliarity may increase the likelihood that the babies would need to clarify their wishes in order to make themselves understood. (This assumption contrasts with Harding, Kromelow, & Touris's, 1984, finding that infants produced more instrumental and intentional communication attempts toward their mothers than toward their day-care providers. However, in that study, the adults were instructed to ignore the infants in a frustration situation. The infants' greater instrumental and intentional communications may be a function of their greater expectation that their mothers would respond.)

Another way in which use of these criteria may underestimate infants' attempts to use adults instrumentally is that they require infants to be somewhat persistent and not distracted from their goals—and young infants are not known for their persistence. Older infants are able to withstand longer delays in carrying out their intentions (Diamond, 1985). Such differences in resistance to distraction could limit the appearance of instrumental episodes at early ages.

Thus, these criteria specify a certain kind of instrumental use of adults, one that involves great responsibility on the part of the infant to make the goal clear and to persist in trying to reach it, but without requiring the infant to demonstrate an intent to make the adult understand—just to demonstrate an intent to make the adult act.

THE NATURE OF THE DATA

We observed two middle-class U.S. infants as they interacted one at a time with 21 different middle-class adults, from the time the infants were 4 to 15.5 months old. The infants were a girl and a boy twin who were each observed with one adult every 2 or 3 weeks over the 11.5 months of the study. Each adult interacted only once with each baby. The data analyzed in this study consist of videotape recordings of each adult's interaction with one of the two babies. (An earlier study reported by Rogoff, Malkin, and Gilbride 1984, used the data from these same adults with the other baby in a parallel but different data set.) Twelve of the interactions are with the boy and nine are with the girl; the two babies appear in equal proportions in the early and later months of the study.

The adults were recruited through personal contacts, and were an assortment of relatives, acquaintances, and strangers to the babies. None of them were very familiar with the babies at the time of the observation, and 14 were complete strangers. They were either college students or had already completed college, and ranged in age from about 20 to 75. Most were natives of the United States. Thirteen of the adults were female and eight were male. Only nine of them were parents themselves.

The interactions occurred in a playroom in the babies' home, with the baby usually placed in a high chair facing the adult, who was asked to "get the baby to talk and smile and play with toys." A box of 11 toys was available beside the adult. The camera was placed at a right angle to the dyad, so that expressions and movements of both participants were available. The interactions continued until the adult or baby seemed to lose interest, and either the adult or sometimes the experimenter suggested that it was enough—usually after about 5 to 7 minutes.

Each videotape was viewed from beginning to end by two of four observers (the authors, two of whom are U.S. natives, one from India, one from Poland), paired at random but working independently. They used the criteria discussed above to extract instrumental episodes from the flow of the interaction. Each episode that an observer identified as providing convincing evidence of instrumental use of an adult was described in detailed narrative identifying the evidence for the decision. These narrative episodes were examined for agreement between the two observers. The transcripts were analyzed in terms of the nature of the baby's goal, the means the baby used to influence the adult, and the outcome of the baby's efforts.

AGREEMENT REGARDING THE EXISTENCE AND NATURE OF EPISODES

In addition to providing a check on the agreement between observer's judgments, data on the extent of agreement provided evidence regarding developmental changes in the clarity of the infants' instrumental efforts. We were interested in early hints of instrumental episodes, despite lack of agreement, to get a picture of what might be the precursors of infants' instrumental use of adults. To try to catch all possible episodes in a situation in which it was easy to miss one lasting only a few seconds in a 5- to 7-minute session, two independent coders evaluated each session. The ambiguity of the evidence at the youngest ages made for lack of agreement on whether or not an episode was convincing.

When the total footage of the sessions is considered, the agreement between observers is high, in that only 9% of the total footage consisted of actual disagreements (one observer identifies as instrumental an episode that the other observer does not identify). However, this figure is inflated by the footage consisting of agreements that *no* instrumental episode occurred. While this information is not irrelevant, it is important to consider the relation between videotape footage that both observers identified as the same instrumental episode, and footage on which there was disagreement (please refer to Table 1).

From 4 to 6 months, there was no footage containing episodes on which both observers agreed. (In two cases, observers agreed that no episode had occurred, and in the others, observers identified up to three

Table 1. Observers' Agreement That an Instrumental Episode Occurred

Age (months)	Number of dyads	Average footage	% of footage		# agreed episodes per 100 feet
			Agreed	Disagreed	
4–6	6	105	0	13	0
6.5–8	5	110	6	7	0.7
9–10.5	5	167	18	10	1.1
11–15.5	5	111	19	7	1.6

episodes per session, but no episodes were chosen in common by both observers.) From 6.5 to 8 months, there was roughly an equal amount of footage involving agreement and disagreement. From 9 to 10.5 months, there was almost twice as much agreement as disagreement footage. And from 11 to 15.5 months, there was almost 3 times as much agreement as disagreement footage.

When agreement is considered in terms of number of episodes rather than footage, it increases similarly with infant age. At 4 to 6 months, there is no agreement; at 6.5 to 8 months, 36% of the episodes are identified by both observers; and after that, approximately 50% of the episodes are identified by both observers (and the remainder were identified by only one observer).

To correct for varying session length at the different ages, we also examined the number of episodes per 100 feet of videotape (which was about the average length of a session for the ages with the shortest sessions). There was an increase with age in the average number of episodes per 100 feet of videotape that were identified by both observers (see Table 1).

This increase in agreement with increasing age of infants suggests that evidence of instrumental interaction is very unclear in the first half of the first year, and becomes more explicit with each 2-month advance. Consistent with this developmental pattern, Bruner, Roy, and Ratner (1982) found 8 months to be the age at which they could first consistently code their two subjects' requesting behavior. However, the frequency of instrumental episodes found here was approximately double that reported for requests at the same ages by Bruner et al. (1982). The difference may be due to the fact that their subjects interacted with mothers and ours interacted with strangers, or to differences in focus on requests versus instrumental interaction.

When both observers agreed that an episode existed, their description of the evidence of instrumental interaction, the baby's goal, and the outcome were highly congruent. Almost all of the episodes coded by two observers were the same except for slight differences in the degree of detail recorded by one or the other observer. Thus, we were able to use either observer's transcript to analyze the baby's goals and means, and the outcome of the baby's efforts.

For subsequent analysis, disagreements between observers were resolved by having a third observer decide whether the episode in question was or was not a convincing case of instrumental interaction. There were 22 episodes that observers agreed upon initially, and 31 episodes that only one of the observers noted. When a third observer voted on the disputed episodes, 16 of them were considered to have strong enough evidence of instrumental interaction, and 15 of them were discarded as having insufficient evidence. This results in a corpus of 38 episodes that were initially or finally agreed upon by two observers.

DEVELOPMENTAL CHANGES IN THE EXTENT AND NATURE OF INSTRUMENTAL INTERACTION

Frequency of Instrumental Episodes

The frequency of instrumental episodes (agreed upon initially or eventually by two observers) increased with age, as shown in Table 2. The youngest children had the most dyads with no episodes at all, and had the fewest episodes on the average. With greater age, there was an increase in the number of episodes and number of episodes corrected for length of session (i.e., per 100 feet of videotape; see Table 2). At 4 to 6 months, there was an average of a half an episode, while at 6.5 to 8 months, there was an average of one and a half episodes, increasing to an average of over two episodes by age 11 to 15.5 months. The greatest change appeared to occur between the first two age spans (4–6 months and 6.5–8 months).

Consistent with these findings, Bruner (1983) reports that Pratt, in an Oxford thesis, found a transition at about 6 months in British mothers' interpretation of the intent of infants' cries. Before 6 months, mothers regarded cries as indicating physical needs, and infants were more likely to stop crying when the mother responded physically by feeding, re-settling, or comforting the child. After 6 months, however, mothers added more "psychological" interpretations, and infants were more likely to respond to the "psychological" interventions of being offered an object or being engaged in interaction.

Using the observers' narratives of each episode, we examined the purpose of the infants' interaction, the means applied, their persistence, and their success.

Table 2. Frequency of Instrumental Episodes at Each Age

Age (months)	Number of dyads	Dyads with no episodes	Number of episodes	Mean episodes per 100 feet
4–6	6	3	3 ($\bar{X}=.5$)	.5
6.5–8	5	1	9 ($\bar{X}=1.8$)	1.6
9–10.5	5	0	13 ($\bar{X}=2.6$)	1.6
11–15.5	5	1	13 ($\bar{X}=2.6$)	2.3

Purpose of the Instrumental Interaction

The babies' goals were classified according to whether they involved access to an object, an activity with an adult, or an activity with an object, and whether the baby wanted the object access or activity to begin (or continue) or to cease. An example of each type of purpose appears in Table 3, along with the frequencies.

The most common purpose was to get the adult to assist with an activity with an object. The purposes involving access or activity with objects predominantly demonstrated interest; the babies never tried to get the adult to take an object away and seldom tried to get the adult to stop an activity with an object. On the other hand, the purposes involving activities not involving an object were generally avoidant; the baby often tried to get the adult to stop doing something social but seldom requested a purely social activity with the adult.

For the most part, the percentages of the various types of purposes were the same across the four age categories. Activities involving objects was an exception. There were no activities involving objects at 4 to 6 months; activities involving objects increased to equal the other purposes at 6.5 to 10.5 months; and at 11 to 15.5 months the babies began to engage in activities involving objects to a much greater extent than the other purposes. At 11 to 15.5 months, there were nine episodes involving activities with objects, two episodes involving access to an object, and two episodes involving activities with the adult. The emergence of object-offers in infants' repertoires at about 8 or 9 months—both in infants within Western industrial societies and those in hunter–gatherer groups (Bake-

Table 3. Frequency and Examples of the Purposes of the Episodes

Purpose	Number of episodes	Example
Access to object: begin/continue	8	The baby tries to get the adult to give him the jack-in-the-box.
Access to object: cease	0	(hypothetical) The baby refuses an offer of an object.
Activity with adult: begin/continue	2	The baby tries to regain the adult's attention and continued interaction.
Activity with adult: cease	11	The baby tries to get the adult to stop blowing in his hair.
Activity with object: begin/continue	14	The baby tries to get the adult to work the jack-in-the-box.
Activity with object: cease	3	The baby tries to get the adult to change activities.

man, Adamson, Konner, & Barr, 1990)—may be associated with similar instrumental intentions.

Related to this shift is a focus at the oldest ages on purposes that predominantly involved beginning or continuing (11 episodes) rather than avoiding (2 episodes). At the earlier ages, the babies had a roughly equal distribution of purposes involving continuation versus cessation. It may be that at older ages the babies' greater communication skills precluded the need for persistent avoidance efforts, and the adults may have been more certain what the babies' cues meant so they would discontinue unwanted activities before the baby needed to insist.

The Manner in Which the Babies Attempted to Influence Adults

Nature and Frequency of Different Means of Influence Used by the Babies. The means which the babies used to attempt to influence the adults were classified into the following categories:

- Changing posture toward or away from the adult or ongoing activity (such as turning the body away).
- Moving body in interest or distress (such as wiggling feet eagerly).
- Smiling at adult or indicating distress through facial expression.
- Nonword vocalizing of interest or distress.
- Gesturing with nondirect motions to indicate interest or rejection.
- Gazing fixedly at object.
- Making self-initiated versus responsive eye contact or avoiding eye contact.
- Slapping palm of hand against high chair tray in frustration.
- Pointing.
- Touching object to draw attention to it.
- Offering object.
- Demonstrating activity with object.
- Using words or symbolic moves such as affirmative or negative nods.

The total number of means used in each episode was greater for episodes involving cessation than those involving beginning or continuing an activity or access (10.9 cessation actions vs. 8.4 continuation actions). At different ages, the babies used roughly comparable numbers of actions, except that they used more actions at the oldest ages than at the other three ages (11.9 vs. 7.5 to 9.3), and more actions for purposes involving continuation at the oldest than the younger ages (11.5 vs. 5.6 to 6.5). So in addition to greater involvement in positive continuation activities with objects, at the older ages the babies engaged in much more extensive directions to the adults regarding what to do with the object.

The number of *different* means used per episode was not much greater for purposes of cessation than for purposes of continuation (5.7 vs. 4.9 different actions). Here too the babies at the oldest ages used more different means per episode when pursuing a positive purpose (continuation) than did the babies at the other three ages (5.8 vs. 4.0 to 4.5 different actions).

In the next sections we consider developmental changes in the use of several key means of influencing adults: self-initiated eye contact versus gaze avoidance, stylized gestures, and conventionalized communication. These are means of influence that appear increasingly sophisticated, and have attracted attention in previous work on prelinguistic communication.

Use of Self-Initiated Eye Contact versus Gaze Avoidance.   In the literature on intentional communication, infants' coordination of attention to an object and the person manipulating it has been used as an indicator of person-oriented intentional communication (as opposed to use of adults as tools). We examined the babies' use of eye contact that was not elicited by the adult as an indicator of the babies' interpersonal communication in the service of using adults instrumentally. This is somewhat broader than the coordination of attention to object and person, since we wanted to examine instrumental acts that did not necessarily involve objects.

Table 4 presents developmental changes in the use of self-initiated eye contact. The use of self-initiated eye contact is compared with the use of avoidance of eye contact, which may be a more rudimentary use of gaze that instrumentally breaks communication without as much effort required as for initiating contact with gaze. We distinguish episodes involv-

Table 4.   Comparison of Episodes with the Purpose of Continuation or Cessation Using Self-Initiated Eye Contact or Avoidance of Eye Contact

Age (months)	Number of episodes		% of episodes with self-initiated eye contact		% of episodes with avoidance of eye contact	
	Continue	Cease	Continue	Cease	Continue	Cease
4–6	2	1	50	0	0	100
6.5–8	5	4	60	100	0	75
9–10.5	6	7	50	86	0	57
11–15.5	11	2	100	50	0	0

ing a purpose of beginning or continuing an activity (continuation) from those involving an attempt to stop an activity (cessation).

In our data, it appears that the use of self-initiated eye contact as a means of influencing an adult begins as early as 6 months of age. At least half of the episodes after that age used self-initiated eye contact. It appears that the use of eye contact increased with age for episodes in which babies tried to influence an adult to begin or continue an activity (going from 50% to 100% of the interactions), while it decreased with age after 6 months for attempts to get an adult to stop an activity (going from 100% of the episodes at 6.5 to 8 months, down to 50% of the episodes at 11 to 15.5 months).

The onset of instrumental self-initiated eye contact that we observed may occur somewhat earlier than the ages reported for coordinating eye contact and object manipulation in the literature on the development of intentional communication (Sugarman-Bell, 1978). Bruner (1983) found that only at 9 months did his two subjects glance at their mothers concurrently with extending a hand toward an object in a request. Harding and Golinkoff (1979) found that most of their subjects aged 8 to 11 months intentionally used eye contact and gazing at an object when their mothers stopped working an object for them in a frustration episode. The discrepancy may be partially explained by the fact that our self-initiated eye contact episodes before the age of 9 months did not necessarily involve coordination of attention to an object and a person, since some of the episodes involved attempts to get the adult to continue or cease an activity that did not involve an object. However, of the eight episodes in which the baby initiated eye contact between 6 and 8 months, three did involve objects.

An episode involving a 6-month-old demonstrated the use of self-initiated eye contact (as well as other means of influence) as the baby attempted to attract the adult's attention and resume interaction:

> The adult had been whistling, to the baby's delight, but quit when the baby bumped her chin. The adult looked over into the box of toys. The baby immediately looked at the adult, straightening from her bent position and turning to watch him. The adult looked back at the baby questioningly, glancing back and forth between baby and toy box uncertainly, as if trying to decide whether to return to the baby or to go on to get a toy. The baby sat silently gazing at the adult, almost in anticipation, with her mouth open in an expectant almost-smile.
>
> As the adult turned back to the toy box, the baby called out to him, loudly, "Hey!" as she looked intently at him, eyes widened and body making emphatic movements. As the adult continued to look in the toy box, the baby called again loudly and with emphasis "Hey-ey-ey!" making excited motions with her upper body. The adult put a toy in front of the baby, and

the baby commented "Ah!", looking at the toy, then at the adult, then at the toy with less excitement but apparently satisfied, ceasing vocalization.

The early appearance of social acknowledgment of the adult's role was also apparent in the babies' initiation of eye contact when they accomplished their goals. On some occasions when the babies were successful, they acknowledged the adults' involvement when the goal was accomplished by making eye contact with the adult and smiling as they, for example, began to play with a toy they had requested. Acknowledgment of satisfaction using eye contact occurred as early as 6 months of age, and occurred in three of nine episodes at 6.5 to 8 months, and in five of twenty-six episodes from 9 to 15.5 months. On occasion, of course, the baby simply engaged immediately with the object, or the attempt failed, so such social acknowledgment did not occur.

An example of acknowledgment using self-initiated eye contact occurred at the end of an episode in which the 9-month-old baby had solicited an adult's assistance in taking a stuffed plush frog out of the toy box. (In addition, the baby used other means of eliciting the adult's help, including instrumental use of eye contact at the beginning of the episode. Such coordination of various means to use adults instrumentally is characteristic of most of the episodes.)

> The baby reached into the toy box and touched several toys. She looked up at the adult with her hand on the frog, which was wedged between other toys in the box. As soon as the baby looked at her, the adult reached for the frog, whispering "What's that?" The adult began to pull the frog out of the box, with the baby gazing at the frog.
>
> At this point, the adult was interrupted by the experimenter. The baby straightened up suddenly, staring fixedly into the toy box, and exclaimed "A ha ha *ha!*" as if saying "What's going *on!*" At the baby's exclamation, the adult looked back at her quickly, but the experimenter continued talking and the adult turned back to the experimenter. The baby then looked up at the adult, still holding onto the frog, waiting until the interruption ended.
>
> When the adult turned back to the baby, the baby proceeded to bang her hand on the frog, looking down at the frog now. The adult moved other toys out of the way to get the frog out of the box, as the baby watched. The baby looked appreciatively, shyly, toward the adult, and after knocking the frog over a few times, the baby got hold of it and laughed wildly, clutching and chewing on the frog.

The use of avoidance of eye contact as a means of influencing the adult was limited (for obvious reasons) to episodes involving attempts to get an adult to stop an activity, and decreased as the babies grew older. It may be that avoidance of eye contact is a means of influence that is easy enough to implement at early ages but drops out as more sophisticated strategies for influencing others become possible. While avoidance of eye contact may be instrumental without indicating that the baby intended the action as communication, our criteria for inclusion of episodes required gaze aversion to be apparently directed toward the adult as communication rather than simply avoidance of the irritating action of the adult.

In the following interchange, the baby's use of gaze aversion appeared to be quite pointed communication with the adult. The interchange appears to involve extensive negotiation of the adult's activity through gaze aversion as well as self-initiated eye contact, as a baby of 6.5 months attempted to get an adult to stop blowing in his hair:

> The baby seemed pleased the first time the adult blew into his hair, but the second time, the baby looked from side to side and not at the adult. The baby's face was serious. When the adult blew again, the baby effortfully pushed his body to turn entirely away from the adult, sitting slumped over the arm of the chair facing 90 degrees away, looking down with a serious expression.
>
> At this, the adult stopped the cadence of blowing and looked at the baby, gently touching his hand, saying "Huh?" The baby immediately turned back to face the adult, pulling both arms back onto the high chair tray. He still did not look at the adult however. When the adult blew on the baby's hair again, the baby sighed deeply and glared up at the adult for a long intense gaze, putting his head back against the chair with his eyes squinted. The adult looked at him for a while, then asked sympathetically, "Want me to stop doing that now? Don't want me to blow on your hair anymore?" At this the baby smiled and sat upright again, as if indicating readiness to interact.

Stylized Gestures. Stylized gestures include instrumental actions in which the baby refers to an object or action through a gesture that is a stylized version of an action that would be performed if the baby were trying to attain the object or do the activity independently. Stylized gestures, in our terminology, also include pointing, touching an object to draw attention to it, and offering an object as a request to operate the object. Stylized gestures were used at all four ages, increasing somewhat with age (from 33% to 78% to 46% to 77% of the episodes at each age, in order). They were used in roughly equal proportions of the episodes with continuation versus cessation goals.

Bruner (1983) noted that his two subjects began at 8 months to use a stylized symbolic reach—open-handed, noneffortful, and with distinctive vocalization, and Acredolo and Goodwyn (1988) noted that stylized gestures occurred commonly within the second year. We found a similar stylized indication of an object at 5.5 months, as a baby seemed to use a rudimentary point and stylized effort vocalization (an effortless grunt) in an attempt to get an adult to hand him a toy:

The baby took the ring (which he had been gumming) out of his mouth and looked intently to the side, saying "Uhhnn" as if to attract the adult's attention toward an object. The adult was busy trying to put the baby in a comfortable position while the baby continued to look fixedly at the object, with his hand moving sort of in the direction of the object. Finally the adult was satisfied with the baby's position and called the baby's name. The baby still looked intently at the object, then reached out toward it with his index finger raised slightly above the rest of his spread out fingers so that it looked like an approximation of a point (and definitely not an attempt to grasp), as he vocalized "uhhnn." The adult responded, "Do you want Bugs?" and brought the Bugs Bunny jack-in-the-box closer. The baby grasped and held it.

The most sophisticated stylized gestures that we saw involved babies holding toys out to adults as invitations to work toys, or actually demonstrating actions that they wanted adults to perform. Demonstrations by the baby showing what to do with an object fit into the concept of instrumental referencing studied in the social referencing literature, except that in that literature it is the mother who shows the baby what to do with an object.

Stylized gestures involving offers or demonstrations occurred almost exclusively in the episodes involving an activity with an object. There were no such gestures (nor any activities with objects) at 4 to 6 months. At 6.5 to 8 months, there was one episode in which the baby offered an object (out of four episodes at that age involving an activity with an object, 25%). At 9 to 10.5 months there were two episodes with offers (out of four involving an activity with an object, 50%). At 11 to 15.5 months, there were nine episodes involving an activity with an object; in seven of them there was an offer (77%), and in three the baby demonstrated the activity to be performed (33%). In addition, at this upper age, there was one episode of demonstration of an activity involving the adult but not involving an object.

The earliest episode involving an offer of a toy to get the adult to carry out an activity occurred when a 6.5-month-old seemed to attempt to get an adult to work the jack-in-the-box by stretching to hold the box out toward the adult:

The baby pushed the jack-in-the-box slightly toward the adult across the high chair tray, looking up fixedly at the adult with a little smile, and vocalizing softly in a request tone, "Nnnh!" The baby continued to look at the adult, stretching to hold the box out to the adult. The adult reached for the handle, asking "What happens when we *do* this?" and the baby looked down at the front of the box as the adult began to wind the handle.

When the babies were older, there were numerous lengthy examples of a baby and adult negotiating an activity, in which the baby clarified his or her wishes through demonstrations of the desired activity. Over the course of an extended interaction, an 11-month-old trying to get an un-familiar adult to help him get the bunny to pop out of the jack-in-the-box offered the toy as an invitation for the adult to act, and attempted to indicate what he wanted the adult to do. The extensiveness of the inter-action at times resulted from misreading of messages between adult and baby, requiring both participants to seek and provide clarification of their intent. Contributing to the need for negotiation in this episode was the adult's uncertainty about how to work the toy (especially, which direction the handle should be turned) and her preference to change to another activity, and the baby's occasional conflicting messages that appeared to result from great eagerness to get the box open.

Several times during this episode, the infant offered the jack-in-the-box to the adult as an invitation to wind it, either by pushing the box toward the adult while looking at the adult, or by touching the box with one hand and indicating the handle with the other. He also seemed to try to clarify his request to the adult to open the box with a stylized gesture of trying to get into the box, scratching and scrabbling his fingers at the outside of the box until the adult began to try to wind the handle again. In previous episodes the baby had indicated he wanted the box opened with a stylized attempt to pry up the lid, but early in this episode the adult had taken the baby's hand off the top of the box, so he appeared to invent an alternate way to demonstrate getting into the box to avoid touching the top of the box. The baby was persistent and flexible, though occasionally inconsistent, in his efforts to enlist the adult's involvement in getting the box open, even when the adult tried to distract the baby from his goal by offering another toy. The baby insisted several times on returning to the jack-in-the-box activity after interruptions, and escalated his attempts to get his request for help across by insistent vocalizations, indicating that he wanted the box opened with a stylized gnawing on the corner of the box, and what appeared to be a negative nod when the adult tried to distract him. Here, specifically, is how the event occurred:

> The baby touched the top of the closed jack-in-the-box with one hand and the handle with the other, vocalizing softly "Hnh!" The adult assisted the baby in turning the handle, then moved the baby's hand off the top of the box, probably to allow the lid to open freely. The baby was surprised at this "instruction" to keep his hand off the lid, and looked around for another place to put his hand, first putting it back on the lid but immediately removing it. (Henceforth he appeared to try to avoid touching the lid, which may account for his strategy of "scrabbling" his fingers at the front of the box instead of prying at the lid as a way of indicating that he wanted it opened.)
>
> The baby reached for the handle and looked up at the adult very directly. She let go of the handle and said, "OK, you can turn." But as soon as she let go, the baby took his hand off the handle also. The adult wound

a few tentative notes, uncertain of the direction to wind. Then the baby reached for the handle again, and the adult withdrew her hand. The baby made a soft friendly growl sound (ggg) and reached for the top of the box as if to pull at it. He then looked up at the adult and moved his hand down to the front of the box, vocalizing softly with a questioning intonation as if remembering her moving his hand off the top of the box previously, and proceeded to scratch softly at the front of the box. When the adult began to wind the handle again, the baby ceased fiddling his fingers on the box, and watched her wind.

Suddenly he sat up straight and enthusiastically grasped the box with both hands, fingers again moving as if trying to get into the box, exclaiming in a deep voice "Ga ga ga ga ga ga ga!" The adult took her hands off the box uncertainly. The baby broke into a smile and looked up at her, holding his hands on the box. She asked "What are you saying?" and he immediately pushed the box toward her, looked down at it, and scrabbled at the front of the box with his fingers.

The adult tried to switch to a mouse puppet, but the baby put his hands back on top of the box and exclaimed "Ga ga ga ga ga ga ga!" in a friendly growl, then moved his hand and fiercely scrabbled at the front of the box with his fingers. The adult distracted the baby using the puppet, and then wiped the baby's nose.

After the nose wipe, the baby returned his attention to the box, scrabbling at the front. When the adult tried to distract him again with the mouse puppet, the baby turned his head from side to side about 8 times, looking at the box, in what appeared to be a very effortful and deliberate negative response to the adult's suggestion to change activities. Then the baby picked up the box and began to *chew* on the bottom corner! (Another stylized indication of wanting the box open? By this age he no longer put things in his mouth for exploration.)

This successfully attracted the adult's attention, and the baby grinned at her and pushed the box energetically toward her. He grinned, took his hand off the box, then looked down at the handle, which he held with the other hand. Eventually the adult turned the handle again, and the baby smiled and watched, contentedly looking at the box, then at the adult.

The adult continued trying to wind, but was uncertain which direction to turn the handle, and quit, encouraging the baby to try. The baby tried, but as soon as the adult turned her attention away, the baby picked up the box and again chewed on the bottom edge of it, vocalizing loudly "Ga ga ga ga ga!" He then looked up at the adult with a very mischievous grin. But it was for naught, as the adult was now talking with the experimenter. The baby pushed the box away from him on the tray, and eventually let go and turned away, leaning dejectedly over the side of the high chair. He continued to look away from the adult for some time.

Primarily through nonconventionalized means of communication, this baby managed an extensive battery of attempts to communicate his intent to an adult who was sympathetic but preferred changing activities, since she was unfamiliar with how to work the toy. In addition to showing how persistent and resourceful the baby was in trying to use the adult instrumentally, this episode shows how interwoven the baby's efforts were with the adult's, and how the baby's instrumental actions were embedded in a temporal and interactional context. Most of the lines in this long episode could be identified as efforts by the child to enlist the adult's help, but they would lose a great deal of meaning if the adult's actions and the interactional sequence were not also available for interpretation.

Conventionalized Communication.   It was only at the upper age range that the babies used the sophisticated strategies of conventionalized communication: uttering words or nodding affirmatively or negatively. In using conventionalized communication, the child must be able to manage the use of arbitrary sounds or motions that carry meaning shared with others in the culture, so it is not surprising that such sophisticated means should only occur later in infancy.

Conventionalized communication occurred in 36% of the episodes having a purpose of continuation at age 11 to 15.5 months (see the rudimentary example in the previous episode, when the child seemed to effortfully produce a negative nod to reject the adult's offer to change activities). Conventionalized communication never occurred in the episodes with a purpose of cessation at that age, nor in any episodes at previous ages.

An example of conventionalized vocal communication (along with offers of an object) occurred when a baby aged 15.5 months tried to get an adult to wind the handle of a jack-in-the-box to make the bunny come out. The episode was extended by the adult's teasing efforts to get the baby to clarify his already clear message, a language socialization technique that may appear when the baby begins to show competence in conventionalized communication, to encourage greater use of the conventional terms and gestures. Over the course of the episode, this baby confirmed his intent with simple but conventional words and nodding:

> After successfully turning the handle of the jack-in-the-box, the baby glanced at the adult and took his hands off the box momentarily. The adult began to put the box away. The baby looked surprised and reached for the box with his hands and his glance. The adult asked, "You wanta still play with this?" holding it up. The baby seemed to say "Mm hm," and the adult asked "Yeah?" The baby extended his arm, looked at the adult, and grasped the box. The adult still didn't put the box on the tray, so the baby grasped the box with both hands and put it on the tray with conviction, and the adult responded "MmKay."
>
> The baby banged the box on the tray, then held it out toward the adult, saying "Mo?" [More?] as he turned to look at the adult (who had been off task for a moment). The adult said "What?" and the baby pushed the box

further toward the adult, smiled, and looked down at it. The adult said, "You want me to do that?" The baby responded by looking intently at the handle, putting his fingers on it, cocking his head and saying "Mo?" The adult said "No?" and nodded her head negatively. The baby instantly looked up as if misunderstood. The adult asked "Do you wanta do it?" nodding yes and smiling, seeming to hold out for clarification from the baby. The baby looked at her intently, and with effort nodded no. The adult grinned, tickled the baby's leg, and asked again "Do you wanta do it?" The baby pushed the box toward the adult, looking at it.

The adult teased, "Don't want to play with that anymore?" and took the box off the tray. The baby opened his mouth wide, leaned to look over the tray to the box, and pushed at it with his foot. The adult lifted the box and turned the handle while the baby watched intently, hands very still, opening and closing his jaw [shades of Piaget's daughter with the matchbox?].

Summary of Developmental Changes in Instrumental Means. The data on the manner in which babies attempted to influence adults suggest that even as young as 4–6 months, babies may use multiple means to get adults to implement their goals. While most of the means at the earliest ages involved using the adult as a tool, without obvious acknowledgment of the existence of the other as a person, as young as age 6 months babies may use more sophisticated strategies that are less direct and more communicative, such as self-initiated eye contact and stylized gestures. It was not until the end of the first year, however, that the babies used sustained and complex conventional symbols such as symbolically demonstrating the action to be performed or using words or nods.

Persistence and Success of the Babies' Instrumental Efforts

Even at the youngest ages, the babies were persistent in their attempts to influence adults, and appeared to adjust their strategies to clarify their goals and fit their means more appropriately to the goals. We coded the episodes in terms of either (1) showing adjustment of means to be increasingly effective, intense, or clear; (2) showing persistence without adjusting the means to the situation; or (3) using a single effective means or simultaneous cluster of means. Most of the episodes at all ages were coded as showing adjustment (100%, 66%, 62%, and 69%).

It is interesting that the use of a single means or a simultaneous cluster of means occurred primarily in the older two age groups (in five episodes after 9 months, and in one episode before 9 months). This may indicate that such simplicity of means is less effective at the earlier ages. Or it may indicate that the observers required more evidence than this at the early ages to be convinced that an episode was indeed an example of instrumental interaction (rather than an adult imposing an action on the baby, or the baby accepting whatever action the adult offered without having a specific goal). At the younger ages, the observers may have required evidence of persistence or adjustment in the application of means to be convinced that the baby was attempting to influence the adult. This interpretation is consistent with the data on developmental changes in the success of the babies' efforts.

At all ages, the babies' efforts were generally successful. It appeared that success was more frequent at the younger ages than the older ages. Of the episodes from 4 to 8 months, 92% were successful, but only 69% of the episodes from 9 to 15.5 months were successful. It is unlikely that younger babies meet with greater success in general in getting their way or influencing adults than do older babies. A more likely explanation is that in order to infer the intent to influence an adult at younger ages, observers depended on the information provided by the baby's confirmation when the goal was satisfied. In cases of failure, the baby's reaction may be less useful than the acknowledgment of reaching the goal that is common in the successful episodes, since the baby may simply look away from the adult or "fret out" when efforts fail. Hence, we feel that the apparently greater success of the younger children is best viewed as an artifact of the observers' probable need for greater evidence from younger children, eliminating many of the younger children's unsuccessful episodes from consideration.

Our interpretation of the differential success ratios in our observations of younger and older children underlines the importance of remembering that comparisons across ages involve inferences based on operationalizations of constructs that may fit more closely with the skills of the more sophisticated individuals.

A related caveat should be applied to the broader findings of developmental changes in instrumental efforts. Our developmental findings can be safely summarized as showing that at older ages, the babies more frequently met our criteria of instrumental interaction, and that the means employed differed with the age of the babies. But it would not be appropriate to make the inference that younger babies are less likely to use adults instrumentally. While that would be an easy conclusion to make, it must be remembered that as observers we had more difficulty interpreting the behavior of the babies when they were younger. It is possible that they attempted to use adults instrumentally but had difficulty in communicating their goals, implementing effective means to use adults instrumentally, or pursuing goals in the face of distraction.

SUMMARY

In this study we have examined developmental changes in two babies' efforts to use adults instrumentally, from 4 to 15.5 months of age. The findings indicate that observers had more difficulty in agreeing on episodes of instrumental interaction until the second half-year of life.

The number of episodes of instrumental interaction increased four- or five-fold from age 4 to 6 months to age 11 to 15.5 months. The goal of getting the adult to facilitate an activity employing an object did not occur at the earliest months, but by the end of the first year of life, it became much more prevalent than the other goals (getting an adult to carry out an activity not involving an object, or to provide access to an object). At 11 months and later, the babies used more total means per episode to try to enlist an adult's help and more different means per episode than they did at earlier ages. The babies' strategies for influencing adults became more sophisticated with age: they increased their use of self-initiated eye contact and decreased their avoidance of eye contact. And they increased the use of sophisticated stylized gestures and conventionalized communication such as offering an object to invite assistance, demonstrating the desired action to be performed on the object, and using words and head nods.

While the use of these stylized gestures, conventional vocalizations, and self-initiated eye contact increased with babies' age, it is important to note that stylized gestures and self-initiated eye contact were frequently employed by the babies as young as 6 to 8 months of age.

This study suggests that even quite young infants effectively attempt to employ adults as tools in attaining their own goals. Such instrumental interaction requires skill on the part of adults in referencing the meanings and intents of the babies, and skill on the part of babies in clarifying their purposes and the role the adults are to fill.

The general conclusion of this chapter is that researchers in the areas of socialization of development and social referencing would do well to broaden their scope to consider the mutual involvement of both infants and adults in the influential interactions that appear to be a forum for children's developing skills and knowledge. This chapter emphasizes the role of infants in managing adults as tools to reach infants' own goals, and in attempting to influence adults' understanding of their intent. To attain a more complete understanding of the social context in which children develop, it is important to keep in focus the mutual relations between the efforts of adults with children and the efforts of children to make use of the social world in bootstrapping their development. Child development involves a joint construction of reality.

Acknowledgments: We are grateful for the cooperation of Valerie Magarian and David Magarian and the adults who participated in this study, and for feedback on the paper from Artin Göncü. An early version of this paper was presented at the SRCD Study Group on "Social Referencing, Infancy, and Social Psychological Theory," organized by Saul Feinman, Laramie,

Wyoming. The research reported in this chapter was supported by the National Institute of Child Health and Human Development, Grant no. HD 16793-02.

REFERENCES

Acredolo, L., & Goodwyn, S. (1988). Symbolic gesturing in normal infants. *Child Development, 59,* 450–466.

Azmitia, M. (1988). Peer interaction and problem solving: When are two heads better than one? *Child Development, 59,* 87–96.

Bakeman, R., Adamson, L. B., Konner, M., & Barr, R. G. (1990). !Kung infancy: The social context of object exploration. *Child Development, 61,* 794–809.

Bates, E. (1979). Intentions, conventions, and symbols. In E. Bates, L. Benigni, I. Bretherton, L. Camaioni, & L. V. Volterra (Eds.), *The emergence of symbols* (pp. 33–42). New York: Academic Press.

Bretherton, I., McNew, S., & Beeghly-Smith, M. (1981). Early person knowledge as expressed in gestural and verbal communication: When do infants acquire a "theory of mind"? In M. E. Lamb & L. R. Sherrod (Eds.), *Infant social cognition* (pp. 333–373). Hillsdale, NJ: Erlbaum.

Bruner, J. S. (1981). Intention in the structure of action and interaction. In L. P. Lipsitt (Ed.), *Advances in infancy research* (Vol. 1, pp. 41–56). Norwood, NJ: Ablex.

Bruner, J. S. (1983). *Child's talk: Learning to use language.* New York: Norton.

Bruner, J. S., Roy, C., & Ratner, N. (1982). The beginnings of request. In K. E. Nelson (Ed.), *Children's language* (Vol. 3, pp. 91–138). Hillsdale, NJ: Erlbaum.

Diamond, A. (1985). Development of the ability to use recall to guide action, as indicated by infants' performance on A$\overline{B}$. *Child Development, 56,* 868–883.

Dunn, J. (1982). Comment: Problems and promises in the study of affect and intention. In E. Z. Tronick (Ed.), *Social interchange in infancy* (pp. 197–206). Baltimore: University Park Press.

Feinman, S. (1982). Social referencing in infancy. *Merrill-Palmer Quarterly, 28,* 445–470.

Gunnar, M. R., & Stone, C. (1984). The effects of positive maternal affect on infant responses to pleasant, ambiguous, and fear-provoking toys. *Child Development, 55,* 1231–1236.

Harding, C. G. (1982a, March). *Pre-language vocalizations and words.* Paper presented at the International Conference on Infant Studies, Austin, TX.

Harding, C. G. (1982b). Development of the intention to communicate. *Human Development, 25,* 140–151.

Harding, C. G., & Golinkoff, R. M. (1979). The origins of intentional vocalizations in pre-linguistic infants. *Child Development, 50,* 33–40.

Harding, C. G., Kromelow, S., & Touris, M. (1984, April). *A longitudinal study of infants' communication patterns with mothers and daycare caregivers.* Paper presented at the International Conference on Infant Studies, New York.

Kruper, J. C., & Užgiris, I. Č. (1985, April). *Fathers' and mothers' speech to infants.* Paper presented at the biennial meeting of the Society for Research in Child Development, Toronto.

Lunzer, E. A. (1979). The development of consciousness. In G. Underwood & R. Stevens (Eds.), *Aspects of consciousness* (pp. 1–19). London: Academic Press.

McDermott, R. P., Gospodinoff, K., & Aron, J. (1978). Criteria for an ethnographically adequate description of concerted activities and their contexts. *Semiotica, 24,* 245–275.

Miller, G. A., Galanter, E., & Pribram, K. H. (1960). *Plans and the structure of behavior.* New York: Holt.

Newman, D., Griffin, P., & Cole, M. (1989). *The construction zone: Working for cognitive change in school.* Cambridge: Cambridge University Press.

Piaget, J. (1952). *The origins of intelligence in children.* New York: Norton.

Rheingold, H. L. (1969). The social and socializing infant. In D. A. Goslin (Ed.), *Handbook of socialization theory and research* (pp. 779–790). Chicago: Rand McNally.

Rogoff, B. (1986). Adult assistance of children's learning. In T. E. Raphael (Ed.), *Contexts of school-based literacy* (pp. 27–40). New York: Random House.

Rogoff, B. (1990). *Apprenticeship in thinking: Cognitive development in social context.* New York: Oxford University Press.

Rogoff, B. (1991). The joint socialization of development by young children and adults. In M. Lewis & S. Feinman (Eds.), *Social influences and socialization in infancy* (pp. 253–280). New York: Plenum.

Rogoff, B., Malkin, C., & Gilbride, K. (1984). Interaction with babies as guidance in development. In B. Rogoff & J. V. Wertsch (Eds.), *Children's learning in the "zone of proximal development"* (pp. 31–44). San Francisco: Jossey-Bass.

Ross, H. S., & Lollis, S. P. (1987). Communication within infant social games. *Developmental Psychology, 23,* 241–248.

Scoville, R. (1984). Development of the intention to communicate: The eye of the beholder. In L. Feagans, C. Garvey, & R. Golinkoff (Eds.), *The origins and growth of communication* (pp. 109–122). Norwood, NJ: Ablex.

Sorce, J. F., Emde, R. N., Campos, J., & Klinnert, M. (1985). Maternal emotional signaling: Its effect on the visual cliff behavior of 1-year-olds. *Developmental Psychology, 21,* 195–200.

Sugarman-Bell, S. (1978). Some organizational aspects of pre-verbal communication. In I. Markova (Ed.), *The social context of language* (pp. 49–66). New York: Wiley.

Valsiner, J. (1987). *Culture and the development of children's action.* New York: Wiley.

Vygotsky, L. S. (1978). *Mind in society.* Cambridge, MA: Harvard University Press.

Wertsch, J. V. (1979). From social interaction to higher psychological processes: A clarification and application of Vygotsky's theory. *Human Development, 22,* 1–22.

14

A Consideration of Social Referencing in the Context of Attachment Theory and Research

Mary D. Salter Ainsworth

INTRODUCTION

As demonstrated by the chapters in this volume, the concept of social referencing refers to a diversity of phenomena observed by scholars from a variety of disciplines and divergent theoretical positions. Since attachment theory has eclectic underpinnings and is an open-ended theory, it is subject to revision, refinement, and extension in the light of further research. As what is meant by social referencing is better agreed upon, and as research into both it and attachment proceeds, it seems likely that its overlap with attachment will become clearer. Nevertheless, it is evident that there are even now important overlaps and areas of congruence. It is my hope that my comments here may help to clarify the degree of congruence that is already appreciable; there may well be more overlap between social referencing phenomena and attachment phenomena than I have included in this chapter.

MARY D. SALTER AINSWORTH • Department of Psychology, University of Virginia, Charlottesville, Virginia 22903.

Social Referencing and the Social Construction of Reality in Infancy, edited by Saul Feinman. Plenum Press, New York, 1992.

In the literature stemming from recent research in developmental psychology, most attention has been paid to social referencing phenomena as an aspect of interaction between infant and mother. It is this approach that I wish first to discuss. Subsequently, I consider the fit between attachment theory and certain of the concepts of social referencing in more general terms.

INFANT–MOTHER ATTACHMENT RESEARCH AND SOCIAL REFERENCING

Here I wish to focus on social referencing as affective communication (see Campos, 1983; Emde, Chapter 4, this volume; Feinman & Lewis, 1983), not as instrumental communication (e.g., Rogoff, Mistry, Radziszewska, & Germond, Chapter 13, this volume)—thus, on yielding information about how to feel rather than direct information about what to do.

As I understand it, the definition of social referencing in infancy as affective communication (Campos, 1983) implies that an infant may receive from another person—most often the mother figure or principal caregiver—sensory input that either directly or after a cognitive interpretative process influences how an infant feels and, hence, indirectly what he does in a given situation. One major emphasis in current research has been on information conveyed to the infant through visual perception of the facial expressions of the other. However, other information may be involved, such as visual perceptions of gestures and action, not merely facial expression; auditory perceptions of vocal output, perhaps, especially in infancy, tone of voice; and communications implicit in physical contact.

There is much evidence to suggest that visual discriminations, especially across any considerable distance, are relatively late to develop, so that auditory, tactual, kinesthetic, and olfactory discriminations may be more important early on. I would especially like to emphasize the importance of early communication in relation to close bodily contact. The earliest and most effective signal an infant gives of his state is crying, and even in my white, middle-class American sample, in which most mothers had been advised not to pick up a crying baby, the overwhelming majority of mothers responded by picking the baby up and holding him (Bell & Ainsworth, 1972). How the mother holds a baby after having picked him up also was found to be important. Babies who turned out to be securely attached to their mothers at the end of the first year had mothers who more often handled and held their babies tenderly and carefully and/or affectionately (Ainsworth, Blehar, Waters, & Wall, 1978). Such babies also had mothers who responded relatively promptly to crying signals. It may be assumed that what is conveyed from the mother when a baby is picked up promptly when upset and held tenderly is closeness and comfort. Not only do babies responded to in this manner stop crying relatively quickly and sink in comfortably against the mother's body, but also after many repetitions of this scenario they learn to trust their mothers to be accessible and responsive, and they become securely attached to them. (The association of maternal sensitivity with secure attachment has been noted in a variety of studies [Egeland & Farber, 1984; Pederson et al., 1990; Smith & Pederson, 1988]). A different message comes through to babies whose mothers delay unduly in responding to their cries and in offering close contact, or respond without giving the comfort of contact, or handle the baby roughly, impatiently, or tensely. Such babies either learn that they cannot rely on their mothers to give comfort when they need it or, to the extent that the mother is consistent in ignoring or rebuffing their bids for comforting, they come to feel rejected. As far as attachment theory is concerned, this very early kind of emotional interaction is significant because it clearly influences the quality of the eventual attachment an infant forms to the mother.

However, emotional communication between mother and infant does not necessarily constitute social referencing. It is generally agreed that social referencing does not begin until the third or fourth quarter of the first year. Nevertheless, the nature of early emotional communication between mother and infant, whether in the context of close bodily contact or otherwise, does influence the quality of infant–mother attachment (Ainsworth et al., 1978), which seems also to be established at approximately the same time that social referencing has been observed to begin. Therefore, let us consider what attachment research has to offer relevant to this later period, and here I deal with my own research primarily. I focus on infant behavior during the last quarter of the first year, considering first research pertaining to a laboratory situation, and then behavior observed in the natural environment of the home.

Behavior in the Strange Situation

"The strange situation" is a laboratory situation to which the infants of our sample, accompanied by their mothers, were introduced when they were approximately 12 months of age. First, the infant is introduced to the room, which contains a massive array of toys expected strongly to activate exploratory behavior and to override any tendency for infant attachment behavior to the mother to be ascendant. The mother had been instructed to be noninterventive, although if the baby clearly wanted her to respond to one of his initiatives, she was to do whatever seemed to her appropriate. Indeed, it was suggested that she read a magazine, or pretend to do so. After this mother–baby episode when the only common stress was the unfamiliarity of the physical environment, a series of episodes followed that were intended to be cumulatively stressful, the first being the entrance of a female stranger. It is this episode when stranger, mother, and baby are together that is particularly salient to social referencing.

This episode could be predicted by attachment theory to be a conflict situation. At least four different behavioral systems were likely to be activated, the first two having been in potential conflict even in the preceding mother–baby episode, namely: (1) attachment behavior which would lead the baby to seek proximity to the mother, and (2) exploratory behavior which would lead him to approach the toys and to manipulate them. With the entrance of the stranger two more behavioral systems potentially come into play: (3) the wariness/fear system—because the new person is unfamiliar, and in that sense strange, and strangeness is considered to be one of the natural clues to the threat of danger identified by Bowlby (1973)—and (4) the affiliative or sociable system, which would lead an infant to approach even an unfamiliar conspecific with friendly interaction in mind.

This stranger–mother–baby episode was designed to last 3 minutes. During the first minute the stranger said "Hello! I'm the stranger" upon entering, and then sat quietly in her chair, having been instructed not to initiate interaction with either the infant or mother, but to respond appropriately to the infant should he smile, vocalize, or approach her. We wanted her to give the baby a chance to size her up, and thus avoid frightening him as she might do if she approached immediately. Meanwhile, the mother remained noninterventive, and indeed silent. At the beginning of the second minute, however, the stranger was to initiate pleasant conversation with the mother. This was intended to show the infant that this unfamiliar person was one whom the mother could accept positively. We expected that infants would check out the mother's response to the stranger, and that observing her natural positive response might overcome any natural tendency of their own to be wary of the stranger. Then at the beginning of the third minute, the stranger did indeed try to initiate interaction with the baby, through the expedient of offering him a toy.

We certainly expected to observe manifestations of social referencing in this episode, even though "social referencing" was not part of our vocabulary then. We expected that when the stranger entered, the baby might look toward the mother for some clue about how to respond to her. Virtually all of the 106 infants in our sample looked first at the stranger, and in the majority of the cases this look was prolonged for at least 5 seconds, and in one case as long as 45 seconds (Bretherton & Ainsworth, 1974). Then 30% averted their gaze, which implies that they did not then immediately look at the mother. During the first minute when the stranger remained silent, the mean frequency of looks to the mother was 1.7, whereas the mean frequency of looks to the stranger was 4.2. The looks to the mother tended to be brief, and our impression was that infants were merely checking her availability, as indeed babies tended occasionally to do in the preceding episode when most of their time was spent in exploratory activity. In any event, these brief glances were unlikely to yield clear-cut affective information, for the mothers themselves tended to be watching the stranger with a fairly neutral expression. Some babies, upon the stranger's entrance, more or less immediately retreated to their mothers, and most of these turned around, perhaps leaning back against mother's knees to stare at the stranger, and perhaps even to smile at her from that point of vantage. It seems that the main point at issue was mother's availability rather than mother as an agent for helping the baby to interpret the situation, guiding him as to how to feel and thus how to act.

During the second minute, while stranger and mother conversed pleasantly, I had expected that the baby would look back and forth from one to the other, and would indeed be reassured by the positive tone of their interaction. Although some did look back and forth, there were still, on the average, significantly more looks at the stranger than at the mother. In the final minute of the episode, after the stranger had approached with her toy, the babies' attention was almost wholly focused on the stranger. Some glanced at the mother once, but half of the sample did not glance at the mother until the very end of the episode when she was attempting to leave the room unobtrusively—which suggests that the babies were alert to her whereabouts even though their gaze had been directed elsewhere.

There is no doubt that this episode was an uncertain or ambiguous one for the great majority of the babies, for nearly all showed signs of experiencing conflicting reactions to the stranger, evincing both positive, affiliative interest *and* wariness. Of 106, only 12 were fearful or wary, manifesting no affiliative behavior, whereas only 4 displayed affiliative behavior with no sign of wariness. In retrospect it seems to me that the infants were watching the *stranger* and her actions for information as how to resolve their uncertainty, rather than looking at the mother for such information. Indeed, the main issue for the infant seemed to be the availability of the mother rather than any information she might offer him that would resolve uncertainty about how to respond to the stranger. This view is congruent with Emde's (Chapter 4, this volume), based on observation of 1-year-olds in a modified strange situation (see also Clyman, Emde, Kempe, & Harmon, 1986). Both he and Hornik, Mangelsdorf, and Gunnar (Chapter 9, this volume) suggested that for the infant in the second half of the first year the main issue is indeed the availability of the mother.

Bretherton and Ainsworth (1974) did not include in their report how individual differences in the stranger–mother–baby episode related to the security of the infant's attachment to the mother. However, a subsequent analysis showed that 12-month-olds who showed clear-cut fear of the stranger in that episode were proportionally more frequent among anxious–ambivalent infants than among those who were either anxious–avoidant or secure in their attachment to the mother. This seems reasonably congruent with the findings of Dickstein, Thompson, Estes, Malkin, and Lamb (1984), who reported that in their sample of 19.5-month-olds the highest frequency of social referencing (i.e., looking at the mother after having looked at the stranger) occurred with those whose attachment to the mother was anxious–ambivalent, the lowest with those who were anxious–avoidant, whereas those who were securely attached were intermediate. The differentiation among groups was only marginally significant, however, despite the fact that one might expect social referencing in the second half of the second year of life to be less obscured by the issue of maternal availability than it appears to be at the end of the first year. On the other hand, it could be that the strange situation is far from an ideal situation in which to observe social referencing, if only because the instructions to the mother to be noninterventive deter her from intentionally providing clear informational signals to the baby about how to feel about or how to respond to the stranger, and it is unlikely that she would inadvertently express either a strongly positive or a strongly negative emotional response to a pleasant person who is a total stranger to her as well as to the baby.

Behavior at Home

My associates and I undertook longitudinal observation in the natural environment of the home with two samples of infant–mother dyads, in neither of which was the mother's behavior in any way controlled by instructions. In the case of both samples the infant's response to the visitor–observer as a stranger appears to offer the most useful instance of a situation in which social referencing might occur.

One sample consisted of 26 white, middle-class infant–mother dyads in the Baltimore area. They were observed every 3 weeks from 3 to 54 weeks, each visit lasting approximately 4 hours. Nearly always it was the same visitor–observer who came for each visit, so there was clearly the opportunity for the stranger to become less unfamiliar in the course of the first year. Furthermore, from about 3 weeks onward there was clearly a familiarization process in the course of the visit, so that (in all but one case) the baby seemed to become more comfortable with the observer in the course of the visit. Yet also from about 3 months onward, the initial arrival of the observer evoked a staring response, and we did not notice any general tendency for the babies either to check with their mothers before this long stare or to behave decisively in one way or another after subsequently checking with their mothers. In short, we were not struck with a tendency for this situation to be one that evoked obvious social referencing. On the other hand, the response of infants to the observer as stranger in the course of our 72 hours of observation of each has not yet been analyzed, so I can speak only from general impressions at this time. Furthermore, this situation also was perhaps not an ideal one in which to study social referencing, for two reasons. First, the observers bent every effort to avoid upsetting the baby, both because they did not want to damage rapport with the mother, and because their primary goal was to observe mother–infant interaction that was as natural and spontaneous as possible despite the presence of an outsider. Second, the mothers themselves tended to extend welcome to the observers as guests, and thus were initially focused on the observer rather than on the baby, and behaved toward the observer in a generally positive way. Thus the observers tried to present themselves as unambiguously nonthreatening, and the mother tended to give only signals of a positive response to the observer.

The other (chronologically antecedent) sample was of 28 infant–mother dyads observed in their homes in villages about 15 miles from Kampala, Uganda (Ainsworth, 1967, 1977). The only criterion for inclusion in the sample was that the baby be unweaned. Consequently, the ages of the infant at the onset of the study varied substantially. The visits were of 2-hour duration occurring approximately every 2 weeks, and there were two visitors—my Ganda assistant–interpreter and myself. One notable difference between the Ganda and the Baltimore mothers was that the former, as a customary part of their welcome to a guest, gave the baby to one or other of the two visitors to hold. The younger the infant the more readily he accepted the stranger. However, from the third quarter onward fear of strangers emerged, and it was very much more clear cut, more dependable, and more intense than in the Baltimore sample—and this was especially true in the case of infants who were over 8 months old when visits first began. This striking fear I attribute chiefly to the fact that Ganda infants had far less experience with strangers than does the typical middle-class American infant. Be that as it may, the Ganda infants who showed intense fear of the stranger scuttled as fast as they could to the mother, climbed onto her lap, and hid their faces against her body, peeking out occasionally to look at the stranger, only to hide the face again should they catch the stranger's eye. As with the Baltimore sample in the strange situation, the key issue when faced with a stranger seemed to be proximity to or contact with the mother, rather than information derived from the mother's behavior to the stranger.

Another aspect of my longitudinal studies may be worthy of mention here in light of Emde's suggestion (Chapter 4, this volume) that social referencing has an important mediating role in the process of internalizing restraints as a consequence of parental prohibitions. We examined infant responses to maternal commands and prohibitions in the Baltimore sample in the last quarter of the first year (Stayton, Hogan, & Ainsworth, 1971). Many but by no means all of these commands were indeed prohibitions, such as "No! no!" "Don't touch!" or "Stop!"

There were substantial positive correlations (r = .65 to .67) between the proportion of commands complied with and the ratings of the mothers on scales of cooperation–interference, acceptance–rejection and sensitivity–insensitivity to infant signals—scales that were later found to differentiate very significantly between the mothers of babies who were securely attached to them and the mothers of those who were anxiously attached. Babies who by the end of the first year were identified as securely attached complied with 81% of maternal commands during the preceding quarter-year, whereas those who were anxiously attached and avoidant complied with 54%, and those who were anxious and ambivalent complied with 44%. Our observers did not consistently note whether the baby looked at the mother before or while complying with her prohibition, but it is inconceivable to me that they did not. But those who did not comply with a prohibition usually were noted *not* to have looked—except that occasionally a baby might look as though to ascertain if mother really "meant" a command issued in a soft rather than in a sharp tone of voice. In short, it seems that infants whose experience with their mothers had engendered trust and hence secure attachment tended to heed their mothers' commands and (in the course of the heeding) engage in social referencing in terms of which they complied or failed to comply, whereas those who experience had been with mothers who were not well tuned-in to their signals and behavioral communications, and who thus were not securely attached, tended to pay no attention to mothers' commands and thus neither to comply with them nor to engage in social referencing.

Manifestations of internalized control (or self-inhibition) were infrequent at this early age. They were themselves fairly substantially correlated with the maternal ratings mentioned above (r = .40 to .42), and more strongly with the amount of floor freedom allowed the child (r = .47) and DQ (r = .52). Thus there is some evidence here to support Emde's suggestion, in that the same kind of maternal behavior that is associated with secure attachment and with heeding and complying with mother's commands (and thus implying being able to use mother as a referee whose signals guide behavior) is associated with being able to internalize such guidance so that the infant can, for example, when he is about to touch the prohibited base plug draws his hand back, perhaps even verbalizing a "No! no!" and desists, without needing to look to his mother for guidance.

However, our findings also suggest that such capacity for internalized control also depends upon (1) sufficient experience with freedom to explore so that mother has already had occasion to prohibit the behavior at issue, and upon (2) the infant's general developmental level.

RELEVANT ASPECTS OF ATTACHMENT THEORY

As I suggested earlier, attachment theory is an open-ended theory with eclectic underpinnings. It has areas of congruency with a variety of other theoretical approaches, and hence it is not surprising to find much in attachment theory that is akin to concepts of the theoretical backgrounds from which various views of social referencing proceed. Here I wish to discuss several aspects of attachment theory that I myself have found especially pertinent when considering how the concept of social referencing relates to attachment. These four aspects are: (1) feeling and emotion; (2) components of relationships; (3) "working models" of attachment figure and of self; and (4) perspective taking, communication, and mutually agreed plans.

Feeling and Emotion

In Volume 1 of his trilogy, *Attachment and Loss*, Bowlby (1969) espoused an appraisal theory of feeling and emotion, and in this he finds common ground with theories of social referencing. I was particularly struck by the emphasis on emotion as appraisal in Emde's work (Chapter 4, this volume, but especially in Klinnert, Campos, Sorce, Emde, & Svejda, 1983) and in the work by Hornik *et al.* (Chapter 9, this volume). Bowlby holds that the appraisal function of feelings (or affect) has obvious influence on subsequent action, whether the information has been sought or merely received, and whether the appraisal is felt (conscious) or unfelt (unconscious)—that is, whether the information is processed at the highest, conscious level, or at some lower level in the hierarchy of information processing. Because affect influences behavior, it may also communicate information to others. Bowlby stressed the affective components of attachments, whether they be positive (e.g., feeling joyful, delighted, or secure) or negative (e.g., feeling distressed, anxious, sad, angry, or jealous). Implicit in his position is an emphasis on the significance of affective communication between partners in an attachment relationship. Throughout his trilogy, however, it seems to me that the stress is on appraising the implications of the behavior of significant others merely received as input rather than on actively seeking such information from the behavior of the other.

Fear. Insofar as Bowlby conceived the biological function of attachment behavior to be protection, it follows that appraisal of input relevant to the threat of danger is particularly relevant to attachment theory. Indeed, the first third of Volume 2 in the *Attachment and Loss* trilogy is devoted to a theory of fear (Bowlby, 1973). He distinguished between two components of situations that activate fear behavior: (1) environmental stimuli arousing *alarm* and (2) the unavailability of an attachment figure arousing *anxiety*. When both components are present, both fear and the attachment system tend to be activated at high intensity. The individual simultaneously seeks to avoid the alarming stimulus and to regain proximity to an attachment figure, and in this sense the two systems are usually in synchrony. In regard to alarm, he identified certain natural clues to the threat of danger, including clues such as loud noise and sudden approach, but also strangeness and aloneness. Even though such clues by no means always indicate danger, to behave fearfully in response to them is likely to have yielded enough edge of survival advantage for such behavior to have been naturally selected in the course of evolution and thus for members of the species to have become genetically biased to respond in this way. It may be noted that this formulation resembles that of Bandura (Chapter 8, this volume), who specifies that it is features of objects or situations rather than specific classes of objects, animate or inanimate, that arouse fear.

Bowlby acknowledged that fears may also be learned through both one's own painful experiences and observation of the behavior of others, and he held that the intensity of fearful reactions to even natural clues of danger may be considerably reduced by various desensitization influences, and in this connection he cited Bandura's work at some length. Nevertheless, a compound fear situation that combines several natural clues to danger may activate fear even in a normal adult, especially if he encounters them when alone; and any human companionship, but especially the presence of a trusted figure, may mitigate such fear.

All of this seems quite compatible with the notion of social referencing, and yet it still gives the edge to proximity-keeping rather than to active search for clues to action on the basis of the emotional expression of the trusted figure. There seem to be two experimental situations that have been demonstrated to be most likely to increase the search for and/or receptivity to social referencing clues. In the first type of situation, a young child encounters either a stranger or an animated toy, each of which embody in fairly equal balance both (1) natural clues to danger and (2) clues to activate either sociable behavior or exploratory activity. The facial expression of the mother, or indeed her vocal or gestural clues, may tip the balance in one way or the other.

On the other hand, Harlow's infant monkeys, frightened in an open field situation, first dashed to the surrogate mother as a haven of safety, and then, as though being assured of her availability, turned to appraise the situation visually, and then ventured out from mother to explore the previously alarming situation, having used as a secure base a mother figure who, being inanimate, could be accessible but who could provide neither behavioral nor expressive cues. Their behavior was in striking contrast to the behavior they displayed when the surrogate mother figure had *not* been placed in the open field; they appeared to be simply terrified throughout, huddling passively, and exhibiting no exploratory behavior. Similarly, when the infant monkeys were frightened by a toy gorilla beating a drum, they fled to the terry-cloth mother, clung, and then after looking at the gorilla from their secure base, approached the toy, explored it, and in some instances proceeded to destroy it (Harlow, 1961). In these experiments it was clearly the availability of the mother figure that made the difference between fearful and exploratory behavior and presumably also between fear of the unfamiliar and interest in it.

Young children may be sufficiently reassured by the mere presence of the mother, especially if they are secure and confident of her availability, that they will explore an unfamiliar situation or approach a somewhat alarming but interesting object, without even seeking more specific information from her, as may be seen in the "strange situation." Availability may thus be enough, as with the monkeys—which is not to say that initial uncertainty might not be resolved by a glance at the mother (social referencing) followed by exploratory behavior in the absence of a strong contrary signal from her.

The second type of situation is somewhat different—the visual cliff. Here a baby's conflict is between a natural desire to seek increased proximity to the mother and a desire to avoid a natural clue to danger, namely, a visual clue to a loss-of-support situation. Mother's encouragement for him to approach may overcome the natural tendency to avoid the apparent danger, whereas the tendency to avoid may be confirmed if the mother herself displays fear. This kind of situation perhaps provides the clearest demonstration of how emotional information offered by the mother may influence the behavior of an infant. It is of interest, however, that in order to equalize the approach-mother and avoid-danger tendencies it was necessary to decrease the apparent drop of the visual cliff before avoidant tendencies could be overcome. Be that as it may, this situation first makes the mother seem inaccessible to the baby by interposing the danger stimulus between them, and in this it differs from the first type of situation in which increasing proximity to mother and avoidance of perceived danger are synchronous. Thus, even though the visual cliff experiment highlights social referencing, it by no means conflicts with the contention that maternal availability is the chief issue for an infant in an ambiguous situation.

Facial Expression of Emotion.   Before we leave the topic of emotions, let me address the issue of whether, to use Bandura's terms (Chapter 8, this volume), facial expressions are innate vicarious instigators of emotion, and therefore presumably of appropriate action. Attachment theory holds that infant signaling behavior, such as crying, smiling, and vocalizing, has evolved as a class of species-characteristic behaviors because it was of survival value in the environment in which the human species first emerged. It had such value because it tended to activate complementary proximity-keeping behavior on the part of the adult who perceived the signal—who is usually the principal caregiver, the mother figure. This implies that the adult of the species has some genetically biased tendency to respond to such infant signals. Indeed, it is difficult for me to conceive of facial expressions as having taken species-characteristic forms except as they communicate significant information to others. Certainly facial expression *per se* can have no effect on the inanimate environment, and would seem to accomplish nothing except insofar as it conveys information to others, whether the individual intended to send a communication or not. Furthermore, as implied in the responsiveness of adults to infant signals, facial expression could scarcely have evolved to be part of the signaling repertoire of the species without some complementary receptive sensitivity to such signals having been evolved also. Despite the fact that we can learn to control our facial expressions to some extent, inhibiting them or faking them, the occurrence of similar expressions across many cultures suggests that there is indeed some innate basis for both sending such signals and for receiving them and interpreting them.

Species-characteristic signals were perhaps especially evolved as modes communicating emotions and their associated impetus to action, in that they tend to be associated with one or other of the major species-characteristic behavioral systems. Thus they may be considered as especially pertinent to social referencing. Let us consider the case of the attachment system of the infant and the complementary caregiving system of the adult. Once infants have developed locomotor ability, it becomes important that the caregiver be able to exert some control over them from across a distance, whether by deterring them doing something dangerous or by inducing them to approach her, thus both distancing them from the danger and bringing them closer to the chief protective figure. Facial expressions, as well as gestures and vocalizations, may be used as signals in such a situation.

Components of a Relationship

There has been an unfortunate tendency to assume that all aspects of interaction of a person with an attachment figure are somehow pertinent to the nature of the attachment to that figure. Hinde's (1976) view of relationships is instructive in this context. He suggests that a relationship is based on all of the interactions two individuals have had with each other, and that the nature of such interactions may indeed be various. According to attachment theory, the interactions that are focal to attachment are those having to do with proximity maintenance, protection, and other caregiving. However, a mother may indeed play roles other than caregiver in interaction with her infant or young child: the two roles that most readily occur to me are the roles of playmate and teacher. In middle-class American dyads a mother is likely to play all three roles, but this is not necessarily the case in other cultures. Thus, for example, among the Ganda I observed only one mother playing with her baby; among the Ganda the caregiving role is the one that was emphasized almost to the exclusion of the other two roles (Ainsworth, 1967). Ganda infants whose mothers were accessible to them and sensitively responsive to their signals developed to be securely attached, despite the fact that their mothers did not play with them, rarely engaged in face-to-face interaction, and did not supply them with toys or other materials to encourage their cognitive development. And indeed in the first year they did precious little of what one could call teaching or training, except to intervene if the baby strayed into a dangerous situation.

Attachment theory distinguishes between the relationship a child has with a figure who is primarily a caregiver and figures who are primarily playmates or teachers. Infants or young children are almost certain to become attached to their most significant caregivers, but although they may seek proximity to a playmate they are unlikely to become attached to him, unless somehow their interaction fosters something of the same kind of concern with the accessibility and responsiveness of that figure that is inherent in the infant–caregiver relationship. Similarly, an infant or young child may indeed learn from those who merely take a teaching role, but does not become attached to the person solely through the interaction implicit in that role.

These considerations would tend to place the emphasis on affective social referencing rather than on instrumental social referencing insofar as their relationship to attachment is concerned. Mother-as-teacher may indeed give the child guidance as how to act with regard to objects to be manipulated in the physical environment, and perhaps any other pleasant and not too unfamiliar person might do as well. But when it comes to how to feel in an uncertain situation, it seems likely that an attachment figure is most apt to be chosen as a referee, especially in situations in which there is some activation of fear.

Two studies that introduced infants to potentially fear-arousing objects with a familiarized stranger present as well as the mother are pertinent to this issue. Zarbatany and Lamb (1985) reported social referencing in 12-month-olds directed toward the mother but not to a familiarized stranger when faced by a large mobile toy spider. Klinnert, Emde, Butterfield, and Campos (1986) found that when the mother looked puzzled in response to a robot entering the room, the familiarized stranger's affective responses influenced infant behavior. Indeed, it seems reasonable that, when social referencing occurs, one's response may be guided by a relatively unfamiliar referee, if the familiar referee of first choice does not resolve the uncertainty that may be deemed to have led to the social referencing in the first place. But, if the object in question arouses clear-cut fear rather than uncertainty (or wariness), one would not expect social referencing to occur, but rather some direct action whether it be avoidance or signaling for help, without having first made a visual check with a referee. Thus Zarbatany and Lamb (1985) found that the social referencing effect was not found even for the mother when the infant was initially afraid of the spider.

Working Models of Attachment Figure(s) and of Self

One important aspect of Bowlby's attachment theory that many have overlooked until recently is his emphasis on children's gradual development of working models (internal representational models) of their attachment figures and complementary models of themselves (Ainsworth & Bowlby, 1991; Bowlby, 1988). It is my belief that the bases for such models develop very early in the form of expectations of the routines favored by the principal caregiver and of her behavior in response to the infant's signals (Ainsworth, 1983, 1985). Sander and his associates (Sander, 1969; Burns, Sander, Stechler, & Julia, 1972) have demonstrated how even in the first week or so of life babies' sleep–wake activity, and hunger cycles alter in response to the caregiver. My own research convinces me that even during the first 3 months of life babies build up expectations of how their mothers will respond to their crying (Bell & Ainsworth, 1972) or behave in the context of close bodily contact (Ainsworth, 1979). By the time a baby is cognitively capable of conceiving of a person as existing even though not currently present to perception (and this is indexed by the onset of separation distress), he surely has some kind of internal representation of that person. We have evidence that suggests that this occurs sometime in the second half of the first year (Ainsworth, 1967; Stayton, Ainsworth, & Main, 1973), and we have linked it to Piaget's Stage IV of sensorimotor development (Piaget, 1954), at least in terms of its beginnings. Initially, this internal model may be based on expectations. Thus a baby whose mother has been fairly consistent in her sensitive responsiveness to his behavioral signals develops a model of her as dependably available, and to be trusted to continue to be so. Similarly, if she has been only inconsistently accessible and responsive, the baby's model of her is of someone whose whereabouts cannot be depended upon, and whose responsiveness is unreliable even when she is accessible, and so on.

The theory goes on to specify that a child also gradually builds up a working model of self, complementary to his working model of the attachment figure, although it is not yet clear when this emerges. Bowlby, however, suggested that when the model of the principal attachment figure is of an accessible, responsive, caring person who can thus be trusted, the model of the self would reflect self-worth, someone lovable and worthy of care, attention, support, and protection. As Webster and Foschi point out (Chapter 11, this volume), notions of this sort have been around for a long time, for example, in the work of Cooley, Mead, Sullivan, and others. Recently, empirical support has been given to this position by Cassidy (1985), who, using several measures of self-esteem, found that 6-year-olds' self-esteem varied in relationship to the pattern of attachment they manifested toward the mother in a reunion situation after an hour-long separation. Thus, attachment theory is totally congruent with the identification as a social referencing phenomenon that a person's feelings about himself reflect the person's appraisals of the feelings others express to and about him.

However, Bowlby's concept of working models is much more complex than I have so far suggested. When a child's interaction with an attachment figure includes highly contradictory episodes, or when what the child is told by an attachment figure about her feelings to him conflict with what he would conclude from actual experiences with her, two or more incompatible models may be formed, of which one tends to be in ascendance and conscious, although the others that are not readily accessible continue to influence his feelings and behavior (Bowlby, 1980). In other words, an attachment figure may give the child mixed messages about himself, leading to conflicting internal models of the self—and this in turn may lead to variable self-esteem, which makes it difficult to obtain valid and reliable measures of the self-concept.

Furthermore, even in infancy a child is likely to have more than one attachment figure, and interaction with the second (or third) may lead to a working model that differs from that of the principal attachment figure and consequently also a different model of the self. This is suggested by the fact that the quality of an infant's attachment to the mother does not enable one to predict the quality of his attachment to the father (Grossmann, Grossmann, Huber, & Wartner, 1981; Lamb, 1978; Main & Weston, 1981), or, at best, it is only a partial predictor (Easterbrooks, 1989). Similarly, there appears to be no correlation between quality of attachment to substitute caregivers and that to mother or father (Goossens & van IJzendoorn, 1990).

Attachment theorists (e.g., Bretherton, 1985; Main, Kaplan, & Cassidy, 1985) have suggested that eventually there tends to be some kind of integration of these various models into a generalized model of attachment and attachment relationships. Whenever such a generalized model can be achieved (and it is likely that not all people achieve the integration), then presumably a generalized model of the self would be complementary to it. Thus, current attachment theory has something akin to the notion of the model of the self being complementary to the concept of the "generalized other" that Webster and Foschi mention (Chapter 11, this volume).

Perspective Taking, Communication, and Mutually Agreed Plans

It is all too often assumed that attachment theory is concerned wholly with the attachment of an infant to a parent or parents, and thus that attachment pertains only to infancy. Indeed, in the first volume of *Attachment and Loss,* Bowlby (1969) did focus largely on infancy. However, even there he has an important chapter on the fourth and final phase of development of attachment, a phase that he identifies as "the goal-corrected partnership." In the first three phases, which last somewhat beyond infancy, a child may adapt himself to the behavior he has come to expect of a caregiver, but he has no effective way of altering her behavior to make it more congruent with his wishes and plans, except insofar as the caregiver's sensitive responsiveness to behavioral signals prompts her to alter her own plans better to suit what she infers that the child wants. This state of affairs gradually changes as the young child becomes more and more adept in verbal communication. The child becomes better able to convey his feelings, wishes, and plans to her, and to some extent the child can comprehend what she tries to convey in words about her feelings, motives, and plans. An understanding of her is, however, vastly improved when he becomes capable of even simple conceptual perspective taking, which according to Marvin's research generally emerges in the fourth year of life (Marvin, 1977; Marvin & Greenberg, 1982). With improved verbal communication and perspective taking, it becomes possible for the young child to learn more about the mother's feelings, motivation, and plans, and to attempt to negotiate with her until a common plan is mutually agreed upon. The give and take implicit in such negotiation constitutes a partnership. Although there may be developmental changes enabling partners to become increasingly adept in accommodating to each other, this notion of goal-corrected partnership, Bowlby suggests, is characteristic of attachments to specified others throughout the rest of life.

Although one would not suppose that the kind of social referencing that is characteristic of infants would altogether disappear, presumably it becomes a less frequent way of adjusting one's actions upon the receipt of input from significant others. No doubt information continues to be conveyed silently through expressive behavior, including facial expression, and to be received and often acted upon by the partner. But more commonly verbal communication becomes the preferred channel. Some of the chapters in this volume (e.g., Chapter 3, by Bretherton) seem to be geared to the verbal child (and/or adult), and to include within the concept of social referencing the verbal mode of communication. Furthermore, both Emde (Chapter 4, this volume) and Rogoff *et al.* (Chapter 13, this volume) suggest that social referencing becomes more and more a negotiated construction, for which undoubtedly verbal communication is required; this notion is clearly congruent with the notion that the attachment becomes increasingly identifiable as a goal-corrected partnership.

Verbal communication ties in with attachment theory's concept of multiple working models of the attachment figure and the self. Although it is believed to be mentally healthy for the person to be able eventually to integrate these into one comprehensive set of models of self and other, some find their models too conflicting for such integration to be achieved. It would appear that in such cases the conflicting models become separately consolidated, and often enough this is because what has been conveyed by the partner in expressive behavior does not match the semantic content of what is verbally conveyed.

SUMMARY

In summary, the concept of social referencing refers to a variety of processes through which the behavior of another influences one's own behavior. Insofar as the "other" is often an attachment figure, especially during infancy and early childhood, there is overlap and much congruence between the theory and research pertinent to social referencing and attachment theory and research. In regard to social referencing in infancy, attachment theory appears to be far more relevant to referencing based on affective communication than that based on instrumental communication. Attachment theory's concept of working models (or inner representational models) of self and significant others overlaps substantially with the broader view of social referencing relevant to the older child or adult that imply verbal communication.

REFERENCES

Ainsworth, M. D. S. (1967). *Infancy in Uganda: Infant care and the growth of love.* Baltimore: Johns Hopkins Press.

Ainsworth, M. D. S. (1977). Infant development and mother–infant interaction among Ganda and American families. In P. H. Leiderman, S. R. Tulkin, & A. Rosenfeld (Eds.), *Culture and infancy: Variations in the human experience* (pp. 119–149). New York: Academic Press.

Ainsworth, M. D. S. (1979). Attachment as related to mother–infant interaction. In J. S. Rosenblatt, R. A. Hinde, C. Beer, & M. Busnel (Eds.), *Advances in the study of behavior* (Vol. 9, pp. 1–51). New York: Academic Press.

Ainsworth, M. D. S. (1983). Patterns of infant–mother attachment as related to maternal care: Their early history and their contribution to continuity. In D. Magnusson & V. L. Allen (Eds.), *Human development: An interactional perspective* (pp. 35–55). New York: Academic Press.

Ainsworth, M. D. S. (1985). Attachments across the life span. *Bulletin of the New York Academy of Medicine, 61*, 792–812.

Ainsworth, M. D. S., Blehar, M. C., Waters, E., & Wall, S. (1978). *Patterns of attachment: A psychological study of the strange situation.* Hillsdale, NJ: Erlbaum.

Ainsworth, M. D. S., & Bowlby, J. (1991). An ethological approach to personality development. *American Psychologist, 46*, 333–341.

Bell, S. M., & Ainsworth, M. D. S. (1972). Infant crying and maternal responsiveness. *Child Development, 43*, 1171–1190.

Bowlby, J. (1969). *Attachment and loss, Vol. 1: Attachment.* New York: Basic Books.

Bowlby, J. (1973). *Attachment and loss. Vol. 2: Separation: Anger and anxiety.* New York: Basic Books.

Bowlby, J. (1980). *Attachment and loss. Vol. 3: Loss: Sadness and depression.* New York: Basic Books.

Bowlby, J. (1988). Developmental psychiatry comes of age. *American Journal of Psychiatry, 145*, 1–10.

Bretherton, I. (1985). Attachment theory: Retrospect and prospect. In I. Bretherton & E. Waters (Eds.), *Growing points of attachment theory and research. Monographs of the Society for Research in Child Development, 50*, Serial No. 209, pp. 3–35.

Bretherton, I., & Ainsworth, M. D. S. (1974). Responses of one-year-olds to a stranger in a strange situation. In M. Lewis & L. A. Rosenblum (Eds.), *The origin of fear* (pp. 131–164). New York: Wiley.

Burns, P., Sander, L. W., Stechler, G., & Julia, H. (1972). Distress in feeding: Short-term effects of caretaker environments in the first 10 days. *Journal of the American Academy of Child Psychiatry, 11*, 427–439.

Campos, J. J. (1983). The importance of affective communication in social referencing: A commentary on Feinman. *Merrill-Palmer Quarterly, 29*, 83–87.

Cassidy, J. (1985). *The self as related to attachment in the sixth year.* Unpublished Ph.D. dissertation, University of Virginia.

Clyman, R. B., Emde, R. N., Kempe, J. E., & Harmon, R. J. (1986). Social referencing and social looking among twelve-month-old infants. In T. B. Brazelton & M. W. Yogman (Eds.), *Affective development in infancy* (pp. 75–94). Norwood, NJ: Ablex.

Dickstein, S., Thompson, R. A., Estes, D., Malkin, C., & Lamb, M. E. (1984). Social referencing and the security of attachment. *Infant Behavior and Development, 7*, 507–516.

Easterbrooks, M. A. (1989). Quality of attachment to mother and to father: Effects of perinatal risk status. *Child Development, 60*, 825–830.

Egeland, B., & Farber, E. A. (1984). Infant–mother attachment: Factors related to its development and changes over time. *Child Development, 55*, 753–771.

Feinman, S., & Lewis, M. (1983). Social referencing at ten months: A second-order effect on infants' responses to strangers. *Child Development, 54*, 878–887.

Goossens, F. A., & van IJzendoorn, M. H. (1990). Quality of infants' attachments to professional caregivers: Relation to infant–parent attachment and day-care characteristics. *Child Development, 61*, 832–837.

Grossmann, K. E., Grossmann, K., Huber, F., & Wartner, U. (1981). German children's behavior towards their mothers at 12 months and their fathers at 18 months in Ainsworth's strange situation. *International Journal of Behavioral Development, 4,* 157–181.

Harlow, H. F. (1961). The development of affectional patterns in infant monkeys. In B. M. Foss (Ed.), *Determinants of infant behaviour* (Vol. 1, pp. 75–88). New York: Wiley.

Hinde, R. A. (1976). On describing relationships. *Journal of Child Psychology and Psychiatry, 17,* 1–19.

Klinnert, M. D., Campos, J. J., Sorce, J. F., Emde, R. N., & Svejda, M. (1983). Emotions as behavior regulators: Social referencing in infancy. In R. Plutchick & H. Kellerman (Eds.), *Emotions in early development. Vol. 2: The emotions* (pp. 57–86). New York: Academic Press.

Klinnert, M., Emde, R. N., Butterfield, P., & Campos, J. J. (1986). Social referencing: The infant's use of emotional signals from a friendly adult with mother present. *Developmental Psychology, 22,* 427–432.

Lamb, M. E. (1978). Qualitative aspects of mother– and father–infant attachments. *Infant Behavior and Development, 1,* 265–275.

Main, M., Kaplan, N., & Cassidy, J. (1985). Security in infancy, childhood, and adulthood: A move to the level of representation. In I. Bretherton & E. Waters (Eds.), *Growing points of attachment theory and research. Monographs of the Society for Research in Child Development, 50,* Serial No. 209, pp. 66–104.

Main, M., & Weston, D. R. (1981). The quality of the toddler's relationship to mother and to father: Related to conflict behavior and the readiness to establish new relationships. *Child Development, 52,* 932–940.

Marvin, R. S. (1977). An ethological-cognitive model for the attenuation of mother–child attachment behavior. In T. Alloway, P. Pliner, & L. Krames (Eds.), *Advances in the study of communication and affect* (Vol. 3, pp. 25–60). New York: Plenum.

Marvin, R. S., & Greenberg, M. T. (1982). Preschoolers' changing conceptions of their mothers: A social-cognitive study of mother–child attachment. In D. Forbes & M. T. Greenberg (Eds.), *New directions in child development. Vol. 14: Development plans for behavior* (pp. 47–60). San Francisco: Jossey-Bass.

Pederson, D. R., Moran, G., Sitko, C., Campbell, K., Ghesquire, K., & Action, H. (1990). Maternal sensitivity and the security of infant–mother attachment: A Q-Sort study. *Child Development, 61,* 1974–1983.

Piaget, J. (1954). *The construction of reality in the child.* New York: Basic Books.

Sander, L. W. (1969). Regulation and organization in the early infant–caretaker system. In R. Robinson (Ed.), *Brain and early behavior* (pp. 427–439). London: Academic Press.

Smith, P. B., & Pederson, D. R. (1988). Maternal sensitivity and patterns of infant–mother attachment. *Child Development, 59,* 1097–1101.

Stayton, D. J., Ainsworth, M. D. S., & Main, M. (1973). The development of separation behavior in the first year of life: Protest, following, and greeting. *Development Psychology, 9,* 213–225.

Stayton, D. J., Hogan, R., & Ainsworth, M. D. S. (1971). Infant obedience and maternal behavior: The origins of socialization reconsidered. *Child Development, 43,* 1057–1069.

Zarbatany, L., & Lamb, M. E. (1985). Social referencing as a function of information source: Mothers versus strangers. *Infant behavior and Development, 8,* 25–33.

V

Connections and Directions

15

What Do We Know and Where Shall We Go?

Conceptual and Research Directions for Social Referencing

Saul Feinman

Our method in this book has been to examine social referencing in infancy within the context of a diversified and multifaceted framework, in order to see what can be learned by looking at this phenomenon from different perspectives. At this point, it seems appropriate to ask what we have discovered about referencing through this approach, and what we can suggest as to future directions in research and conceptualization. What can we say that sheds new light upon this process in which the infant (the referer) used another person's (the referee) interpretation of an event (the referent) to make sense of that event? This chapter aims to highlight, and present in an integrated manner, the major issues that have been raised and the suggestions for future research which have been made in the chapters of this volume.

The questions that can be asked about any phenomenon, and referencing in particular, can be divided conceptually into issues of *function, structure,* and *process.* First, what are its consequences, contributions, or func-

---

SAUL FEINMAN • Child and Family Studies, Department of Home Economics, University of Wyoming, Laramie, Wyoming 82071.

Social Referencing and the Social Construction of Reality in Infancy, edited by Saul Feinman. Plenum Press, New York, 1992.

tions? Specifically, what are the effects which are produced through social referencing and what impact do these effects have upon infants? Second, how is it organized? With regard to referencing, asking structural questions means inquiring into the social structure of who has the potential to serve as a source of information, and how the social relationship which the infant has with the referee might mediate the outcome of this activity. Third, what are the processes or mechanisms by which the phenomenon operates? In other words, how does it work? For referencing, this means describing the operating mechanisms which allow the infant to gather information from other people about specific environmental events, and then to use this input to construct an interpretation of the event, an interpretation upon which action can be based.

Unquestionably, function, structure, and process are integrally interrelated in social referencing, as they are in any phenomenon. We cannot have one without the others, and their domains overlap and influence each other. Nonetheless, the conceptual distinctions which they emphasize, by reminding us that referencing generates certain outcomes (function) through particular operating mechanisms (process) within the context of the structure of social relationships (structure), is a heuristically useful way in which to organize and present our discussion of this phenomenon. In this fashion, we begin with matters of function and then move on to those of structure and process, respectively.

ISSUES OF FUNCTION

Survival and the Social Construction of Reality

Social referencing's basic function is to serve as a central process in the social construction of reality in infancy, much in the same way that it serves this function throughout the lifespan. That other people assist infants in formulating definitions of the situation, and provide social guidance in such matters, is a theme which generally permeates the chapters of this volume, but especially those of Bretherton, Denzin, and Webster and Foschi. Social referencing is a social psychological process which lies at the interface of the individual and society on the macrosociological level, and the individual and her near environment of family and friends on the microsociological level. Much like Sullivan's (1947) discussion of the role of significant others, we can see here that social referencing serves to enculturate the infant into the ways of family, home, community, and the broader society at large. But, just as the relationship between individual and society is not a one-way street for adults, it can similarly be seen as a process of mutual influence even in infancy, in which the child can come to negotiate meaning in a back-and-forth manner with other people, as is most prominently noted in the chapter by Rogoff, Mistry, Radziszewska, and Germond. Thus, infants participate in the social construction of reality not only as beneficiaries but as benefactors as well.

The human infant lives her everyday existence in the mesh of social networks and social interaction. In this web of sociality, it is reasonable to expect that the way in which she copes with what happens around her is influenced by what others have to say about these happenings. "Since children live in families, frequently the positive or negative aspects of an event are determined for the child by how the adults are reacting" (Farran & Margolis, 1987, p. 70). Sharing knowledge with others, especially dependent children, is a normal and comforting practice, which is sometimes viewed as an essential form of altruism (Trivers, 1971). Indeed, the importance of receiving information from others, which assists in the construction of reality, is reflected in the argument that social referencing serves to reduce stress in infants' daily lives (Lerner & East, 1984). Thus, social referencing is viewed as an integral and salient aspect of the infant's everyday life, which contributes significantly to how she comes to understand her world.

It is this perspective on referencing, this view of it as a social construction of reality process in the workaday world of the infant, which underlies the emphasis placed upon the need for more natural investigation of the role this process plays. Virtually all referencing studies have been performed in the laboratory, often utilizing experimental designs which manipulate informational messages. How this process actually functions in the infant's natural environment is a matter which has received little consideration in previous research. In response to this issue, Lewis and Feiring, and Rogoff and her colleagues have shown us what referencing may be doing and how it may be functioning in the naturally occurring events of the infant's daily life. Along this line, Bretherton has noted the importance of paying less attention to demonstrating that referencing can be shown to exist in the laboratory, and more attention to examining individual differences in how social referencing operates within the young child's social construction of reality. Similarly, Emde's call for studies of infant social referencing in natural settings is based upon his concern that the processes observed in the laboratory may differ from those which operate in the real world.

Although research on how other people influence the individual's response to stimuli in adults has been connected intimately with real-world issues and social problems, such as Milgram's (1974) consideration of how conformity may facilitate some of the most horrifying of historical events, referencing studies have virtually ignored the connection of referencing with the relationship between individual and society. A focus on referencing within more natural settings and in the context of the infant's relationship with family and society will serve to connect it to the actual experiences and issues of which infants' lives are made.

Predictive Validity and Control.   Identifying referencing as a contributor to the social construction of reality then begs the question of why it is important for infants (or individuals of any age) to define reality. The obvious answer is that it assists the individual in predicting and controlling her environment. As suggested by the work of Gewirtz and Peláez-Nogueras, referencing messages which anticipate the event's occurrence serve the function of helping the infant predict the consequences of contact with referent events; thus, others' interpretational cues possess predictive validity. Indeed, it can be expected that infants will cease their reliance upon referees whose referencing communication does not manifest such predictive value. Most broadly, referencing is important because it helps the infant survive and succeed through the definitional assistance provided by others.

Survival and success can be achieved only if the individual formulates an adaptive course of action which takes her out of harm's way. Social referencing aids in the prediction and control of such "injurious agency," as Bandura so aptly notes. It is essential that the individual be able both to predict and to control (i.e., formulate an adaptive response to) environmental events. It has been suggested that referencing contributes to the infant's ability to do both of these—emotional referencing (or more generally, the use of any cues which are correlated, in advance, with occurrence and consequences) to her capacity to predict, and instrumental referencing to how well she can control and cope with the occurrence of these events (Hornik-Parritz, Mangelsdorf, & Gunnar). In the most general sense, referencing cues of any kind allow the infant to anticipate what will happen and what to do when a particular referent event occurs.

Instrumental versus Emotional Referencing, and Self-Efficacy. Although emotional referencing can serve to predict the consequences of an event and, as a result, frame the infant's basic affective reaction, an adaptive response calls for control as well. In addition to determining how to feel, the infant must also figure out what to do. As Bandura notes, it is action, and not affect, which really counts in survival. Although the emotional component may come first temporally, as Užgiris and Kruper suggest, and as I have suggested in an earlier paper (Feinman, 1985), it is still necessary to determine a specific course of behavior. To some extent, instrumental action, at least on the simplest level, may flow directly out of the emotional reaction—feared events are avoided, while joyful ones are approached. But for the infant to respond to the referent stimulus in a more sophisticated and flexible manner, she must receive guidance with regard to particular methods of controlling and coping with the event. Indeed, prediction without control sometimes heightens rather than reduces fear (Hornik-Parritz & colleagues). Since adaptive response depends upon control and coping, as well as upon prediction, it would appear that instrumental as well as emotional referencing plays a key role in survival.

Furthermore, there are some suggestions that learning what to do may actually be the more potent form of referencing. Both Bandura and Hornik-Parritz and her colleagues note that learning how to deal with a stimulus event can, through the achievement of control, have an impact upon the emotional definition which the infant forms of that referent. If the infant can learn how to cope with an event, then she may subsequently not find it fear provoking. In this view, it may be instrumental referencing which is the temporally prior process, in that emotional definition follows instrumental mastery. Interestingly, it is instrumental referencing, in which the infant can learn how to master the referent event, that is viewed as the factor which enhances her self-efficacy, her sense of confidence that she is competent to handle the situation (Bandura; Hornik-Parritz & colleagues). Nonetheless, it is also possible that even a purely emotional message about the referent, with no indication of coping mechanisms, such as in the visual cliff studies (Sorce, Emde, Campos, & Klinnert, 1985), can strengthen the individual's sense of self-competence (Webster & Foschi).

Without further comparative investigation of the relative effects of emotional versus instrumental referencing, the most sensible approach at this time would be to pay considerable attention to both. In this light, Emde's emphasis upon the role of emotional referencing and Rogoff and her colleagues' discussion of how referencing can demonstrate what to do (as when the infant scratches on the top of the bunny-in-the-box to indicate to the adult that she should make it pop out) speak as complementary rather than contradictory voices.

Ainsworth's suggestion that only an attachment figure will do for emotional referencing, while a wider range of potential referees is acceptable for instrumental referencing, is interesting to consider in this perspective. It may be that people other than attachment figures make perfectly good instrumental referees for stimuli that are of moderate relevance but not for those of high relevance, especially when the stimuli possess cues of danger. The suggestion, in imitation studies (which rarely are stressful), that it is the mother who defines the situation emotionally, while the experimenter (a familiarized stranger) defines it instrumentally (Užgiris & Kruper), is consistent with the assertion that Ainsworth's prediction operates in circumstances of moderate relevance. On the other hand, when environmental events place the infant in harm's way, learning what to do as well as how to feel may be most welcome from a trusted source of

information. In that case, attachment figures may be selected for instrumental as well as emotional referencing, thus further accentuating the
importance of attachment relationships in social referencing.

The Dark Side. Because referencing plays a role in survival, it has
the potential to generate maladaptive as well as adaptive consequences.
Thus, if the infant is receptive to the interpretations provided by others,
and these interpretations encourage the infant to define a dangerous situation as a safe one, or to reject a perfectly acceptable toy, then referencing
messages can lead to behaviors which work counter to adaptation. It is this
possibility which Bretherton (1984; this volume) terms "the dark side," and
it is to prevent this dark side of the force from directing infant behavior that
biological boundaries which delimit the influence of referencing may exist
(Feinman, 1985). That messages in experimental studies of referencing
typically are more or less faked has been noted in several chapters (Bandura; Bretherton; Feinman, Roberts, Hsieh, Sawyer, & Swanson; Užgiris &
Kruper). Receptivity to faked messages can serve both as a blessing and a
curse. If, for example, the mother is not afraid of the heat from a wood
stove, but wishes to teach her baby to avoid it, then the child's receptivity
to an artificial message of fear would be beneficial to survival. On the other
hand, it would allow a message which is inappropriate or even cruel to be
influential. Research on how well infants are able to resist outrageous
and/or truly dangerous messages would be of value in investigating the
dark side of referencing. Human history certainly has indicated that the
social construction of reality detracts from, as well as it contributes to,
survival. Prediction and control can be removed as easily as they can be
bestowed through the efforts of others to define the situation for the
individual. Social referencing in infancy particularly can be a double-
edged sword—which is not especially surprising, in view of the consensual belief that referencing is a process which operates in basically the
same way during infancy (despite developmental quirks) as it does
throughout the lifespan.

The Nature of the Referent

If social referencing is to contribute to adaptive response during infancy, then it must influence the way in which salient events, people, and
objects are interpreted and handled by infants. Clearly, the events which
the extant research indicates can be defined and/or redefined through
referencing (toys of questionable meaning, people whose intentions are
not known, places to fall off of) are salient in infants' lives and may even
be directly relevant to the avoidance of physical injury. In contrast, as
noted in the discussion of referencing and conformity (Feinman), much of

the study of definitional influence in adults has focused (with rare exceptions, e.g., Milgram, 1974) on referent stimuli which are not particularly central to most people's lives.

Referencing research has focused primarily upon referents which are of greatest importance during the first year of life—matters of safety, and the basic issue of how to feel and what to do with regard to environmental events in general. As the infant develops, referencing messages become effective not only with regard to objects which are present, which can be seen, heard, and touched, but also to those which are not manifestly in evidence, which can be discussed through representational conversation (Užgiris & Kruper). Thus, the range of referents is likely to expand as infants grow into toddlerhood and beyond.

Referencing serves a role in language development as well, as in the naming of new objects. The labeling activity, or "Great Word Game" (Brown, 1986), which makes up a significant share of adult–toddler conversation about objects and events is, in essence, social guidance. Naming *per se* can be considered to be instrumental referencing (what to call it), while the tone of voice usually associated with the mentioning of that label conveys the basic affective definition of the object. As Užgiris and Kruper noted, the naming of a "flower" will most likely be spoken in a rather different tone of voice than the naming of a "rag."

As infants navigate the passage into their second year of life, standards and expectations may come to be the referents of definitional messages from adults, just as roles and relationships will emerge as referents during the third year (Emde; Webster & Foschi). It seems most reasonable to assume that this developmental progression is additive rather than substitutive. The newly emergent referents do not take the place of the developmentally prior ones. Rather, in the second year toddlers will be influenced about standards as well as objects. The extant research, however, in examining referencing in the second year and beyond, has focused primarily upon issues of object safety, of whether to approach or avoid, cuddle or strike a new object, of whether to be concerned or pleased about a new person. The developmental sequences suggested by Emde, Užgiris and Kruper, and Webster and Foschi imply that research on referencing beyond the first year of life would do well to enlarge the scope of referents which are considered. Such an expansion to the examination of standards, expectations, roles, and relationships would certainly contribute to an understanding of the part that referencing plays in the real-life processes of early childhood socialization.

The Self as Referent.   How might the self and the self-image be connected to referencing? As noted earlier, self-efficacy can be enhanced as the result of learning how to cope with environmental events. Emde notes, generally, that social referencing can facilitate the emergence of the self, and Denzin points out that a theory of self, and of self and other, needs to be incorporated into our perspective on referencing. It has also been suggested that the self *per se*, the child's self-image, can be the topic of referencing communication. Webster and Foschi tell us that self-evaluation is the key dependent outcome in source theory, intimating that it is a relevant referent in referencing as well. Citing the social psychological tradition of symbolic interactionism (e.g., Mead, 1934), Ainsworth reminds us that internal representations about the self can come from other people. Furthermore, she indicates that multiple attachment relationships—and therefore multiple bases of information as well as of emotional security—could lead to different images of the self, and eventually to the integrated image reflected by the generalized other. Thus, referencing can guide the definition of the inner as well as the outer environment, influencing what the young child thinks and feels about her self as well as about the world which exists around that self.

When the self is the referent, the usually routine distinction between referer and referent becomes confounded. In this case, the toddler is both referer and referent, subject and object. In the view of referencing as an indirect effect, in which one person influences another with regard to a third person or event (Lewis & Feiring), the situation in which the self is the referent is especially intriguing. It can still be thought of as an indirect effect, but only if we view the self dualistically, and divide it into the components of objective versus subjective self, distinguishing the self as object (referent) from the self as subject (referer).

It has long been realized that, in children and adults, self-definition is influenced by other persons' reactions, expectations, and evaluations (Rosenberg, 1979)—a point that has been noted in earlier discussions of the conceptual origins of referencing (Feinman, 1982, 1985). Indeed, the very title of George Herbert Mead's classic work, *Mind, Self and Society*, reflects the role which other people play in what we think, and particularly in what we think about our selves. Webster and Foschi review much of this research on the sources of self-evaluation—indicating, for example, that school children's educational self-concept can be shaped by adults' reactions.

Exactly when such evaluative input is initially provided to very young children, and when these self-defining messages first come to have an impact on self-image is not well known. Since the most salient expectations and standards which a child learns are likely to be those which govern her own behavior, Emde's suggestion that standards emerge as a major focal topic of referencing during the second year would imply that the self comes to be a salient referent then too, during the period when self-awareness seems to develop as well (Lewis & Brooks-Gunn, 1979). It would seem that being able to divide up the self so that it can serve as both referer and referent at the same time is an ability that would not be operational until this point in developmental time.

What has been referred to as "affective social checking" (Hornik-Parritz & colleagues; Hornik & Gunnar, 1988) may be one way in which other people provide the young child with definitional messages about herself. Thus, the sequence in which the child does something with regard to the referent object, then turns to smile at the mother, and receives a message of "Oh, you are so brave!" seems to be one which could not only enhance self-efficacy with regard to the particular situation but also fortify a positive self-image more generally. It also is interesting, in this light, to examine procedures which Bandura describes as facilitating mastery learning. By observing a model demonstrate how to handle a stimulus event or object, the individual comes to feel more self-efficacious in that situation. A change has been induced in the person's self-concept (at least in this particular circumstance), but it is effected through an indirect, roundabout channel in which the apparent referent was the stimulus to be controlled, and not the individual's self-concept *per se*. The suggestion that social referencing affects the self-concept indirectly through the enhancement of self-efficacy, and directly through the conveyance of definitional messages about the self, can serve to open up new frontiers for social referencing research which focus on the impact of this process upon one of the most important referents—the self.

ISSUES OF SOCIAL STRUCTURE AND RELATIONSHIPS

Who Is the Referee?

The Selectivity Postulate.   There has been interest in the matter of selectivity since the beginning of thinking and research about social referencing (e.g., Feinman, 1982), when this feature was hypothesized to be one of the characteristic attributes of the process. Clearly, selectivity is an important issue in the more general consideration of how the individual comes, through social construction, to understand the world inside and outside of her self. For Lewis and Feiring, selectivity is inherent in the fundamental mechanism of transitivity by which the child can learn about one person through another's reaction (e.g., "I like Mom, Mom likes the doctor, so I guess I like the doctor too"). In this scheme, if a referee who is disliked conveys her disgust with a new person, than it is to be expected that this third party will be liked by the referer (because the multiplicative result of two negatives is a positive). Referencing research has not considered this possibility. All potential referees who have been available in referencing studies have been either primary caregivers (who are assumed to be trusted intimates) or familiarized strangers who typically are not disliked. The general principle which has guided work on selectivity in the study of infant social referencing is more a matter of whether the referee is perceived by the infant as capable and trustworthy than of whether she is liked *per se*, although liking and being liked may be proxy measures of trustworthiness. Nevertheless, adults seem to be capable of using transitivity mechanisms to learn that their enemy's enemy is actually their friend. Whether infants could make the reversals called for by a negative relationship with the referee, rather than simply just reject this source of information out of hand, is an intriguing question for empirical consideration.

The qualities which theories about evaluation and vicarious processes identity as being features of good models (Bandura) or sources (Webster & Foschi) bear much resemblance to referencing's focus upon expertise. Status characteristics, as Webster and Foschi note, are often accepted as surrogates for actual measures of ability and experience, which are the more reliable, but not always observable, indicators (hence the reliance upon proxies) of expertise. Similarity, especially in the form of correlated social experience, is likewise taken as an indicator of the ability to provide information relevant to our own situation (Bandura). But perceived ability, status, and similarity are better reflections of expertise than of trustworthiness. A source or model may have the ability to help us define the situation adaptively, but may be someone who cannot be trusted to refrain from deceiving us. Although research on source theory and on vicarious modeling has clearly delineated the features which lead us to perceive a person as expert and capable, it has been less energetic in delineating matters concerning trust, especially as these reside in relationships with significant others. Some of the work on selectivity in social referencing has directly concerned the matter of trust, of determining who can be counted on not to deceive us. This may reflect a broadly based general difference between social psychology and the study of development in infancy—the former being more interested in what happens in relationships with people in general, most of whom are not intimates, and the latter paying more attention to how children interact with caregivers and other intimates. Social referencing research and theorizing, because it derives from developmental *and* social psychology, reflects a strong concern for both sets of issues.

The salience of close relationships, rather than of interaction with the broader social world, in the study of infant development can be seen in the discussions of how referencing is related to attachment and imitation. The restriction of emotional referencing to attachment figures (Ainsworth) seems to be driven more by the trust that is found in the intimacy of attachment relationships than by any assumption that caregivers possess more expertise than other people. Užgiris and Kruper's suggestion that selectivity has been more of a factor in the extant social referencing research—which has been concerned primarily with emotional referencing—than in studies of infant imitation—which have focused more on instrumental matters—gets at essentially the same point, namely, that guidance in more important matters is reserved for referees who can be trusted. Because imitation research has concerned itself with referents of lesser consequence, it makes sense that individuals other than intimates would be accepted readily as referees. Like Ainsworth's discussion, Užgiris and Kruper's analysis of selectivity emphasizes the importance of the trust which resides in intimate relationships. The discussion of indirect effects (which also is an idea that emerged more from developmental than from social psychology) also reflects this stress upon trust. In combination with social psychological research on source theory and vicarious modeling, which has highlighted the factors that indicate varying degrees of expertise, we get a full picture of what is involved in the important matter of selecting a referee. Putting together the developmental psychological orientation to the salience of early intimate relationships with the social psychological emphasis upon ability and status generates a comprehensive picture of what selectivity in social referencing is based on—the multiplicative function of the expertise to provide accurate interpretations of the situation and the trustworthiness to be motivated to do so. Regardless of whether a referee's credibility is lowered in the infant's eyes because of perceived lack of expertise or because of a sense of mistrust, the outcome will be essentially the same, namely, the discounting and perhaps even disregard of that person's interpretational messages (Feinman; Gewirtz & Peláez-Nogueras).

The possibility that selectivity may vary as a function of domain, which my colleagues and I discussed in Chapter 2, indicates the importance of considering both elements of credibility—expertise as well as trust. Even if an intimate caregiver is more liked and trusted, an experimenter may truly be the better source of definition in the laboratory, assuming that she is not antagonistic to the infant. The finding that the infant is more likely to look to a peer's mother than to her own mother when the peer is upset (Hay, Nash, & Pedersen, 1981) suggests that infants may not rely completely on the criteria of trust when they seek out and accept referencing information (Feinman). Similarly, infants' willingness to be influenced by a friendly stranger who appears knowledgeable, especially when the mother seems to lack expertise, also reflects the complimentary roles of ability and trust in referee selectivity. These factors have not been systematically varied or manipulated in previous referencing research; a fuller and richer understanding of selectivity will call for such studies to be done.

Developmental Issues in Referee Selection.   Referencing research has told us very little, as of yet, about how the potential range of referees varies as the young child matures. The suggestion that the first sources of referencing information are likely to be parents and other familiar intimates (Denzin; Užgiris & Kruper; Webster & Foschi) certainly is consistent with empirical evidence that infants between 9 and 12 months will accept influence from their mothers and fathers. The preference for these close relatives over strangers (Zarbatany & Lamb, 1985) is in line with this proposition as well.

Although referencing studies have reflected some concern about the degree to which other people's interpretations are accepted, there has been little in the way of systematic consideration of how the child's range of referees may expand or shift as she develops. Užgiris and Kruper have given us a place to begin considering this issue by hypothesizing a developmental progression of potential referees over the first year of life: familiar caregiver, familiar person, knowledgeable person, target of identification. They argue that the range of referees cannot expand beyond close relationships until communication becomes at least somewhat more conventionalized. Because early dyadic interchange is rather idiosyncratic, influence attempts from people with whom the child has not had a lot of social experience are likely to fall short of the mark. Instead, familiar caregivers, and to a lesser but still meaningful extent, other familiar persons, would be the likely sources of referencing messages. By the end of the first year, the emergence of conventionalized communication, stylized gestures, and the beginning of simple expressive language would allow the infant to interact effectively enough with unfamiliar people to be able, if she so desired, to engage in social referencing with them.

Along this line, the increased sophistication of infants' efforts to engage, during the second year, in mutual referencing, in which they discuss definitional meaning in a give-and-take fashion with a relatively unfamiliar adult, is noticeable in the descriptions provided by Rogoff and her colleagues. The finding that infants can be influenced by familiarized, friendly strangers ("knowledgeable people" in Užgiris and Kruper's terminology) by the end of the first year is consistent with the expectation that unfamiliar people can serve as referees once young children are able to engage in more conventional communication, and do not have to rely solely upon the idiosyncrasies of established relationships. For instance, an experimenter whom the infant had only just met was able to influence 10-month-olds' interpretation of attractive toys (Bradshaw, Campos, & Klinnert, 1986). Bandura's suggestion that, as infants mature, they may come to be influenced through vicarious modeling of what they see and hear in the symbolic environment, for example, television (also noted by Feinman, 1985), would seem to require that the child understand communication in a more generic manner. The finding of imitation of televised models in 14-month-olds (Meltzoff, 1988) is consistent with this expectation.

Referencing studies typically use relatively simple and stylized messages; the use of complex communications is found only in studies in which a parent is the referee. Although it is clear that infants can make sense of these richer messages from familiar caregivers, can they do so with unfamiliar persons also? Perhaps receptivity to influence from unfamiliar but knowledgeable persons is restricted, at the end of the first year, to situations in which the referencing message is expressed simply and briefly. Furthermore, the virtual lack of research on referencing with familiar persons who are not caregivers (Feinman & colleagues) makes it impossible to appropriately examine the distinction which Užgiris and Kruper make between these two classes of referees.

The Relationship with the Referee

Development of the Referencing Relationship.   As infants mature, changes can be observed in the way that they engage in referencing. Not all that long after the onset of referencing, infants become capable of beginning to engage in a more mutual, negotiated form of this process. As suggested in Emde's discussion of this developmental progression, infants first are not cognitively capable of referencing; then, during the second semester of the first year, they come to be influenced by what others have to say about environmental events; finally, in the second year, referencing becomes a bidirectional, "conversational" matter in which meaning is clarified. Thus, the contours of the referencing relationship are transfigured over the course of the first 2 years of life.

The first indications of referencing, at around 10 months or so, seem to be pretty much a matter of the infant accepting, more or less, what the adult thinks and feels about the referent. One sees very little in the way of "back talk" at this age. By the middle of the second year, however, there are indications of a more negotiated, discussional construction of reality. The emergence of a more mutual character to social referencing is reflected in the finding of some disagreements between mother and child as to whether the referent in Hornik and Gunnar's (1988) black rabbit study was a "bunny" or a "doggy," the report of toddlers in the second year contacting the fear-defined toy, and then turning to smile at the mother (Walden & Ogan, 1988), and even some mention of 12-month-olds attempting to persuade their parents that a toy which had been defined as fear-provoking was really quite pleasurable (Hirshberg, 1988).

In giving an account of the developmental changes which transpire between 4 to 15 months in the way that infants interact with an adult,

Rogoff and her colleagues noted that efforts are made by the child to define the situation for the adult. These attempts seem especially apparent in the older infants. There are instances in which infant and adult have somewhat dissimilar interpretations of the situation; such differences of opinion are resolved by the ensuing conversation about how they shall jointly interpret it. These encounters have a negotiated, give-and-take quality to them, strikingly illustrated in the examples provided in that chapter. Although such negotiations evidently are facilitated by the child's maturing verbal proficiency (Ainsworth), stylized gestures seem to work quite well in earlier service of much the same purpose, if admittedly on a simpler level. Furthermore, there are other exchanges in which, clearly, it is the adult who is confused about what to do, and the infant who is defining the situation for the adult. This is not a matter of negotiation but, rather, of a reversal of the roles which we typically expect in a referencing situation involving an adult and a very young child. It is the adult who has become the referer, and the infant the referee.

This facet of the referencing relationship during the second year—that either partner can influence the other, and that they can mutually engage in dialogue of a sort in order to achieve intersubjectivity—parallels a corresponding shift in the broader scope of their relationship. As Ainsworth so aptly points out, mutually agreed plans and negotiated referencing reflect the same ethos as has been described for the later form of attachment known as goal-corrected partnership (Bowlby, 1969), in which the balance of power and dependency has become less one-sided, and the direction of influence more reciprocal. Referencing's transformation, in the second year and beyond, into an affair of mutual guidance may be part and parcel of the overall evolution of a guided partnership between adult and child.

Individual Variation and Patterns in the Referencing Relationship.   Considerable variation can be detected in infant receptivity to definitional messages. It is very rare indeed for there to be uniformity in how individual infants respond to others' interpretation of the situation. Although there have not been any studies which have investigated whether these are stable individual differences which transcend particular situations and referents, there seems to be good reason to believe that this indeed is the case, and that the differences may be associated with the relationship that the infant has with the referee. Thus, in noting the differences in how particular infants responded to apparent parental disagreement as to whether a new toy was one to be liked or feared, Hirshberg (1988, 1990) found that these variations were correlated with features of the relationship and experiences which the infants had with their parents. Similarly, the finding that adolescent mothers were considerably less likely than adult mothers to offer comfort and information when their 20-month-olds were distressed after encountering a robot (J. Osofsky & A. Eberhart-Wright, personal communication, May, 1987) seems most reasonably attributable to differences in the nature of the toddler–mother relationship. Emde's suggestion, that unusual patterns of social referencing could serve as a marker of relationship disorders, presumes that there is enough stability in the character of referencing between an infant and a caregiver to be able to use particular observations as a barometer of the general functioning of that relationship. Indeed, relationship disorders and psychopathology might be reflected in some patterns of referencing.

It makes a good deal of sense to believe that there is a reasonably consistent style of social guidance generally and social referencing in particular within the relationship which an infant has with another person. Variations in this style may be the consequence of how expressive, sensitive, expert, trustworthy, and reliable the referee has been over the course of past experiences with the infant. Perhaps a caregiver who is an unreliable guide will come to be perceived as being a questionable, anxiety-producing base of information—one who sometimes is very helpful, but cannot be counted on consistently. On the other hand, a caregiver who regularly provides the infant with maladaptive interpretations would probably be viewed as a base of information to be avoided. Thus, infants may come to feel comfortable, anxious, or avoidant within the context of a referencing relationship.

Assessing the overall style in which the infant uses particular people as bases of information may open up to our inspection an important dimension of the relationships which infants form with other people. Much has been learned over the last several decades through assessment of the styles in which infants utilize caregivers as bases of security. But, these relationships may serve functions other than that of emotional comfort. As Ainsworth notes in her chapter, mothers can play multiple roles: caregiver, teacher, or playmate. The Ganda mothers whom Ainsworth studied provided care but did little teaching and no playing, suggesting that the quality of the attachment relationship may differ from that of the referencing relationship. Although mothers (and other caregivers) in American society seem to discharge all three of these roles to some extent, it is reasonable to expect that individual adults vary as to how much they emphasize each role, how sensitively they handle each role, and how strongly their performance in one role correlates with that in the other two.

It is essential that we acknowledge that important functions other than care and comfort can exist in the infant's intimate relationships. Although the term *significant other*, as currently used in everyday lexicon, typically brings to mind images of close, meaningful, trusting relationships, Sullivan's (1947) original formulation of this concept (actually, he used the term *significant individual* or *significant adult*) explicitly included not only caregiving functions but socializing and enculturating functions as well. The significant adult was the person whom the infant depended on not only for nurturance and comfort, but also for illumination and instruction. In studying very young children, perhaps we have emphasized caregiving at the expense of enculturation (Feinman & Lewis, 1991). Just as infants (and older children as well) need comfort and care, so too do they need information about environmental events from other people. Not only does the very young child derive emotional and nutritional succor from relationships with adults, but she derives knowledge, social definition, and guidance as well.

Assessing the infant's relationship with the adult as a base of information may tell us something quite different from, and just as important as, what we can learn from examining the infant's style of utilizing the caregiver as a base of attachment. The possibility that security in one of these realms may not imply security in the other further highlights the importance of independent examination of how each of these roles is performed. Perhaps the style of referencing and social guidance generally is correlated with a different set of antecedent and consequent variables than is style of attachment. On the other hand, it may be that there is a *general relationship factor* (gr), analogous to the g factor proposed for intelligence, which guides the overall, correlated performance of the various relationship functions. In this view, an adult who sensitively and reliably provides care and comfort would also be expected to be a good play partner and a good information provider. On the other hand, if these functions represent separate realms, then we would expect that dimensions of relationship performance and security could be essentially unassociated with each other. Indeed, the realm of information gathering and utilization might even be composed of two constituent components which are only minimally correlated: that in which the adult constructs the environment so as to facilitate solitary learning by the child (guidance through structure), and that which involves the social conveyance of definitions and coping strategies (guidance through meaning; Feinman, 1991). Perhaps adults who are proficient in one of these realms might not be as good in the other. Indeed, these realms might even be negatively correlated, in that they may each call for rather different definitions of the desired level of self-reliance with which the child should develop.

All this suggests that it would be worthwhile investigating the regularities in how individual infants gather and use information about the environment from particular people. Just as such patterns have been found to exist with regard to how securely infants feel with the comfort-and-caregiving realm of their relationships, so might we reasonably expect to find at least a moderate degree of commonality among the informational experiences which an infant has with a particular adult. With such a data base, variations in the style of how information about the world is conveyed within the infant–adult relationship could be assessed, and clusters or typologies, if they exist, could be identified. Just as attachment classifications emphasize the security of the caregiving relationship, it may be that one basic dimension, perhaps the most important dimension, of the infant's style of using a particular adult as a base of information will turn out to be the security with which she can count on getting reliable input about environmental events. But there may be other dimensions as well, perhaps reflecting the degree of independence versus dependence which the adult encourages in information conveyance. Identification of the various styles by which young children obtain and exchange information with their relationship partners would aid us in formulating a fuller picture of the multiple functions served by infants' social relations.

ISSUES OF PROCESS

The "Astounding Claim"

The assertion that children who have not yet celebrated their first birthday can participate in the complexities and subtleties which the process of social referencing inherently entails is, in some respects, a rather bold declaration. Indeed, Bretherton points out that the most striking feature of the conceptualization of referencing is "the astounding claim that infants as young as 10 months can make deliberate and specific use of another person's judgment to form their own appraisal of a situation." What makes this claim astounding is its proclamation that infants are capable of a level of social and cognitive sophistication, of an ability to handle complexities, which was thought to be beyond their reach (Užgiris & Kruper). Nonetheless, there appears to be strong evidence in support of this "social cognitive hypothesis" (as Bretherton calls this model), both from referencing research *per se* and from other areas of infant behavior and cognition (Bretherton; Užgiris & Kruper). That referencing outcomes have been shown to be specific learning about particular target referents, deriving from sophisticated information processing—and not merely a matter of contagion—and that similar specificity can be found in other processes during infancy (Bretherton; Feinman & colleagues; Lewis & Feiring; Užgiris & Kruper), indicates that this astounding claim is indeed valid.

The Infants as Sophisticate.   With all due respect for developmental differences, it can be noted that in social referencing—and other activities which involve intentional communication, intersubjectivity, and deliberation—infants function pretty much in the same basic way that adults and older children do. Although technique and style do vary according to age (e.g., the greater emphasis on nonverbal messages during infancy), the fundamental dynamic is, in many respects, essentially the same. The finding of mutuality in referencing by the second year of life (Hornik & Gunnar, 1988; Walden & Ogan, 1988; Emde; Hornik-Parritz & colleagues), and the rudiments of the negotiation of meaning at the end of the first year (Hirshberg, 1988; Rogoff & colleagues), certainly suggests that even very young children possess at least some of the sociocognitive savoir-faire which is usually attributed to adults.

Although recognition of developmental differences—the acknowledgement that individuals of different ages are, in some ways, different beasts—is certainly healthy and appropriate, sometimes we seem to be guided excessively by this "developmental relativism." Too much respect for such variations can cloud our vision in examining the commonalities which exist across all or at least most ages. This point is illustrated in Bretherton's discussion of the use of a rich interpretation of language, that is, the construction of linguistic meaning through the elaboration of what is actually expressed. As she notes, embellishment is needed not only for very young children, such as in elucidating the meaning of one word sentences, but for adults as well, since they too often express themselves in incomplete phrases which do not explicitly label the referent. Despite language use and comprehension differences between adults and infants, the commonalities are significant and basic, and must be given their due.

It is much the same in looking at social referencing in infancy. Despite the variations in the ways that this process operates through the lifespan, the basic functional and structural similarities are fundamental and salient, reflecting, in 10-month-olds, 8-year-olds, and 40-year-olds, the use of others' interpretations as specific information about particular objects, events, and people. One does not have to abandon a healthy sense of developmental relativism and respect, to go so far as to see children as "miniature adults," as in a Renaissance painting (Gelis, 1989), in order to acknowledge that very young children and adults share much in common in the ways that they process information and respond to their environments.

The deliberateness and finesse with which very young children can process intricate and often perplexing information is reflected in the ways that they repair failed messages (Bretherton; Rogoff & colleagues; Užgiris & Kruper). The narrative accounts provided by Rogoff and her colleagues concerning how infants attempt to influence adults' definitions of the situation, and the ways in which they engage adults in conversations about meaning, reflect the persistent, and repetitive if necessary, presentation of their point of view, and the elicitation of the adult's perspective, until intersubjectivity is achieved. For example, if the child's initial effort to get the adult to stop touching her does not succeed, then she typically persists in communicating her desires, often conveying this message a bit differently the next time.

Similarly, if the infant is trying to get the adult to make a bunny-in-the-box pop out, but her initial attempts to define the situation in this instrumental manner leaves the adult thinking, erroneously, that the infant doesn't like the toy or wants to play with it herself, then the infant persists in communicating the desired interpretation, and in attempting to figure out how the adult is viewing this situation, thus repairing the failed message several times if necessary. Despite the ease with which misconstruction of meaning (what Lacan, 1977, calls *méconnaissance*) occurs when communication is based upon, at best, simple verbal cues and stylized gestures, the infant perseveres in her goal-directed behavior, communicating her intent and meaning to the adult, repeating the message in slightly varied ways which convey the same essential theme.

The interpersonal signaling cues which are utilized in social referencing could easily be misconstrued. The specific identity of the referent could go astray. In an even more radical departure, the message could be seen as nonreferential, simply reflecting the referee's basic overall mood. The adult's efforts to catch the gaze of the infant, and even her conveyance of definitional information about the stimulus, could be construed by the infant as an invitation to interact. Similarly, if the infant orients to the referent, and then looks toward her mother's face, this sequence could be interpreted by the mother as a request for mediated control rather than the solicitation of referencing information.

All sorts of things could go wrong here, but usually they don't. Whether the infant is functioning strictly in the role of referer, or a more mutual and reciprocal ethos is operating, both members of the dyad seem to engage in sufficient efforts at clarification of meaning, and at the repair of failed messages. Certainly, misconstruction of meaning, and confusion among alternative competing processes, does occur, as when the young child takes the mother's greeting to the stranger as a threat to her availability rather than as a message about the stranger (Feinman & colleagues; Lewis & Feiring). An interesting topic for future research might be to examine the degree to which such *méconnaissance* can account for individual variation in how readily and strongly the conveyed message is accepted. Nonetheless, the finding that referencing, as specific and deliberate learning about a referent event, does occur to a considerable degree in infancy clearly indicates that the social cognitive hypothesis of this phenomenon is supported empirically. The "astounding claim" is, indeed, firmly planted in the empirical soil.

When research on infant referencing first began a little more than a decade ago, one of the main causes for critical concern was the assumption that infants as young as 10 months were not cognitively or socially up to what this process required. That they could be influenced broadly and nonspecifically by a more primitive, less cognitive dynamic of mood contagion or resonance was not doubted. The particular issue in contention was whether they could take in not only the basic gist of the message *per se* but also the referential nature of that communication. It must be remembered that most of what we now know about the capacity to comprehend and express referential gestures comes from research which emerged at about that time, in the mid to late 1970s (Butterworth & Cochran, 1980; Murphy & Messer 1977; Scaife & Bruner, 1975), and had not yet been well integrated into the corpus of knowledge about infancy. As can be seen in Bretherton's chapter, much has been learned about intentional communication, intersubjectivity, and dyadic interaction with objects over the last 10 to 15 years. Thus, it is not terribly surprising (through hindsight at least) that, at the time of social referencing's debut in the world of infancy research, there was considerable skepticism about the social cognitive hypothesis which was proposed as its operating mechanism (Campos, 1983; Feinman, 1982). With what we have learned over the last decade about referencing, and about other related phenomena of intentional, referential communication in very young children, this claim, while perhaps still astounding, is now somewhat easier to accept.

The Infant as Rational Actor.   Much of the evidence concerning the selectivity and ambiguity postulates, and about how infants cope with conflicting definitional signals, suggests that they are acting with a degree of logical sense beyond that which typically is attributed to them. It is quite sensible to accept interpretative messages from a knowledgeable and friendly, albeit unfamiliar, adult, especially if the trusted caregiver appears bewildered (Klinnert, Emde, Butterfield, & Campos, 1986; Feinman). Similarly, selecting referees on the basis of apparent ability, expertise, and trustworthiness (Bandura; Feinman; Webster & Foschi) is most eminently reasonable. Inhibiting approach to stimulus toys, while signaling to the referee for clarification after receiving internally contradictory signals from her (Barrett, 1985), would certainly seem to be a hallmark of the rational actor. Attempting to discuss the meaning of what appears to be a perfectly respectable toy, after receiving a fear message about it from a parent (Walden & Ogan, 1988) or conflicting messages from mother and father (Hirshberg, 1988), most assuredly reflects a good deal of logical sense. In these respects, infant behavior in social referencing situations possesses a quality which most strikingly resembles what is expected from rational actors who are engaging in logical thought processes.

The conservative interpretation of these observations is that infants, much like their older counterparts in the lifespan, behave logically and rationally. That they do so is suggested by much of the evidence concerning the manner in which infants go about discovering contingencies and connections in their environments (Bower, 1989). A more controversial, but nonetheless intriguing alternative notion is that infants display some patterns of behavior and cognition which reflect greater logic and rationality than that exhibited by adults. As Webster and Foschi note, adults often resolve conflicting messages from two sources through accommodative means, resulting in a compromise solution which lies somewhere in the middle. While this strategy could be the outcome of logical thinking, it may also reflect a desire to avoid conflict or to try to please both parties. Faced with conflicting messages from mother and father about a toy which seems friendly enough, 12-month-olds, instead, often try to "discuss" this matter with the parent who reacted fearfully. This approach, which could certainly incur the ire of the parent if she did not wish to be disputed by her child, nonetheless seems a quite reasonable way to resolve the conflict.

It may be that, while adults often find themselves torn between the desire to be correct and the desire to please other people, infants may uniformly be more relentless seekers of truth. Although compliance, the form of conformity which is motivated by the wish to gain social approval, is often seen in adults, infants may be incapable of the deceit involved in doing something that is not internally felt. For them, behavior and interpretation may be more integrally packaged. Indeed, the suggestion that the behavioral conformity displayed in infant social referencing may more consistently be a matter of internalization than it is among adults (Feinman) reflects what could be construed as a downward rather than upward developmental progression. Along a related line, the reliance of adults upon the status characteristics of a source person as an indication of the capability of that person to deal effectively with the task at hand (Webster & Foschi) can easily become a matter of overgeneralization, so that status blinds the perceiver as to the actual skill level of the other person. Perhaps infants, if examined with respect to this issue, would be found to be less "status conscious" than adults and children.

This interpretation suggests a conceptualization of development as a process of "growing down," in which we become less rather than more capable, less rather than more rational (Feinman, 1991). The finding that adults' eating behavior reflects a less adaptive response to satiety cues than do the reactions of young children (Birch & Deysher, 1986) and the notion that, through the constraints of adult guidance, children can be twisted in "unnatural" ways (Rousseau, 1750/1911) reflect this theme of "development as a process of growing down." Although it is possible that this hypothesized downward progression unfolds naturally, the culprit typically held to blame for this "fall from grace" is the manner in which children are raised—how they are treated and what they are encouraged to do (and discouraged from doing) by family, community, and society. While these social forces are assumed to have a facilitative as well as an inhibitive potential, usually they are seen to serve the latter more than the former cause. Indeed, the very first sentence in Rousseau's treatise on child rearing, *Emile*, is a stark expression of this sentiment: "God makes all things good; man meddles with them and they become evil" (Rousseau, 1750/1911, p. 5). The notion that development, and the influence of society on development, restricts rather than elaborates our faculties, that it dulls rather than polishes our sensibilities, was perhaps most eloquently expressed by Goethe (cited in Handley & Samelson, 1988, p. 18): "If children grew up according to early indications, we should have nothing but geniuses."

It is worth examining, in this perspective, Bower's (1989) contention that infants are more comfortable than adults with a four-valued system of logic, which tolerates ambiguity and complexity more comfortably than the two-valued logic system typically utilized by adults. In the two-valued system, a particular contingency is either true or false. The four-valued system, on the other hand, accepts two additional and more subtle possibilities, namely, that something can be both true and false, or neither true nor false. These two logical possibilities reflect a sense of conditionality, that is, the idea that an event may occur in some circumstances but not in others, thus rendering it sometimes true and sometimes false. As Bower notes, adults can function epistemologically within these more complex systems, but typically they revert to the simplified dichotomy of true or false (right vs. wrong; yes or no; if you're not part of the solution, you're part of the problem, etc.).

The transition from the more open and tolerant four-valued logic of younger children to the simpler two-valued system of adults can be seen as an instance of development as a process of growing down. Or it could be understood, in a more developmentally relativistic perspective, merely as a change (no better, no worse) to a different way of making sense of the world, a different form of rationality. Regardless, the four-valued scheme seems more sensitive to the complex, gray, fuzzy nature of reality. Imposing a true or false dichotomy on the between-the-lines subtleties of real life is a cognitive simplification often practiced but, nonetheless, perhaps not the most rational or adaptive way to understand environmental events. What we do know about how infants handle some of the twists and turns that referencing situations take, how they deal with conflict and ambiguity, suggests that they may be acting in more logical and appropriate ways, perhaps driven by the four-valued system of logic which Bower (1989) attributes to them.

Since the four-valued system of logic is inherently more tolerant of complexities, subtleties, and conditionalities, it is reasonable to assume that it may dispose its user to be more tolerant of ambiguity. As noted in the review of referencing research (Feinman & colleagues), the evidence about how ambiguity affects referencing is equivocal. Perhaps this mixture of results—as compared to the consistency of the finding that adults resist social definition more in clear-cut than ambiguous situations—suggests that infants are, indeed, more comfortable and accepting of ambiguity than adults are (Feinman). In adults, receptivity to social influence seems to operate according to the "Goldilocks Principle," in that maximum influence of others' messages is achieved when the stimulus is not too scary ("not too hot"), not too pleasurable ("not too cold"), but somewhere in the ambiguous muddle of the midrange ("just right"). Such a pattern is just what would be expected from two-valued logical thinkers, who are most comfortable with clear-cut distinctions. On the other hand, four-valued logical thinkers, who are less distressed by vagueness and equivocation, may not experience a heightened need to be assisted in ambiguous rather than in clear-cut situations.

Another way of approaching this matter is to suggest that four-valued logical thinkers, even when they are well convinced that they have established the truth or falsity of a contingency, will remain receptive to additional evidence. Thus, they would be operating according to the rational principle that, although they have solved the problem, their solution may not be correct. Such thinkers would probably be more receptive to additional evidence, including interpretive messages from other people, in clear-cut, open-and-shut cases, than would the more steadfast two-valued thinkers. When ambiguity is a privilege rather than a problem (Azuma, 1979), as it seems to be in epistemological systems which accept conditionality as a tolerable end state for information processing, then subjective and situational uncertainty are less likely to have a strong influence upon receptivity to social influence. In this perspective, the way in which infants deal with uncertainty in referencing situations may reflect a more open manner of dealing with the complexities and subtleties that are the stuff of which reality is made.

How Does Social Referencing Operate: The Clockwork Mechanisms

In referencing, infants appear to be performing cognitive and social tasks which call for sophistication and rationality. Although these social cognitive features of referencing seem to be fairly well established, and to be supported by tangential evidence from related phenomena, it is still necessary to describe the particular mechanisms by which social referencing operates. It is an entirely legitimate commentary on referencing to say that while we have a substantial amount of evidence indicating *that* it works, we know considerably less about *how* it works, as suggested in one manner or another by Bretherton, by Denzin, and by Webster and Foschi. Knowing more about "that" then "how" is a common characteristic of the study of many phenomena, especially when investigation is comparatively new. The examination of social referencing in infancy would seem to be at the age when more consideration of process issues is appropriate. Clearly, this state of affairs implies that greater research effort be devoted to issues of underlying process. However, knowing that one needs to dig, but not knowing where in particular to plant the shovel, is not especially useful. Fortunately, some pieces of the treasure map have been provided.

Let us examine the basic sequence of steps which occur in social referencing. Referencing appears to be an information-and-action process in which information about an environmental event is gathered, and action is subsequently based upon those acquired data (Feinman, 1986). First, the infant must be interested in the stimulus, whether on her own or by having her attention drawn to it. Second, she must become receptive to information about the stimulus. In referencing, it is a particular interest in socially conveyed information about the situation that is aroused. Third, these messages must be attended to and assimilated. Fourth, the input, once received, is then utilized to formulate an understanding of the stimulus, being integrated with what the infant may already know about the situation. Finally, this interpretation becomes the basis for action taken with regard to the event. With this structure in mind, let us first examine the information-gathering phase, composed of steps one, two, and three, and then the interpretation and action phase, which consists of the fourth and fifth steps.

Information Gathering.   How do infants gather information from others in social referencing situations? What do we know and what is there still left to learn? First of all, with the exception of the work of Hornik-Parritz and her colleagues (Hornik & Gunnar, 1988; Hornik-Parritz & colleagues), we know very little about the manner in which "what to do" instrumental messages are conveyed. The apparent significance of instrumental referencing (Feinman & colleagues; Hornik-Parritz & colleagues) makes it imperative that more be learned about this side of referencing. With regard to emotional referencing, there is much evidence that decodable messages can be transmitted through simple unichannel communications of either voice tone or facial expression. Much more is known about facially than vocally expressed messages, reflecting what Emde notes to be the possible overemphasis upon vision in the study of referencing. What is especially troublesome about this gap in our understanding is that referencing messages in natural environments may be more likely to be conveyed vocally than visually, especially in situations of impending danger, as in the prevention of household accidents. Furthermore, we know nothing whatsoever about the single-channel effects of gestural and body language cues, since these have not been investigated.

Omnichannel, typically more free-form messages which operate through a combination of facial expression, tone of voice, and paralinguistic gestures, have been found, in many studies, to arrive safely at their destination. How the various component parts and the gestalt of such communications are processed by the infant and come to be integrated into the new understanding of the situation is not at all known. Furthermore, there is no evidence whatsoever—either in unichannel or multichannel studies—of how tactile, tension, and kinesthetic cues may be conveyed in referencing messages. The concern, in some studies of infants' individual response, when the infant sat on the mother's lap or close enough to feel her tension, that such cues might influence how the infant interprets the stimulus (see Feinman, 1982, for a brief review) suggests that referees can convey, through direct physical contact or "vibes," their relaxation or uptightness about an encountered stimulus.

The focus of the lion's share of the referencing literature on the end of the first year and beginning months of the second has taught us much about how infants become receptive to and receive nonverbal messages. But, as we should expect, the communication of referencing messages seems to take on a more verbal quality by the middle of the second year (Ainsworth; Emde; Feinman & colleagues; Hornik-Parritz & colleagues; Užgiris & Kruper0. It is also reasonable to expect that conventionalized gestures such as head shakes and nods also come into play a more significant role. The developmental sequence suggested by Užgiris and Kruper—in which the means of communication expands from expressions of emotion to idiosyncratic actions, to conventional gestures, and finally to linguistic forms—may characterize the shifting sands of referencing as young children mature.

Although comparatively little has been done to determine how effectively young children of various ages may process verbally conveyed messages about a referent, it appears that the use of simple language and conventionalized gestures in the negotiation of meaning begins to show up with reasonable consistency between 11 and 15 months (Rogoff & colleagues). Since we know that referencing processes, even in children who are only a few years older, are strongly reliant upon verbally conveyed messages, it is sensible to suggest that verbal conduits of information will become more heavily utilized during the second year and beyond and, as Ainsworth suggests, may become the preferred modality. The paucity of evidence about how the conveyance of referencing messages evolves as the child matures, and especially the virtual lack of information about the hypothesized transition from nonverbal to verbal means of communication, indicates quite clearly a direction for future research.

How does the very young child signal her wish to have referent information conveyed, if it is not being offered? The primary gesture that has been identified in the first year is the "social referencing look," which prototypically involves a glance to the referent followed by looking to the referee with an expression of puzzlement, interest, or mild concern. Although this gesture has been studied and observed in laboratory settings, little is known about its frequency and function in the infant's everyday life. There is evidence, also in laboratory settings, of the use of the verbal modality to request referencing information by the middle of the second year (Hornik & Gunnar, 1988; Hornik-Parritz & colleagues). Furthermore, conversations in which meaning is discussed and negotiated also incorporate greater use of verbal communication by the second year (Rogoff & colleagues). More detailed examination of the developmental changes in the format of information request, especially as it apparently shifts to a greater emphasis upon verbal solicitation, clearly is needed.

Although some of the initial conceptualization of referencing had included only the solicited form within the definitional parameters of the phenomenon (Campos, 1983; Klinnert, Campos, Sorce, Emde, & Svejda, 1983), and despite the strong research interest in this more "active" form of referencing, referencing information is conveyed in other ways as well. Clearly, as Užgiris and Kruper so aptly note, the infant must have, or come to have, some interest in obtaining socially constructed definitions of the situation if these messages are to affect her. Nonetheless, the finding that studies in which referencing messages are offered have produced essentially the same behavior regulation effect as those in which the message must be solicited (see the review in Chapter 2, this volume) suggests that these are two sides of the same phenomenological coin. Furthermore, the frequently utilized practice, in studies where the message must be initially requested, of then offering the message continuously for up to 2 minutes further blurs the differentiation between these two variations on the referencing theme.

The realization that the supposedly quintessential initiation of a referencing bout, through the infant's solicitation of the referee's input, actually occurs rather infrequently both in studies of referencing and in the examination of data from other areas of investigation (Ainsworth; Emde; Feinman & colleagues; Lewis & Feiring) further reinforces the suggestion that the conveyance of referencing messages can take on more than one form. The observation, during infancy and toddlerhood, of socialization episodes which open with the caregiver's offer, or perhaps even imposition, of her message, and the finding that such communication often leads to internalized, self-policed, and enduring definitions of the situation (Stayton, Hogan, & Ainsworth, 1971; Ainsworth; Emde) provides additional evidence of the salience of nonsolicited referencing messages. Bowlby's comment, noted by Ainsworth, that young children often learn more through what caregivers offer than by specifically requesting such input suggests that if there indeed is a prototypical trigger for referencing message conveyance, it is more likely to be the caregiver's concern for socializing the child than the child's active search for such input.

Typically, we have distinguished between offered versus solicited messages (Feinman, 1982). Nonetheless, it would seem that this classificatory scheme is too simple to adequately describe the array of methods through which messages are communicated. Lewis and Feiring, in describing what goes on when a family eats dinner together, note that a lot of the referencing information which the young child can utilize is derived from observation of interactions and conversations in which she is not participating. Because she did not instigate these incidents, it would not be appropriate to classify them as solicited. But, because the participants did not stage these conversations for the intended purpose of providing the target child with definitional information, a decision to classify them as instances of offered referencing would not be appropriate either. The messages were simply *available* for the child utilize if she wished to do so. Available messages would seem to fall somewhere on the continuum between the expectation for infant self-reliance implied by the requirement of solicitation (Feinman, 1991), and the more proactive stance taken in offering a message. Even more forward than the offered message is the insistence and often highly arousing nature of what can be thought of as *imposed* messages, such as those used in prohibitions, especially when the infant is heading away from the caregiver and into harm's way. The situations described by Ainsworth, and by Emde, seem to fit this classification. An imposed message is one which the referee strongly insists *is* the interpretation of the situation. In contrast, an offered message is one which the referee makes sure that the infant receives, but without pushing the infant to accept that definition. The continuum would then be marked by four increasingly proactive and more forward regions of message conveyance: solicited, available, offered, imposed. This elaborated classification scheme should offer a more sensitive and valid way to describe the range of variation that exists in the manner in which referencing messages are conveyed.

Regardless of the way in which interpretative input is provided in referencing situations, infants seem to spend surprisingly little time in visual regard of these displays, even when no vocal cues are offered (Feinman & colleagues). The implication of this finding is that infants are learning enough in what seems to be a remarkably short amount of time to form an interpretation of the referent. The information harvest seems not to take very long. Very little of a more definitive nature is known about this mechanism, despite its obviously great importance for understanding how referencing works. Are infants, indeed, getting a lot from a little? In studies where vocal cues also are being provided, how much do infants attend to these signals (a more methodologically difficult issue, perhaps, than the examination of visual attention)? It would seem remarkably adaptive for infants to learn a lot from brief glances, given the nature of the everyday communication and interaction which they have with other people. Nonetheless, there needs to be further documentation indicating that this indeed is the case, that infants truly gather the referencing information which they need through relatively fleeting visual glances or momentary auditory snatches.

Finally, although infants do seem to be able, by 10 months, to use other persons' interpretative messages as they were intended (Bretherton; Lewis & Feiring), namely, as information about one particular object, event, or person, we know relatively little about how they do this. It seems reasonable to assume, because understanding of referential gestures emerges in most infants toward the end of the first year, that specificity probably operates through the exercise of that skill. Nonetheless, the paucity of research which looks at the correlation of individual differences in referential gestures with social referencing prowess makes it impossible to be more confident in this matter. Similarly, there is evidence which suggests that referencing is a complex juggling process in which the infant has to pay attention to two or more visual or auditory displays at once, coordinate them, and not get confused. For example, touching the infant while giving the message may distract her attention from the cognitive and social balls which she is juggling and, as a consequence, allow some other alternative process to interfere. But without studies which experimentally manipulate such distracting gestures, we cannot be certain whether it is these distractions *per se*, rather than relationship variables which covary with the natural use of such actions, which account for the observed individual variation.

Interpretation and Action

The Construction of Meaning.   We probably know even less about how referencing messages (once received) are transformed into interpretative meaning, than about how these cues are elicited and obtained. Because interpretative processes are, manifestly, much less palpable than the information-gathering activities of referencing, this is not all that surprising. Nonetheless, there are some interesting possibilities to consider. Strikingly, there is some similarity between what seems to be happening in referencing and the basic process of adaptation described by Piaget (Piaget & Inhelder, 1966/1969) in which data are first taken in and then integrated into existing schema (assimilation), sometimes with an expansion, constriction, or alteration of that schema, thus resulting in a change in how the infant perceives that particular situation (accommodation). Although Piaget emphasized the utilization of sensory input from direct experiential contact, while referencing clearly is powered by the fuel of socially created and acquired data, the basic mechanism through which informational input metamorphizes into understanding seems to be rather similar. Perhaps the interpretation and action stages of referencing operate according to the adaptational processes of assimilation and accommodation described by Piaget.

It has been noted that referencing messages appear to enable the infant to anticipate the nature of environmental events, and to foresee how a particular manner of interacting with that event will turn out. Just how this process transpires has not been investigated in detail. Nonetheless, some possible mechanisms can be delineated. If the referee's expressed emotion possesses intrinsic meaning to the infant referer, then the association of such cues with a referent event would lead the infant, in a more or less prewired fashion, to interpret the event in a manner consistent with that emotional signal (Campos, 1983). This does not mean that all infants will, on all occasions, automatically accept the referee's emotional definition of the situation. Rather, what it does suggest is that if and when the infant does accept this emotional definition, then a biologically based process would lead her to define that referent in a manner consistent with the emotional cues received from the referee—and not in accordance with some other emotion. Thus, for example, if the infant hears her father speak happily about a novel toy, and she accepts this definition, then she will come through prewired mechanisms to see the toy as a joyful stimulus, and not as fearful or disgusting. Since the adult referee typically possesses at least some degree of free will as to the emotion which she displays to the infant in association with a particular referent (as reflected in the utilization of faked emotional messages in almost all studies of referencing's regulatory function), then what we have here is a process which is a combination of social constructive and biological mechanisms (Feinman, 1983).

But, as noted by Gewirtz and Peláez-Nogueras, it is possible for referencing messages to convey a basic affective definition of the referent through an apparently different pathway. The finding that cues which have no intrinsic emotional meaning can assist the infant in predicting the consequences of contact with a referent, and in acting accordingly, suggests that the sheer association of the referee's gesture with the referent event which follows imbues this gesture with referencing power. Thus, it would appear that referencing can operate through a classical conditioning process, particularly when the messages do not in themselves trigger the operation of any prewired mechanism. It is the reliable, conditioned association of a specific cue with particular consequences which leads the infant, over time, to permit this cue to shape her response to the referent. Thus, the pathway from referencing cue to interpretational meaning proceeds, most simply, through the predictive validity of such cues—rather than through any biological mechanism. If the gesture does not validly predict the nature of what is to come, then it will not serve a referencing function.

What we have, then, are two hypothesized mechanisms by which referencing messages can be transformed into interpretation. In one, the definitional emotional cue, once accepted by the infant, is translated into interpretation through a more or less prescribed course. In the other, it is the conditioned and predictive association of referencing messages with later referent consequences which empowers this transformation. It is by no means unreasonable to consider the possibility that these two pathways exist side by side, so that referencing can influence infants' interpretations through more than òne avenue. It would be intriguing, however, to design studies in which an apparent opposition is created between these two mechanisms, in order to see how they interact. Consider, for instance, what might happen if emotionally negative referencing cues were continually associated with favorable outcomes, or positive cues with unfavorable outcomes. If, as Gewirtz and Peláez-Nogueras suggest, infants are inclined to discount the cues provided by referees whose messages lack predictive validity, then we would expect that negative messages about what are obviously favorable outcomes (and positive messages about unfavorable outcomes) would come to be ignored by the infant. The consideration, in future investigations, of such alternative and perhaps oppositional mechanisms would be of considerable benefit in understanding the processes which govern the operation of social referencing in infancy.

Because of the paucity of research which has focused upon instrumental referencing *per se*, we know even less concerning how infants learn what to do, than of how they learn what to feel about referents. Yet, the importance attributed to such instrumental processes (Bandura; Hornik-Parritz & colleagues) implies that an understanding of this side of referencing is very much needed. The most likely possibility as to how infants learn from others what to do about a referent event is through observation of the use of particular coping methods which lead to an ensuing successful result. Thus, the infant would need to see not only how the demonstrated method is executed but also that it does indeed generate a desirable outcome. Unlike the predictive validity proposed by Gewirtz and Peláez-Nogueras—as the basis of how infants learn the basic affective and approach–avoidance response to an object or person—this mechanism for the operation of instrumental referencing requires that the infant come to associate, through vicarious acquisition, her own actions (and not just those of the referee) with the successful outcome. Thus, learning the particulars of what to do may operate through a more vicarious process than learning to predict what to expect from referent events.

From Meaning to Action. How does interpretation become translated into action? The hypothesis that referencing represents an internalization form of conformity (Feinman) implies that interpretation in social referencing is connected in a noncontradictory fashion with action. Clearly, in adults and older children, attitudes, interpretations, opinions, and values do not necessarily translate directly and automatically into action. Rather, other factors often intervene, as noted in the voluminous literature on attitudes and behavior. The further examination of the extent to which similar processes occur in infant social referencing would be an interesting direction for future research.

The translation of interpretation into action can, perhaps, be influenced by the nature of the action that is called for in the situation. When an unfamiliar person is the referent stimulus, how the infant's interpretation is expressed behaviorally varies according to whether the stranger is nonintrusive, tries to talk to the infant, tries to touch the infant, or tries to pick her up (Boccia & Campos, 1983; Feinman, Roberts, & Morissette, 1986; Feiring, Lewis, & Starr, 1984). Similarly, the lived-body experience is rather different for the visual cliff study than for the toy studies because the infant is being asked to crawl across the stimulus rather than touch it (Denzin). Furthermore, the geometric configuration of the visual cliff study is different from that used in any other investigation, because by crossing over the referent, the infant reaches the mother (Ainsworth). In all other studies, the referee and referent are in separate corners or, at least, in different directions from the infant. Generally, examination of the specific features of particular actions and physical configuration seems to be a good technique to utilize in exploring the operating mechanisms through which interpretation is translated (or not) into action.

CONCLUSIONS

Research and thinking about social referencing in infancy over the last decade or so has taught us a good deal about the basic functions, structures, and processes of this phenomenon. The analyses, ideas, and commentaries presented in this book suggest different ways to think about referencing, and indicate new directions for future research. Cutting across the heuristic classification of function, structure, and process are another set of overall themes which often surfaced.

First of all, it can be noted that questions about referencing's *definition and scope* surfaced often. There was much discussion of such matters in the earlier years of referencing research, and some of these issues linger still. Nonetheless, there seem to be some valid indicators that referencing is a fairly broad phenomenon which offers guidance about the construction of instrumental as well as emotional reality, in which informational messages can be conveyed in a wide range of ways, and in which the understanding of clear-cut situations is not necessarily immune from social influence. Issues of instrumental versus emotional, solicited versus offered, ambiguous versus unambiguous are, fundamentally, matters of empirical consideration. In this light, it is noteworthy that much of the data that were not available 10 years ago, but to which we now have access, suggest that referencing is broader than was originally thought. Although some variation with regard to definitional matters still remains, we seem to have a more consensual sense of definitional clarity now than there was in the past.

Second, many of the issues discussed can help us in refining the *procedures utilized in studying* social referencing in infancy. For example, we would benefit by modifying our methodologies so as to better discriminate information-seeking looks from other types of visual regard. Similarly, it would be wise to test consistently for whether the observed behavior regulation effect is characterized by the referent specificity which the social cognitive hypothesis claims is a feature of referencing. Better understanding of the impact of neutral versus control messages would aid us in the more precise design of message conditions, and in investigating hypotheses about the relative potency of these different conditions. Methodological implications surface throughout this book; taken together, they can serve as a source of modifications and revisions which have the potential to make the investigation of social referencing a more rigorous, incisive, and enlightened enterprise.

Third, further consideration of *developmental* issues and progressions related to referencing is essential for formulating a fuller understanding of the phenomenon. Most of what we know about referencing focuses on a limited, although very important, age span, from around 9 to 18 months. Furthermore, even within this age range, little work has been done to determine what developmental changes occur. Clearly, examination of developmental issues needs to be both wider and deeper if we are to construct a more comprehensive understanding of how referencing emerges and develops over the first years of life.

Fourth, there is a strong need for systematic examination of the extent to which *individual differences* exist in the ways that referencing information is gathered, integrated, and utilized by very young children as they construct reality. A phenomenon, when it is first investigated and its existence established, is likely to be studied more normatively than variationally. The use of a variational approach (Valsiner, 1984) will be especially important in investigating the mechanisms by which errors occur in referencing situations, such as when infants connect the message with an unintended referent. The state of our knowledge about how referencing operates in infancy is such that we are now at the point where greater consideration of variations around the theme is in order.

Fifth, the almost complete lack of any examination of how referencing functions in young children's *natural environments* outside of the laboratory is a serious limiting factor in establishing the ecological validity of the extant research. We know what referencing can do, but it now behooves us to investigate the form that these effects and processes take outside of the laboratory. The choice of referees, referents, and message conveyance techniques in extant research appears, at face value at least, to have been made with due concern for mundane as well as experimental realism. Nonetheless, investigation in more natural settings is essential. It is sobering to realize that social referencing has not been studied in infants' home environments.

A related need is for studies in which referencing can be observed without experimental manipulation of messages or other conditions. We have not, as of yet, observed the nature of social referencing which transpires when infants and their caregivers are left to their own devices. Those studies which did not manipulate message variables did, however, ask the caregiver not to initiate interaction with the child, thus severely restricting the utility of such data for investigating the natural frequency, context, and nature of referencing in everyday interaction. The importance of beginning to observe referencing in natural settings cannot be overstated. It may be the most pressing issue to be considered in new studies of infants' social referencing.

Looking back at the decade or so in which social referencing was first defined and its existence demonstrated in infancy indicates what we have learned about this phenomenon, and the twists and turns which this body of research has taken during that period of time. What we have tried to do here is to assess what has been done, and provide suggestions and critical commentary—especially from the perspective of other research and theoretical traditions—in order to offer some suggestions as to the directions in which research and thought about social referencing in infancy might want to go in the future. The degree to which our efforts have been successful will be, most probably, best measured in that future.

REFERENCES

Azuma, H. (1979). Culture–education interaction and the problem of a changing society. In S. Doxiadis (Ed.), *The child in the world of tomorrow: A window into the future* (pp. 251–254). New York: Pergamon.

Barrett, K. C. (1985). Infants' use of conflicting emotion signals. (Doctoral dissertation, University of Denver, 1984). *Dissertation Abstracts International, 46*, 321B–322B.

Birch, L. L., & Deysher, M. (1986). Caloric compensation and sensory specific satiety: Evidence for self regulation of food intake by young children. *Appetite, 323–331.*

Boccia, M. L., & Campos, J. J. (1983, April). *Maternal emotional signals and infants' reactions to strangers.* Paper presented at the biennial meeting of the Society for Research in Child Development, Detroit.

Bower, T. G. R. (1989). *The rational infant: Learning in infancy.* New York: W. H. Freeman.

Bowlby, J. (1969). *Attachment.* New York: Basic Books.

Bradshaw, D. L., Campos, J. J., & Klinnert, M. D. (1986, April). *Emotional expressions as determinants of infants' immediate and delayed responses to prohibitions.* Paper presented at the Fifth International Conference on Infant Studies, Los Angeles.

Bretherton, I. (1984). Social referencing and the interfacing of minds: A commentary on the views of Feinman and Campos. *Merrill-Palmer Quarterly, 30,* 419–427.

Brown, R. (1986). *Social psychology* (2nd ed.). New York: Free Press.

Butterworth, G., & Cochran, E. (1980). Towards a mechanism of joint visual attention in human infancy. *International Journal of Behavioral Development, 3,* 253–272.

Campos, J. J. (1983). The importance of affective communication in social referencing: A commentary on Feinman. *Merrill-Palmer Quarterly, 29,* 83–87.

Farran, D. C., & Margolis, L. H. (1987). The family economic environment as a context for children's development. In J. H. Lewko (Ed.), *How children and adolescents view the world of work* (pp. 69–87). San Francisco: Jossey-Bass.

Feinman, S. (1982). Social referencing in infancy. *Merrill-Palmer Quarterly, 28,* 445–470.

Feinman, S. (1983). How does baby socially refer? Two views of social referencing: A reply to Campos. *Merrill-Palmer Quarterly, 29,* 467–471.

Feinman, S. (1985). Emotional expression, social referencing, and preparedness for learning in infancy—Mother knows best, but sometimes I know better. In G. Zivin (Ed.), *The development of expressive behavior: Biology–environment interactions* (pp. 291–318). New York: Academic Press.

Feinman, S. (1986, July). Social referencing as social attention. In M. L. Boccia (Chair), *Social attentional processes in human and nonhuman primates.* Symposium conducted at the XIth Congress of the International Primatological Society, Gottingen, Germany.

Feinman, S. (1991). Bringing babies back into the social world. In M. Lewis & S. Feinman (Eds.), *Social influences and socialization in infancy* (pp. 281–325). New York: Plenum.

Feinman, S., & Lewis, M. (1991). Influence lost, influence regained. In M. Lewis & S. Feinman (Eds.), *Social influences and socialization in infancy* (pp. 1–19). New York: Plenum.

Feinman, S., Roberts, D., & Morissette, P. L. (1986, April). *The effect of social referencing on 12-month-olds' responses to a stranger's attempts to "make friends."* Paper presented at the Fifth International Conference on Infant Studies, Los Angeles.

Feiring, C., Lewis, M., & Starr, M. D. (1984). Indirect effects and infants' reaction to strangers. *Developmental Psychology, 20,* 485–491.

Gelis, J. (1989). The child: From anonymity to individuality. In P. Aries & G. Duby (Eds.), *A history of private life. Vol. III. Passions of the renaissance* (A. Goldhammer, Trans.) (pp. 309–325). Cambridge, MA: Harvard University Press.

Handley, H., & Samelson, A. (1988). *Child.* Wainscott, NY: Pushcart Press.

Hay, D. F., Nash, A., & Pedersen, J. (1981). Responses of six-month-olds to the distress of their peers. *Child Development, 52,* 1071–1075.

Hirshberg, L. M. (1988, April). *Patterns of coping with conflict in infancy: 12 month olds' response to conflicting parental emotional signals.* Paper presented at the Sixth International Conference on Infant Studies, Washington, D.C.

Hirshberg, L. (1990). When infants look to their parents: II. Twelve-month-olds' response to conflicting parental emotional signals. *Child Development, 61,* 1187–1191.

Hornik, R., & Gunnar, M. (1988). A descriptive analysis of infant social referencing. *Child Development, 59,* 626–634.

Klinnert, M. D., Campos, J. J., Sorce, J. F., Emde, R. N., & Svejda, M. (1983). Emotions as behavior regulators: Social referencing in infancy. In R. Plutchik & H. Kellerman (Eds.), *The emotions* (Vol. 2, pp. 57–86). New York: Academic Press.

Klinnert, M. D., Emde, R. N., Butterfield, P., & Campos, J. J. (1986). Social referencing: The infant's use of emotional signals from a friendly adult with mother present. *Developmental Psychology, 22,* 427–432.

Lacan, J. (1977). *Ecrits: A selection* (A. Sheridan, Trans.). New York: Norton.

Lerner, R. M., & East, P. L. (1984). The role of temperament in stress, coping and socio-emotional functioning in early development. *Infant Mental Health Journal, 5,* 148–159.

Lewis, M., and Brooks-Gunn, J. (1979). *Social cognition and the acquisition of self.* New York: Plenum.

Mead, G. H. (1934). *Mind, self and society.* Chicago: University of Chicago Press.

Meltzoff, A. N. (1988). Imitation of televised models by infants. *Child Development, 59,* 1221–1229.

Milgram, S. (1974). *Obedience to authority.* New York: Harper & Row.

Murphy, C. M., & Messer, D. J. (1977). Mothers, infants and pointing: A study of a gesture. In H. R. Schaffer (Ed.), *Studies in mother–infant interaction* (pp. 325–354). London: Academic Press.

Piaget, J., & Inhelder, B. (1969). *The psychology of the child.* New York: Basic Books. (Original work published 1966)

Rosenberg, M. (1979). *Conceiving the self.* New York: Basic Books.

Rousseau, J. J. (1911). *Emile* (B. Foxley, Trans.). London: Dent & Sons. (Original work published 1750)

Scaife, M., & Bruner, J. S. (1975). The capacity for joint visual attention in the infant. *Science, 253,* 265–266.

Sorce, J. F., Emde, R. N., Campos, J. J., & Klinnert, M. D. (1985). Maternal emotional signaling: Its effect on the visual cliff behavior of 1-year-olds. *Developmental Psychology, 21,* 195–200.

Stayton, D. J., Hogan, R., & Ainsworth, M. D. S. (1971). Infant obedience and maternal behavior: The origins of socialization reconsidered. *Child Development, 42,* 1057–1069.

Sullivan, H. S. (1947). *Conceptions of modern psychiatry.* New York: Norton.

Trivers, R. L. (1971). The evolution of reciprocal altruism. *Quarterly Review of Biology, 46,* 35–57.

Valsiner, J. (1984). Two alternative epistemological frameworks in psychology: The typological and variational modes of thinking. *The Journal of Mind and Behavior, 5,* 449–470.

Walden, T. A., & Ogan, T. A. (1988). The development of social referencing. *Child Development, 59,* 1230–1240.

Zarbatany, L., & Lamb, M. E. (1985). Social referencing as a function of information source: Mothers versus strangers. *Infant Behavior and Development, 8,* 25–33.

Author Index

Subject Index